Phenomenology of Tea

Bloomsbury Introductions to World Philosophies

Series Editor:
Monika Kirloskar-Steinbach

Assistant Series Editor:
Leah Kalmanson

Regional Editors:
Nader El-Bizri, James Madaio, Ann A. Pang-White, Takeshi Morisato, Pascah Mungwini, Mickaella Perina, Omar Rivera and Georgina Stewart

Bloomsbury Introductions to World Philosophies delivers primers reflecting exciting new developments in the trajectory of world philosophies. Instead of privileging a single philosophical approach as the basis of comparison, the series provides a platform for diverse philosophical perspectives to accommodate the different dimensions of cross-cultural philosophizing. While introducing thinkers, texts and themes emanating from different world philosophies, each book, in an imaginative and path-breaking way, makes clear how it departs from a conventional treatment of the subject matter.

Titles in the Series:

A Practical Guide to World Philosophies, by Monika Kirloskar-Steinbach and Leah Kalmanson
Daya Krishna and Twentieth-Century Indian Philosophy, by Daniel Raveh
Māori Philosophy, by Georgina Tuari Stewart
Philosophy of Science and The Kyoto School, by Dean Anthony Brink
Tanabe Hajime and the Kyoto School, by Takeshi Morisato
African Philosophy, by Pascah Mungwini
The Zen Buddhist Philosophy of D. T. Suzuki, by Rossa Ó Muireartaigh
Sikh Philosophy, by Arvind-Pal Singh Mandair
The Philosophy of the Brahma-sūtra, by Aleksandar Uskokov
The Philosophy of the Yogasūtra, by Karen O'Brien-Kop
The Life and Thought of H. Odera Oruka, by Gail M. Presbey
Mexican Philosophy for the 21st Century, by Carlos Alberto Sánchez
Buddhist Ethics and the Bodhisattva Path, by Stephen Harris
Contextualizing Angela Davis, by Joy James
Yorùbá Art and Aesthetics, by Barry Hallen

Phenomenology of Tea

A Dialogue on Japanese Aesthetics

Adam Loughnane

BLOOMSBURY ACADEMIC
LONDON · NEW YORK · OXFORD · NEW DELHI · SYDNEY

BLOOMSBURY ACADEMIC

Bloomsbury Publishing Plc, 50 Bedford Square, London, WC1B 3DP, UK
Bloomsbury Publishing Inc, 1359 Broadway, New York, NY 10018, USA
Bloomsbury Publishing Ireland, 29 Earlsfort Terrace, Dublin 2, D02 AY28, Ireland

BLOOMSBURY, BLOOMSBURY ACADEMIC and the Diana logo are trademarks of
Bloomsbury Publishing Plc

First published in Great Britain 2026

Copyright © Adam Loughnane, 2026

Adam Loughnane has asserted his right under the Copyright, Designs and Patents Act,
1988, to be identified as Author of this work.

Series design by Louise Dugdale
Cover image © Ainul Azhar / Getty Images

All rights reserved. No part of this publication may be: i) reproduced or transmitted in any form, electronic or mechanical, including photocopying, recording or by means of any information storage or retrieval system without prior permission in writing from the publishers; or ii) used or reproduced in any way for the training, development or operation of artificial intelligence (AI) technologies, including generative AI technologies. The rights holders expressly reserve this publication from the text and data mining exception as per Article 4(3) of the Digital Single Market Directive (EU) 2019/790.

Bloomsbury Publishing Plc does not have any control over, or responsibility for, any third-party websites referred to or in this book. All internet addresses given in this book were correct at the time of going to press. The author and publisher regret any inconvenience caused if addresses have changed or sites have ceased to exist, but can accept no responsibility for any such changes.

A catalogue record for this book is available from the British Library.

A catalog record for this book is available from the Library of Congress.

ISBN: HB: 978-1-3502-4661-4
PB: 978-1-3502-4657-7
ePDF: 978-1-3502-4658-4
eBook: 978-1-3502-4659-1

Typeset by RefineCatch Limited, Bungay, Suffolk
Printed and bound in Great Britain

For product safety related questions contact productsafety @bloomsbury.com.

To find out more about our authors and books visit www.bloomsbury.com
and sign up for our newsletters.

For our mother, Anne-Marie

Contents

List of Illustrations		viii
Series Editor's Preface		ix
Introduction		1
1	What is (not) Tea?	5
2	Water for Tea	19
3	Urasenke Institute	33
4	Tetsugaku Michi	55
5	Kyoto Daigaku I	73
6	Kyoto Daigaku II	91
7	Tea Garden	113
8	Outer Roji	143
9	The Un-named Artist Copying Copies	153
10	Inner Roji	175
11	Wabi-Sabi, Raku and Zen	199
12	Space and Time	211
13	The Tea Hut	221
14	Alcove and Hanging Scroll	231
15	Flowers for Tea	253
16	Sitting	277
17	As if in a Dream	295
Notes		311
Bibliography		327
Index		341

List of Illustrations

2.1	Rikyū's Well, Sakai, Japan. (*Rikyū no I*, 利休の井).	19
2.2	Fresh Water Bucket. (*Mizusashi*, 水指).	20
2.3	Portrait of Myōan Eisai. *c.* 1150.	27
2.4	Portrait of Dōgen Zenji. *c.* 1253.	29
2.5	Daisu (台子) Tea Shelf.	32
3.1	Urasenke Institute, Kyoto.	33
3.2	Murata Shukō. (村田珠光; 1423–1502).	35
3.3	*Mu* (無), "emptiness".	38
3.4	*Sōan* (草庵) style tea hut.	40
3.5	Takeno Jō'ō (武野 紹鴎, 1502–55).	42
3.6	Sen no Rikyū (千利休; 1522–91).	45
4.1	Philosopher's Walk, Kyoto. (*Tetsugaku no Michi*, 哲学の道).	55
4.2	Cherry blossom-lined path of the Philosopher's Walk. (*Tetsugaku no Michi no sakura namiki*, 哲学の道の桜並木).	56
4.3	Kamikaze Attack on USS *Missouri*, April 11, 1945.	64
4.4	*Ginkaku-ji* (銀閣寺), Kyoto.	65
7.1	Outer Garden Door. (*soto-mon*, 外門).	114
7.2	*Yin yang* symbol (阴阳)	123
7.3	*Shimenawa* ropes (しめ縄).	135
10.1	*Qi* energy patterns in mountain landscape.	187
10.2	Barrier Stone. (*sekimori ishi*, 関守石)	188
11.1	Raku Pottery. (*raku-yaki*, 楽焼).	200
13.1	"Crawling in space" (*nijiriguchi*, 躙り口).	228
14.1	Alcove. (*tokonoma*, 床の間).	232
14.2	*Kana* (仮名).	235
14.3	Sesshū Tōyō. "Splashed Ink Landscape" (破墨山水図, *Haboku-sansui*), 1495. Ink on paper.	242
16.1	First Charcoal Ceremony. (*shozumi*, 初炭).	277
16.2	*Book of Changes*. (*I Ching*, 易经).	279
16.3	Tearoom Floor Plan.	279
16.4	Traditional Japanese Confections. (*wagashi*, 和菓子).	286
16.5	*Fukusa* Folding Ritual.	293

Series Editor Preface

Bloomsbury Introductions to World Philosophies offers plural, hitherto unexplored pathways into the study of world philosophies. Instead of privileging a single philosophical approach as the basis of comparison, the series provides a platform for diverse philosophical perspectives to accommodate the many different dimensions of cross-cultural philosophizing. While the choice of terms used by the individual volumes may indeed carry a local inflection, they do not foreclose critical thinking about philosophical plurality. Each individual volume strikes a balance between locality and globality.

Adam Loughnane's *Phenomenology of Tea: A Dialogue on Japanese Aesthetics* unravels the multilayered philosophical, aesthetic and religious aspects of the Japanese tea ceremony step-by-step. The approach to this salient facet of Japanese material culture is ingenious: creatively exploring the experience of undertaking a tea ceremony through the genre of a philosophical dialogue. Loughnane guides readers through the ceremony's complex background in Buddhism, Daoism, Confucianism and Shinto, while simultaneously reading the experience through the lens of philosophical and phenomenological theories of Nishida, Heidegger, Ueda, Merleau-Ponty, and Nishitani. This intercultural reading is a sustained engagement through the tea ceremony of a simple question: "How can one experience a foreign culture?", and in its unique approach offers a novel proposal for intercultural encounter. *Phenomenology of Tea* opens the way to a rich philosophical immersion into a seemingly simple aesthetic ceremony.

Monika Kirloskar-Steinbach

Introduction

Over the years I spent working on this project, I was often asked: *"Why a dialogue?"*, and at the request of the series editors, I promised an answer.

After returning from a research stay in Japan—where I had the chance to learn about and take part in the tea ceremony—I began teaching a course on Japanese aesthetics at University College Cork, Ireland. While the course did not begin this way, it gradually evolved over several years into a guided tour through the various stages of the tea ceremony. As anyone who has experienced it knows, the ceremony immerses one in a great deal of Japan's major artistic traditions and aesthetic practices: calligraphy, flower arranging, gardening, pottery, dress making, architecture, and more. And, looking deeper, one finds many of the major Japanese aesthetic concepts woven into the garden paths, the many ritual objects, and the tea hut—also shaping how bodies move, see, touch, taste and smell, and also how one speaks, gestures, or remains silent and still in the unique way the Japanese tea ceremony affords.

Because of how comprehensively the ceremony brings together so many elements of Japanese art and culture, it became an ideal framework for structuring an undergraduate class on Japanese aesthetic and, in turn, for structuring the present work.

This was one reason I chose to frame the book as a tour, but that alone did not require writing in dialogue. The dialogical format allowed for two possibilities that traditional academic forms could not, which turned out to be crucial for approaching the main questions the work grapples with.

First, a recurring question in class was whether the tea ceremony should be understood as an artistic, religious, or even philosophical ritual. The dialogue—which includes a Theologian, a Philosopher, and an Artist—allowed me, as author, and hopefully you, as reader, to see the ceremony through a diverse set of eyes. The characters' varied backgrounds are meant to open a space for the ceremony to be experienced and interrogated from several perspectives without reducing to any one.

Secondly, while this book offers an overview of the Japanese tea ceremony and its philosophical influences—Buddhist, Daoist, Confucian, and Shinto—it was not conceived strictly as an introduction, but was shaped by a programmatic intent. This aim would not have been possible without the dialogical form and the use of literary devices not available in conventional academic prose. Without revealing too much, the dialogue format allowed—however minimal of an attempt—for the development of a position and the provocation of an experience concerning intercultural encounter that I don't believe would have been possible otherwise.

The intention was to provoke a question of whether, and to what extent, it is possible to truly experience the tea ceremony today. As a centuries-old tradition that evolved within a world profoundly different from our own, how might we avoid reducing the ceremony to an aestheticized object, one consumed through the same habits of attachment and objectification pervading our late-modern, deeply materialist world? This present world of ours runs, in many ways, in direct opposition to the ethos the tea ceremony was meant to cultivate: a non-objective space where guests could loosen their attachments to the world.

What I came to realize—only late in the writing process—is that the underlying premise of this project must have been that such an experience might no longer be possible, or at least exceedingly remote. And yet, insofar as I wrote the work and insofar as its characters do partake in the ceremony, a modified question emerged retroactively: What can we do in the face of this impossibility? What possibilities remain for aesthetic experience within, or despite, the various obstructions complicating intercultural experience? And if there might be a way forward, can our attempts to have an experience of the Japanese tea ceremony tell us about intercultural methods to encounter another culture's arts and rituals more generally?

This question brought me to an intellectual tradition that, though foreign in origin, has become deeply entwined with the Japanese philosophical world; that is, phenomenology. Phenomenology offers some of the most refined tools for thinking about embodied, aesthetic experience and provides, I believe, a meaningful way forward in the face of the possibilities and impossibilities—not only for experiencing the tea ceremony today—but for intercultural encounter more broadly.

And, for the space to explore these questions and support for this unconventional approach, I would like to thank Monika Kirloskar-Steinbach for the invitation to this series, and to the team at Bloomsbury—Colleen Coalter,

Aimee Brown, Suzie Nash—the anonymous reviewers for their greatly appreciated feedback, and to my research assistant, Meghan Troha. Lastly, a big heartfelt thanks to Annette and Étienne for their support and patience while I finished this work.

Carrigadrohid, Ireland. July 2025

1

What is (not) Tea?

Guide: Welcome everyone. *Hajimemashite, douzo yoroshiku*! I'm so glad you're all here today! To begin our tour of the Japanese tea ceremony, let me start by saying that I can't take you on a tour of the Japanese tea ceremony!

~ *All three participants appeared puzzled.*

Artist: How's that? We're beginning our tour, but . . . you can't take us?

Theologian: Do we take ourselves, then?

Guide: No, you can't take yourselves either. But, don't worry, we'll still go.

Philosopher: Is this a riddle or . . .?

Theologian: You can't take us, we can't take ourselves . . . then, what will we do?

Artist: I like contradictions, but I'd also like to go to a tea ceremony.

Guide: *I* can't take you to a Japanese tea ceremony, and no, you can't take yourselves. And, that's simply because none of us are selves, the tea garden is not a place, and the tea ceremony is not a thing. So, we'll have to find another way.

~ *The three were no less mystified, but a glint of curiosity flickered in their eyes.*

Guide: Shall we?

Theologian: So, we are going to the tea garden, then?

Guide: Yes, absolutely.

Artist: But, if we're not selves, who will go?

Philosopher: And, if the tea garden isn't a place, *where* will we go?

Guide: Don't worry, it will all make sense as we get on our way. And yes, something like your selves will be in some place like a tea garden undertaking what we call a Japanese tea ceremony. We'll learn all about the rituals, aesthetic objects, as well as the philosophic, religious, and artistic principles involved in the ceremony, but we'll do our best to revise some of our ideas about selves, places, and things along the way.

Philosopher: Sounds straightforward enough.

Guide: In a sense, yes. It's the simplest thing we can do. But, in another sense, some of our ideas make it almost impossible.

Artist: But, thousands of people do these ceremonies every year. It can't be completely impossible.

Guide: No, of course not. We can definitely participate in a tea ceremony, but we have to ask ourselves, is just being there and going through the motions going to ensure we actually experience the ceremony as it was meant to be experienced? We bring a whole landscape of assumptions from the Western world—the intellectual tradition we typically trace to Europe, with its origins in Greece—many of which we can't even see. These might get in the way of the ceremony appearing on its own terms.

You're going to gain a lot of new knowledge over the next several days that will help you think better about the ceremony, but what if thought itself can get in the way of our having something like an *authentic* experience? Or, what if grasping for authenticity is the problem?

The rituals we're going to learn evolved within a deeply foreign culture. A different language, different ideas of art, different religions and philosophies. Even for present-day Japanese citizens, we might say that the tea ceremony evolved in a different "world". How or whether we can get access to that world is by no means a simple question.

There are a lot of ideas in the West about rituals, about aesthetics and fine arts, but until historically very recently, Japan didn't even have a concept of fine art and maybe not even a concept of aesthetics as we know it. It's a real question whether we in the twenty-first century can experience a complex ritual from such a different world. I've been learning about and going to tea ceremonies for almost twenty years: I don't even know if I've experienced one yet. Whether we can get beyond our tradition and our deeply engrained cultural biases to have an experience of this kind of ritual as anything other than foreigners or tourists, it's a tricky question.

Theologian: It does sound almost impossible.

Guide: Nah, you're overthinking it. In the end, it's just a cup of tea. What the Japanese call *Chanoyu* (茶の湯)[1] is the most simple thing. The great tea master, Sen no Rikyū (千利休, 1522–91) said, *Chanoyu* is merely to "heat water, make tea, and drink".

We can all heat water, right? We've all made tea. We all know how to sit with friends and drink.

Philosopher: Okay, that sounds possible.

Guide: There's nothing difficult at all, but that in itself can be the biggest challenge. Making tea is one of the most simple things a human can do. But, in another sense, tea is as complex as the entire universe. Many tea masters have dedicated decades to performing this most simple of tasks, and maybe they'll do it perfectly, just once in their life, if they're lucky.

But we're thinking about the challenge of experiencing the tea ceremony in terms of our own limitations—the issue could also lie within the ceremony itself.

Artist: A problem with the ceremony making it difficult for us to experience the ceremony?

Guide: Yes, maybe it's not just us. Some Japanese intellectuals have argued that the tea ceremony has stagnated, that it's no longer a living tradition but something like a museum piece, a formalized reproduction of the past—or even a dead or dying tradition.

There's a twentieth-century philosopher, Zen Buddhist scholar, and tea practitioner named Hisamatsu Shin'ichi (久松 真一, 1889–1980), he wrote a book *Philosophy of Tea* (茶道の哲学, 1987, p. 36) where he laments the decline of the contemporary version of ceremony. He called for "killing the ancestors" (「祖を殺す」) of the ritual to bring it back to life.

Artist: Who are the "ancestors"?

Guide: Literally, that term "ancestors" (*sō* 祖)—sometimes translated as "patriarchs"—refers to the great figures of the Buddhist tradition.

Theologian: We should kill these people?

Guide: In a sense. What Hisamatsu means is that when we become too enamored with the past, we start reproducing it rather than engaging with it in the present as a living, evolving tradition. "Killing the ancestors"—overcoming attachment to one's spiritual lineage—would revitalize the ceremony, he thinks, at least.

Keep this in mind for later. We'll have the chance to kill a few Buddhas along our way.

Philosopher: But, isn't Buddhism an important part of the tea ceremony?

Guide: A very important part.

Theologian: How exactly will we kill the Buddha?

Guide: We can't. But, we'll try.

Artist: When do we kill the Buddha?

Guide: As soon as possible. But, not before we learn about the non-duality of life and death.

Theologian: I don't understand—the tea ceremony is dead? And we have to kill it to bring it back to life?

Guide: To be alive, things have to grow and evolve. If the ceremony becomes overly formalized and conservative, it risks becoming a mere reproduction of the past rather than a dynamic, living practice. A Russian-French philosopher, Alexander Kojève (1980), made this exact point after visiting Japan—that the ceremony had become an empty formalism.

To foreshadow a Buddhist concept we'll revisit later, "clinging" or "attachment" (Skt. *upādāna*. Jp. *shūshu* 執著) to something as a fixed object might be one sense in which something dies for us.

And, if the tea ceremony has been so formalized that it can only be consumed as an object rather than experienced as a living practice, then this is another big obstacle to our ability to experience it.

Philosopher: But, what is the tea ceremony if it's not a thing? It's not a person or a place, what else is left?

Guide: Ah, the classic "what is?" question. That's a favorite of Western philosophy. Let me propose this: why don't we ask, "what is *not* tea?"?

Theologian: But, we came to learn about tea.

Philosopher: Wouldn't we then be talking about something else? Everything that *isn't* tea.

Guide: All completely reasonable assumptions. The Western intellectual tradition trains us to think that if we want to learn about something, let's call it "A", we figure we should ignore what "A" is not; forget about what is "not-A".

Artist: . . . seems pretty straightforward.

Theologian: If we want to learn about the tea ceremony, then we learn about the tea ceremony.

Guide: Let me share a quote with you from the tea master and founder of the Edosenke School, Kawakami Fuhaku (川上不白 1719–1807). He says "the essence of *Chanoyu* lies precisely in what isn't *Chanoyu*" (Hiroichi 1982, p. 58).

"*Chanoyu*" (茶の湯) is one of the several words for the tea ceremony, by the way.

I realize it probably seems completely innocuous to ask "what is?" questions, but when we ask this question, we're actually making substantial, implicit philosophical commitments to a certain logic, metaphysics, epistemology, and aesthetics, and we're mostly doing that in a Western way.

Philosopher: So, we should bracket our Western ways of thinking to experience a tea ceremony?

Guide: Yes and no. There's nothing wrong with Western ways of doing philosophy or asking questions,—the mistake is to think that it's the *only* way. Especially when trying to experience something like the Japanese tea ceremony, Eurocentrism would be another substantial obstacle in our way.

But, Western ways of thinking are deeply ingrained, so even if we wanted to, we can't just discard them. If we're going to try to really experience the tea ceremony, to feel its profound beauty, then we need to learn some different ways of thinking that tea practitioners who created the ceremony might have adhered to.

Artist: Okay, let me try to understand. You've said that you can't take us to the ceremony, but we will go. That it's impossible to experience, but not to worry, not to overthink it. That we'll kill the tea ceremony ancestors to keep it alive. And, now, to learn about the tea ceremony we'll focus on what is *not* tea?

Guide: Exactly.

~ *None of the three seemed satisfied.*

I think you might be noticing that I'm giving several answers to the same question, and some of those answers seem to contradict each other.

Artist: Yeah.

Guide: I've done this tour several times and there's always a bit of a resistance to the idea of there being more than one truth. Mostly, we want there to be just one and for it not to involve any contradiction. *Chanoyu* is *this* and not *that*. A self is *this* or *that*. Time and space are *this* and *not that*. The Western tradition hasn't given us great tools to imagine things being this *and* that. A *and* not-A. We're taught to expect and work towards a single truth.

Philosopher: But, if truths contradict each other, doesn't one have to be false?

Nāgārjuna—Two-fold Truth

Guide: Have any of you heard of the Buddhist philosopher Nāgārjuna?

~ *All three shook their heads.*

Okay, he was a second-century CE philosopher and founder of the Mādhyamika school of Mahāyāna Buddhism. He had an idea he calls the "Two-fold Truth" (Skt. *dvisatya*).

The Two-fold Truth distinguished between what he calls "conventional" truth (Skt. *saṃvṛti*) and "ultimate" truth (Skt. *paramārtha*). Consider that quote, "the essence of *Chanoyu* lies in what is not *Chanoyu*", and the couple of contradictions I've already thrown at you.

We can say that in a "conventional" sense, of course *Chanoyu* is simply *Chanoyu*, just as a self is a self, the tea ceremony is a thing, and we are all selves. These things all have a form, an essence, we can define them—no problem. We can speak about these things meaningfully, define them in A=A, *non-contradictory* ways, and we'll all understand each other just fine. This is one level of truth.

In this "conventional" sense, the question of whether we can actually experience a Japanese tea ceremony as foreigners isn't even a question. Of course we will.

But, at the same time, in an "ultimate" sense, things are more complicated. In the "ultimate" sense, Nāgārjuna says all things are "empty", or his Sanskrit term, *śūnyatā*. As empty, we are *not* selves, the garden is *not* a place, and the ceremony is a *not* a thing. So, the question of whether or how we can experience the tea ceremony, or experience *anything* becomes more complicated, but a lot more interesting, I think.

In a conventional sense, "what is?" questions are great. Tea is tea, the self is a self, A is A. But, if we want to talk about how things are in an ultimate sense, then we also might ask "what is not?" kind of questions—we have to bring A in relation to not-A, or let's say the positive in relation to the negative.

Artist: I don't understand. The negative, how?

Guide: That's precisely what we need to sort out before we get going. The idea of the negative doesn't show up too often in the Western tradition. Philosophers who are part of this lineage have mostly focused on the positive. Let me give you a set of terms we're going to use throughout to distinguish the positive from the negative. Look here:

~ *The guide showed the participants his notebook.*

	Positivity:	**Negativity:**
	"being"	"nothing"
	"essence"	"empty"
	"presence"	"absence"
	"form"	"formless"
	"substantial"	"relational"
	"permanence"	"impermanence"

~ *Each of the participants scribbled the table into their own notebooks.*

Great, yes good idea to write these down. We'll come back to them a lot and you'll likely want to add to it, and then probably throw it away.

Philosopher: Throw it away?

Guide: Yes, this is an embarrassingly over-simplified taxonomy, and ultimately, we'll need to think in a more nuanced way—specifically to go beyond the implicit duality—but for now, it's helpful to get us started. I'm sure it all looks completely abstract, but don't worry—we'll spend the next few days unpacking these ideas. Once the negative comes into view, we'll start to see how we're *non-selves*, how we speak in the mode of *non-speaking*, and act in the mode of *non-acting*.

Let's get started unpacking these ideas of "positivity" and "negativity"—or, what I'll refer to as the "ontological positive" and "ontological negative".

Let's begin with the ontological positive and back to the "what is?" kind of questions. Who was famous for this kind of question?

Theologian: Socrates? He would walk around Athens getting citizens to answer "what is justice?", "what is knowledge?", "what is virtue?", that type of thing. The Socratic method, right?

Guide: Exactly. And, what was his aim?

Artist: Finding definitions?

Philosopher: And, those definitions were supposed to indicate the essence of things.

Guide: Great. Look back. That's another term on our table, "essences".

Yes, Western philosophy has been very concerned with essences. The philosopher was the one who knew or could see essences and the Socratic method was a way of questioning that was supposed to lead us to define the world, things or the kind of beings we are as having an un-changing, permanent essence.

Artist: That's another term on our table. "permanence"

Guide: Yes, good. Even for many who have never studied philosophy, and even for places we consider "non-Western", when we want to know something—even if we never think of this explicitly—we naturally follow ways of thinking and questioning that expect we can find definitions and essences. This is crucial for approaching many questions, scientific questions in particular, but we're going to have to slightly modify this approach to come more in line with ways of thinking associated with the tea ceremony. Or, ways of *not* thinking.

Theologian: . . . think of ways of not-thinking?

Guide: Another way the Western intellectual tradition has shaped our expectations is that contradiction signals an error in our thinking. Contradiction is a mistake and demands clarification, disambiguation or correction. A cannot equal not-A. The self can't be a non-self.

This is partly because at the very beginnings of Western philosophy, when Aristotle was formalizing the laws of logic, he made the "Law of non-contradiction" foundational. According to this law, A cannot equal not-A. ($A \neq \neg A$): You are not her. The sky is not the river. My shoes are not your nose. And *Chanoyu* is *not* not-*Chanoyu*. Without ever having studied any philosophy, almost everybody takes this logical rule for granted.

Philosopher: But, can we speak meaningfully about anything without accepting Aristotle's logic?

Guide: Yes, we can, and we do. The question is, can we use language *without* using the not-A part, what I referred to as the negative. To understand *anything*, we need both A *and* not-A. But, to see this, we'll have to learn more about the "ontological negative" and we'll see why we *have to* ask "what is not?" questions for anything to be intelligible at all.

Theologian: But, what about Western philosophers like Plotinus or Aquinas? Didn't they define God in the negative? Isn't that a not-A kind of description?

Guide: Great point. That's what's called the *via negativa*. These philosophers, sometimes called "negative theologians" used this approach, yes. There are some interesting parallels between this and some Asian philosophies we'll explore, but let me highlight one key contrast.

The *via negativa* acted as a kind of constraint on *descriptions* of God. They believed language couldn't adequately capture God's perfection, so they resorted to the "linguistic negative", to define God they said what he wasn't. Rather than saying God is this or that, we have negative sentences like God is *not* material (*non materialis*), *not* changeable (*immutabilis*), God is *not* in time (*non in tempore*), God has *no* potentiality (*actus purus*).

We'll see this negative linguistic approach in some Asian philosophies as well, but they take the negative a few steps farther from logic to ontology.

Artist: I'm still not clear about what you mean by the "ontological negative". So, it's not just Asian philosophers who used this concept?

Guide: This is why the table I showed you—and *any* simple binary opposition—is ultimately problematic. I'll use the words "Eastern" and "Western" a lot, and juxtapose the positive and negative, but we have to be careful about taking these too literally. These are provisional oppositions that are useful in a sense, but ultimately, we have to see that they are generalizations. We'll come back to this table throughout our lectures, but keep in mind that this is mostly an introductory course, so we'll mostly work on a high level of generality, but I'll point out exceptions and nuances when I can. So, please try to remember the terms on this table, but don't hold onto the oppositions too tightly. Especially terms like "East" and "West". They might point to some broad historical differences, but the distinction becomes less and less meaningful as time goes on. There is no monolithic Eastern or Western tradition. Some scholars have even stopped capitalizing "East" and "West" to reinforce that exact point. I'll sometimes refer to the "Western" lineage as the "European" tradition to reflect its origins in Ancient Greece.

But, do keep in mind that even some of what we call "western" or "european" philosophers invoke the "ontological negative", with concepts like "nothingness", "emptiness", "abyss", "void", or "negation", even terminology like "non-object" or "non-willing".

Artist: But, what does that "non-" refer to? It can't mean that there literally is *nothing*—no self, no garden or ceremony *at all*?

Guide: Not exactly. When we append negative prefixes to terms like the self, language, or objects, we're not saying they *exist in no way at all*, but rather that they *exist in a different way*.

The various "non" terms we'll learn, these indicate how selves, language, objects, etc., exist *as constituted by both the ontological positive and negative*. We need *both* sides of our table.

Philosopher: But, when we use negations like *non-self* or *non-thing*, does that mean the terms we negate become *less than* they would be without the negation? Is there an ontological kind of subtraction?

Guide: Great question. Many philosophers do treat negation as a *less than* position—sometimes referred to as a "deflationary" account of whatever is being discussed. But what I want to show you is that when we bring *both* sides of that table together, the interplay between negativity and positivity doesn't lead to deflationary "less than", it actually gives us a radically expansive "more than" understanding of the self, objects, and phenomena.

And the tea ceremony, with its intricate rituals, offers an extraordinary way to experience this kind of expansive possibility. But at the same time—it's just a cup of tea. So, don't get too caught up in philosophical technicalities or let expectations and concepts get in the way.

This brings up a lot of what we call "inter-cultural" issues. The question about how to encounter foreign cultures is a complicated one, and we'll actually have a few lectures on just that topic in later meetings.

Artist: Would you say that we are being inter-culturally sensitive if our definitions of the tea ceremony include *what it is?* and *what it is not?*, the positive and the negative?

Guide: It's one part of the inter-cultural puzzle.

Theologian: In the most abstract sense, is killing the ancestors a negation?

Guide: Hmm, maybe but it's not so simple. For now, let's say, it's a negation of a negation, but we'll come back to this in a later talk.

Philosopher: But, is there anything we can say about the tea ceremony that is straightforward and positive?

Guide: What do you have in mind?

Philosopher: I don't know, just the most minimal thing. It seems like we can at least say that it's a ceremony, that there's tea, that it's Japanese.

Guide: Let me ask you all—do you associate the tea ceremony with Japan?

Theologian: That's what I've always thought.

Artist: I'm pretty sure that they didn't invent it, but systematized it in a fashion people associate with a "Japanese" way of doing things.

Guide: Okay, great. Let's have this one last discussion before we head off today.

Let's apply some of our new logic and say that the tea ceremony is both Japanese and not Japanese.

Many do consider the tea ceremony quintessentially Japanese. Even those who haven't visited or lived in Japan have encountered representations in films, literature, poetry and in paintings and even sculptures in art galleries all over the world. Tea has played a complex and significant role in Japanese culture for over five hundred years. At different times and for various reasons, it has been part of Buddhist monasticism, Zen meditative practice, and ritual ceremonies—it was even employed as a tool in war. Later, it became associated with samurai and the pursuit of self-discipline, as well as Japanese Buddhist monks and their pursuit of salvation.

Tea culture has profoundly shaped Japanese identity, influencing art, architecture, and more concretely, food, clothing, etiquette, politics and everyday life. It has provided new ways to think about the self, the world, and, in a philosophical sense, space, time, the body, perception, materiality, and spirituality. It's a major factor in the manners and etiquette of everyday Japanese life, and has also played a crucial role in sociality, solidarity, and class dynamics—both reinforcing social hierarchies and, at times, challenging them.

As a convergence of a multitude of practices, *Chanoyu* is an intricate and beautiful synthesis of major aspects of Japanese art, culture, craftsmanship, philosophy, and religion—some originating in Japan, others imported and gradually transformed into distinctly Japanese traditions.

Studying the tea ceremony connects us with nearly all of Japan's major philosophical, religious, and aesthetic traditions, including Buddhism, Daoism, Shinto, and Confucianism, all of which we'll explore together in the coming weeks.

The ceremony encompasses a wide range of traditional Japanese art forms, including calligraphy, gardening, architecture, poetry, dressmaking, pottery, flower arranging, and highly aestheticized cuisine. As we make our way through the garden and into the hut, we'll also encounter key Japanese aesthetic principles such as *wabi-sabi*, *yūgen*, and *mono no aware*.

Philosophically, we might say that the world of tea has its own ethics, metaphysics, and ontology, as well as a unique conception of space and time. Artistically, it has its own aesthetic world. Religiously, it is a deeply sacred ritual—while at the same time all these terms are problematic and demand more and less from our thoughts and actions.

We still have to be careful with importing western categories. Until quite recently, Japan had no terms corresponding to what is called "aesthetics" or even "fine art" in the European tradition. Some scholars have even argued that nothing akin to western aesthetics has ever existed in Japan. (Ōhashi 2010)

The two main Japanese terms now used for "aesthetics" were introduced only in the late nineteenth century as translations of western concepts. Nishi Amane first used *Kashuron* (佳趣論, "theory of good and beautiful taste") in a lecture in 1870. Later, in 1877, he introduced *bimyōgaku* (美妙学, "doctrine of sublime beauty"). The term for "fine arts", *bijutsu* (美術) was only adopted during the Meiji period to approximate European notions.

So, when we ask, "What is *Chanoyu*?"—we might debate whether it is art, religion, or philosophy. Again, we want to say that it is *this* and it is *not that*. But categories like philosophy, art, and religion hold different meanings in Japan than they do in the European traditions. If we expect our experience to fit neatly into western categories, this could get in the way of experiencing the ceremony on its own terms.

What makes *Chanoyu* remarkable is that it incorporates all of these categories while resisting reduction to any single one. In many ways, the tea ceremony challenges our tendency to seek clear-cut definitions, refusing to be confined by any single framework or un-ambiguous definitions.

Philosopher: That's not something we're taught to be comfortable with in the west.

Guide: Yes, that's right.

Let me share another quote I have in my notebook here. This is from Hisamatsu Shin'ichi, again:

> *Sadō has a synthetic cultural unity which cannot be found in other fields. It not only includes art, ethics and morality, philosophy, but even religion, in short, all manner of different aspects of culture. It absorbs all of these into one cultural system.*
>
> (1970, p. 9)

This synthetic aspect makes the ceremony unique but also difficult to define using our usual categories—or difficult to experience if we are overly constrained by those categories.

The ceremony's resistance to taken-for-granted ways of thinking and categorizing is one of its greatest virtues. Throughout the class, we'll work on cultivating this different way of thinking and philosophizing.

Artist: So, in that way of thinking, the tea ceremony is and is not Japanese?

Guide: I think so, but it's nuanced. There's no denying that, over centuries, the tea ceremony has become a complex and beautiful expression of some of Japan's most refined cultural and aesthetic impulses.

But we'll also see how framing the tea ceremony as *quintessentially* Japanese—or even speaking of a singular "Japanese identity"—is problematic and sometimes even dangerous. The tea ceremony has been appropriated at times to bolster a version of Japanese identity that has had disastrous consequences, which we'll need to consider carefully.

There's no simple answer to how Japanese the tea ceremony is. In many ways, we'll have to be satisfied with—and learn to sustain—a *yes* and a *no* to this question, as well as many others we'll encounter.

And remember, we don't have to settle on any one answer. No single identity or essence defines or limits what tea has been—or, perhaps more importantly, what it might become. It is many things, none of which reduce to a single definition.

The traditions having touched the tea ceremony at different moments of its evolution—Buddhism, Daoism, Shinto, and to a lesser extent, Confucianism—have sometimes engaged with definitions and *"what is?"* questions. But these were almost always instrumental—serving not as fixed answers but serving a practice of living harmoniously, reducing suffering, minimizing social friction, and, in some cases, aiding in the pursuit of enlightenment.

Does anybody know what the terms "epistemology" or "soteriology" mean?

Philosopher: I don't know the second one, but epistemology means the study of knowledge.

Guide: Exactly. The western philosophical tradition has been, at times, obsessed with acquiring certain or absolute knowledge, whereas traditions like Buddhism and Daoism—they obviously thought about knowledge, they wouldn't reject it—but striving for certain knowledge wouldn't have been their main interest. They were more "soteriological" than epistemological. "Soteriology" means something like, "doctrine of salvation". The idea being that to exist is to suffer and philosophies aim to diminish or modify that suffering.

Of course, soteriology isn't completely absent from western philosophy. The Stoics, some Hellenistic schools, theological philosophies and existential thinkers would have been less concerned with certainty and knowledge and more focused on improving one's well-being.

For our purposes, the important thing to keep in mind as we explore philosophical aspects of the tea ceremony is that it didn't evolve to help practitioners gain knowledge, to prove a theory or formulate a definition. It's not speculative or theoretical the way European philosophy has been for most of its history. And, the version of the tea ceremony we'll partake in, which is closely aligned with

Zen Buddhism, is a set of rituals meant to bring peace and well-being. How that approach remains philosophical is a question we'll return to throughout our meetings.

Artist: So, the idea isn't just to define what well-being is, but to actually *experience* well-being, to reduce suffering?

Guide: Yes, exactly. If there's anything philosophical about the tea ceremony, it's more about experiencing than *theorizing about* experience. That being said, we will discuss the ceremony in the abstract quite a lot before we actually undertake the ritual. We just need to keep in mind that answering "what is tea?" kind of questions, and *defining* what the various aspects of tea are won't be our main goal. Everything we learn will be in service of preparing us to experience *Chanoyu*. And, this isn't unlike the actual tea masters who likewise dedicate an incredible amount of time and energy for preparing the ceremony in hopes that their guests can have some hint of an experience, however fleeting, of the profound sense of well-being that can come by the simple act of sharing a drink together in a beautiful setting.

So, that's a lot for one day. Unless you have any questions, we'll meet in Osaka tomorrow for our second class.

See you there!

2
Water for Tea

Figure 2.1 Rikyū's Well, Sakai, Japan. (*Rikyū no I*, 利休の井). R. Loughnane.

Guide: Welcome back, everybody.

As you know, most of our tour will take place in Kyoto. Can anyone guess why we're starting here in Osaka today?

Artist: I guess, if we stick to what you've said, we're not here.

Philosopher: And this spot isn't a place, so how could we be here?

Guide: I love this group already.

But, this *non*-place we're *not* at has some interesting history. This is the "Camellia Well" (*Tsubaki-no-ido* 椿の井戸), which is also known as *Rikyū no I* (利休の井) or, "Rikyū's Well".

Sen no Rikyū (千利休, 1522–91) was Japan's most famous tea master, and some of his most important ceremonies used water from this very well. Over there was one of his early residences before he moved to Kyoto.

Philosopher: What was special about this well?

Guide: Tea masters placed exceptional value on water, so much that they would sometimes travel long distances to collect it for a special gathering. There are several famous water collecting spots throughout Japan—and more than a dozen in Kyoto.[1]

Aside from having water that was supposed to make better tea, there were other factors that contributed to the elevated status of certain wells, let's call them spiritual aspects tied to Buddhism, Shintoism or Daoism, which we'll talk about more in the next few days.

Artist: Did our tea host take water from here for the ceremony we'll do?

Guide: No, but we will. Here, take these. Fill them up and we'll take some water with us to the garden.

Normally, tea hosts would have collected water in wooden fresh-water containers called *mizusashi* (水指), but since we're going to be walking throughout Kyoto for

Figure 2.2 Fresh Water Bucket. (*Mizusashi*, 水指). R. Loughnane.

most of the day, these glass bottles will do. Our host will be very happy to have water from this source.

It's a nice sunny day, so why don't we sit on that patch of grass and get to know each other a bit. Let me ask you, what interests you about the tea ceremony? What made you decide to take this course?

Theologian: I was actually a practicing minister, but over the years I've realized that I'm more interested in reading and researching about religion, so in my forties I turned slightly away from practice and more towards study, towards theology. I'm mostly interested in religious rituals of different cultures, and always wanted to learn about the tea ceremony. I've traveled to a lot of countries to learn about different rituals, but still know very little about Japan. There seems to be something so unique about how the Japanese do things, so I'm really excited to learn more.

Guide: Right, this is a big question that will come up for us. About this Japanese way of doing things . . . about whether the Japanese tea ceremony is even Japanese.

What about you?

Artist: I've been a painter my whole life and, to be honest, until recently I hadn't considered many Asian art forms or practices. I was born here in Japan but moved to America when I was young. I've recently moved back and am trying to figure out where my practice fits between the culture I was born into and the one I lived in for almost twenty years. I've been visiting a lot of galleries and museums since I returned, but a Japanese friend told me that if I wanted to experience traditional Japanese arts, I had to do a tea ceremony.

Philosopher: . . . but, can we say that a tea ceremony is art? It has some artistic elements, but wouldn't you say it's a ritual?

Theologian: . . . a Catholic mass also has many artistic elements, but you wouldn't say that a mass itself was art.

Guide: Great questions! Is it art? Or, a ritual with artistic elements? I don't know. These are deeply complicated questions. But, what I do know is that we shouldn't expect to properly answer that question if we remain strictly within western ways of defining what art is, which is a shift we have to try to make over the next few days.

What about you, what brought you here?

Philosopher: I study philosophy and came to Japan for a post-doctoral fellowship. I didn't have any intention of looking into Asian philosophies but after a few years of getting to know Japanese history and culture, and visiting some Buddhist temples and Shinto shrines, I've gotten curious about the Japanese aesthetic and intellectual traditions. I'm still learning but I find it all very intriguing. I don't know if I'd consider them philosophies, or not, but definitely worth learning more about.

Guide: Oh yes, great. Is the tea ceremony art, is Buddhism philosophy? We'll get into all of this.

Artist: . . . why wouldn't they be philosophies?

Theologian: It's not so easy to classify them as philosophies because they have some elements we typically associate with religion, right.

Guide: Exactly. And, in western ways of thinking, philosophy and religion don't mix so well. We generally want to keep them separate. I sometimes refer to traditions like Buddhism and Daoism as "philosophy-religions". It's a clunky term but it's one way to avoid forcing western binaries onto these traditions. They don't fit neatly into either philosophic or religious categories, because they include elements of both.

Philosopher: And, as you said, those of us who are descendants of the European intellectual tradition tend to want things to be one thing or the other. Philosophy as philosophy, not as *non*-philosophy.

Guide: . . . and it's possible that the tea ceremony could be two things, or many things, even contradictory things. In the end, we don't need to decide for it to be one thing or another. But, we should guard against assuming that their resistance to western terminology means that there's something problematic or deficient with this tradition. It doesn't. If we assume that all ways of thinking should be judged by western standards, then the problem is our own. But, not to worry, a lot of what we'll learn in this tour should help us get beyond these limiting ways of thinking, and the reduction of philosophy to western definitions. We'll speak a lot about how there are philosophical, artistic, *and* religious aspects within the tea ceremony.

So, thank you, it's great to learn more about all of you. Let's hold onto your great questions for now and talk a little about the history of the tea ceremony.

We'll need to catch a train to Kyoto before noon so maybe we can continue our discussion on the way.

> ~ *The group gathered their things and the water they collected and together began making their way across Osaka to the Namba train station.*

Tea History: Which Cha?

Guide: Does anybody know the Japanese term for tea?

Theologian: I know this one. It's the "*cha*" like in *matcha* and *sencha*.

Guide: Yes, right. *Cha* is the Japanese term that comes from the Chinese, *chá* (茶). And, as you said, it's the suffix in the name for powdered tea, *matcha* (抹茶), but it's also used in many different forms of tea, including *sencha* (煎茶)[2] *hikicha* (挽茶), *bancha* (番茶), *kamairicha* (釜炒り茶), *shiracha* (白茶), and *dancha* (団茶).

Among all of these different varieties, whether it is green, brown, oolong, yellow, white or red, and regardless of what form it takes; leaves, powder, fermented, or roasted, all of these come from one single species called the Camellia sinensis, or "Chinese camellia". The one we tend to use for tea is among 220 other known species of camellia and around 3,000 hybrid species.

Cha is also heard in a bunch of other terms describing the many ways of enjoying tea. For example, *Okensha* (御献茶) was a ritual offering to Shinto tea gods; *Okucha* (御供茶) a memorial for the dead in Buddhist temples; *Chaji* (茶事) a vehicle for enlightenment with seven different forms.[3] *Chakai* (茶会) is mostly closed to participants and *Ōyose* (大寄せ), on the other hand, was a tea event that could include hundreds, sometimes even thousands of participants. And, *Chakai ōyose* (茶会大寄せ) was a public ceremony with anonymous guests. In all cases, we hear the "cha" sound.

But, among all the different ways of meeting to partake in a simple cup of tea, the one we'll be learning about and eventually partaking in is called *Chanoyu* (茶の湯). This is the tradition that arose within a heterodox group of highly cultured figures in Japan who venerated the Chinese literati tradition of Song China. Several different schools of tea branched off from *Chanoyu*. Our focus will be one step more specific: the most highly aestheticized form of tea, *Wabicha* (侘茶).

Artist: Was tea always an aesthetic ritual?

Guide: No, in fact it wasn't. Tea was treated sometimes as an elixir or medicinal concoction, sometimes used within a game or competition, other times as a meditative aid, or some thought, to give one magical powers.[4] Politicians and warlords employed the ceremony and expensive teaware to display and wield power, while at other times it was used simply as a pretext for gathering and passing time together in an informal social setting. Only very late in its history did it become a form of aesthetic self-cultivation, as it did with *Wabicha*.

You might have also heard the term *Chadō*, which translates as "the way of tea". This represents tea as a Daoist "way". We'll speak more about all of this terminology throughout our tour.

The question we're going to discuss now is, how tea drinking evolved from its origins, where it was used mostly for medicinal purposes or to keep one awake while meditating, all the way to such a sophisticated ritual practice that came to include architecture, pottery, poetry, painting, gardening, flower arranging, and eventually drawing inspiration and influence from Buddhism, Daoism, Confucianism and Shintoism.

We already spoke about how the tea ceremony originated in China. Does anybody know when it arrived in Japan?

Philosopher: In medieval times, right? Around the fourteenth and fifteenth centuries?

Guide: The version we'll experience, *Wabicha*, arose during the Muromachi period, around 1336 and 1573. So yes, the medieval period of Japanese history. But it actually existed here earlier. Does anyone know when tea itself, not the ceremony but just the drink first started being consumed?

Theologian: I think the origins are quite a lot earlier, in India.

Guide: Good, yes. There are records of tea being consumed in India before the Common Era. And, its spread outside of India is tied to the spread of Buddhism, which took root throughout the continent, in Tibet, Central Asia, even in the north coast of Africa, before it later migrated east to China, Korea, and Japan.

But before we get into the historical details, let me share with you some mythology about the origins of tea and its movement into China.

There are a few mythological accounts, but one of the more fantastical has to do with Bodhidharma (菩提達摩), an Indian Buddhist monk thought to have lived in the fifth or sixth century CE who brought Buddhism to China, and who later became the first patriarch of the Chinese school of Chan Buddhism. The story goes that he was among the first to bring tea from India into China.

And, here's the mythological part. He was said to have spent nine years meditating facing a wall and one day fell asleep during meditation. So angry with himself, he cut off his eyelids to ensure his eyes would never inadvertently close again while practicing. Where he threw his eyelids to the ground is said to be where the first tea plants grew.

While that's clearly fantastical, it does highlight an important part of tea history as it relates to Buddhist meditative practice. Tea spread rapidly throughout monastic communities in India and later China because of its vivifying effects helping practitioners stay awake and alert throughout long periods of meditation. Now we know that tea has these effects because of its caffeine content, but the mythological aspect sometimes went far beyond depicting that energetic boost we're all familiar with. If you look back through the historical accounts of tea drinking in Buddhist and Daoist lore, you'll find stories extolling not only the medicinal but even magical qualities of tea, which was said to cure diseases, give wings to fly, or render the dedicated drinker immortal.

We find the first accounts of tea drinking in China in the early Han dynasty, around the third century BCE, where it was mostly used as a medicinal concoction. Much later in the T'ang dynasty, around the seventh century CE, tea began spreading widely throughout Chinese culture. Around this time, tea shops sprung up in villages selling cakes of moistened tea leaves known as "brick tea" (Ch. *tuánchá* 團茶).

It's also during this time that we find one of the most important early texts explaining the practice of drinking tea and associated virtues. The *Chajing*, (茶經) or the *Tea Classic* was written around 772 by the Chinese tea master Lu Yu (陸羽, 733–804). One of the text's more fascinating aspects is that already in the eighth century, tea was being practiced and written about as a synthesis of Buddhism, Confucianism and Daoism.

In the *Chajing*, there is a strong emphasis on social etiquette and ritual, invoking Confucianism; highly sophisticated codification of procedures for ceremonial preparation of tea, which characterized Chan Buddhist monasticism; and Daoist influence, where tea was thought to improve the individual's relation to nature and the cosmos.

Lu Yu also brings the well-known *yin yang* symbol into the tea world. According to his system, tea is part of the *yin* category since it lowered the body's heat.

Theologian: You were going to say when exactly tea arrived in Japan. I heard that it was also Japanese Buddhist monks who were traveling to China and visiting monasteries—that it was them who first started importing tea to Japan.

Guide: Yes, exactly. It was during the Chinese T'ang dynasty, which in Japan corresponded to the late Asuka (538–710) and early Nara periods (710–94), that Buddhist monks traveling to China began bringing "brick tea" (団茶 Jp. *datcha*) home. The Asuka period was one of the three great phases of cultural importation from China, but some speculate that tea bricks might have come to Japan not directly from China but via Korea (Isozaki 2007; Ludwig 1974, 1981). Likewise, the precursor to Zen Buddhism, that is Mahāyāna Buddhism, also arrived through Korea around this time and along with it came practices and rituals associated with preparing, serving, and drinking the concoction.

We have some unverifiable accounts in the later Nara period of the priest Gyōki serving tea to Emperor Shōmu,[5] and more reliable accounts of Japanese priests Saichō (最澄 also known as Dengyō) and Kūkai[6] (空海, also known as Kōbō Daishi) who studied in T'ang China and likely brought tea back to Japan.

But, it's in the later Heian period (794–1185), a time of the highest cultural and aesthetic achievement that we find the first historically reliable accounts of tea in the Japanese archipelago. One story involves the abbot Eichū (永忠) cultivating tea plants planted by Saichō and then serving them to Emperor Saga on the shores of Lake Biwa around 815 (Sen Sōshitsu XV, 1997). The emperor was apparently so impressed by the refreshing beverage that he ordered tea be cultivated throughout the surrounding provinces of Kyoto. It's also believed that he held tea gatherings with similarities to what is depicted in Plato's *Symposium*, where learned citizens gathered to discuss literature, philosophy, and the arts (Kikawada 1973).

Around this time in mid-Heian, tea history goes a little dark. In the late ninth century, interest in China was in decline and officially interrupted by a break in relations between the two countries in 895. But, tea culture re-emerged in the late Heian period, around the mid-twelfth century, the Japanese once again looked to the Chinese continent, now in its Song dynasty, and find tea flourishing in what was the high point of tea culture in China. Tea now begins spreading beyond monasteries throughout the Japanese population by way of tea houses and through the emergence of tea festivals and tasting competitions called *cha awase* (茶合わせ).[7]

In this period, for the first time the Chinese started grinding their hard bricks of tea to produce a fine powder. What we now know as *matcha* (抹茶), and which we'll drink in our own ceremony.

Philosopher: I tried *matcha* recently. Was it always the main form of tea for the Japanese ceremony?

Guide: No, different teas have been popular at different periods and with various schools. Loose tea leaves were popular at times. Though, *matcha* is the main form used today. And, since you've had it, you'll know why. As a finely ground powder it has this amazingly deep green color. This is because the tea leaves are shade grown, which increases their amino acid content, making them extremely chlorophyl rich, and deeply green.

It was actually a Zen Buddhist, Myōan Eisai who brought powdered tea to Japan around the late twelfth century where it was used in monastic ritual and later in the upper echelons of society. Around this time, tea took root in monastic communities, alongside artistic practices that were becoming highly synthetic, fusing Buddhist practices of selflessness and Daoist ideas of harmonization with nature. And, the synthesis of Buddhism and Daoism brings us to our next topic, that is, Zen.

Zen and Myōan Eisai

Myōan Eisai (明菴栄西, 1141–1215), who I just mentioned, was one of the key early figures in the history of the tea ceremony in Japan. Eisai studied in China within the Southern Song school of Chan Buddhism and after four years returned to Japan to found a Japanese version of Chan, which is now known around the world as Zen.

Figure 2.3 Portrait of Myōan Eisai. 1198. Artist Unknown.

Eisai is renowned for founding the *Rinzai* (臨済宗) school of Zen Buddhism. During his time in China, he learned the practices and rituals associated with *matcha* and brought this knowledge back to Japan. In 1211 he authored "The Account of Drinking Tea and Prolonging Life" (*Kissayōjōki* 喫茶養生記), a two-volume text modeled on Lu Yu's *Tea Classic*. In it, Eisai details tea's medicinal properties and the various ailments it was thought to cure.[8]

Eisai was deeply influential in Japanese culture beyond the Rinzai monastery. His enthusiasm for tea helped spark a revival, which three centuries later would grow into one of the greatest Japanese aesthetic practices, and the one we'll immerse ourselves in throughout this course. However, the evolution from Eisai's time to the later development of *Wabicha* was not linear.

At the start of the Japanese medieval period—spanning the Kamakura (1185–1333) and Muromachi periods (1336–1573)—Japan took a decisive turn away from the refined aesthetics of Heian court life. The rise of medieval feudalism, with the military and samurai class becoming de facto rulers, led to many artists feeling alienated from the increasing military dominance over culture. Samurai was not only the most powerful social stratum, but as the imperial court went into decline, the feudal lords heading various samurai clans became increasingly dominant in the cultural sphere.

Even in the hands of powerful lords and samurai, tea remained a highly materialist expression, used to show off one's wealth through opulent ceremonies, tasting contests (*tōcha* 闘茶) and parties (*chayoriai* 茶寄合). These events would typically showcase highly-prized Chinese teaware (Ch. *míngwù*, Jp. *meibutsu* 名物), often with exorbitant prizes for competing participants. The minimalist Zen aesthetic most have come to associate with the tea ceremony was nowhere to be found. Early medieval tea ceremonies took place in luxurious palaces meant to display the wealth and power of the aristocracy. Tea was deeply entrenched in the luxury and excess associated with gambling and entertainment. This indulgent version of tea was referred to as part of a broader "*basara*" (婆娑羅) attitude of materialist superficiality associated with extravagance, individuality, and a rejection of traditional norms. Nothing could be more at odds with the austerities and minimalism of what would later evolve into Zen-inspired *Wabicha*.

This brings us to a second major Zen school, this one sought to counter the indulgences of "*basara*" as it spread not just through the tea ceremony but throughout Buddhism and Japanese culture in general. Does anyone know what this school was, or who founded it?

Dōgen Zenji

Figure 2.4 Portrait of Dōgen Zenji. *c.* 1253. Artist Unknown.

Theologian: Is it the Pure Land school of Buddhism?

Guide: Good guess. We'll talk about Pure Land later. It does have a little-known influence on *Wabicha*. But the school I'm thinking of was *Sōtō* Zen Buddhism, and its founder, and one of my favorite philosophers, the irreverent and astonishing Dōgen Zenji (道元禅師; 1200–53).

Like many monks at the time, Dōgen made a pilgrimage to China to study and practice in Buddhist monasteries. In 1223 he boarded a vessel at Hakata (present day Fukuoka) to make the perilous journey across the East China Sea in search of the *Jingdisi* (景德寺) monastery where Eisai had trained. But, Dōgen was disenchanted with the teaching he received and began searching for new mentors, leading him to the Mount Tiāntóng monastery and the great master Rújìng (如淨; Jp. *Nyōjo*), the thirteenth patriarch of the Cáodòng (Jp. *Sōtō*) lineage of Zen Buddhism. In 1228 Dōgen returned to Japan to establish the *Sōtō* (曹洞宗) school of Zen Buddhism. His brand of Zen will be an important topic for us later, not just for his particular Buddhist interpretation, or his impact on the tea ceremony, but because he's actually one of the Buddhist philosophers who has gained a lot of attention from contemporary scholars who engage his work in dialogue with western philosophies, particularly the school known as phenomenology.[9] More on that later.

Regarding the "*basara*" attitude, Dōgen was deeply frustrated with the growing materialism of his age, a time known as *mappō* (末法), or the "degenerate age of the dharma". During this time of conflict, war and natural disasters, there was a growing and pervasive social malaise. These conditions led to relaxation of Buddhist discipline to make it more accessible to the ruling and wealthy elite. Dōgen would have nothing to do with this. He sought to counter this drift by re-interpreting Buddhist scripture and reinstating stricter rules for Buddhist monasticism and also for tea practice.

As is typically the case, periods of decline give rise to great artistic movements, philosophies and cultural flourishing. At this time, many artists retreated from cities to contemplate the beauty of nature outside courtly life, developing an aesthetic language to express Japan's previous cultural high point. Figures like Kamo no Chōmei (鴨長明, 1155–1216) and Saigyō (西行法師, 1118–90) left the city and established an artistic language to express the feeling of reclusion and melancholy that would later inform several Japanese arts. And, to give you a bit of foreshadowing, it's in response to the calamities of Kamakura Japan that some of the most important and enduring aesthetic principles arose, including *yūgen* (幽玄) and *wabi-sabi* (侘寂), the latter of which you can probably guess, is going to be central for *Wabicha*.

As the Kamakura period ended, the military and samurai classes gained even more power and Zen became the predominant school of Buddhism, thanks in part to the samurai predilection for its practices and aesthetics. Zen cultivated a system of etiquette, complicity, and self-discipline that suited the samurai's ascetic lifestyle.

An important evolution of the tea ceremony began at this time, crucial for the version we're familiar with today. Tea lost popularity after the decline of Heian court life and through the tumultuous Kamakura period. Slowly, as Kamakura came to an end around the fourteenth century, Japan became increasingly enamored with its earlier cultural zenith. The ceremony then enters a new period of evolution where it begins moving in the direction of the highly systematized and codified practice we know it as today.

Around the fourteenth century, tea ceremonies come to be held in specially designed and constructed tea pavilions, contests and tea gatherings are flourishing and the practice is gradually refined, not just for displaying wealth and power but as an aesthetic pursuit for its own sake. It now begins evolving into what will become a deeply religious practice.

At this point of medieval history, tea began spreading beyond Buddhist monasteries and palaces of the nobility and was becoming a broader cultural phenomenon transcending the strict caste system of feudal Japan. The merchant class and low-ranking courtiers previously excluded by virtue of their low rank began partaking of tea, which was gradually coming within their means, even available to commoners in shops and on the streets. There was a surge in popularity between the fourteenth and sixteenth centuries extending tea beyond hedonistic materialism and power politics, and eventually in the way of a highly aestheticized and deeply religious practice. But, we still have a little ways to go before we get to *Wabicha*.

In late Muromachi Japan, around the fifteenth century, in a time known as the Higashiyama period, a movement called *Shōin Daisu* (書院台子) emerged within the tea world, which would eventually lead to the *Wabicha* style and the aesthetics we'll discuss and eventually experience.

In the *Shōin Daisu* tradition, *matcha* was part of ostentatious gatherings held in the opulent residences of the military elite who were so enamored with the tea ceremony and its etiquette as to appropriate the practice as an expression of warrior culture, and often, an expression of political and military power. Chinese teaware and utensils (*meibutsu* 名物) were most highly prized. These utensils had a sophisticated aesthetic of their own but also served as symbols of wealth and power reinforcing the strict social hierarchy prevailing at the time (Slusser 2013).

Shoin refers to a living room in the household of the nobility where tea parties were held rather than in tea pavilions separate from the domicile. *Daisu* refers to the split-level, Chinese shelving unit designed to carry tea utensils. These stands were the aesthetic center of the *Shōin Daisu* ceremony.

Despite its ostentation, *Shoin* practice began evolving in a more refined and subtle aesthetic direction. In the mid-fifteenth century tea became swept up in a broader artistic development towards a quality referred to as "elegance" (*fūryū*, 風流).[10] It too was later criticized for indulgent aestheticism, as an artistic pastime divorced from moral or medicinal principles, and came to be referred to negatively as "vulgar tea" (*Fūryū-cha* 風流茶). It was, nevertheless, an important step towards the eventual austere and sophisticated subtleties of *Wabicha*.

With *Shōin Daisu*, tea was neither a party nor a competition, not a military exercise nor a religious ritual, but became a secular, deeply aesthetic practice. While not yet the full expression of *wabi* tea with its small hermit-style hut we'll

Figure 2.5 Daisu (台子) Tea Shelf. R. Loughnane.

eventually partake in, *Shoin Daisu* was, nevertheless, a decisive step in that direction, partly through its increasing association with Zen Buddhism.

Tea had been many things throughout its history: a magical elixir, medicinal concoction, refreshing beverage, ritual center of social gatherings, art practice, pursuit of refinement and elegance, and aid to meditation. But in the final years of Muromachi Japan, in the Momoyama period, it becomes what Hisamatsu Shin'ichi (1993, p. 16) calls a "comprehensive cultural system, or a cultural life which has Zen as its essence."

Now, around the late fifteenth century, Zen sensibilities begin entering the tea ceremony. The *Shoin*-style shifted from the power politics of samurai public life towards the austerities of their private life, which were heavily influenced by Zen Buddhism. But, it would take a significant thrust to fully extricate tea from all of its unnecessary encumbrances and to align with Zen principles. That process, which eventually led to *Wabicha* in the later medieval period, began with a thorough simplification or we might say "Zennification" of tea.

That pretty much covers the early period of tea ceremony history in Japan. We're just about to arrive at the station. Let's get our tickets and we'll pick this up when we arrive in Kyoto.

3

Urasenke Institute

~ The group arrived at the Jingū-Marutamachi Station and began making their way across Kyoto to the Urasenke Institute.

As they arrived, they were greeted at the door and led into the Konnichian library, where their next teacher was waiting.

Figure 3.1 Urasenke Institute, Kyoto. R. Loughnane.

Sanada-sensei: *Ohisashi buri*! Nice to see you again!

Guide: Yes, it has been a while! Great to see you!

Everybody, this is Sanada-sensei. He is one of the instructors here at the Urasenke Institute and has a wealth of knowledge about the history of the tea ceremony.

Sanada-sensei: Welcome back to the Institute.

Guide: Thank you. It's great to see you again after so long.

Could you tell our students a little bit about the Urasenke Foundation?

Sanada-sensei: Yes, of course, I would be very happy to. Can I please ask, what have you spoken about so far?

Guide: We've already discussed the origins of tea in India and China, the early years in Japan, including some discussion of Saichō, and the *Shoin Daisu* style. We finished our discussion about the Zen appropriation of tea and Myōan Eisai and Dōgen Zenji. Basically, we've covered Asuka to around the end of Kamakura.

And, since we began our tour at Rikyū's Well, I think we're all very excited to learn from you about the greatest Japanese tea master and his *Wabicha*.

Sanada-sensei: Oh, that's most excellent that you had a chance to visit *Rikyū no I*. Did you collect some water for your ceremony?

Guide: Yes, we did. And we have one bottle for you.

~ *The Guide and Sensei bowed in unison as the water changed hands.*

Sanada-sensei: Please, let me first share with you some history of our humble organization. The Urasenke Foundation is one of the most important centers of tea knowledge and practice in the world. Established in 1949, its history stretches back much farther. We trace its origins all the way to Rikyū himself. He wasn't necessarily the originator, but he is known for having perfected *Wabicha*. After his death, the Japanese tea world split off into the "three Sen houses" (三千家) or sometimes referred to as the "head houses" or "head families" (*sōke* 宗家) of Japanese tea, which are the *Urasenke* (裏千家), *Omotesenke* (表千家), and *Mushakōjisenke* (武者小路千家) schools.

Rikyū was the most important tea master in Japanese history, but two crucial precursors to his version of the ceremony paved the way for him to bring *Chanoyu* to its greatest expression as *Wabicha*. Those are Takeno Jō'ō (武野 紹鴎, 1502–55), and the one we'll begin with now, Murata Shukō (村田珠光, 1423–1502. Also known as Jukō).

Murata Shukō

Shukō was a Zen priest from the *Shōmyō-ji* temple near Nara. He was commonly thought to be the founder of *Chadō*, or tea ceremony as a "way", and the originator of the *Wabicha* style. Many elements of the tea ceremony we recognize today come from his innovations. We have him to thank for several of the aesthetic objects and rituals you'll experience in your own tea ceremony, including: conducting the ceremony in a small grass-roofed hermit-style hut (*sōan* 草庵); the 4.5 tatami mat room (*yojohan* 四畳半); the use of a hearth cut

Figure 3.2 Murata Shukō. (村田珠光; 1423–1502). R. Loughnane.

into floor (*ro* 炉); and one of the greatest aesthetic innovations, the shift in emphasis away from the *Daisu* tea stand towards the hanging scroll in the alcove.[1] All of these can be traced back to Shukō.

Not only did he shift the tea hut's symbolic orientation, he also transitioned the ceremony from its focus on scrolls depicting nature scenes to calligraphy; an innovation for *Wabicha*, which cannot be under-estimated. You'll see in your own ceremony how the scroll is very much the nexus of all the aesthetic relations throughout the tea garden and hut.

But, perhaps most importantly, aside from the material innovations Shukō brought about, he initiated the eventual drift away from *Shoin*-style ostentation, away from the warrior ideal of tea towards what eventually became a deeply religious and aesthetic ritual practice.[2]

Shukō rejected the hedonistic elements still associated with tea competitions. But, above all, under the tutelage of the radical and iconoclast Zen Buddhist Ikkyū Sōjun (一休宗純 1394–1481),[3] Shukō began approaching the ceremony in a decidedly artistic "way" and sought to develop and codify aesthetic principles to guide practitioners along that way.

You might have heard the terms *Chadō* or *Sadō* (茶道), usually translated as "the way of tea". That *dō* suffix you hear has profound philosophic and religious significance. Essentially, this term speaks to the Zen and even Daoist core of the *Wabicha* tea ceremony, and the bodily cultivation the tea ceremony came to represent.

Guide: Yes, please everybody keep that *dō* principle in mind for later. This Daoist element is absolutely central to the tea ceremony we'll experience.

Sanada-sensei: What you're going to see in your ceremony is a highly choreographed set of ritualized bodily movements and gestures called *temae* (点前). Shukō is credited with developing this system based on Zen-style disciplines for bodily cultivation. *Temae* translates roughly as "point in front", indicating specific points in space in front of the practitioner who must learn a complex and highly choreographed set of movements.[4] In *Wabicha*, almost every inch of the tea hut is codified, and the tea master's movements fit meticulously into the hut's various spaces and transitions.

Temae codified movements became understood as Zen-style spiritual practices or even meditative exercises to help practitioners focus and concentrate their minds in a spontaneous and un-self-conscious way. This is how the tea ceremony became an embodied practice aiming to achieve a Buddhist version of salvation for both tea host and guest.

In his "Letter on Heart's Mastery" Shukō (1980) emphasizes many Buddhist ideals, and also warned against the dangers of tea leading to self-attachment, veneration of costly teaware, or over-adherence to tea conventions. He also severely castigated those who would envy masters while ignoring or scorning beginners.

Artist: It sounds like he had a sense of "kill the tea ancestors" idea we spoke of.

Guide: Yes, Shukō was definitely an innovator. In no sense was he simply reproducing the tea of his ancestors.

On the way to *Wabi*: Chill and Withered

Sanada-sensei: Although he's credited as one of the main forerunners of *Wabicha*, Shukō didn't yet use the term "*wabi*", but had a precursor to that term known as "chilled and withered" (*hiekareta* 冷え枯れた). This term harkens back to Chinese aesthetic notions of the austerity and restraint seen in the mountain hermit's reclusive lifestyle of poverty, and was first prevalent in *Renga* and *Waka* poetry and also Noh drama. The Japanese poet Shinkei (心敬 1406–75) originally formalized this concept in his writings (1991), and it became one of Shukō's main aesthetic principles.

As for the term itself, it's made up of two parts; first "Chill" (*hie* 冷え), referred to the austere bareness of winter, and the beauty of ice, while "Withered" (*kare*, 枯れ) evoked the muted color palette of nature during winter, as opposed to the multicolored flourishing of spring and summer, and the desire for grasping their vibrant colors provoke.

Hiekareta is sometimes referred to as a "seasonal aesthetic", but it also has deep philosophical implications. When colors are muted things cease appearing as distinct objects, the lines dividing them from each other are blurred, thus highlighting the Buddhist notion of emptiness. (Hirota 1995)

Have you discussed this idea already?

Guide: We did mention it, but haven't gone into a lot of detail about the underlying ontology yet. But, everyone, please keep in mind what Sanada-sensei is telling us about erasing the distinctions between things, this will be important when we speak more about ideas like non-self and non-object.

Philosopher: If "emptiness" refers to the ontological negative, what concepts refer to the ontological positive?

Guide: Great question. Whereas notions like "emptiness" or "nothingness" are typically considered the ontological negative, the main concept associated with the ontological positive is "being". We'll get into these ontological terms in later talks, but there is one related idea that is important for the concept Sanada-sensei is speaking of, that we might mention.

Again, there are some important exceptions, but typically, western thinkers who developed philosophies we could include within the category of the "ontological positive", they have tried to find permanent features of reality to serve as the foundation for their philosophies. In contrast, Asian philosophers we include within the category of the "ontological negative", those whose main concept was "emptiness", these philosophers went in the opposite direction. When they looked to the world, they didn't see anything permanent. For them, the main quality of reality was its *impermanence*.

You don't need to know any Japanese for this course, but let me just write out the characters for "impermanence" or what in Japanese is *mujō* (無常). And, take note of the first character, *mu*, as it's going to come up throughout our meetings.

Figure 3.3 *Mu* (無), "emptiness".

Sanada-sensei: Yes, that's a good character to remember. And yes, as you said, the idea of impermanence was crucial to the early moments of *Wabicha*. Shukō followed Shinkei in advocating for an attunement with the impermanence of all things. This was a major aspect of their *hiekareta* aesthetic. For them, attachment to permanence was the cause of suffering and traps one in cycles of desire and aversion.

By embracing the impermanence of all things, including the self, abiding with the "chill" aspect of existence, one feels part of the non-differentiation of all things—on this basis one can be deeply moved by the world's beauty without the forms of attachment that perpetuate suffering.

What is important to note is that by following Shinkei—who aligned Renga aesthetics with Buddhist principles—Shukō begins a process of evolving the tea ceremony as a religious practice. And, in doing so, he introduced what became one of the most essential principles of *Wabicha*, that being equality. Shukō's version of the tea ceremony began to deliberately oppose the highly stratified social rank system, which excluded many of the lower classes from the ceremony, and became a practice available to all strata of medieval Japanese society. This was truly revolutionary, but still in its early stages.

As *Chanoyu* underwent many advances under Shukō, Japan became embroiled in the long and costly Ōnin wars (1467–77). But, the tea ceremony actually gained increased relevance as the general population needed an escape from the strife and conflict in the wider social-political spheres. The samurai also sought respite from the conflict and death they were experiencing daily. This further spurred on the shift of tea from the private sphere of *Shoin*-style gatherings to the tiny grass-roofed hut as a venue available to all, where fellow citizens could meet under one modest roof without the divisions otherwise dividing society. All were unified by an ethos transcending social station, which Shukō formalized as a set of core tea values: reverence (*kin* 欽), respect (*kei* 敬), purity (*sei* 静), and tranquility (*jaku* 寂). These were another key contribution of Shukō to the still embryonic *Wabicha*. We'll speak later about how these four values are slightly modified by the lesser-known Yabanouchi school, and ultimately by Rikyū.

During this time of war, one economic factor came to have a decisive and lasting impact on the tea ceremony. As is typical during times of conflict, weapons production ramps up and those responsible, the lowest class merchants within feudal Japan, became more and more powerful as the wars dragged on. Still ranking as the lowest class—and on this basis were previously excluded from *Chanoyu*—merchants gained increased wealth and power. Although they were not able to take steps up the social ladder, they nevertheless gained vast wealth and influence.

There was one part of Japan that benefited greatly from wartime production; the port city and trading hub of Sakai. Along Osaka Bay, Sakai was one of the largest ports with the greatest exposure to European trade and culture. An inordinate volume of manufacturing happened there but almost none of the conflict. As a safe haven with expanding resources, a context arose where the newly wealthy merchants and their powerful guilds could counter samurai influence and shape what grew into a new tea ceremony and a lasting expression of Japanese culture.

Somewhat paradoxically, during this moment of growing merchant wealth, a diminutive tea hut aestheticizing poverty emerged. This was the *sōan* (草庵) hut, and it became part of a new tea ideal.

The Sōan Ideal

Despite Sakai's economic boom and the shifting social strata, townspeople's houses remained quite small. As merchants began participating in the ceremony, they would hold their tea gatherings in a room separate from their dwelling known as a *machiya* (町家) (Keane 2014).

To establish a refuge for enjoying aesthetic pleasures away from the city's bustling trade, merchants also began to acquire small plots of land outside the urban centers and built tiny huts to enjoy tea.[5] These were typically six or even four-and-one-half

Figure 3.4 *Sōan* (草庵) style tea hut. R. Loughnane.

tatami mat-sized rooms; not yet the complete spatial reduction later achieved by Rikyū, but this was a long way from the military lord's expansive *Shoin* banquet-rooms, which could be hundreds of tatami in expanse.

Guide: Sanada-sensei, I wonder if I could add something at this point.

Sanada-sensei: Yes, by all means.

Guide: I'd like to share a contradictory provocation for our students to keep in mind for later. Although there was a drastic reduction in tea hut size initiated by Shukō, as you've rightly explained, I want us to imagine that his tea hut was actually much more expansive than the previous *Shoin*-style halls.

I have a quote here from Furuta Shokin.

> One should not interpret this act of Shukō's as an attempt to create something small, to counter the spacious shoin-zukuri tearoom. Small and cramped though his four-and-a-half-mat chashitsu might have seemed, for him it embodied the spaciousness of a vast chamber of dozens or even hundreds of mats . . . The four-and-a-half-mat room ceases to be small and becomes a place of infinite space and freedom.
>
> (1989, p. 8)

Philosopher: How could this be? Something can't be both spatially small and large at the same time. And certainly, a tea hut's smallness couldn't possibly make it large.

Theologian: Could we say, along the lines of the "two-fold truth" we discussed, that in a "conventional" sense, a smaller tea hut is simply a smaller tea hut. Small is small. A is A. But, in an ultimate sense that A is not-A. Small is large?

Guide: That's one way to look at it, yes. And, to grasp that ultimate sense, we're going to have to revise our conceptions of space and even challenge some metaphysical principles by way of Buddhist ideas. Then, we'll be able to see how the reduced *objective* size of the tea hut gives one a significantly expanded *subjective* experience of space.

Artist: Can we understand space according to the ontological positive and negative?

Guide: Yes, absolutely. And, this is how phenomenology is going to be important for us. With that methodology, we'll see how our experience of space has some interesting ambiguities, some that allow us to grasp the tiny tea hut as spatially expansive. But, we'll come back to that in a later discussion. Let's let our sensei continue.

Sanada-sensei: That's very interesting. I don't know anything about phenomenology, but there's some Buddhist mythology I can share with you that seems to invoke this contradictory experience of space you're referring to.

The tearoom Shukō designed was said to reflect the tiny hut of Vimalakīrti, who was a famous lay practitioner and contemporary of the Buddha. His hut measured only ten by ten feet, but despite these objective dimensions—or maybe we could use your terms, despite these "positive" dimensions—the room was said to be infinitely expansive. In the *Vimalakīrti Nirdeśa Sūtra* (वमिलकीर्तनिर्दिश), a text much venerated by Zen adherents, you'll even find a conception of enlightenment where one goes beyond finite space and time to an "empty" or "infinite" spatial experience.

Guide: That's fascinating. Yes, in many ways Buddhist ideas of space and time—or maybe I should say ideas of spatial and temporal *experience*—turn out to have intriguing similarities with contemporary phenomenological accounts we'll eventually get to.

Sanada-sensei: I wish I could join the rest of your tour to learn more about that.

To return to the historical picture we're drawing, despite the spatial austerities of Shukō's newly reduced *sōan*-style tea hut, elite merchants remained enamored with using and exhibiting costly Chinese teaware. The expenses associated with such utensils constituted a quite significant barrier to entry for lower classes. What this meant was that despite initiating an egalitarian ideal within the tea ceremony, the early *sōan* movement did in some sense remain an exclusive venue for the wealthy; a barrier to equality that would later be overcome as *Wabicha* evolved (Slusser 2013).[6]

The next step along the way to the culmination of *Wabicha* was undertaken by a second great tea master—also from the city of Sakai—that is Takeno Jō'ō.

Takeno Jō'ō

Sanada-sensei: Takeno Jō'ō (武野 紹鴎, 1502–55) was a student of Shukō's. Like Shukō, he grew up in Sakai. Although his family were wealthy, he abandoned that lifestyle and became a priest in Kyoto. He continued Shukō's movement towards the austerities of hermit life and Zen-style ritual. One of his biggest contributions to the development of a distinctly Japanese ceremony was his shift to commission Japanese poets to scribe calligraphy for the hanging scroll in the tea hut's alcove, whereas costly Chinese versions had previously been the norm. And, perhaps even more importantly for the history we're tracing, he was the first to use the term "*wabi*" in association with the tea ceremony.

Figure 3.5 Takeno Jō'ō (武野 紹鴎, 1502–55). R. Loughnane.

While his teacher Shukō found inspiration in the literary world of Shinkei's "chill and withered" aesthetic, Jō'ō had a distinct aesthetic influence, also a literary figure, the poet Inō Sōgi (宗祇, 1421–1502). Inspired by Sōgi, Jō'ō brought *Chanoyu* within the realm of *wabi*. And, as you probably are aware, *wabi* is one of the central principles of Japanese aesthetics. I'm sure you'll speak about *wabi* at length in your coming meetings, but let me say by way of foreshadowing that the turn away from "chill and withered" towards *wabi* involved a veneration of the beauty of the mundane world, an appreciation of insufficiency represented in the lifestyle of the hermit recluse living in nature with material possessions reduced to the absolute bare minimum so as not to interfere with the appreciation of the beauty of the human condition and the natural beauty of all things.

To embody the austerities of the *wabi* aesthetic within the tea ceremony, Jō'ō persisted in questioning the dominance of expensive Chinese utensils, and although transcripts show he did not abandon them entirely, he did begin to incorporate Japanese-made utensils (Hirota 1995). He had an inclination for plain unfinished rather than varnished or lacquered wood, and clay instead of papered walls.

On his path to *wabicha*, Jō'ō popularized a term that has entered popular culture of late, that is "*ichigo ichie*" (一期一会). Has anybody heard this phrase?

Artist: I was actually in an amazing restaurant in Ireland a few years ago named Ichigo Ichie. I think the term refers to something like the life-changing potential of once-in-a-lifetime chance meetings.

Philosopher: . . . how fortuitous events or encounters can change the direction of our existence, but can't be controlled or repeated.

Sanada-sensei: I think you have the basic idea. Jō'ō employed the term to emphasize the deep spiritual significance of the exchange transpiring between tea host and guest, which has the potential to affect one's heart deeply, but may never happen again, at least not in the same place, or in the same way between the same two people.

While *ichigo ichie* is often associated with the tea ceremony, its popular usage can be misleading. Many take it to mean any poignant, chance or even random encounter. But this overlooks the tea ceremony's deliberate nature. The spiritual intensity of the meeting between host and guest arises not from coincidence, but from the meticulous planning of every detail. In this sense, nothing is left to chance. Yet, paradoxically, within this precision emerges a unique spontaneity—that's where the true magic lies.

Philosopher: Does *ichigo ichie* have a relation with impermanence?

Sanada-sensei: Possibly. Can you say more?

Philosopher: When I think about the European philosophical tradition and its search for permanence, it seems like what it wants are truths that should apply to all people in all places and times. If we were to achieve this kind of truth it should be always repeatable by virtue of its permanence. The truth we look for isn't the truth of *one time*, but *all times*. It seems like the truth of *ichigo ichie*, on the other hand, rather than reinforcing permanence actually highlights the impermanence of all things. It's the truth of one time. Just this time.

Sanada-sensei: That's very insightful. Within *Chadō*, the spiritual state of the deepest significance vanishes completely the moment the ritual concludes. Nothing lasts. Nothing can be taken away. If we try to grasp it, or if we become attached to the truth revealed by the experience and try to make it permanent, we realize that there is nothing to hold on to. So yes, I think you're right that the truth of *ichigo ichie*, if we can call it that, is a singular rather than universal truth, and in that singularity, we can find the idea of impermanence you've nicely invoked.

Getting back to our historical sketch, we could say much more about Takeno Jō'ō, but I know you have to get on with your tour so let's move on to discuss the figure said to be the "last man" of medieval Japan, the greatest of all tea masters, Sen no Rikyū.

Sen no Rikyū

Sanada-sensei: Rikyū was not only a tea master, he was a painter, poet, an *ikebana* practitioner, calligrapher and gardener, and eventually a major government official. But, the achievement he is most renowned for is having brought *Wabicha* to its highest expression.

Rikyū trained as a Zen Buddhist right here in Kyoto not far from the Urasenke Foundation, in the Daitoku-ji monastery. Of course, he is associated with the tea ceremony but his status as a cultural figure was much broader. We might go as far as to say he helped advance new visions for human existence, for religious salvation, initiated new social virtues, and aesthetic ideals that forged Japanese identity and culture for his generation and far beyond.

As his predecessors Shukō and Jō'ō had, Rikyū continued bringing *Chanoyu* within the Buddhist path. Let me read you a passage from "Memoranda of the words of Rikyū" attributed to him.

Figure 3.6 Sen no Rikyū (千利休; 1522–91). R. Loughnane.

Chanoyu in a small room means first of all to practice the austerities of Buddhism. To enjoy a splendid dwelling or a meal with rare delicacies is a trivial pleasure. A house suffices if it does not leak; a meal, if it satisfies hunger. Such is the teaching of the Buddha and the essence of chanoyu. We carry water, take firewood, boil the water, and make tea. Next we offer it to the Buddha, serve our guests and drink it ourselves. We arrange flowers and light incense. All of these are ways to pursue the teachings of the Buddha and his elders.

(Sen Sōshitsu XV 1979, p. xxv)

It's true that Rikyū did help bring tea onto the Buddhist path, yet to say that he merely imported existing Zen practices within *Chanoyu*, wouldn't fully capture the momentous quality of his contribution. Some claim the direction of influence also went in the other direction: that Rikyū deeply influenced Zen. As one of Japan's greatest modern philosophers of art, Hisamatsu Shin-ichi has said, "Rikyū was not bound by conventional forms of Zen. Instead, it appears that he aspired to use them as a steppingstone to develop an entirely new type of Zen" (1993, p. 24).

Let's consider some more of his background that led to his eventual breakthroughs. As his teacher and the teacher before him had, Rikyū grew up in the vibrant tea city of Sakai and was included as one of the great "masters" (*sōshō* 宗匠) of tea.

To use a contradiction, we might say that Rikyū helped give tea a highly sophisticated simplicity, or a complex uncomplicatedness. Doing so, he resolved some of the main tensions emerging in tea culture at the time; between the indulgent *Shoin* and the austere *Wabicha* traditions; between the Zen aesthetic and the merchant–warrior sensitivities.

Rikyū's main concern was to bring attention to the everyday and the mundane, to cultivate an appreciation for the great beauty of the imperfect and impermanent; both deeply rooted in Buddhist soteriology.

Rikyū's Innovations

Sanada-sensei: His innovations are almost too numerous to list, but we can discuss a few since you'll definitely encounter many of these throughout your ceremony.

Rikyū is known for augmenting Jō'ō's emphasis on the hanging scroll, making it the central art object and the symbolic heart of the ceremony. Before Rikyū, the scroll in the alcove (*tokonoma* 床の間) was typically scribed by a Chinese calligrapher, which meant it was very scarce and costly in medieval Japan. Rikyū began commissioning Japanese calligraphers to make scrolls for his ceremonies.

In a similar turn towards his native land, he substituted the elaborately decorated bowls from Tang and Song China and used simple and unadorned earthenware. He even worked with local potters, specifically of the *Raku* clan, to develop a pottery style perfectly suited for the overall *wabi* aesthetic he was honing. I think you'll learn more about *Raku* ware later in your course, won't you?

Guide: Yes, we'll actually begin one of our later meetings at the Raku Museum and Workshop. We'll see some classical pieces and also tour the workshop to see how descendants of the *Raku* clan continue to make pottery according to medieval practices and aesthetic principles.

Sanada-sensei: That's excellent. Please say hello to Raku Oie from me.

Aside from the beautiful pottery you'll get to see and touch in your own ceremony, you'll also notice another feature Rikyū instituted. He is known for having developed what is called an "aniconic" tea ceremony, which means that there were no images displayed in the tea hut. Prior to Shukō, images of various sorts were the norm, as were colorful flowers, but these were excluded from *Wabicha* as it evolved under Rikyū.

Another quality you should be on the lookout for when you finally get inside the tea hut is the texture of the walls. Like Jō'ō, Rikyū preferred a rustic interior but went beyond his master in a few ways. In line with the Shinto preference for purity of natural, un-worked materials, he not only used unfinished wood but even left the bark on the timber beams. And, he didn't simply leave the walls without paper, as Jō'ō had, he even skipped the final coat of plaster, meaning that cobs of straw mixed into the mud remained visible. You can even see the black charcoal seeping out of the walls and staining the surface of his huts.

His taste for natural materials meant he chose bamboo for flower containers and tea scoops, which in the *Shoin*-style ceremony were fashioned out of the finest ivory. And, perhaps most importantly for the aesthetics of the exterior of the hut, to more closely approximate the homes of hermits or farmers, Rikyū chose grass thatch instead of wooden roof shakes.

Rikyū's Tea Values: Religious/Philosophic Synthesis

Theologian: Our teacher mentioned that he would refer to Asian traditions as "philosophy-religions". Rikyū was a Zen practitioner, would you say that the ceremony he developed also had elements of philosophy and religion?

Sanada-sensei: *Arigatou*, that's a very good question. Do you remember we spoke about how Shukō had established the main values of *Chadō* as reverence, respect, purity, and tranquility? Rikyū's innovation was to substitute reverence for harmony and thus, his four tea values were harmony (*wa*, 和), respect (*kei*, 敬), purity (*sei*, 清), and tranquility (*jaku*, 寂), which endure as the foundations of the tea ceremony and of the Urasenke Foundation to this day.

To answer your question, let me tell you how these values achieved a synthesis of the four major philosophic-religious traditions prevailing in Japan at the time, including Buddhism, Daoism, Confucianism, and Shintoism.

To begin with *Wa*, or "harmony", this ideal developed from the Daoist, Buddhist and Confucian pursuit of harmony between the celestial and terrestrial spheres. As in other traditions, even the ancient Greeks, when looking to the heavens, ancient Chinese witnessed a perfectly harmonious order. They saw no evidence of the kind of friction or conflict experienced on earth, especially with the social-political chaos and war characterizing periods of medieval Chinese history. Observing the orderly procession of stars, moons, and planets inspired them to seek a similar regularity and harmony in the social sphere on earth. Although Confucian and Daoist adherents would have pursued this ideal in very different ways, both use the term *Wa* to refer to that harmony.

The second value, *Kei*, or "respect" was more specifically a Confucian ideal. *Kei* was an interpersonal dynamic obtaining when they treated each other in accord with the harmony associated with *wa*. You can think of the tea ceremony as a simulation of an ideal human interaction. The ideal is to be respectful, to manifest *kei*. And, further reinforcing the egalitarianism Rikyū strove for, *kei* was equal regardless of one's social station. Independent of any marks of distinction outside the hut, all were treated with the same respect in a *Wabicha* ceremony—host and guest, commoner and nobleman alike.

The third value, *Sei* or "purity" is associated with Japan's folk religion, Shinto, which aims to please spirits called "kami" (神) that were thought to animate nature. These natural spirits were believed to be particularly dense in beautiful natural settings and within pure elements. This explains Rikyū's turn towards unadorned raw materials.

You'll put the *sei* value to practice as you make your way through the garden and into the tea hut when you purify yourselves and when the tea host purifies the tea implements. You'll also notice that many of the tea utensils, clothing, and architecture display this love of purity with beautifully unfinished materials left in their natural state.

The last of Rikyū's tea values *jaku*, or "tranquility" comes from Buddhism. And, rather than *wa* and *kei*, which focus on an external and inter-personal order, *jaku* refers to cultivating an internal state of peace. The simplicity and minimalism of the garden and hut help avoid clutter, promoting tranquility and mindfulness. In this sense, Rikyū's *wabicha* promotes the state of tranquility associated with meditative rituals as they would have been practiced in Zen Buddhist monasteries in his day.

Philosopher: It seems like there's a bit of a contradiction between *jaku* and other Buddhist ideals. I don't know that much about Buddhism, but one thing I remember is that it's about overcoming one's attachment and desire. Can we achieve tranquility while immersed in such a beautiful setting? Won't all the aesthetic elements just make us attached to them, won't desire undermine our tranquility?

Rikyū and Sukiya

Sanada-sensei: Very good question. Have any of you heard the term *suki*?

Theologian: Yeah, that was one of the first Japanese words I learned. Doesn't it just mean "to like" something. Or, to want something?

Sanada-sensei: Yes, that's right. There's this everyday meaning you're referring to, but the notion of *suki* was also a cultural ideal with more meaning built into it. It was a culture of refined enjoyment of the beauty of the natural world and how it was reflected in the various arts. And, the hut that evolved within *Wabicha* was also referred to as a *sukiya* (数寄屋).

The origin of the word we use in an everyday sense when we say "*suki*" (好き), or "I want this or that" isn't entirely clear. The "*suki*" in "*sukiya*" uses the compound 数寄.[7] *Suki* is the noun form of *suku*, which means to be fond of, to love, to delight in or be devoted to. In that sense, as you pointed out, this seems to go against the Buddhist ideal of tranquility by overcoming desire. But, we should be careful to distinguish the "*suki*" we want to talk about from the sense we employ in everyday use, which suggests a *personal* preference of liking.

Let me read you a quote from Rikyū, where he makes this point:

> *Suki has come to mean only a taste for things, or architecture and utensils ruled by a liking for things, and this is now regarded as the essence of chanoyu. How sad it is that the two characters, "su-ki", have been buried in the dust of the world for more than a hundred years.*
>
> (Hirota 1995, p. 278)

The evolution of this more specific aesthetic sense of the word, is actually quite important for the tea ceremony and Japanese arts and culture more generally.

In the Heian period (794–1192) "*suki*" referred to amorous feelings within a courtly setting. By the Kamakura period (1392–1573) it gained increased aesthetic meaning, referring to a fondness for various artistic pleasures, or even an aesthetic ideal, suggesting something more elevated, like being devoted to an art, and chiefly to poetry. At this time, we have terms such as "*uta suki*" (歌数寄), referring to having a taste for poetic verse. It lent an aura of eccentricity to aesthetes living according to the *suki* ideal. In late Kamakura and early Muromachi Japan—particularly in the Azuchi-Momoyama period (1568–1600)—we find the development of the term essential for our purposes.

At this time, *waka* poetry was declining in popularity just as tea culture was on the rise. "*Suki*" came almost fully within the domain and nomenclature of the tea ceremony and evolved to be virtually synonymous with *Chanoyu* itself. There was a proliferation of associated terms such as *sukimono* (数寄者), a person with refined tastes; *chasuki* (茶数寄), one with a deep appreciation for tea who likely owns their own tea utensils; *sukisha* (数寄者) a connoisseur deeply but not professionally dedicated to tea; and *wabisuki* (侘数寄), a practitioner devoted to tea in the mode of *wabi*.

Rikyū was likely the first to use "*suki*" to describe not just the tearoom, but to characterize the entire ceremony, and its religious and aesthetic ethos. He represents the pinnacle of *sukiya*'s evolution, but also a return to some Pure Land ideals. And, this is the important point for your question about how we can have a beautiful ceremony without becoming attached to and desiring that beauty. In Pure Land, *suki* wasn't an individual preference, but referred to a life attuned to the impermanence of all things. So, within the *suki* ideal, there was a reminder to avoid attachment to the transient things in the world. It expresses a desire, but perhaps we could say a desire to overcome desire.

Let me share one last etymological twist that elaborates this contradiction. Rikyū insisted on a distinction between "*suki*", which was written with the characters 好き and the root of that character, the 好,which was pronounced "*ko*". Rikyū claimed that "these two terms, however, differ vastly in meaning" (Hirota, 1995, p. 277). *Ko* evoked a passionate or even indulgent form of desire. This is the type of desire I think your question expressed a concern about. Whereas *suki* was associated with a detached, non-grasping appreciation, the kind one might have for the waning moon or the flowers falling from a cherry blossom tree.

Guide: Does that "*ko*" have any relation to the term "*Konomi*"?

Sanada-sensei: Yes, indeed it does. "*Konomi*" (好み), translates as something like a "preferred object", but it has a more interesting origin. Originally, it referred to a stamp of approval tea masters would bestow upon utensils they judged met the highest aesthetic standards. But, Rikyū rejected the elitism surrounding the *konomi* system of aesthetic authorization. Favoring *suki* and rejecting *ko*, was one way to understand how and why Rikyū distanced himself from the exclusionary practices associated with expensive Chinese utensils.

Artist: Was part of the reason Rikyū reduced the size of the hut to avoid the *ko* form of attachment?

Guide: It could be. What was unique about the *sukiya* was that it was a stand-alone structure. Previously, *Chanoyu* was conducted in special and often extravagant rooms, but they weren't yet separated from the main residential domicile. Starting with the Sakai masters, the tendency was to conduct *Chanoyu* in the small, unadorned huts.

If we consider the various meanings associated with the term *sukiya*, we see that it has further philosophical, religious and aesthetic significance. "Abode of fancy" (数寄屋) is a translation of *sukiya*, where "fancy" invokes the poetic and ephemeral nature of the material world. There were also related terms like "the abode of the asymmetrical" (*hi-taishō no sumai*, 非対称の住まい), referring to the avoidance of symmetry in the tea hut, also invoking Buddhist and Daoist view of reality as an ever-changing process of becoming. And then there's the "abode of the void" (*kū no sumai*, 空の住まい), where "void" invokes Buddhist ideas like "emptiness" and "nothingness". We referred to these earlier as the "ontological negative".

Rikyū's Egalitarian Ideal

Sanada-sensei: Great, thank you. Before you head off for your ceremony, there's one last element of Rikyū's *Wabicha* we must touch upon.

As I've mentioned, Rikyū truly realized his predecessor's attempts to instantiate egalitarianism within his version of *Wabicha*. In the highly stratified society of medieval Japan, he designed a ceremony, including aesthetic and architectural features, which counteracted the divisions otherwise strictly maintained outside the hut. In the text purporting to transmit his word, the *Nampōroku* (南方録),[8] we read the master exhorting that "worldly rank is ignored" in the *sukiya*.

Competitive displays of wealth and power, or any signs of class or political station, including dress, weapons or elaborate teaware, were strictly excluded from Rikyū's hut. Thus, the prevailing materialist tendencies of *Shoin* tea were decisively excluded while significantly undermining the indulgent "*basara*" attitude.

No longer were rare imported Chinese tea implements used. Rikyū favored simple, unadorned, and locally produced pottery reflecting the agrarian lifestyle surrounding him at the time.

Tea scholar Denis Hirota even speaks of Rikyū's deployment of the *wabi* sensibility as a "non-hierarchical awareness of the real" (1995). Although Zen aimed to reach the lay community, it often remained confined to monastery walls. Rikyū was given by Hideyoshi the title "*koji*" (居士), a Buddhist term for a devoted but secular adherent. As Hisamatsu (1993) commented, Rikyū was able to "develop a tea ceremony by transforming it into *wabi* tea, which could spread widely among the laity, thus leveraging the popularity of tea to help transmit Zen outside the monastery."

The *sukiya*, while a great architectural innovation, also had a profound social and political impact within the highly stratified feudal Japan. Society was arranged hierarchically with the samurai at the top, followed by farmers, artisans, and merchants at the bottom. These divisions were absolute, with virtually no mobility possible between strata. In a quiet but radical intervention into this hierarchy, the very structure of the *sukiya* undermined such stratification. All present within the tearoom were considered equal. With the *sukiya*, we have the beginnings of an ongoing movement throughout Japanese society towards a classless society.

Egalitarianism wasn't simply an ideal for Rikyū—not something tea guests could decide to adhere to or not. The architecture of the tea hut enforced the ideal. For example, the tiny entry way into the hut by way of the *nijiriguchi* (躙口) disallowed samurai from entering with their most visible mark of distinction, their katana sword. Likewise, the large top hats worn by nobility could not fit through the tiny aperture. The typical markings of social rank and political station were stripped away. They couldn't even get into Rikyū's *sukiya*.

A further outcome was that this erasure of class distinctions allowed samurai and merchants, nobility, and the poor to mix. Some have questioned the extent of the equality attained in mingling classes and have warned not to forget the exclusive elitism persisting within *wabicha*, nor mistake the equality attained with modern forms of egalitarianism (Slusser 2013).

A final crucial point I'd like to share with you before you head on your way is that the austerities which embedded an egalitarian ideal within *wabicha* might have led to Rikyū's untimely demise.

His influence was so grand that during a period of political turbulence he became the chief tea adviser to the great Shogun Oda Nobunaga and later Toyotomi Hideyoshi. This was a position of great influence. Perhaps predictably, his attempts to erase class distinctions rubbed the Shogunate the wrong way in that they threatened to subvert or even erase the social hierarchy, which legitimated Hideyoshi's power and position at the top of the social hierarchy (Slusser 2013).[9] Especially since the Shogun used extravagant tea ceremonies to establish and exhibit his power, modifying *Chanoyu* was a threat to the entire social-political structure sustaining his rule. Rikyū's subversive efforts invoke what you've referred to as the "killing the ancestors", but those efforts came with consequences for Rikyū.

Sadly, after his many astonishing contributions to Japanese culture, Rikyū met a tragic end. Hideyoshi had Rikyū build a golden tearoom (黄金の茶室), thus contravening the core of his *Wabicha* philosophy. Rikyū did undertake the commission but, there must have been some disagreement. Some claimed that Rikyū had planned to poison Hideyoshi, or alternatively, that the warlord wanted samurai to be recognized in their superior station within the ceremony, to which Rikyū would not abide. Whatever the case may be, Hideyoshi sentenced Rikyū to death. To preserve his honor, the ruler permitted the great tea master to conduct one last ceremony, his "death tea" after which he committed *seppuku*, or ritual suicide.

Rikyū's contributions were not lost, however. Like other great teachers such as Confucius and Socrates, Rikyū didn't commit any teachings to paper. He followed the Zen principle of eschewing textual learning in favor of one-to-one teacher to student transmission. What we know of his style of tea came from his followers and students who wrote about their great teacher.

Following his death, those students placed different emphasis on various aspects of his system, eventually splintering into three separate schools, the "three Sen houses" (三千家). Each differs in detail but retains the core spirit of Rikyū's practice and his four tea values.

The Urasenke school was initiated by Rikyū's grandsons and to this day is headed by his direct descendants, the most current being Sen Sōshitsu XVI, the sixteenth generation descendant of Rikyū and the grandmaster of the House of *Urasen*.

The Foundation keeps alive one of Japan's greatest cultural traditions. But, there's one last detail worth mentioning, lest we make the mistake of assuming that *wabicha* remained some kind of aesthetically pure institution, free from the messy world of power politics.

Following Rikyū's death, the aims of his practice were tragically subverted and used as a political tool serving the militaristic interests of political rulers (Cross 2013). This continued until historically very recently. During the Second World War the narrative of his life as well as his death were appropriated to glorify suicide and to justify sacrificing one's life for the nation. His memory was stained by using his life story and the aesthetics he developed to support an ideology justifying hyper-nationalistic tendencies and the disastrous narrative of the Japanese unification of east Asia, which led the empire into some of its most catastrophic brutalities.

But, I must emphasize, all of these appropriations of Rikyū's life and art could not be more deeply at odds with the values he had developed as the foundation of his *Wabicha*, and the values we keep alive at the Urasenke Institute.

Now, unless there are any questions, I think you're all very well equipped with a good bit of tea history to help you appreciate the ceremony you'll soon experience.

Guide: Dear Sanada-sensei, *arigatou gozaimashita*! We're so deeply fortunate to have had this amazing overview of Japanese tea history with you. Yes, I think we're perfectly prepared after your very generous lecture, so let us all thank you from the bottom of our hearts before we're off to our next stop.

Sanada-sensei: I'm very glad I could meet you all and contribute to your tea journey! Good luck with your ceremony!

> ~ *The group bowed deeply to express their gratitude. One by one, they followed their Guide out of the Urasenke Institute.*

Guide: I hope you all enjoyed this great talk. That's it for today. Tomorrow, we'll meet at the Kumano Nyakuōji-jinja shrine in Sakyo Ward, and we'll walk together from there to Kyoto Daigaku campus.

4

Tetsugaku Michi

Cherry Blossoms: Impermanence and *Mono no aware*

Figure 4.1 Philosopher's Walk, Kyoto. (*Tetsugaku no Michi*, 哲学の道). R. Loughnane.

Guide: Welcome back everybody. I hope you've had a chance to look around a bit while you were waiting.

Artist: I came a little early and wandered around the shrine. It's quite impressive. Are we having our next lecture here? On Shintoism, perhaps?

Guide: We will have a lecture on Shintoism, but not today. I wanted to meet here because of its proximity to an actual philosophic landmark of Kyoto. Let's head over to the pathway along the canal.

Does anyone know what this says?

Theologian: I recognize that last kanji. It's the character for the *dao* (道), isn't it?

Guide: It is. In this case, the wording is "*michi*", which refers more literally to a pathway. But, the first two kanji read as "*Tetsugaku*". Has anyone heard that term?

Philosopher: Ah, right. That's the Japanese term for philosophy, right?

Guide: That's right. Altogether what we have here is *Tetsugaku no michi* (哲学の道) or the "Philosopher's Path". The route was named to honor several of the main proponents of the Kyoto School of Japanese Philosophy such as Nishida Kitarō and Hajime Tanabe who would often stroll on the banks of the river between classes at the nearby Kyoto University. That's the philosophy aspect of the path, I think the aesthetic aspect should be quite obvious. As you can see, it's one of the best places in all of Kyoto for *hanami* (花見), or cherry blossoms viewing.

The path first opened in the late Meiji era as an irrigation channel leading into the Lake Biwa canal, and besides the stunning expanse of cherry blossoms lining the canal, there are several temples and shrines along the way.

I assume cherry blossoms aren't new to any of you. Can anyone say what they represent in Japanese culture?

Artist: They're a kind of an aesthetic treasure in Japan, aren't they?

Guide: Yes, absolutely. And, does anyone know why they're so cherished?

Philosopher: I don't know exactly what they represent, but I've attended a couple of gatherings during cherry blossom season and it's clearly a big deal. There seems to be a high value placed on the timing of viewing the blossoms.

Figure 4.2 Cherry blossom-lined path of the Philosopher's Walk. (*Tetsugaku no Michi no sakura namiki*, 哲学の道の桜並木). R. Loughnane.

Guide: Yes, that's right. *Hanami* (花見) is a short period around the end of March and early April where the cherry trees are in bloom, and millions gather in parks and alongside bodies of water to view them.

It's a tradition dating back to the Nara period (710–94). If you read Japanese literature, poetry, or see any of the great works of Japanese painting or even cinema, you'll often see cherry blossoms and people gathering to view them.

And, you're right, timing is crucial. Catching the blossoms at the right moment is of such importance that you'll even hear radio announcements from the Japan Meteorological Agency called "blossom forecasts" (桜前線, *sakura-zensen*) detailing the precise increments of blooming in different parts of the country. Literally reporting that, for example, the trees are seven-tenths bloomed in the Shukkeien Garden in Hiroshima, or only four-tenths at the Kaege Incline in Kyoto. Even this class today was timed so we'd be here, on this particular path on this very day in late March.

Let's begin our stroll and we can discuss some of the aesthetics elements surrounding cherry blossoms.

~ *The group made their way onto the pathway, stopping to admire and snap photos of themselves under the blossoming trees.*

Artist: Did cherry blossom viewing originate with the tea ceremony?

Guide: Flowers do play an important role in some versions of the tea ceremony, but cherry blossoms aren't actually associated with the tea ceremony. But, as a class on Japanese aesthetics, they're an important element of that tradition.

Philosopher: The trees seem like they're slightly just beyond peak blooming. The petals are already beginning to fall.

Guide: Precisely. Had we come earlier, we would have only seen them in full bloom, which would have been unfortunate.

Philosopher: Wouldn't that have been perfect?

Mono no aware and Impermanence

Guide: This brings us to one of our first Japanese aesthetic principles, *mono no aware* (物の哀れ). Like cherry blossoms, this concept wasn't related directly to the tea ceremony. It evolved within Japanese literature and poetry long before, maybe five or six centuries before *Chadō* was formalized in Japan. But, within the context of Japanese aesthetics, it's an important aesthetic idea we should discuss.

The term is typically translated as "the pathos of things", and it refers to the beauty associated with sadness felt when witnessing something being lost, fading away, or in some cases, even dying.

Philosopher: It sounds like the aesthetic dimension of impermanence.

Guide: In many ways, yes. When we experience something beautiful, we generally want to hold onto it, we want it to last, to be as permanent as possible. So, when cherry blossoms shed their petals, as we see today, we don't just feel their beauty, we feel our own desire for them to stay the way they are. The beauty is tinged and augmented by an element of sadness.

There are endless references in Japanese culture to this feeling of sad beauty which cherry blossoms evoke. If you ever wanted to look into this deeper, there was one Japanese aesthetic thinker in particular, Motoori Norinaga (本居 宣長, 1730–1801) who popularized the idea of *mono no aware* through his analysis of Japanese literature, particularly in his extensive studies of the *Tale of Genji*. Does anyone know that novel?

Theologian: Yeah, I think it was actually one of the first novels ever written, wasn't it?

Artist: And, it was written by a woman, right?

Guide: Exactly. The author, Murasaki Shikibu (紫式部 973–1014) wrote the text around the early eleventh century, during the highpoint in Japanese culture we've already discussed, the Heian period. *Genji* is an extremely significant text not just in Japanese literature or Japanese studies, but in world literature. And, at around a thousand pages and with intricate detail of the minutiae of courtly life, it's one of our best historical sources of knowledge of this period. Although we're a long way from Heian Japan, the concept of *mono no aware* underwent a bit of a renaissance in the eighteenth century thanks to Norinaga's commentary, which remains a major force in Japanese literary and cultural studies to this day.[1]

Does anybody recognize any of the components of the term?

Theologian: "*mono*" means "thing", or "object", doesn't it?

Guide: Right. You probably hear it most often in the Japanese word for shopping, *kaimono* (買い物). Literally "thing buying". *Kakemono* (掛物), the term for a hanging scroll we've mentioned, is "hanging thing". And, "*kimono*" is "wearing thing".

The "*aware*" part refers to the emotional reaction or pathos provoked when witnessing something beautiful yet transient, like cherry blossom petals falling.

Can anyone guess what exactly we're sensitive to when in a state of *mono no aware*?

Artist: Maybe it's like beauty infused with a bit of suffering.

Guide: Perfect, yes. The idea of suffering was exactly what I had in mind. One reason the Japanese have been so gripped by cherry blossoms at the moment when they begin to die is because it's more than just an aesthetic event: their passing exhibits one of the fundamental qualities of existence, and that is its transience, ephemeral quality, or its impermanence.

Philosopher: And, impermanence causes suffering?

Guide: Yes, but maybe more specifically, our grasping for permanence within an impermanent world is what causes suffering.

Cherry blossoms are particularly evocative of impermanence because almost as soon as they come into their fullest bloom, at the moment they reach the peak of their vibrant beauty that we desperately want to endure, just at this moment they begin to die. Their beauty has almost no duration. Their life cycle undermines our desire to grasp for permanence.

As opposed to the self, which endures long enough to give us the *illusion* of permanence—for long enough that we become attached to and grasp for prolonging existence—cherry blossoms have no such moment we can hold on to—virtually no time allowing us to fool ourselves that their beauty can be permanent.

Here's a bit of a philosophical claim we'll unpack throughout our classes. In this case the *aesthetic is ontological*. What I mean is that the sadness we feel when the beauty of cherry blossoms is slipping away—which is an aesthetic experience—this shows us something about existence, about how all things are impermanent—which is ontological, something true about reality itself. Cherry blossoms remind us that all things are transient and part of the reason their transience has been aestheticized is to remind us to appreciate reality without becoming attached to any particular moment.

On this point we really have to read some passages from a famous Japanese Buddhist monk and author Yoshida Kenkō (吉田兼好, 1283–1350). In his *Essays in Idleness* (*Tsurezuregusa* 徒然草) he asks:

> *Are we to look at cherry blossoms only in full bloom, at the moon only when it is cloudless? To long for the moon while looking on the rain, to lower the blinds and be unaware of the passing of the spring—these are even more deeply moving. Branches about to blossom or gardens strewn with faded flowers are worthier of our admiration.*

(Kenkō 1967, p. 115)

And, he extends this appreciation of beauty beyond cherry blossoms, to human existence itself, when he writes that

> *if man were never to fade away like the dews of Adashino, never to vanish like the smoke over Toribeyama, but lingered on forever in the world, how things would lose their power to move us! The most precious thing in life is uncertainty.*
>
> (p. 7)

Once we can recognize the quality of *mono no aware*, we start seeing it everywhere in Japanese art. Of course, in the *Tale of Genji*, but it's also in haiku poetry, Noh drama, painting, and very often in cinema.

But, because *mono no aware* reflects the Buddhist principle of impermanence—because it invokes something ontological through the aesthetic—we can recognize this sad valence of beauty not just when viewing cherry blossoms but in all of our own everyday experience.

Artist: This really contrasts so strongly with what I've learned about European philosophy and art. That tradition started with a search for permanence, and a lot of its great artworks reflect and reinforce that.

Guide: Can you elaborate?

Artist: Well, think about making a sculpture out of stone. The point hasn't been to accentuate how it will eventually fall apart. The idea is actually to avoid that, to create the illusion that a body will last forever. That it will be permanent.

Guide: Yes, very good. It might be worth pausing for a second to discuss how different the world is according to *mono no aware* and the principle of impermanence as opposed to how it's seen in our western philosophic and aesthetic worlds, which, yes, you're right, often operated according to principles of permanence.

Let's think in broad strokes about western art history.

Many great sculptures often depict human bodies in their youth. Think of Michelangelo's *David*. Have any of you seen it?

~ *All three nodded "yes".*

Guide: And, did it make you feel sad?

Theologian: No, not at all.

Philosopher: I'd say it was more of a positive feeling. Like this is how beautiful and perfect the human body can be.

Guide: Right. And, at this moment of the Renaissance, beauty was associated with perfection. In this case with Michelangelo's "David", and in many attempts to represent the perfect human body, the choice is often to depict that body on the verge of full maturity. The perfect human form is not yet decaying, not yet showing the signs of aging. Or, we might say, not yet displaying its impermanence. In a way, depicting that moment can trick us into thinking that the nature of reality, or of beauty is permanent. So, you probably didn't feel any sadness because there's nothing deliberately built into works like *David* to provoke that feeling.

Can anyone think why western artists have prioritized this moment as one of the highest expressions of natural beauty?

Philosopher: I guess, it's like we already spoke about. The early European philosophers began looking for a reality that was permanent. The world we perceived with our senses was constantly in flux, constantly impermanent, and thinkers like Aristotle and Plato wanted to find some realm of existence that never changed, something permanent to be the foundation for knowledge and philosophy. Nietzsche (1999) even criticized Plato for creating the dream of a permanent realm, saying that he was too frightened by the world of change.

Guide: Yes, although there are some exceptions with philosophers like Heraclitus and some Sophists, western philosophy began with and remained for most of its history in pursuit of permanence. Plato began asking what are the metaphysical principles that are universal, trans-historic and thus *always* true, *permanently* true. He didn't want to base his philosophy on the physical world, which was constantly changing and thus impermanent, a world where our bodies and all objects decay and eventually pass away, so he theorized a different realm of existence, one where things didn't change, a realm of permanence. Like you said, for him we could only have knowledge of a world that was permanent, so it was the one the philosophers chased, or some might say, the world they invented.

Even though Plato knew that all bodies break down and decay, he nevertheless posited a kind of human permanence, the idea of an immortal soul.

A lot of western philosophy is "Platonist" in the sense that it assumes some permanent metaphysical realm beyond the world of change we're immersed in. When we think about European art history in broad strokes, we can understand why so many artworks depict bodies in their perfect youthful state. Like we said with *mono no aware*, aesthetics and ontology are coupled. Western artists were also informed by philosophy. Especially in the Renaissance when Greek learning was revived, artists often sought to create artworks where beauty represented perfect forms, and those forms should be just as perfect in any moment throughout history. A beauty that didn't change; a beauty that was permanent.

This is the significance of cherry blossoms and the aesthetics of *mono no aware*. Yes, the Japanese too probably would have liked to experience permanence, to avoid the body's decay and death. As humans we're all terrified by life's transience. But, instead of creating artworks that gave the comfort and illusion of permanence, some Japanese artists and literary figures recognized something I think is quite unique in global art history. They realized that sadness actually *elevated* our experience of beauty, that if we can be attuned to the passing of all life and the impermanence of all things—an *ontological* fact of reality—then we also find an elevated form of beauty—an *aesthetic* fact of reality.

Artist: It seems right to point out that impermanence plays an interesting role in Japanese aesthetics, and that *mono no aware* seems unique in ways, but having studied art in the west, I can say that death has been a quite constant aesthetic subject throughout European art history. From *natura morta*, to *memento mori*, there's centuries of depicting crucifixions and funerals, there's David's "The Death of Marat", Picasso's "Guernica" and Damian Hirst's "The Physical Impossibility of Death in the Mind". There's really no lack of depictions of death and mortality in western art.

Guide: You're absolutely right. And, you're much more of an authority on art than I am, but wouldn't you say that maybe not all, but *most* depictions of death in western artworks—maybe we have to limit ourselves to before the twentieth century—but isn't death mostly depicted as something bad, something undesirable and to be avoided?

Artist: I would have to think about it more. There are obviously lots of beautiful works where death is represented, but I'm not sure that death itself is often depicted as beautiful.

Guide: It's very possible we could find some instances of western artworks where death itself is depicted as beautiful. Think of the many astonishing depictions of the crucifixion. But, even if death itself is depicted as beautiful, it's the *human act* that is beautiful—I'm not sure, though, that we'd find the further aspect that the beauty of dying tells us something about the fabric of reality. Or, we could say, the aesthetic isn't really ontological in these cases. The point is to show the human act of sacrifice, for example, that that has its own beauty, but not that all reality is beautiful in a sacrificial kind of way. It's Christ who is depicted as dying and impermanent, not the fabric of reality.

Theologian: But, isn't that good? Shouldn't we avoid aestheticizing death? We don't make a painting of Jesus on the cross to make him look beautiful, but to tell us something important about religion, about forgiveness and redemption.

Aestheticization of Death

Guide: You raise a deeply vexed issue, with tragic implications in Japanese history.

Mono no aware is an important and unique aesthetic principle in that it brings our attention to an aspect of reality, which many other aesthetic and philosophic principles want to overlook. But, the aestheticization of death has had disastrous consequences in Japanese history, particularly in terms of self-sacrifice, but in a very different sense than western religious depictions of Christ's sacrifice.

During wartime, the aesthetics of cherry blossoms were even used as a symbol to legitimate sacrificing one's life at a time of war. Giving one's life for the nation was construed as a way of extending life, not in the western sense of an immortal soul, but as the dissolution of one's self that fulfilled a destiny of assimilation into the body of imperial Japan. Sacrifice in war was seen as a gift to the nation and ultimately to the Emperor, where one integrated oneself into Japan's "community of shared destiny" (*unmei kyodotai* 運命共同体).

Furthermore, ritual suicide of high-ranking aesthetes—such as Rikyū's state-sanctioned *seppuku*—fueled the idea of joining a community of artistic elite; a narrative deeply ingrained in Japanese culture to this day. The aesthetics of cherry blossoms and aestheticization of impermanence were appropriated, or let's say *mis*-appropriated to turn suicide into an honorable, heroic, and ultimately an aesthetic act.

You've probably heard of one of the more well-known examples of aestheticizing death with the Second World War *kamikaze* (神風 "divine wind") bombers. Their slogan "the total suicidal death of one hundred million" (*ichioku gyokusai* 一億玉砕, literally "100 million shattered jewels") gave pilots a narrative to justify and glorify the ultimate sacrifice.

So, you're right to worry about how Japan has aestheticized death. To this day, we see the heart-breaking implications of this tradition in the many images of ritual suicide in Japanese literature, film, and in many dreadful cases, in the news. Although it's an extremely complicated issue, this history of valorizing

Figure 4.3 Kamikaze Attack on USS *Missouri*, April 11, 1945. U.S. Navy photograph (public domain).

suicide partly explains why Japan continues to have such a problem with suicide to this day. It's a dilemma many Japanese philosophers have struggled to comprehend.[2]

Theologian: It makes the question of "killing tea ancestors" even more complicated.

Guide: Absolutely. And, we have to get started with that shortly. And, as I mentioned, we're going to have to complicate this life–death binary along the way.

For now, let's walk over there and we'll talk a bit more about how the theme of death comes up in the Buddhist philosophy-religion it inherited from abroad.

~ *The group crossed over the canal on a small footbridge and wandered towards Ginkakuji Temple where they sat in the shade of some old cherry trees in the cool draft rising off the canal.*

What you see now is one of Japan's aesthetic gems from its Medieval period. *Ginkakuji* (銀閣寺, lit. "Temple of the Silver Pavilion") was built in the late fifteenth century. This Rinzai Zen temple is a prime example of Higashiyama culture from the Muromachi period. These stunning gardens surrounding the pavilion are believed to have been designed by the great landscape painter Soami. It's one of the most important pieces of Japan's cultural heritage so, let's forget this and go across the canal to get some pizza.

Figure 4.4 *Ginkaku-ji* (銀閣寺), Kyoto. R. Loughnane.

~ *The three classmates paused in disbelief that they heard correctly.*

Guide: You look somewhat surprised.

Artist: I suppose you could say that. We're at this cultural landmark and we're going to skip it and get pizza?

Philosopher: I could understand going to get some sushi, or ramen, but pizza seems like a slightly odd choice.

Guide: Yes, in a superficial sense, what we're going to do is to get pizza. But, in a more philosophic sense, we'll be killing the Buddha. Shall we?

~ *The Guide took the footbridge across the canal and led the three down Tetsugaku Michi to the Monk pizza restaurant.*

Buddhism: Philosophy, Religion and Art

Guide: So, here we are. I can tell you're all slightly perplexed, and understandably so. But, I'm going to try to show you that coming to this restaurant can actually keep us engaged with Japanese aesthetics in a way that going to the temple might not have.

And, we'll get there by speaking about the Buddhist influence on Japanese aesthetics. We've already touched on some Buddhist principles like non-selfhood and impermanence, but haven't yet delved into Buddhism itself. So, while we wait to be seated, let me ask you, what do you know about Buddhism?

Theologian: It's one of the major religions in Japan, Korea and China. But, it actually originated in India.

Philosopher: And, they don't go to church or pray but have monasteries where they meditate, like the one we just left. And the goal isn't so much to gain knowledge or grasp the truth but to become enlightened. "Soteriological", I think you called it.

Guide: That's all exactly right. Although there's some debate about his historical existence, the figure we call "the Buddha" is thought to have been an actual person who lived in South Asia near present-day Nepal during the sixth or fifth century BCE. Siddhartha Gautama was a prince who led a privileged but sheltered life within a walled palace where he enjoyed every luxury. Only after venturing beyond the palace grounds did he first see examples of human suffering.[3] Rather than retreating back into the safety and comfort of the palace, he made it his life's mission to explore the nature of suffering. And yes, meditation was one of the main practices he employed. He supposedly meditated under the Bodhi tree for forty-nine days before becoming a "Buddha", which means "an enlightened being". Following his realization, he became an itinerant spiritual teacher traveling around South Asia spreading his teachings and gaining adherents for what became one of the world's great religions, now with more than 520 million adherents worldwide.

Does anyone know how Buddhism spread from India?

Philosopher: Didn't it first travel into China? But, there are also Buddhists in places like Afghanistan and as far east as Myanmar and the Philippines aren't there?

Guide: Yes there are. Buddhism first reached China before spreading to Korea, Japan and South-East Asia. For our discussion on Japanese aesthetics, we'll focus on Zen Buddhism, since this was one of the major schools that evolved in Japan. To give you a brief context, Zen (禅) means "meditation" and it is actually a transliteration of the Chinese word "*Chan*", which is itself derived from the Sanskrit term "*Dhyāna*", which meant "meditation".

Aside from the Zen lineage, if you trace Buddhism all the way back to its origins, you'll find dozens of schools. After the Buddha passed away in the fifth century

BCE, what we call the "pre-sectarian" period ended, and the movement splintered into many different sects each with their own interpretation of the Buddha's teachings. For our purposes of discussing Zen, we'll consider Mādhyamika Buddhism, which was one school within the broader Mahāyāna lineage, the other being the Yogācāra school. We won't dwell too much on the particularities of these schools, but there's one small point to keep in mind. First, that Mādhyamika is known as "middle way" Buddhism. And, remember when I mentioned the "Two-fold truth" earlier? The origins of that notion are also found in Mādhyamika Buddhism.

If we think back to our discussion of *mono no aware* and the beauty tinged with sadness—or let's say the suffering associated with impermanence—we see that there's a connection between this aesthetic principle and the foundations of Buddhist philosophy. Buddhism doesn't theorize a permanent reality or comfort itself with the idea of an immortal soul. Instead, it embraced impermanence from the very beginning, and thus it didn't seek to hide from human suffering or its causes. Just as many western artists based their practice on the prevailing philosophies of their time, likewise many Buddhist artists would have created their works not just to depict, but to embrace impermanence. To be an artist was, in many senses, to be a Buddhist practitioner.

Theologian: But, there are lots of artists in the Europe that follow Greek or Christian principles, you wouldn't say that they were religious or philosophic practitioners.

Guide: Good, this brings up a unique aspect of Buddhist and Japanese aesthetics, which isn't strictly speaking "aesthetic" the way we tend to understand that term in our western tradition. To be a Japanese aesthetic practitioner, a calligrapher, a landscape painter or an ikebana artist were ways of being a Buddhist practitioner. And since Buddhism has elements of philosophy and religion, being a Japanese artist meant your practice could embrace art, philosophy and religion.

Again, speaking very broadly, in the west we have tended to cordon domains of knowledge off from one another, and that's partly because our philosophies began this way, looking to know about things that were self-subsistent, existing on their own, something "in itself". Likewise, we have tended to want to avoid overlap between philosophy, religion and art. There are endless debates about whether something is philosophy or religion or art. Lots of disciplinary boundary policing. And, these debates can be very interesting, but in Asian traditions it's not so problematic that someone or some practice could be philosophic, religious, *and* artistic, without needing to strictly delineate between these aspects. Graham Parkes, a great philosopher of intercultural aesthetics wrote that in "Japanese traditions, philosophy is generally interfused with poetry and music, psychology and religion, as well as with training of the body and self-cultivation" (Parkes 1996). You didn't have to choose one pursuit over another. To be a Japanese aesthetic practitioner was a way of practicing Buddhism.

Many important artists were serious Buddhist practitioners, no less than any other monk. Take Sesshū Tōyō for example. He's one of Japan's most famous artists and as head abbot at a Zen Buddhist monastery was known not only for painting but for meditating every day of his adult life. Whereas this would be quite an exception in the west, there was nothing special about being an "artist-monk" or "painter-priest" in Japan. Those went together perfectly fine in Zen Buddhism because the goal for the monk and the artist were the same, to modify one's suffering by diminishing attachment to the illusion of a permanent world or self.

When I think of it, a western author might really like having three distinct characters such as yourselves to represent different intellectual, spiritual or artistic dimensions of a single practice. But, in the Japanese tradition, you three could be different dimensions of one single practitioner's character.

Artist: But if all three of us were one person, would we do philosophy or make art differently than in the western tradition, where these are kept separate?

Guide: Interesting question. The important thing to keep in mind is that, although making visually beautiful art was certainly the outcome of many Japanese aesthetic practices, it wasn't necessarily the goal. And, this is perhaps worth considering. To be an artist was one way of working with one's suffering. This is another sense in which art and aesthetics differed from how we tend to understand them in the west. Our tradition has mostly focused on the *outcomes* of artistic work and demanded that it be beautiful, but we haven't been overly concerned with the question of whether the practice of making the work contributed to the artist's well-being.

As a Buddhist practice, being an artist had a soteriological dimension. It was a way of cultivating non-selfhood. Soteriological philosophies don't merely seek to define reality or beauty, create metaphysical theories, or cultivate knowledge—although they might also do all of those—they're primarily oriented towards cultivating means for living well and for diminishing suffering for oneself and all beings.

Philosopher: This doesn't seem entirely foreign to the European philosophic tradition. I mean, Socrates wanted us to learn how to live the "good life", and

Aristotle said that we study ethics not "to know what virtue is, but in order to become good" (1103b26–1104a1). Other schools of Greek philosophers, such as the Stoics were oriented towards living well. Pierre Hadot has a book on this where he reads ancient Greek schools as what he calls "Philosophy as a way of life".

Guide: Yes, you're absolutely right. But, tragically, this element has been mostly lost as philosophy evolved into an academic discipline that is focused almost exclusively on speculation and theoretical knowledge. Great work is carried out in these domains, but we have to see that it's not a discipline that cultivates concrete practices to work with everyday life and suffering. Like the art world, western academic philosophers are evaluated based on the outcome of their work, the practice of getting there is most insignificant.

Artist: But, have art and religion always been so separate in the west? I know that there are many "religious artists", in the Renaissance, for example, who sought communion with God through their art practice.

Guide: You're absolutely right. There are more differences between Japanese and western aesthetic worlds, but let's pause that discussion for now and come back to it later. I'd like to talk about the present setting we find ourselves within.

You were all quite understandably surprised to have ventured in the opposite direction of that great monument of Japanese architecture and Zen Buddhism. Can anybody explain why?

Theologian: The temple seemed like the obvious choice. We're speaking about Buddhism and aesthetics, and there's a magnificent Zen temple right in front of us. I would have assumed that the temple would have illustrated the ideas we're talking about.

Artist: But, you proposed that coming to this restaurant actually lets us remain engaged with Buddhism and aesthetics, and having gone to the temple might have obstructed that experience.

Guide: Yes, that's right. Let me explain because this raises some important elements of Zen we should understand. Especially in the west, we're habituated to expect that the highest religious experiences should come along with the kind of sophisticated art and architecture we saw across the canal, not the dust under our feet. And, in the Mādhyamika lineage of Mahāyāna Buddhism Zen arises from, we find a deterrent to help one avoid the suffering associated with this particular form of attachment.

The radical feature of the Mādhyamika philosophies that inform Zen is that they realized very early on that their central principle called "emptiness"—

which should itself help us avoid attachment to ideas like a permanent self—*can itself become a locus of attachment*. It sounds simple but it's important we grasp this point. "Emptiness" or *śūnyatā*—a principle that guides us towards non-attachment—can itself become a locus of attachment.

Emptiness and Attachment

Philosopher: Ok, I'm a bit lost. Non-attachment can become attachment?

Guide: Let me try to put it another way. I think we already know that we should not become attached to the self or to things. Let's say this is one Buddhist principle. But, Mādhyamika realized that philosophical principles could also themselves become a source of attachment. The danger is, we can become *attached* to the principle of *detachment*. We subvert the meaning of emptiness when we make it into a static thing. And, this would subvert one's soteriological aims.

In preaching detachment, Nāgārjuna realized that he had to go one step further. To avoid our becoming attached to "emptiness" (*śūnyatā*), he went beyond construing reality as empty, and articulated a theory—or maybe we could say a non-theory, or "theory against theory"—he called the "emptiness of emptiness" (*śūnyatāyāh śūnyatā*). What that means is that, as a philosophical principle, emptiness *was itself empty*. So, even if you tried to turn emptiness into a static thing, even if you objectify it, Nāgārjuna's move to the "emptiness of emptiness" reminds us that emptiness too is empty, just like all things, and also not something to be attached to.

Philosopher: . . . I'm starting to see how we're killing the Buddha.

Guide: There's several Zen stories that might sound funny or fantastical but they have this same idea, the need to avoid attachment precisely where it becomes most intransigent, when we become attached to philosophies, or to great teachers of a religious or philosophical lineage. The most famous such story is where the Rinzai Zen sage Linji says, "If you meet the Buddha, kill the Buddha."

Theologian: So, maybe, soteriologically speaking, we're better off here in this unexpected place where we have no attachments than on the other side of the canal at a famous Buddhist temple.

Artist: Where it's almost impossible not to be attached to our assumptions about such a place.

Guide: Right, the temple is clearly an aesthetic masterpiece, but it's also now a tourist attraction that's been very nicely packaged for mass consumption. So yes, the potential for attachment is very high with such cultural masterpieces. Visiting the temple might give us a sense of having consumed some culture, but it's not likely that any of us derives any of the soteriological value it was originally constructed for. But, coming here to a restaurant serving pizza, a very *non*-Japanese dish most likely appears to be of lesser aesthetic or soteriological value.

What you don't know is that the chef of this Michelin star restaurant, Yoshihiro Imai, is a philosophically trained Buddhist practitioner. His pizzas fuse Italian and Japanese culinary culture in the masterpieces we're about to enjoy. In a very Japanese way, he's taken something from a foreign culture and re-interpreted it to make a new and beautiful creation. He illustrates the Mahāyāna principle that the means for enlightenment are always immanent, always in the everyday mundane circumstances surrounding us. We don't need palaces and jewels, sophisticated texts or architecture. Even in what Buddhists refer to as "the dust of the marketplace", there is all the soteriological potential needed for realization. The potential for enlightenment is always right beneath our feet.

And, because we're going to get deeper into the complications of intercultural encounter, the amazing beauty of Imai's dishes shows us there are indeed bridges between eastern and western aesthetic worlds. As he's doing a Japanese interpretation of a very European dish, he's giving us this important lesson with some of the intercultural flavor we're looking for.

Philosopher: So, having come here is one way of avoiding the attachment potential of the temple?

Theologian: Killing the Buddha with pizza.

Guide: Exactly. But, next time, go to the temple or do something else. No sooner will we take a bite of our delicious pizzas than we're forming new attachments.

Philosopher: Don't become attached to detachment from attachment?

Guide: Perfect.

Theologian: But, attachment to the idea that we can be anything other than selves attaching to things, is also a problem, isn't it?

Guide: Precisely. This is the main Mādhyamika point. This is why it's a "yes" and a "no" to the question of whether we can experience a tea ceremony. We mustn't replace attachment to selfhood with attachment to non-selfhood. The latter is potentially more precarious.

Theologian: But, when does it end? Detachment from attachment to detachment . . . doesn't it keep going on and on?

Guide: It doesn't matter.

Philosopher: Because of the two-fold truth?

Artist: Or, the emptiness of emptiness?

Guide: No, because our pizza is here. It would be foolish to worry about philosophical speculation when we have these masterpieces of intercultural aesthetics waiting to be enjoyed. And, these philosophical questions will all be answered by someone who is a much better authority on the subject than myself, who we'll visit at Kyoto University just as soon as we're done killing the Buddha in the most delicious way possible.

Itadakimasu!

> ~ *The group enjoyed their pizzas, later strolling again together down Tetsugaku Michi towards Kyoto Daigaku for their next lesson.*

5

Kyoto Daigaku I

Guide: Welcome back, everyone. We're now at *Kyoto Daigaku*, home of Japanese Philosophy. You might have heard of the "Kyoto School". Let me tell you about how it all began before we head in for our lecture.

During the late nineteenth century, when Japan was still an empire, the Imperial Universities (帝国大学, *teikoku daigaku*) were established, with Kyoto Daigaku being the second, founded in 1897. Previously, Japan didn't have any university departments where philosophy was studied. The Department of Philosophy was established here in 1906, the first of its kind in Japan. Among the prominent philosophers of that time, Nishida Kitarō (西田幾多郎, 1870–1945) is generally regarded as the founder of the Kyoto School.[1] This was a very significant moment for the Japanese intellectual world since before the formation of the Philosophy Department, western-style academic philosophy wasn't practiced in Japan.

And, to learn more, let's head into the Philosophy Department and meet our next teacher.

Foreigners in the Tea Hut: Interculturality and Nationalism?

Guide: It is great to see you again! Please come meet our group. Everyone, this is Professor Atallah. She is a specialist in east–west intercultural philosophy and has been working here in the department for over a decade. Professor, would you please tell us a little bit about yourself.

Dr. Atallah: Yes, of course. Very nice to meet you all. I was born in Nigeria into a devout Muslim family and although my early life was steeped in the practices and rituals of Islam, I became more and more interested in the philosophic and religious principles of the Islamic faith. This interest led me to studying religion and philosophy at the University of Lagos and then later to

France for my master's degree. While in France, completely unexpectedly, I developed a fascination with Japanese culture, so much so that I began learning Japanese. By the time I started formulating a doctoral project, I was already deeply immersed in Japanese philosophy and began a dissertation exploring intercultural issues in dialogue between French and Japanese philosophies. Specifically, I compared French phenomenologists with those who had sprung up in Japan in the twentieth century.

Guide: Apologies for interrupting, but I should say, our professor is very humble and would never mention that not only is she one of only very few women to be hired as a professor in the Department of Philosophy here at Kyoto Daigaku, much more significantly, she is the only foreigner and person of color to ever do so. Her tenure here has transformed the department, which had otherwise only ever been staffed by native Japanese, and almost exclusively male scholars.

Having foreigners on staff very much aligns with the Kyoto School's goal of developing a global approach to philosophy. This makes our teacher the perfect ambassador for the Kyoto School in the twenty-first century and the ideal scholar to help us develop the cultural sensitivity we need for experiencing the tea ceremony.

But first, Professor Atallah, I wonder if you might answer a question that has come up in our discussions. We wanted to know about the "ontological negative" and the principles of "emptiness" underlying the negations in concepts such as *non*-selfhood, *non*-object or *non*-action.

Dr. Atallah: Certainly. This is a critical issue for intercultural philosophy and also to help prepare you for your tea ceremony. It might sound difficult to understand the ontological negative, but please trust me, in ways this is a completely straightforward idea according with many of our intuitions about experience.

But, let's go back to the early days of western philosophy, back to Plato and his student Aristotle and draw the contrast between how they thought about the self and objects and how we need to think of them to follow the Buddhist principles informing Japanese aesthetic practices like the tea ceremony.

I'm going to introduce two slightly different but related terms from the ones you've used, those being "substance ontology" and "relational ontology".

Guide: Yes, great. Remember everybody, these were on our original table where we divided the ontological positive from the negative.

Dr. Atallah: These are very important terms, but it's vital to keep in mind that they're western terms. "Ontology" is a Greek word so it wouldn't have been part of the Buddhist tradition. "Onto" means "being" and the "ology" part is the suffix you're familiar with in all of your studies like psychology, geology, biology; it denotes "logic of", or "the study of". So, ontology is the logic or study of Being.

Especially with Aristotle, when he undertook ontological speculation, what he thought was most real were substances, what the Greeks called *hypokeimenon* (ὑποκείμενον) and *hypostasis* (ὑπόστασις).

Philosopher: I think "substance" was on our table from an earlier class where we divided the "ontological positive" and "negative".

Dr. Atallah: Yes, where you're using "ontological positive", I'm using "substance ontology". They're related terms, but emphasize slightly different aspects of a similar way of doing philosophy.

Substances are self-subsistent things, separate from all other things, not dependent on anything else for their existence, or so Aristotle thought. To view the world through the lens of substance ontology is to study reality as though what is most true, most definitive of things is their *independent existence*. Not how things *relate* to other things, but how things are defined as *individuated beings*.

You'll often hear philosophers say things like "what is the chair like *qua* chair" or "human *qua* human". Or, an object "in itself". All of these mean, a chair or a person or any object *with an essence* or another term is a form. It is an object *not* in relation to other things external to it, but something that can exist and thus be known *in itself*. This is substance ontology. Based on this "substance" way of thinking, an entire logic was formalized to describe things in the world.

Artist: We spoke about Aristotle and the law of non-contradiction. Does that apply here?

Dr. Atallah: Yes, very much so. What did you learn?

Artist: That A equals A, and A cannot equal not-A. So, a chair is a chair. A tea bowl is a tea bowl. A self is a self. A=A. And conversely, a tea bowl does *not* equal a non-tea bowl, that is, it doesn't equal a shoe or a book. A does *not* equal not-A.

Dr. Atallah: Yes, good. You'll definitely want to try to think beyond these logical constraints today and especially for the tea ceremony. But, don't think too hard. In the absence of theorizing about things, the quality of our experience usually goes beyond A=A kind of logic, anyway.

Philosopher: But, what's the alternative. If substance ontology tries to describe things as they are *in themselves*, independent of all other things, what is "relational ontology?

Dr. Atallah: Good question. Let's turn to Buddhism to see how we can understand relational ontology, and how that brings with it a different logic.

Artist: And "relational ontology" was in the column of the ontological negative?

Guide: Yes, correct.

Dr. Atallah: When Buddhists looked to the world, they didn't notice things being permanent or unchanging. They saw constant change and flux. Instead of looking for an essence, which remains the same as things change, the Buddhist approach would assume that all things are "empty" of any essence. So, now we're back at that idea we've already touched on—emptiness, or *śūnyatā*.

For something or a self to be empty means that when we investigate it, we don't find an unchanging and independent essence making it what it is, we find nothing. It is "empty" of any essential nature. Another term is formlessness (Skt. *arūpa* अरूप, Jp. *mushiki* 無色).

Artist: But, how exactly does something like a tea bowl become a tea bowl? How does it remain a tea bowl as it changes?

Theologian: How do we all know what we're talking about when we talk about tea bowls?

Dr. Atallah: Good questions. You're expressing a common apprehension about the ontological negative. Many people assume that if something is "empty" it wouldn't exist at all *in any way*, as though there is simply nothing, a complete annihilation of existence. But, this is a big mistake. If you take one thing from this class, let it be this: *emptiness does not mean that things don't exist, they just exist in a different way.*

In your example, a tea bowl doesn't exist because of some inherent essence isolated from everything else. Instead, it exists because of its *external causes*, its relationships and connections to all other things.

This is "relational ontology", the ontological negative: defining them not in relation to themselves, not as tea bowl *qua* tea bowl, but through its relations to other things. Theories of emptiness can get quite technical, but remembering one key idea will be enough. *Something that is empty still exists, it just exists as a relational thing not an independent thing.*

You are you, but not by virtue of some intrinsic essence. You're you by virtue of your relations to things that are not you. You are yourself in not being yourself. Or, as the Kyoto School philosopher Ueda Shizuteru puts it, "I, in not being I, am I".[2]

Theologian: So, this is non-selfhood? The self considered within negative or relational ontology is the "non-self"?

Dr. Atallah: Precisely. This is the relational structure of the empty self, the non-self—just as it is the structure of all things that exist as empty. We aren't defined by an internal essence like an ego or soul. Instead, we exist relationally, sustained by countless non-self causes.

And, if the self is sustained by non-self causes, perhaps you can see how this demands an alternative logic. A equal A falls short. Emptiness—or more generally the ontological negative—demands that A can and *does* equal not-A. This means that "I" as A exist only through what is not me, what is not-A.

Philosopher: But, can we really do philosophy based on this kind of contradiction?

Dr. Atallah: We tend to assume that contradiction should be avoided, and if we encounter one, it signals a flaw in our thinking or logic. The law of non-contradiction (A=A and A≠not-A) makes sense if things exist based on an internal unchanging essence, as a substance ontologist would believe. But, when we define things through their external relations—based on emptiness, as a relational ontologist would—then the law of non-contradiction might actually blind us to an important aspect of the existence of all things.

Take the tea bowl again. To say it's defined by its relations is to say it's defined by what is *not*-tea bowl. This includes the vast web of contexts that bring the bowl into existence and sustain it as what it is, how it is. The not-tea bowl elements—the not-A that defines the A—comprise the minerals forming the bowl, the tools and techniques shaping it, the structure of our hands and mouths that demand certain shapes, even the forces like gravity, all of these determine what a bowl must be to function as a bowl for us. Only through this precise constellation of external relations does a bowl become what it is. The bowl exists as a relational nexus—an impermanent meeting point we call "bowl", where all the not-bowl elements, causes and conditions adhere for a time.

If we approach a tea bowl as a substance ontologist might, confined to A=A logic and defining the bowl *qua* tea bowl, only in relation to itself, we strip away the vast relational context. This approach actually reveals *less* about the object, much less. By shifting to the negative and bringing relations into view, we gain a greatly expanded perspective, and it's one that reflects our actual experience. After all, we never experience anything in a vacuum, as an object *qua* object divorced from its relations to other things. The self-subsistent object is a bit of a dream.

Philosopher: Okay, I think I get it, but I have a bit of a technical question. I understand that the ontological negative brings relations into view. But, does "emptiness" refer to the *thing* and how it exists or is "emptiness" the field of relations outside the thing?

Dr. Atallah: That's a sharp and important question. There are nearly as many interpretations of "emptiness"—or what we're calling the "ontological negative"—as there are Buddhist philosophers. To answer your question precisely, we'd have to investigate particular thinkers, but for today's class, we can say that the term is used in both senses. Emptiness can refer to the nature of the thing *or* the field of relations, but these amount to almost the same thing. It's likely more of a question of emphasis rather than distinct meanings. Let's focus for a moment on this second sense, "emptiness" as a relational field, this will help us get a different view of what *śūnyatā* is.

Co-dependent Origination

Imagine visualizing any object alongside the relational causes sustaining its existence. These relations extend infinitely. Take the bowl: even at the mineral level, we don't stop. The minerals themselves are empty, constituted by their own relational nexus. Trying to grasp them leads outward—to geological events that ground stones into fine grains for pottery. This brings us to sedimentation, erosion, volcanism, plate tectonics, and planetary formation, all shaping what particular minerals are. The relations keep expanding. There's no fixed point where an object can be circumscribed or its relations ended. So, in viewing how the tea bowl "arises", we don't reach an end-point in an essence, only an infinitely proliferating web of relations upon which the bowl depends. This is precisely what Buddhism means by "emptiness" and "co-dependent origination".

The Sanskrit term is *Pratītyasamutpāda* (Skt. प्रतीत्यसमुत्पाद, Jp. *engi* 縁起). It's also translated as "inter-dependent arising" or "dependent co-arising".

In the *Flower Garland Sūtra* (*Avataṃsaka Sūtra*), this relational field is beautifully illustrated by the metaphor of Indra's Net. Has anyone ever heard of this?

Artist: Yes, I think that's the infinite network of jewels, isn't it? Where each reflects all others?

Philosopher: It sounds like Leibniz's monads.

Dr. Atallah: Yes, very good. Indra's Net is an infinite network of jewels, each reflecting all others, which is meant to illustrate the causal web of relations constituting "co-dependent origination". And yes, some scholars have pointed out the similarities with Leibniz's concept of the "monad", but there are also some important differences we don't have time to go into now.[3]

But, if you can picture that kind of field where everything reflects everything else, that gives you an idea of how things exist in the relational field of emptiness. The infinite reflecting is the quality of things as "co-dependent arisen".

Philosopher: I feel like I was taught almost the opposite approach when trying to know or define things. Like, we had to abstract things away from their relational context in order to really know them.

Dr. Atallah: Yes, that's typical of the western substance ontological approach. Although his student Aristotle later challenged him on this, Plato used the verb "*chōrizō*" (χωρίζω), which means "to separate" or "to divide" to explain how we should understand the essences of things as existing independent of one another.[4]

Theologian: So, we would have a drastically different picture between the western substance ontological view that wants to isolate things and separate them from their contexts to define them, and the Buddhist view from emptiness, which includes the context.

Artist: If we shift from the tea bowl to ourselves, we must get a very different picture of who we are.

Philosopher: Or, who we are not.

Non-Self

Dr. Atallah: The key point most Buddhist philosophers would agree on is that humans are not defined by a separate, isolatable essence, ego, soul or even a mind. This doesn't mean that we lack something resembling these. Rather, when we explore the self, we don't uncover some unchanging permanent essence, but a network of relations sustaining us—not forever, not permanently. Just as the tea bowl depends on non-tea bowl causes and conditions, likewise, the self is sustained by many non-self causes. And, this is where we get the concept of the "non-self" (Skt. *anatta*, अनात्मन् Jp. *muga* 無我). Referring to one another as non-selves is just to describe our existence in a different way, as beings who exist relationally, empty of any internal unchanging or permanent essence.

Artist: This is why you said that *you* couldn't take us to a tea ceremony. Neither we nor the tea ceremony exist as permanent, unchanging things with essences.

Theologian: And, the self you were when we met isn't the same as the self that would eventually arrive at the garden.

Guide: And, if we can grasp how we all exist based on relationality, how we're *empty* of any permanent essence, then it's entirely possible and unproblematic for us non-selves to experience a non-object like the tea ceremony.

Artist: But, if we enter the tea ceremony, won't we then be in relation to all the things we encounter? Will this then become part of our empty definition, another way that not-A comes to define us as A?

Dr. Atallah: Yes, brilliant observation. That's exactly right. And actually, the tea ceremony is already part of who you are. To introduce more terminology related to the ontological negative—even in its "absence", the ceremony is already part of who you are.

Guide: "Absence" and "presence". Also on your tables. Keep these in mind for our upcoming discussions on Daoism and also phenomenology.

Dr. Atallah: You're right, anything we come in relation with becomes part of who and what we are. That said, we have to be cautious. In one sense it's the most simple thing we can do,—being a non-self encountering non-objects. It's completely mundane. But when it comes to a ritual like the tea ceremony, to truly manifest emptiness at that elevated level is a challenge. There are many things that get in our way, what Buddhist philosophers refer to as "obstructions" (Ch. *wuai* 礙).

Guide: That's a great point, and ties directly to the question I've been trying to articulate since the beginning of our class. How can we really encounter the tea ceremony and not be obstructed by all of our attachments, assumptions, and biases?

Dr. Atallah: You're invoking a core paradox Zen highlights: if we all possess Buddha nature, why is such enormous effort needed to achieve enlightenment? Similarly with the tea ceremony. Anybody can make a cup of tea and share it with others, so why is it near impossible for a tea master or guest to experience the simplicity of a single cup? Why does it take a lifetime of practice to overcome obstructions and host just one truly exceptional tea ceremony?

But, there are ways to deal with intercultural obstructions. Has anybody heard of a movement in western philosophy called "phenomenology"?

Comparative Philosophy and the Intercultural "double bind"

Philosopher: That's the school started by Edmund Husserl, right?

Dr. Atallah: Husserl got the movement off the ground and then it was advanced by his student Martin Heidegger before branching off in several different schools. We'll focus on the branch known as "existential phenomenology" as it's the one that's given us the most dialogue with Asian philosophies.

Artist: It's a western movement, though. Are they not substance ontologists like most of that tradition?

Dr. Atallah: Not necessarily. From my perspective, the moments when phenomenology approaches the relational ontology and the ontological negative are some of the most important and intriguing. But, we shouldn't expect that philosophy to unfold exactly the same way they do in Buddhist philosophies. Phenomenology, after all, is a relatively recent invention, and yes, a western one, a product of modern Europe. Scholars such as myself and my colleagues who do intercultural philosophy have made a career out of building bridges between phenomenology and the Buddhist philosophers we'll discuss today. And we'll consider the moments of ontological negativity, particularly in existential phenomenology.

That said, we have to keep in mind that phenomenology is not directly related to the tea ceremony in any way. Before diving deeper into this topic, we need to address a more basic set of questions before you step into the tea garden.

Your question brings up several issues in intercultural philosophy. And, although most academics overlook these issues, there's a lot at stake with how we engage— or fail to engage—with other cultures and their intellectual or artistic practices. Philosophy, in particular, has remained one of the slowest university disciplines to internationalize, but the good news is that there has been great progress in the last few decades, so we can hope that it will continue to overcome what has been a deep and persistent Eurocentrism (Van Norden 2017).

But, not all academics share this concern. Many are happy doing only European philosophy. Some even question whether intercultural or comparative philosophy is "real" philosophy. You can argue with them, but one of the best questions I've heard was in a lecture from the intercultural philosopher, Thomas Kasulis (2011) who asks, "it's not philosophy *compared to what*?", in effect, demonstrating how all philosophy has a comparative element.

Philosopher: But, when you compare two thinkers, if you're just putting two similar philosophers side by side, this doesn't seem like philosophy to me.

Dr. Atallah: If that were only what comparative philosophy were doing, you're right that it might not be that useful.

But, firstly, it's a common misconception that comparative philosophy places "similar" thinkers in dialogue. In his collection of essays on *Heidegger and Asian Thought*, the intercultural philosopher, Graham Parkes (1992, p. 1) writes that "comparative philosophy [is] generally more enlightening between un-connected philosophies."

And, Kasulis (2011) addresses your concern about putting thinkers "side-by-side". He calls this "juxtapositional comparative philosophy" and while it has its virtues, he outlines how the discipline has evolved to include "hermeneutic comparison" and the more advanced "transformative comparison" where dialogue between two thinkers aims to create a third concept out of the confrontation.

This is where intercultural scholarship is most fascinating and valuable, I believe.

Let me ask the three of you: can you think of any potential dangers in our attempts to encounter foreign intellectual or artistic traditions or cultures. Any thoughts?

Philosopher: There's been a lot of debate in academic humanities recently about cultural appropriation. Some people are getting a lot of friction for misusing or mis-appropriating the customs or practices of other cultures; their clothes, hair styles, ways of speaking or making art, these have become sensitive topics recently.

Dr. Atallah: Right, yes. It's definitely something we need to keep in mind. But, what is the actual danger? Many cultures very much want foreigners to engage with their traditions and practices. Many actively spread their culture around the world to attract visitors by promoting the most tantalizing aspects of their history, customs or art. The western world is constantly seeking to attract foreigners. Japan is no exception. So, what's the real concern about appropriation?

Artist: I think there's a bit of an asymmetry, historically speaking at least, between how the west has appropriated other cultures and how it has encouraged the spread and uptake of its own culture globally. The term I've heard that describes this is "cultural imperialism". I don't fully understand it, but one of the main points seems to be that after the period of colonial exploitation through military force and violence mostly ended, a less visible but still damaging cultural form of exploitation has persisted. This involves powerful western countries maintaining unequal relations between nations by imposing their cultures on them, taking what they want from those nations without respecting the history or the contexts that made them meaningful, or acknowledging the people or traditions who developed the practices.

Dr. Atallah: That's a really good summary. Learning about other cultures, fostering curiosity and wanting to participate in their traditions is *not* a bad thing. It is, in fact, a great thing, and we need more of it. But we have to recognize that the west hasn't always approached this with the best intentions for the other cultures involved. This is particularly true of the history of relations between the west and Japan.

Philosopher: But, we *are* trying to learn about the ceremony, its history and background. Isn't this kind of approach mostly free of the dangers of cultural imperialism? We're not imposing anything on the culture here.

Dr. Atallah: That's a fair point. But, even when we look back at the history of early encounters with Japan—by academics, anthropologists, historians, or missionaries who participated in the tea ceremony—none were entirely free of the biases and exploitative tendencies of the colonial era. Many imposed their own beliefs, religions, or philosophies onto what they encountered. This is why we need to be particularly cautious when considering phenomenology in the context of the tea ceremony. We don't want to simply impose western frameworks that obscure or distort the ideas developed indigenously alongside the tea ceremony.

This raises an important question for us. Of course, you want to avoid exploitative behavior. But we can also ask: how can foreigners participate in the tea ceremony without allowing their biases to cloud what they see and experience?

There's actually a recent academic, a Palestinian-American, who made a significant contribution to analysing how academics tend to obscure their view of various Asian worlds. Does anyone know who this is?

Philosopher: Ah, yeah. I've heard of him. Edward Said, right?

Dr. Atallah: Yes, and does anyone remember the main text he's known for?

Artist: *Orientalism*. We studied that in an Asian Studies class I did in my undergrad.

Philosopher: Oh yeah? We read a section of it too, but in a graduate class on International Relations.

Dr. Atallah: Yes, that's not surprising. Said's text (1978) is often considered the work that kicked off post-colonial studies. He's widely studied across disciplines, as academia has been conducting a critique of its colonial past for the better part of half a century. One of the main points of that text is that academics have obscured their vision of other nations through a self-serving exoticization and othering.

Does anybody remember how Said makes this argument?

Artist: Well, in my Asian Studies class, we didn't focus on Japan in particular, but highlighted how, western interpretations of Asian cultures often amounted to a narcissistic discourse. Asia was framed as an exotic, fundamentally different land—impenetrable but tantalizing to the western intellect. From what I understand, Said argued that this narrative was largely fabricated by westerners to serve their own entertainment and justify or even enhance the value of their colonial exploits.

Dr. Atallah: Great, yes. Said's concept is crucial to keep in mind. Even for those who grew up partly in Japan or spent significant time in Asia, it can be challenging to avoid this kind of exoticization. And, even more challenging because Japan itself has, at times, been complicit in shaping its identity to titillate western fantasies. Especially today, we need to critically examine this exoticization if we want to experience the tea ceremony beyond orientalist biases.

But, bracketing our biases is not so simple as it might seem. As you're probably starting to realize, we have to hold two seemingly opposing ideas in a tricky balance. We're in a kind of intercultural "double bind" (Loughnane 2022b): On the one hand, we must avoid exoticizing the ceremony. But, on the other, we can't ignore the fact that the tea ritual, as it has evolved in Japan, possesses a quite extraordinary uniqueness. While we should be cautious of imposing cultural assumptions onto Japan, we must also remain open to appreciating the distinct beauty that the Japanese tea ceremony offers.

Philosopher: It's maybe an abstract way to put it, but it sounds like we can neither fully assert identity *or* otherness. We don't want to over-ascribe difference nor simply erase those differences.

Guide: That's a great way to put it, and it reflects the more abstract ambiguity we've been discussing regarding negativity and positivity.

Dr. Atallah: That brings us to our next topic, an equally thorny philosophic and aesthetic topic, the question of Japanese identity.

Japanese Identity and Nationhood

Dr. Atallah: Many scholars, both native and non-native, have argued that the tea ceremony represents something uniquely Japanese or expresses the nation's identity.[5]

Artist: Yes, we've spoken about this. About how we impose a monolithic notion of identity onto Japan, and possibly, the tea ceremony as a Japanese ritual.

Dr. Atallah: Right, but this perspective isn't merely a western construct imposed upon Japan—some very prominent Japanese intellectuals have fueled this way of thinking. Perhaps the most well-known among them is Okakura Kakuzō, whose work *The Book of Tea* (1964) framed the tea ceremony as quintessentially Japanese. The slightly ironic fact is that Kakuzō wrote this work not in Japanese but in English, while living in the US, for an audience of high society New Englanders eager to exoticize Japan, but mostly uninterested in learning the Japanese language.

Others, such as Kobori Nanrei Sohaku, the abbot of the temple Ryōkō-in, reinforced this view by describing the ceremony as a unique "expression of the mind of Japan" (1988, p. 7). Some have even claimed that non-Japanese can't truly understand or experience the tea ceremony's beauty. One towering figure of Japanese aesthetics, Shin'ichi Hisamatsu, was not only a tea master, but a Zen Buddhist practitioner and scholar of philosophy at Kyoto University. While he has shaped much of what the world knows about Zen aesthetics, he insisted that the tea ceremony was so unique to the Japanese that westerners couldn't grasp its true meaning.

The drive to self-mythologize is strong in many cultures, including Japan. There are undeniably elements of the ceremony that seem to express something unique about the Japanese people and nation. We shouldn't deny that. But we also need to recognize that the role the ceremony plays in today's Japanese self-image is a carefully curated one. It emerged in the Meiji period, a time when the nation was eager to assert not just a national identity, but also brutal nationalist endeavors. Scholars have shown that, to a certain extent, the idea of the tea ceremony as a symbol of Japanese identity was a deliberate invention (Kumakura 1980; Tanaka 2007) with several scholars invoking the "invented tradition" thesis[6] (Hobsbawm 1983) when discussing chanoyu as a ritual that was formalized in the early modern period and later recast as "quintessentially Japanese.".

Let me ask this: how can we use Japan's own thinking to challenge its own idea of its unique identity?

Philosopher: Because the idea of identity is exactly contrary to the ways of thinking that were prevalent in the traditions informing Japanese culture.

Theologian: Identity is aligned with selfhood, not non-selfhood. A=A thinking.

Dr. Atallah: Exactly, that's it. Identity is very much of the A=A logic. So, to even begin considering Japanese *identity* is slightly problematic insofar as that tradition has been deeply influenced by its Buddhist inheritance, which should problematize identity not just at the level of the self, but also the nation, and really, everywhere.

Can anybody think of how we might challenge this idea of Japanese *identity*?

Philosopher: I think it's commonly acknowledged that Japan has been a country, not so much of innovators, but of perfectors.

Dr. Atallah: Oh yes, good. Can you say a little bit more about how that relates to its identity, or lack thereof?

Philosopher: It may be a generalization, but throughout much of its history, the Japanese were remarkably open to learning from other cultures. Many Japanese arts—painting, poetry, calligraphy, architecture—emulated Chinese principles. The Japanese often went abroad enthusiastically, returning with techniques and practices learned from others, especially from China. Much of what is "Japanese" wasn't originally so, including Buddhism and the writing system. Many elements shaping Japanese identity come from outside Japan—so it's almost not "identity" at all. Or, using the A=not-A logic we've been exploring, we might say Japan was constructed out of not-Japan.

Dr. Atallah: Yes, Japan was exceedingly skilled at learning from other cultures. Some scholars have challenged this particular trope (Lucken 2016), but what is true is that for long periods of its history, Japan has been a very outwardly-looking nation. Or, we might say that Japan developed more based on "otherness" and "alterity", that's why the notion of "Japanese identity" is awkward. They often learned from other peoples and then innovated, systematized and codified practices and techniques until they began to take on what we tend to look back and attribute a Japanese quality to. The tea ceremony is one of the great examples of their particular way of assimilating the foreign.

This pattern extends to philosophy, too. Buddhism, Daoism and Confucianism were all brought from outside. But, the Japanese didn't simply reproduce what they had encountered abroad, but almost always worked to refine and systematize what they learned, giving their appropriations a unique Japanese character.

Up until medieval times, China was very much seen by Japan as the more advanced civilization, much like the Latin world was for Europe for centuries. Japanese monks and traders would travel to China and return with practices, technologies, teachings and texts on Chinese religions and philosophies. This is how foreign traditions of Buddhism, Daoism and Confucianism got to Japan.

All this considered, I think we can see why the idea of a Japanese identity is complicated. It's difficult to pin down what is truly Japanese. If being Japanese is the ability to incorporate what is not-Japanese, then the concept of a fixed Japanese identity or "Japanese mind" is problematic. But, that position between

Japanese and not-Japanese aligns nicely with a fluidity between identity and difference—which is consonant with the ways of thinking Japan is actually well-known for.

Artist: If we apply this to the tea ceremony, then, likewise, it's difficult to say that it's purely Japanese, I guess.

Dr. Atallah: Right. When we dig down into any of its aspects, we find very little that is *strictly* Japanese. Certainly, throughout the centuries, it has taken on qualities that seem to be part of a unique Japanese way of thinking, but we should question our own desire to construct some kind of identity for this nation, or really, any. Not only are there philosophic problems with that way of thinking, Japan has gotten itself in trouble through an over-assertion of its identity.

Does anyone know what I'm talking about here?

Theologian: I saw a documentary about the Second World War where Japan justified its actions and some brutalities based on a hyper-nationalist idea of Japanese identity.

Philosopher: I think there are instances where philosophers got wrapped up in debates about the role of the Japanese nation during the war.

Dr. Atallah: Yes, exactly. This was a very complicated moment in Japanese history—one that scholars and historians are still trying to come to terms with. But, you're absolutely right: the ideas of Japanese uniqueness had disastrous consequences, and we have to keep this in mind when speaking about the tea ceremony as an expression of Japanese culture or identity.

While there's nothing wrong with being proud of one's national character or achievements, these ideas were taken much too far during pivotal moments in history. What you referred to as hyper-nationalism had a specific term in Japanese, that was *nihonjinron* (日本人論), which were ethnocentric discourses about Japanese nationalism. A sense of uniqueness was felt so strongly that Japan felt justified in appointing itself the leader of the entire East-Asian world. This took the form of colonial exploits, bloody conflicts, and even war crimes. In some cases, intellectuals even got mixed up in complicated ways with the government's hyper-nationalist projects, which continues to be a controversial topic dividing scholars to this day.[7] While we shouldn't allow this to deter us from enjoying the tea ceremony, it raises a set of questions we must take seriously. It's not just Japan itself that has perpetuated the idea of its own uniqueness, we foreigners are also part of a tradition benefiting from this perception.

Theologian: But, what do we do? I'm convinced that we need to take seriously the dangers of nationalism, and the flip side of cultural imperialism, but is the answer to simply forego experiencing foreign cultures at all? Is the right answer for foreigners not to do Japanese tea ceremonies?

Philosopher: But can't we attend to these rituals without being complicit in reinforcing dangerous aspects of identity or, on the other side of the coin, undermining legitimate aspects of identity through typical western chauvinistic forms of cultural appropriation?

Guide: If I can interrupt for a second, I want to echo back exactly what you've both just said, but at one level of abstraction. Part of avoiding the "double bind" of cultural appropriation and cultural imperialism is finding a way to encounter the ceremony without objectifying it.[8] Both Japan's nationalist appropriations and the west's mis-appropriations can be seen as forms of objectifications of the ceremony. If we can find a way to approach the ceremony beyond objectivity—perhaps as a non- or negated object—we open ourselves to the possibility of an extraordinary experience, while hopefully minimizing any harmful impositions.

Dr. Atallah: Yes, great point. These are all serious issues that are debated endlessly, along with related questions about tourism, cultural exoticism, essentialism vs. relativism and authentic vs. inauthentic cultural encounter. These all deserve serious attention, but soon you'll face not abstract or theoretical questions, but a very special concrete phenomenon. And, if approached with humility and an open mind, your partaking is a great benefit both to yourselves as foreigners and the Japanese practitioners of the tea ceremony.

"The Spirit of Tea is Global"

And, if we listen to the ambassadors of Japanese tea, we find that they enthusiastically support the idea of foreigners learning the ceremony. The former head of the Urasenke Foundation, the *iemoto* (家元) Sen Sōshitsu XV, Hounsai (十五代千宗室, 1923–) strongly endorsed foreigners not just partaking in but actually learning the practice. He set the Institute definitively on the path towards internationalization, and in 1970 established a course for non-Japanese students. By 1973 this class expanded into *Midorikai* ("Green Society") becoming the official non-Japanese wing of the Urasenke Gakuen Professional College of Chadō. Soon after, another branch of the Institute was set up in China at the Junior College Urasenke Way of Tea housed at Tianjin University. To date, over

400 students from more than thirty countries have graduated from these programs.

Furthermore, the present *Iemoto*, Sen Sōshitsu XVI (十六代千宗室, 1956–) has continued this global vision, emphasizing intercultural exchange. He travels extensively throughout the world donating to institutions to promote *Chanoyu*. Throughout his tenure as *Iemoto*, he has set up Urasenke institutes in almost forty countries. Remarkably, he has even conducted a tea ceremony for priests at the Vatican's Church of Sant'Anselmo.

Let me read you some quotes from Sen Sōshitsu XV. You can find these in a great little journal the Urasenke Institute used to publish, called *Chanoyu Quarterly*.[9] In an introduction entitled "The Spirit of Tea is Global" Sōshitsu writes;

> *It has been more than forty years since I went alone to the United States carrying with me some tea utensils and a tatami covering, thinking to spread Tea abroad. To date, I have now visited about fifty countries of the world – countries in every region, every continent. The number of trips I have made abroad must be over one hundred and seventy.*
>
> *Even though our languages and customs may differ, let our hearts touch and communicate by our sharing a bowl of tea. Thus, it might be called the international catch phrase of Tea.*
>
> *In the Way of Tea, however, there is no difference between whether one is Japanese or not; the only difference that exists in Tea is whether one is a chajin or not.*
>
> (1992, pp. 5–6)

While it's not so controversial to assert that the Japanese have played a significant role in refining tea into a highly sophisticated ceremony distinct from its Chinese origins, Sōshitsu claims that tea "knows no boundaries and can be applied anywhere in the world".

The Urasenke school not only ventures into other nations to share its wealth of culture, it also brings people to Japan to study the tea ceremony. I myself learned about tea through the Midorikai *fellowship* at the Urasenke Professional College of Chadō, which trains around a dozen foreign students every year.[10]

Some have argued that the tea ceremony is precisely an ideal intercultural "in-between" space where people from diverse cultural and religious backgrounds can enjoy the profound aspect of our shared humanity (Hioki 2013).

Guide: I hate to interrupt again, but we're just about out of time.

Dr. Atallah, we can't thank you enough. You've given us so much that's going to help us understand and experience the tea ceremony. We are deeply grateful.

Dr. Atallah: You're all very welcome! I understand you're going to have another lecture here tomorrow with Professor Leander. I'm sure you'll enjoy your time with him and will be very well prepared to enjoy your ceremony.

> *~ The group left the lecture hall feeling rich from all the insights they had gained, with a growing excitement to eventually experience the upcoming ceremony. They assembled in the courtyard outside the Philosophy Department before going on their way.*

6

Kyoto Daigaku II

Phenomenology

Dr. Leander: Welcome everyone. I'm very glad to have you here for today's lecture. As I think you might already know, we're going to speak about a philosophic method called phenomenology. Has anyone heard this term?

Philosopher: I've heard it a lot in philosophy circles, but also hear sociologists and even art historians using it.

Artist: Yeah, I've actually heard roboticists and archaeologists working with phenomenology.

Dr. Leander: It is a term that's being used quite widely in many academic domains, which is great. It's applicability to a variety of disciplines might come by virtue of it being not just a philosophic doctrine or theory, but also a methodology.

Theologian: Is it a methodology that tea masters also use? Or the philosophers who informed the formation of the tea ceremony?

Dr. Leander: It's possible that some tea practitioners might know about phenomenology, but no, it hasn't been part of that tradition. It's very much a philosophy that arose in the western academic world. But, it's a method that has been uniquely useful in building bridges between western and eastern philosophies.

Philosopher: We learned about cultural imperialism in our class with Dr. Atallah yesterday. Can we avoid those dangers if we impose phenomenology on the tea ceremony?

Dr. Leander: That's exactly the right place to start. Imposing a western philosophical framework on an Asian ritual inevitably creates intercultural challenges we can't ignore. Interpreting other cultures through our own philosophies and concepts, as you said, risks falling into intellectual imperialism, a trap we must work hard to avoid.

Please keep in mind, we absolutely do not need phenomenology to understand or engage with the tea ceremony. And yes, it could be an obstruction if we aren't careful.

For one thing, anyone can have a perfectly great experience of the tea ceremony even without a philosophical guide or without knowing a single thing about philosophy. It's an amazing and beautifully intricate set of rituals, objects and experiences, and everyone can take something away from it with little or no specialized learning.

But some, like yourselves, have chosen to work on your interpretive tools to augment your understanding. These tools need not include phenomenology. There are many entirely valid interpretive frameworks one could use to interpret the tea ceremony: religious, anthropological, sociological, or art historical. The ceremony is the focus of ritual studies, and many feminist scholars have recently examined the gender dynamics of the ceremony and its institutions.[1] Scientists are even using high-tech equipment to study hand and bodily movement, eye movements, light patterns, and cognition within the tearoom.[2]

Even within a western philosophical lens, multiple interpretive angles are available. It doesn't have to be phenomenology. We could explore the ritual's metaphysical or ethical dimensions, analyse the epistemological underpinnings of the institution, or theorize about virtues or forms of hospitality cultivated within the practice.

So no, we don't need phenomenology or any western framework. But, here's our dilemma: We don't want to engage with the ceremony *purely* as foreigners—confined by our worldview and cultural expectations—but neither can we fully bracket our cultural backgrounds and experience the ceremony as though we belong to the Japanese world.

Philosopher: We spoke about this yesterday in terms of an intercultural "double bind" between cultural imperialism and cultural appropriation.

Dr. Leander: That's a great way to put it.

We've all grown up in a particular world, and whether we're aware of it or not, we are profoundly shaped by its intellectual tradition in ways that can be difficult to see.

Just keep in mind, it's not a bad thing that we're conditioned by our European heritage, or any. We can work with this. We go wrong if we assume that other cultures must accommodate us or conform to our worldview. Or, if we ignore how we're conditioned, this has given rise to a lot of the well-intentioned chauvinism in intercultural encounter; assuming that our western perspective is somehow closer to a universal perspective, as if we somehow escape cultural determination altogether.

Artist: So, how do we account for our cultural determination without that obstructing our experience of other cultures, or the tea ceremony?

Dr. Leander: There's potentially many possible approaches, and numerous scholars have articulated intercultural methodologies to address this exact question.[3] What I propose is that to navigate the "double bind" you mentioned, we need a method that both acknowledges our cultural determination, while also providing a bridge to other cultures. And, this is why I choose phenomenology to teach to foreigners wanting to engage the tea ceremony. It's a movement that arises from the European tradition, but it has proven to be an excellent bridge, I think one of our best bridges to Asian philosophies, particularly those emphasizing aesthetic and embodied experience like the tea ceremony.

It's not perfect—no intercultural framework could be—but in some ways, phenomenology actually emerged from interactions between Europe and Asia, and on that basis, it has facilitated a growing body of scholarship placing the two traditions in dialogue.

Philosopher: I notice you've referred to the western or Japanese "worlds" a few times. But, I'm a bit confused with the idea that we're in a different "world". I mean, they speak a different language here and have different traditions and history of course, but strictly speaking, in the end aren't we all part of the same world? Could we come to know about and engage in other cultures if that weren't the case?

Dr. Leander: That's a perfect segue into the next topic I'd like to explore with you. You're absolutely right that, in one sense, we all share the same world, but "world" is also a technical term in phenomenology with a nuanced meaning, and now is a great time to delve into that concept.

"World": Phenomenology and the Pre-reflective

Dr. Leander: When phenomenologists use the term "world" they're not referring to the chunk of rock we see from space. What they're talking about is something more like a shared context of meaning. When we speak about the Japanese "world", of course we don't mean that they're literally on a different planet, but that their understanding is somehow different from other "worlds". That said, phenomenologists take this term even further, exploring subtler dimensions of how our "world" impacts our experience.

Husserl—"Lifeworld"

To give you a bit of background, phenomenology is a movement initiated by the German philosopher Edmund Husserl. He was among the first to use the term "world" in the technical sense. In one of his most significant early works, the *Logical Investigations* (2009), he analysed perception, and noticed that we never perceive anything as an isolated object, but always experience it within what he calls a "horizon" or a "background" of other meaningful things.

For instance, a chair is meaningful in relation to a desk, to a table, and the human body. Without those relations, a chair wouldn't carry the meaning it does. Moreover, a chair is meaningful in terms of a wider background of meaning, such as sitting, resting, working, or eating, but even more broadly in relation to rooms, windows, buildings and so on. Husserl's central insight is that when we seek the meaning of things, we don't encounter isolated objects, but always things accompanied by what he calls a "horizon" of co-meanings.

Philosopher: Is this one way of thinking of non-objects as relational entities?

Dr. Leander: That's a great observation. That isn't a term Husserl used, but there would be some similarities. The idea of a non-object, an object that is "empty" and exists by virtue of external causes, we could say, broadly speaking, is a relational object. Husserl is emphasizing that we *perceive* within a web of relations, and that all meaning emerges in terms of relations. But we have to be careful not to make too simple comparisons. While he explains that perception and meaning are relational, Husserl might not go as far as Buddhist philosophers would and say that things actually *exist* relationally. But, great question. Some phenomenologists will actually go farther in the direction of a negated object or "non-object" and relational ways of thinking.

Let's return to our chair example to see how this leads to the "world" concept. If we continue to expand outward,— from chair, to table, to room, to house— and continue broadening out to the most general context, if we move from chair, to desk, to room, to building, to city, to work, to income, to shelter, to well-being ... and so on, the widest context we would arrive is "world", or what Husserl called "lifeworld" (*Lebenswelt*).

For him, all of our perceptions, but also our actions, beliefs and values are meaningful relative to this embracing "world". "World" isn't simply the physical environment; it's the meaning-giving human community, which underpins our learning, socialization, our dealings with relationships and exchanges, including those from foreign "worlds".

So, we all carry a "world" with us into our experiences and this shapes how we experience everything, including something as simple as a chair, but also more complex phenomena like the tea ceremony. Because we have such a "world" and bring it along as a lens through which we experience everything, there's no neutral "view from nowhere" position available to us for encountering the tea ceremony.

Artist: Is "world" kind of like a worldview? Like, some people speak about our modern "scientific worldview"? Would that be the world we could say we live in as westerners?

Dr. Leander: This brings up an important phenomenological concept. Husserl aimed to return to that world as it is experienced before being shaped by the natural sciences—the world as it appears in an "everyday" sense, or in German *"Alltäglichkeit"*. Husserl's student Martin Heidegger really expands this "everyday" dimension of phenomenology in ways we'll discuss. But, Husserl and later Heidegger were both careful to distinguish the idea of the *Lebenswelt* from what we tend to call a "worldview". A worldview suggests something we could actually become conscious of and maybe also work to change or refine. We might, for instance, decide to adopt a more humane worldview, we might want to cultivate a religious or atheist worldview. In contrast, the phenomenological conception of world isn't something we can so easily see, choose or can even be fully conscious of.

Philosopher: But, wouldn't anyone who expands to the widest horizon of meaning end up at the same world?

Dr. Leander: In an increasingly globalized world, the answer would seem to be "yes". Historically, however, the meaning-giving quality of the "worlds" humans have inhabited appear to have maintained some distinctiveness. But, to grasp this, we need think historically and geographically quite large scale. For instance, we might imagine that people in ancient Greece or medieval Mesopotamia likely had quite different meaning making "worlds" than our own with distinct sets of relations giving meaning to events, rituals, exchanges, objects, etc., For our purposes, we might consider how our "world" today differs from the one tea practitioners and tea guests might have inhabited when the ceremony was developed in medieval times.

Theologian: But, I never really think of my world, and I imagine most Japanese don't either. When I encounter a tea cup, I don't then move from the table, then the room, then the building, eventually arrive at a meaning-giving world, and I don't imagine that's how anybody arrives at meaning.

Dr. Leander: That brings us to a core tenet of the phenomenologies we'll consider. The world isn't something waiting to be pieced together through deliberate investigations uncovering meaning relations. For our illustrative purposes in this class, we can, somewhat artificially, choose to go through object by object and expand to wider and wider relational horizons, but it's very important to realize that our "world" is always already there. We don't need to do anything to import it in to color our experience—it's the starting point of our experience, not the end point of a chain of deductions.

Phenomenologists often use this term "always already" (*immer schon*) to express this idea that the world gives meaning to any object we encounter—like a tea cup—without requiring us to consciously think about it. As soon as we encounter a tea cup, or any other object, it's "always already" shaped by our "world".

Meaning doesn't arrive first by conceptualizing things, or reflecting on them: our "world" infuses things with meaning in what phenomenologists call a "pre-conceptual", or "pre-reflective" way.

Artist: The "pre-reflective"? Before something is reflected back to us?

The Pre-Reflective

Dr. Leander: Not exactly. You can imagine "reflection" simply as thinking about experience. How we often say that we "reflect" on an experience after the fact.

This brings us to a central phenomenological concept that sets this method apart from most western philosophies—one you'll want to keep in mind before embarking on the ceremony.

Western philosophy has traditionally favored the "reflective" mode of engagement. The idea is simple: to reflect means to think about something that has typically already happened. The key implication is that the event has finished, and we're now analysing or interpreting it after the fact.

There are some exceptions, but the western tradition has overwhelmingly maintained, at least implicitly, that the best way to access reality, conduct metaphysical, ethical, logical or epistemological analysis, the best way to be a philosopher was to submit experience to reflection.

And, it isn't that many philosophers would have explicitly argued for this position. The predilection towards reflective intellection exerts a stronger hold on our philosophical world precisely because it remained an unquestioned assumption for so long. We could say that this assumption has operated in the background, as part of our "world", and ostensibly up until the late nineteenth and early twentieth century when phenomenology began to challenge this most basic assumption about philosophical method.

Existential phenomenologists recognized this assumption about reflection and several of the major figures explored how we might access reality in the moments *before* reflecting on it, asking if we have any access to the "pre-reflective". Phenomenologists like Husserl, Heidegger, Merleau-Ponty, de Beauvoir and Sartre turned their attention to the quality of experience *before* we break it apart with the dissecting reflective intellect, before we invoke binaries like subject and object, self and other, good and bad. Different philosophers referred to this moment of pre-reflective experience in various ways. For Emile Lask, it was "primal something", Husserl used terms like "primal impression", "primal apprehension", "living present" and "primal source". Merleau-Ponty called it "flesh" and "wild being", and Heidegger had a whole set of "fore structures"[4] referring to a world that was "always already" there before we submit it to reflection.

Artist: I was thinking that we have to question our *explicit* cultural assumptions to avoid imposing them on the tea ceremony, but it sounds like the way our "world" determines our experience makes it even more complicated, maybe impossible to get out of our "world" and into the one appropriate for the tea ceremony.

Dr. Leander: Yes, but please let me emphasize, it's unlikely that we can just leave our "world" behind. That shouldn't be our goal.

Theologian: A slightly more abstract question. Before we reflect on the world, isn't it just a meaningless stream of perceptual experience?

Dr. Leander: Heidegger is important on this point. He argued that the pre-reflective moment was not an indistinct chaos or meaningless stream of experience. Even before reflecting on experience, he found that the "pre-reflective" was already historically and categorically laden already meaningfully determined by one's world.

That particular insight is why Heidegger's philosophy is often referred to as a "*hermeneutic* phenomenology"—it emphasizes how the world is already meaningful before we undertake any act to make it so.

To back up for a second, can anyone think of why these philosophers were so interested in accessing experience before it's reflected upon?

Philosopher: Maybe because they felt that reflecting on experience changed experience or distorted it in some way?

Dr. Leander: Yes, that's basically it. One of the primary motivations for exploring the pre-reflective was the concern that the intellect imposes categories, binaries, dualities and concepts onto experience—which might misrepresent or in the worst case, actually distort reality.

And here we find a touchpoint between the two worlds we're considering today. Buddhist philosophy, much like phenomenology, holds that reflective intellection imposes concepts and binary oppositions onto existence, which misalign with the way reality truly is.

Theologian: This is why you mentioned that our table of categories from your notebook were too simple. They're all binary concepts.

Guide: Precisely.

Dr. Leander: According to Buddhism, one of the most nefarious illusions the intellect imposes is that we are isolated selves. Across all strands of Buddhism, there is a shared understanding that *nothing* exists in isolation—all things are interrelated and the nature of reality is emptiness.

But, the problem is that language, especially conceptual or theoretical language is inherently dualistic and thus can't capture the fluid, dynamic flux of existence. Zen, in particular, is cautious of reflective intellect and, in ways distinct from phenomenology, evolved practices to engage in the world that do not objectify it, cast it in dualist terms, or arrest the flow of experience.

But, to go back to your questions, Buddhism, like Heidegger, would likely agree that this pre-reflective experience would *not* be a random "worldless" stream. Do you know why this would not be the case?

Artist: Because for Buddhism, the nature of reality isn't a bunch of disconnected individual entities, selves or objects, but things characterized by their relations?

Dr. Leander: Exactly.

Theologian: To be worldless would be to stand outside of the web of relations, not "co-dependently originated".

Dr. Leander: Right. What makes a thing real is how it is related to all other things. Worldless experience is like what phenomenologists often call a "God's eye viewpoint", by which they mean, it's a perspective that doesn't exist.

Philosopher: But, how can you have a philosophy that tries to think about the pre-reflective. Ultimately, they'll just be *reflecting* on the pre-reflective, won't they? Isn't that self-defeating?

Dr. Leander: That's precisely the challenge Lask, Husserl and Heidegger knew they had to address. But, first of all, we should say that neither phenomenology nor Buddhism aims to *eliminate* reflective intellection. Reflective intellection is not problematic—the issue arises when we take the concepts and binary oppositions of reflection to disclose what the world is really like. Buddhism recognized this danger early on and developed practices to ensure that we had other means of engaging with the world, which inevitably frames the self as divided away from the world.

And, regarding your question about the self-defeating nature of *reflecting on the pre-reflective*, this was actually a significant challenge for the early days of existential phenomenology. The German philosopher Paul Natorp raised this exact criticism against Husserl and his idea of "non-objectifying language".[5] Heidegger later formulated a response—which we don't have the time to go into now—but he essentially reformulated the relation between experience and language enabling phenomenology to carry out research into the pre-reflective, despite the seeming self-defeating aspect of reflecting on the pre-reflective you've pointed out.

Philosopher: Is the idea that if we can somehow shift our focus away from how we reflect on the world, we might stop imposing the assumptions of that "world" onto our experience—and so we can experience it more like a Japanese person would?

Dr. Leander: I'm glad you brought that up. No, that's not quite the point. But, this is very important to get right.

I want to be clear that nobody expects that you should experience the ceremony as someone from the Japanese "world". That's not the goal. Nobody can bracket their world and experience as someone in a far off time or land. Placing that kind of pressure on yourself might actually hinder your ability to engage with the ceremony meaningfully.

The aim isn't to inhabit another world entirely—that would be unrealistic—but to negotiate an in-between position as best as we can.

Theologian: But then, what exactly does phenomenology give us? Isn't it ultimately just another part of our western "world" that we can't step outside of? Doesn't that mean we ultimately never have access to the "world" of the tea ceremony?

Dr. Leander: It might be a good idea to resist thinking that your world and the Japanese world are completely separate. Especially in our globalized world, there's more than enough overlap that allows us to experiment with taking steps, not out of our world into another, but maybe in what we can think of as a world somewhere between the two.

And, it's unlikely that worlds are absolutely fixed—something Husserl and other philosophers like Gadamer recognized. Husserl argued that an awareness of our own world already involves a pre-understanding of other worlds.

And, even when cultures evolved separately over a long period of time, we have many examples of worlds melding, or what Gadamer (2004) calls a "fusion of horizons" (*Horizontverschmelzung*). If this weren't possible, neither the tea ceremony nor Buddhism would have ever become part of Japanese culture since these were both foreign imports. So, worlds can definitely change and morph into each other.

Japan and Phenomenology

Dr. Leander: Phenomenology is actually a compelling example of Asian and western philosophical worlds combining. Here's an often-overlooked episode of intercultural philosophical history. During Japan's Edo period, the country isolated itself, remaining in a feudal state while the rest of the world modernized. With the Meiji Restoration (1868), Japan opened up and sent scholars abroad to study foreign sciences, technologies, medicine, engineering, etc.

Some of these scholars encountered and studied with major European phenomenologists—Husserl, Heidegger, and Sartre—and brought their learning back to Japan. In some cases, the influence went in the other direction, these Japanese scholars actually influenced the European philosophers. Heidegger, notably, showed a strong interest in Asian thought, frequently hosting Japanese and Chinese students. He even spent two summers translating the *Daodejing* with a Chinese student and once said of D.T. Suzuki, "If I understand [Dr. Suzuki] correctly, this is what I have been trying to say in all my writings" (Kreeft 1971, p. 522). He also wrote a dialogue with a Japanese intellectual and once noted in a letter: "Again and again, it has seemed urgent to me that a dialogue take place with thinkers of what is, to us, the eastern world." (1969, 721)

Surprisingly, Japan was the first country to engage deeply with Heidegger's work. The first commentary and full translation of *Being and Time* appeared there in 1939—twenty-three years before the English version. Heidegger claimed to have been better understood by Japanese scholars and even considered a position at Tokyo University, asking Karl Jaspers for advice.

Given Heidegger's vast influence on later European thought, there is often an east-west thread running through much of modern phenomenology. It is what allows researchers like myself to pursue "comparative" or "intercultural" philosophy. Phenomenology, in this sense, forms a bridge—perhaps a small one—between Asian and western philosophical worlds.

Phenomenology and Aesthetics

Dr. Leander: Let me add one more thought demonstrating how phenomenology is a bridge between western and Japanese worlds, and towards the world of the tea ceremony in particular.

Unlike most philosophies that arose in Europe, which typically first lay out their main concepts and then as a secondary step apply those to interpret art and aesthetics, some phenomenologists turn this order on its head; they actually derive their concepts from what they learn from artworks and art practice.

In some cases—like with Merleau-Ponty who we will speak of later—artists are not merely exemplars but are actually considered as doing philosophy.[6] Artists can be legitimate philosophers. This perspective is exceedingly rare in western philosophy, but is perhaps the norm in Japan where there is nothing special about art practices being philosophic practices, or art practices constituting legitimate Buddhist practices.

To go back to your original question, yes it does seem that it is possible for "worlds" to grow and evolve, and for "in-between" worlds to emerge. Perhaps it's even inevitable. And, it's not out of the question that phenomenology has some elements of such an east—west in-between status.

Artist: That seems to make intuitive sense—the idea that worlds evolve over time and blend with others.

Theologian: And, it's not just Buddhism becoming part of the Japanese world, it also happens in western philosophy and religion. Greek philosophy, Christianity, Islam, all of these began as unique movements in limited geographical locations, but spread throughout countless different worlds.

Philosopher: What was the idea of Gadamer's you mentioned?

Ueda—"Two-fold World"

Dr. Leander: "Fusion of horizons". It's definitely a very useful concept for thinking about intercultural encounter, but why don't we consider a Japanese phenomenologist who also gives us a way to think about a position "in-between" worlds.

Has anyone heard of Ueda Shizuteru (上田 閑照, 1926–2019)?

Artist: Yes, I actually saw a documentary about him. I think it was called *The Voice of Nothingness* (Roth 2015).

Dr. Leander: Yes, that's a great documentary. While it focuses on Ueda's philosophy, it also explores the lives of students, artists, and others influenced by him. Sadly, Ueda passed away shortly after the film was made, but it stands as a testament to his life and work. New translations and commentaries are also making his thought more accessible (Müller 2022).

Ueda is perhaps the most prominent third-generation Kyoto School philosopher. Though he didn't study directly under Nishida, he offered some of the most insightful critiques of his work (1991, 1993, 1995). He studied under Nishitani Keiji (西谷啓治, 1900–90), whom we'll discuss later.

Ueda exemplifies a scholar working between east and west. His writings bridge these worlds, forming a kind of intercultural phenomenology. Born and educated in Japan, he completed his doctorate in Germany, writing a dissertation on Meister Eckhart (1965), with a well-known introduction linking Eckhart to Zen.

Ueda was also profoundly influenced by Heidegger and engaged deeply with his ideas in Japan and in international academic forums. Yet he also lived the practice: the son of a Shingon priest, he gave weekly talks at Kyoto's Shōkokuji monastery and was the Kyoto School thinker most rooted in Buddhist practice.

His lifelong concern was communication between seemingly irreconcilable worlds: western rationalist traditions (Being, identity, presence) and eastern relational ontologies (nothingness, emptiness, formlessness). His central question was how to bring Zen's non-rational, mystical tradition into dialogue with western philosophy and science.

This is not so far from your own question about intercultural experience in the tea ceremony. Ueda's concept of the "twofold world" (*nijūsekai* 二重世界) captures this in one of his most influential ideas.

Theologian: Does this have any relation to the two-fold truth we spoke about earlier?

Dr. Leander: Curiously enough, I don't know that Ueda invokes the "two-fold truth" idea when speaking of his conception of a "two-fold world". There are definitely some differences between the two, but let's see as we consider the idea whether there might be any similarities.

Ueda develops this concept in an article of his titled "Language in a Two-fold World" (2011), so we're already alerted to the fact that he's pursuing his worldly go-between through the lens of language. And, before getting to Ueda's understanding of language, let's shift for a moment and explore the Daoist approach.

Daoism—Correspondence and Non-Correspondence

The western tradition places considerable faith in the human ability to use language as a tool to express truth. With few exceptions, philosophies within the European tradition have imposed scarce limitations on language's ability to "correspond" with the world. This is evident in one of the dominant conceptions of truth prevailing throughout western philosophy, from the time of the ancient Greeks onward: the "correspondence" notion of truth.

Has anybody heard of this idea?

Philosopher: Yes, it's called truth as *adequatio* in Latin. I guess it's simple. Just the idea that truth happens when language matches up with the things in the world it wants to describe.

Dr. Leander: And, this seemingly innocuous assumption might appear to be unremarkable, maybe even un-noticeable. It's such a foundational part of our western philosophical world as to be almost transparent and beyond question. Yet, it's far from un-problematic.

As we shift to the East-Asian world and the Buddhist and Daoist traditions, we encounter a markedly different relationship between language and truth—one that makes the western correspondence theory appear far less secure.

The best example is in the very first line of the *Daodejing*. At the very beginning of one of the classics of Daoism, Laozi states, "As to a Dao—if it can be specified as a Dao, it is not a true Dao". (2007) If we take these simple lines seriously, they pull the rug out from under much of our western philosophical world insofar as it relies on the correspondence notion of truth.

Can anybody think why that might be the case?

Theologian: Because it's saying that language can't properly describe the Dao. Or, I guess, can't "correspond" to reality.

Dr. Leander: Exactly. If you try to call something the Dao, your language has already missed it. The idea is that language is inherently dualistic. To use language, we have to invoke binaries: self–other, good–bad, subject–object, active–passive, nature–nurture, and countless others. But, the Dao itself is *non-dual*—it transcends these opposites. It's neither big nor small, good nor bad, active nor passive. Because the Dao is non-dual and language is necessarily dualistic, language can never truly "correspond" with it.

But, why would that be so destructive of our western tradition?

Philosopher: If our tradition has relied on the correspondence model of truth, then I suppose this fundamentally challenges aspects of how we use language. Our tradition seems to excel at analysing and refining language and creating theoretical and conceptual frameworks to describe reality. But, I've never encountered any European thinker who questions language's ability to correspond with the world. I mean, our assertions about the world or things might be wrong, but that's our mistake, not a limitation inherent to language itself.

Dr. Leander: That's a helpful description, thank you.

We always want to be careful about over-exaggerating the differences between Asian and western philosophies, but the Daoist critique of language does represent a quite significant alternative.

Zen and Tea

And, this is particularly relevant for your group since one of *Wabicha*'s main philosophical foundations is Zen Buddhism, and Zen is itself deeply influenced by Daoist philosophy. The "world" of tea you're about to experience is largely constructed according to Daoist-inspired Zen Buddhist principles. For instance, a core tenet of Zen is that language—and especially its dualist aspects—distorts our perception of the world. On these grounds, many schools of Zen, with some exception, advocate various practices of silence.

The western philosophical world generally endorses speech as an un-problematic philosophical tool. While there are exceptions,[7] to be a western philosopher is to speak, ideally to speak the truth by making statements that correspond to the world. But, this isn't going to help us much when it comes to the tea ceremony. In the Japanese world of tea, being oriented towards the truth might demand remaining silent, refraining from speaking, and abandoning the search for correspondence between language and things.

Artist: So, best not to speak in the garden or hut?

Dr. Leander: Based on what we've just discussed, it would be entirely reasonable to assume that we should refrain from speaking during the ceremony to respect the principles of Zen. Or, perhaps we might refrain from using language to explain the experience after the fact, given that language's objectifying and dualistic structure can never truly capture the real experience of a non-self and its relationship to the various non-objects involved in the tea ceremony.

But, can anyone see any problems with this?

Theologian: It seems like choosing silence over speech is bringing the speech–silence binary back in.

Artist: To never speak would be to remain in a one-fold world, not a two-fold world.

Dr. Leander: Excellent. This touches on an intriguing paradox within Zen philosophy. Zen offers a radical critique of philosophical language and textual learning. The catchphrase you'll often hear is that Zen has "no dependence on words or text" and is "a special transmission outside the scriptures". But, this is deliberately ironic. While rejecting language and scriptural learning as ultimate authorities, Zen orthodoxy has been shaped by several major sutras, i.e., words, philosophical-religious texts and scriptures.[8]

In this sense, we have a "middle way" in that Zen doesn't entirely discard language but neither does it fully endorse it as a tool for accessing reality. Similarly, you'll learn later that the Daoist notion of "non-speaking" also does not abide the speech–silence binary. Non-speaking is not to remain silent, just as you'll also learn that non-action is not passivity. These are ways of speaking or acting that are in accordance with the Dao, and the Dao is non-dual.

With this in mind, let's go back to Ueda.

Language in a Two-Fold World

You've already discussed the distinction between the "ontological negative" and "ontological positive", or relatedly, substance and relational ontologies. You've associated substance ontology and positivity with the European philosophic tradition, and concepts like form, essence. Relational ontology and the negative are linked to the Asian tradition, with concepts like emptiness or nothingness. Now, moving to Ueda, we'll see how he complicates these too-simple oppositions by finding a middle way between positivity and negativity, a two-fold world bridging Asian and western traditions.

Let me introduce you to some of his main concepts, those being "hollowness" and "actuality".

Guide: This is a good time to take out your notebooks and add to the list we've been constructing.

Dr. Leander. Yes, great. For now, think of "hollowness" (*kyo no koto* 虚のこと) along the lines of the concepts you already have there in your table associated with negativity, such as emptiness or *śūnyatā*.

~ *Each of the participants added the concept to the table they had scribbled in their notebooks*

But, here's the crucial point, if "hollowness" were the *only* quality of existence, we would be in a "one-fold" world. As you know, Ueda wants to show us how we're in a two-fold world.

If we were in a one-fold world, then straightforward silence might be the correct linguistic stance to orient towards the ontological negative, to emptiness or hollowness. In this interpretation of only the ontological negative, we are simply non-selves, things are non-objects and language can never describe anything because all things would be straightforwardly impermanent and empty.

But, Ueda's "two-fold" world also includes the ontological positive, which he refers to as "actuality" (*jitsu no koto* 実の事). You can put that term down in your table on the side of Positivity.

~ *All three added this new concept to their tables.*

Positivity:
"being"
"essence"
"presence"
"form"
"substantial"
"permanence"
"actuality"

Negativity:
"nothing"
"empty"
"absence"
"formless"
"relational"
"impermanence"
"hollowness"

Now, if *actuality* were the only valence of existence, we'd have a one-fold world again. And, philosophy could pay attention solely to the ontological positive. In such a world, there would be no problem with language corresponding to reality. We would be selves, there would be objects with essences, the nature of reality would be permanent, and language could correspond to the things in the world. But again, we know that Ueda wants a two-fold world.

Theologian: I'm a bit confused about the difference between language in the "hollow" or the "actual" world.

Dr. Leander: Okay, yes. This is getting a bit abstract, so let's try to think more concretely. First, let's just start with language and positivity. What would be an example that illustrates this idea?

Artist: Just saying anything, and imagining it can correspond with the world.

Dr. Leander: Good, and language and the negative?

Theologian: Just remaining silent. Like negative theologians who disallow themselves from saying anything positive about God.

Artist: Or, monks who take a vow of silence.

Dr. Leander: Perfect, we now have examples of language oriented to both the positive and negative, actuality and hollowness. Let's say, each example illustrates what language should be in a one-fold world.

But, now, what about language in a two-fold world? Language embracing hollowness *and* actuality?

Philosopher: When we began, our Guide told us he couldn't take us to a tea ceremony, but then invited us to follow him.

Dr. Leander: Please, say more.

Philosopher: In the context of Ueda's world of "actuality", in the ontological positive, we're all selves and language allows us to coordinate our meanings and activities, and we can get to the garden without any problems. But, within "hollowness", or the ontological negative, we are non-selves, the world is made of non-objects and dualistic language can never fully correspond to reality. In this sense, he couldn't truly take us to the garden.

Dr. Leander: I think you've got it.

Remember, the essential point for Ueda is that we're never in only *one* valence of existence or the other. We're always in a two-fold world, always *between* the ontological negative and positive, between hollowness and actuality. And, that means that learning about the Asian philosophical traditions doesn't require us to transition from one world into another absolutely foreign world. The point isn't to leave one world and enter another, not to replace the positive with the negative, but to see the two-fold world where hollowness and actuality overlap.

And, this is still abstract, but it's very easy to see this two-fold aspect in our own experiences. For instance, when trying to be analytic and scientific, we might tend more towards actuality, where language can come close to corresponding with reality. Language does the job, mostly. Conversely, in moments of immersive or ecstatic experiences like playing sports, dancing, musical improvisation, a great conversation, we might tend more towards hollowness, more towards ineffable experiences where we can certainly try to use language to describe those experiences after the fact, but it never satisfactorily captures the beauty or totality of the experience.

But, the crucial point for Ueda—and why I prefer his idea of a "two-fold world" over Gadamer's "fusion of horizons"—is that these worlds don't "fuse", we are always vacillating *between* these valences of reality. The difference or tension between worlds always animates existence and experience. Rather than remaining static in one domain or the other—actuality or hollowness, positivity or negativity— Ueda sees the quality of our experience as a *movement* between the worlds, or what he calls a "double movement". We're never fully in the positive or the negative of language, but always "exiting language and then exiting into language".

Here's a passage from his essay:

> *If we take the original and fundamental structure of human existence which takes place in this dynamic of exiting language and then exiting into language—to be a twofold being-in-the-world, then the being of the human—should be understood as the double movement of going from the world into the-limitless openness, and then back again into the world . . . the human subject becomes the very movement of exiting the world and then re-entering the world.*
>
> (2011, p. 769)

Artist: Can we think of this in-between position as another way of understanding the non-self? Rather than a static and circumscribable positive entity, this is an account of a dynamic self, between positivity and negativity.

Dr. Leander: That's a great way to put it: the non-self as a movement between the positive and the negative. I'm not sure if Ueda used those words but I think he would like that.

It's especially useful because part of the resistance to ideas like non-selfhood or non-speaking is the assumption that including the negative fully erases the positive, which Ueda is explicit is not the case. To conceive of the self as a movement between the positive and negative helps fix that mistaken assumption and overcomes that too-easy distinction I warned you about, where we assume that we are *either* western and ontologically positivists or Asian and ontologically negativist. It's a false dichotomy.

Guide: This is part of why I said that, in the end, you have to throw this table away. To represent the positive and negative, it might be inevitable that we make these kinds of dualistic tables, or think this way, but if we really wanted to picture what Ueda is telling us about the movement within a "two-fold world", we'd have to animate our tables somehow to show the intertwinement and overlapping of the two columns.

And, that kind of two-fold intertwinement is a good way to think about how we're going to be related to everything in the tea ceremony.

Theologian: And, it seems like the idea of a "two-fold world" also might help us solve the problem of how we as foreigners can engage with the tea ceremony.

Guide: It's worth considering, yes. Being a non-self-as-movement between worlds might even be the metaphysical and cultural position *Chanoyu* strives towards as a Zen practice.

Dr. Leander: Let's bring this back to the issues of language, which you might face during or after your ceremony. If we feel that language breaks down, leaving us unable to communicate or understand our experience within the tea garden or tea hut, we shouldn't see this as a failure. It might actually be a really good sign that we're appropriately negotiating an intercultural betweenness, that we're "exiting language". Silence, or the inability to articulate an experience in words might actually be a sign that one is in a respectful and productive intercultural encounter we've been searching for.

Theologian: So, like the negative theologians who refrained from speaking of God, we might take that approach with the tea ceremony?

Dr. Leander: Not necessarily. It's not that language is fully negated. Ueda shows how we "exit language", but the second movement is that we "exit back into language". So, silence does *not* need to be absolute as it might be for some negative theologians or monks who take a vow of silence or formulate a negative theology. Even if we're lost for words in the moment, it's likely that we'll find some language to communicate aspects of our experience.

We might consider the silence associated with Zen not the complete absence of words, but the silencing of the self who typically believes it's in control of language. Maybe we could say that silence is the speech of the non-self.

If we had time, we could discuss how phenomenologists like Heidegger propose a similar position between speech and silence.[9] For him too, "silence" or the "renunciation" of language doesn't mean we relinquish all speaking. He even says that it's a different "way" with language (1982).

Guide: Keep this in mind. We'll elaborate this idea of a "way" with language in more detail when we discuss the Daoist idea of "non-speaking".

Dr. Leander: Yes, that will be a good opportunity to further explain the Zen approach to language and how it was deeply influenced by Daoism.

But, maybe now I'll practice the straightforward positive kind of silence—in a one-world sense—as I've already said so much. And, I think you have a solid grasp of some of the intercultural and phenomenological tools that will help you have a great experience at the ceremony.

Just remember to hold everything you've learned very lightly once you're in the tea hut.

Guide: Thank you so much for this great gift! We're all now richer for having spent this time with you today!

Dr. Leander: You're most welcome. I wish you all a really great experience with your first tea ceremony!

> ~ *The professor bowed in silence.*
> *The group bowed in return, thanked the professor, filed out of the lecture hall one by one and met with their guide under the tree outside the Philosophy Department.*

Guide: We've now completed the theoretical and intercultural sections of our tour. You have a wealth of knowledge about the Japanese tea ceremony and how to navigate the in-between worlds of eastern and western philosophies, so you're all very well prepared to forget it all!

Artist: Forget it all?

Philosopher: Why would we forget it all. Won't that knowledge actually help us have a better experience, and maybe avoid some of the dangers of orientalism and cultural appropriation?

Guide: Yes, absolutely. Everything we've learned is essential. But, the more crucial point to keep in mind is that the tea ceremony, as a philosophic and religious practice, isn't about gaining or deploying conceptual knowledge.

Of course, to be a tea practitioner or even a guest, you do have to have a lot of knowledge of intricate details, aesthetic, historical, and art historical, but in another sense, focusing on the accumulation, definition and recollection of knowledge will obstruct the lived flow of experience. As our teacher explained about phenomenology, we're seeking to remain, as much as possible, in a pre- or non-reflective mode of experience, the moment before we try to invoke knowledge through the reflective intellect. And, if in the middle of the ceremony we get too wrapped up in trying to remember aesthetic principles or definitions, we might lag behind or jump ahead of the lived flow of experience.

But, don't worry about it too much. As the great Zen masters and some phenomenologists knew, we'll never be able to completely quiet the reflective intellect or bracket our "worlds". Their insights are invaluable, but as our lecturer has reminded us today, we should hold them as lightly as possible once our ceremony begins.

Tomorrow, we'll meet at the *Flowers in the Sky* tea garden around the corner from here, and we'll finally begin our intercultural phenomenological experiments! See you all there!

7

Tea Garden

Entering the Gates: *Kire* Cutting Presence and Absence

Guide: Welcome back, everyone. It's a pleasure to finally welcome you to the *Flowers in the Sky* tea garden! I think you'll all see that this is truly a beautiful garden. It's a traditional tea garden in many ways, but at this point you might not be surprised for me to say that it's not even a tea garden.

It was created by a group of artists, scientists, philosophers and tea practitioners who are dedicated to experimenting with the tea ceremony, to explore *Chanoyu* with deep respect for the tradition, but also to thinking about how that tradition might change in ten, a hundred, or a thousand years as it evolves in our rapidly changing world.

In many ways, their question is our question: in this moment of history, with all of the upheavals in our worlds, and with all of our assumptions and pre-conceptions we have about foreign cultures, how can we experience the tea ceremony. In the twenty-first century, globalized world—increasingly dominated by media, the internet, and soon virtual reality, with robots and artificial intelligence about to bring changes we can't even fathom—the *Flowers in the Sky* group is genuinely concerned that the ceremony could become lost, or worse, that it might already be lost, no longer a living, evolving practice. They're working to avoid this fate.

Artist: Are they also looking to "kill the ancestors" of tea?

Guide: They have actually adopted a saying of Nishitani's, which describes the group's relation to tea ancestors: They borrow his idea of "prophesying towards the tradition"[1] as their guiding credo.

Aside from the group's philosophic and artistic orientations, we'll see that the garden itself is also quite exceptional in its design. It's significantly larger than most, which is fortunate because it will provide some extra time and space to linger and take some breaks to discuss everything we'll experience here.

Figure 7.1 Outer Garden Door. (*soto-mon*, 外門). R. Loughnane.

So, shall we begin?

~ *The three nodded enthusiastically in unison.*

Okay, excellent. Come with me to the entryway. What we're now facing is called the *soto-mon* (外門), which means "outer gate" or sometimes *roji-mon* (露地門), the "garden gate". And, believe it or not, there's already significant philosophical meaning right here at this first step, so let's pause for a moment and talk about what's going on.

First, it's important to know the Japanese tea ceremony takes much longer than what we're used to—a formal ceremony can last three or four hours depending on the time of day, season, and type of ceremony. Our next few sessions are a blend of tea ceremony and philosophy class, so we'll move more slowly.

Our focus will be the garden, the tea hut, and related philosophical themes. We'll also begin learning how to perform the role of the tea guest, which is a surprisingly demanding skill. We'll revisit the garden twice before entering the tea hut, so today is just the beginning.

The structure is simple: we'll walk through the garden, stopping at stations to learn about objects and rituals. Since we're simulating a formal *Chaji*-style *Chanoyu*, there will be two rounds of tea, plus food, sake, and sweets. While the form is clear, it contains many stages and intricate details.

We'll pause along the way to discuss the objects and rituals, not something you'd do in a real ceremony. We'll also discuss Buddhist, Shinto, Daoist, and some Confucian elements, as well as Japanese aesthetics. Unlike European traditions, which typically only have one or maybe two terms denoting forms of beauty, Japanese thought includes a rich vocabulary of such terms. We'll explore *wabi-sabi*, *yūgen*, *mono-no-aware*, and also alternatives to western ideas of originality, imitation, and creativity.

Sound good to everyone? Any questions?

Artist: Sounds good. No questions from me.

Theologian: Sounds good. Do we go in now?

Invitation—Space and formlessness

Philosopher: I bet you can't take us in, can you?

Artist: It definitely looks like a place, but I guess that's how it would look to a self, right?

Guide: You're really getting the hang of this. But, what if I said, we're already inside? And, we have been for days.

Philosopher: This is the "the tea garden is not a place" part, then?

Guide: It's part of that part. To get started thinking about space beyond thinghood, objectivity, beyond strict positivity, we can play with this binary between the inside and outside.

Theologian: I thought I was getting the non-self idea, but I'm trying to picture a garden space without inside or outside . . . I can't see it.

Guide: Let me share some etymology with you that might explain your difficulty. The Greeks had a term called *perigraptos* (περίγράφω). The Romans later translated this as *circumscribere*. Can anybody guess their meaning?

Philosopher: Seems like some familiar sounds in there. *Circum*, like in circumference.

Artist: And *peri*, like in perimeter.

Guide: That's right. With *circumscribere* we have the idea of a circumference being "scribed", suggesting drawing a boundary around things, *circum*scribing its form. Similarly, the *"graptos"* in *perigraptos* suggests that we "graph" or "draw" the *"peri*meter", the outer boundaries of an object.

These are more key terms that characterize the idea of western "substance ontology" we've been discussing. They reflect how our tradition began as an attempt to define things as bounded, self-contained, and separate from other things—to deal with things we've tended to think we need a perimeter or circumference that defines a thing and divides it away from other things.

Philosopher: It sounds like the opposite of relational ontology.

Guide: If not the opposite, very different, yes. And what this means is that when we think philosophically or scientifically about things according to these substance ontological ideas, we expect to find definite beginning and end points, the outer edges of objects that distinguish the inside from the outside.

Artist: It sounds like another way of distinguishing A from not-A.

Guide: Yes, great observation.

This desire to find the outer edges distinguishing one thing from another might seem trivial, but it actually represents a deeply significant ontological commitment. These terms *perigraptos* and *circumscribere*, represent how the Greeks thought about the "form" of things.

If we shift to the Asian context, and follow a Buddhist negative or relational ontology, where things are empty, our first step wouldn't be to look to draw outer edges around objects, to divide them away from their surroundings. Because things exist relationally, you can't circumscribe their form, because things are made up of a huge and invisible network of external relations. This disallows us from circumscribing the form of an object. Non-objects are sometimes referred to as "formless" (*musō* 無相), in this sense. There's no perimeter to graph, no circumference to scribe.

Theologian: Could we say that in a conventional sense we're selves outside a space we're calling a garden, and that it's more or less like an object with a form and distinct insides and outsides? But in an ultimate sense, we're non-selves in relation to a formless non-object, with no simple outside?

Guide: Yes, in a way, even before entering the garden, we're already related and thus part of its definition, part of the ceremony waiting for us, part of its relational formlessness.

Tsutsui Hiroichi said of Rikyū that "for him Chanoyu did not begin with the greeting by which the guest is led into the *roji*; it starts at the moment the invitation to the gathering is received" (1982, p. 59). In this sense, we're already participating in the ceremony and how the garden has been arranged, long before crossing any physical threshold.

Here, have a look at this—our invitation. It might seem like a small detail, but as we move through the garden and the ceremony itself, we'll see just how meticulously the tea master has prepared—not for *any* tea ceremony that could happen on *any* day, at *any* time of the year, or with *any* guests.

I arranged our visit months ago because our host orchestrates the entire ceremony for us, tailoring it to this particular visit, aligning it with the season and sometimes even the precise day, since several days on the Shinto calendar[2] will carry special significance that the host will subtly evoke through their preparations.

I also communicated our details to the host in advance. They know some details of your backgrounds, your level of familiarity with the ceremony, as well as the biographical details you conveyed to me when you signed up for the course. All of this has been taken into account in making the fine aesthetic discriminations the host has undertaken for our ceremony.

Ideally, no two tea ceremonies would ever be the same. That's another sense of the *ichigo ichie* principle—*one time, one meeting*. Our ceremony doesn't arise from or contribute to anything permanent. And, if any truth emerges during the ceremony, it's not a truth that corresponds to anything outside of or lasting beyond our brief encounter.

The assemblage of objects, the flowers, the hanging scroll, what plants are in bloom or how close the leaves are to falling, these all fluctuate throughout the season, all of them are provoked or subdued by the tea host, to give us an experience that wasn't constructed for *any* tea goer on *any* date, but for us, on this specific day. In this way, we're already there on the inside of the garden insofar as it's inflected by who we are, literally determined by what is outside—not just the season, the weather or the day, but by us. We are one of the relations constituting the present state of the garden.

Theologian: Could we even go one step farther than Rikyū, and say that the ceremony begins *before* the invitation?

Guide: What do you have in mind?

Theologian: Couldn't we say that this particular ceremony actually began long before we ever planned it—perhaps even long before any of us were born. If I understand the idea of emptiness, then the forces shaping us into the particular non-selves we are, must extend out indefinitely. If there's no *circumference* of the non-self that can be *scribed*, no *perimeter* to be *graphed* for any of us as non-selves, then the tea master has actually crafted all of the numerous details in response to our group within the context of emptiness. So, they're not so much starting even from the point of the invitation, but in the middle of a web of relations that we would find expand infinitely if we were to try to grasp them.

In this way, the garden doesn't have a strict inside or outside. The more specifically what's in there is orchestrated according to our non-selves, the more the outside permeates the inside. The tea master isn't imposing a new order but rather working through these relational forces, weaving the ceremony into the infinite network that exceeds the confines of the garden walls. The space within the garden is a reflection of that network, so the inside is made up of the outside.

Philosopher: And, in that sense, the ceremony doesn't have a definitive beginning or end.

Guide: Right, so not only are *spatial* binaries like here–there, inside–outside ambiguated, now you're undoing *temporal* binaries too, like past–present, now–then, before–after.

Artist: It's making me think of the temporality typical of the western religious idea of creation *ex nihilo*, which still determines a lot of our ideas of artistic creativity—where there's a time zero of creation, which means that there's an unambiguous time *before* and *after*.

When I think about the tea ceremony as a non-object the way we're talking about it now, then the tea master isn't so much creating something out of nothing—beginning something *now* that didn't previously exist *then*—so much as hitching a ride in the middle of a process already unfolding. They're not making something new as much as they're inflecting the direction our existence will travel for a brief moment of time and space.

Guide: I had never thought of it that way, but that's a great way to extend ideas of spatiality and temporality to re-think our ideas about creation. You're definitely right that the traditional Japanese notion of creation and creativity is quite different from the ideas that began in Europe, and we'll actually speak about these issues in much greater detail in an upcoming lecture.

So, maybe it's more appropriate to say, not *"let's begin"*, but *"let's continue"* the ceremony by entering through the gates.

Before we enter, does anybody notice anything peculiar about this area we're standing on now?

Artist: Yes, this is somewhat odd. It didn't rain today, but it seems like the pathway is wet.

Guide: Great that you noticed that—that's not accidental. Once a host has finished their preparations for the day, they come out to splash water throughout the garden. Generally, this is intended to give the garden a fresh and cool feeling, while also signaling to us that the preparations are complete, and we can proceed through the gates.

But, there is even deeper significance. Water is commonly used to symbolize naturalness and purity in Shintoism. Shinto shrines use water as an offering and often have water basins at the entryway of sacred spaces where you can purify yourself before proceeding. Daoism will also play a role in how water is understood and incorporated into various stages of the ceremony.

Another theme tied to water comes from Buddhist lore. You'll often hear the kind of suffering related to desire and attachments invoked by the imagery of "dust" (塵劫)[3]. As we move through the various stages of the ceremony, we'll encounter symbolism and perform several rituals designed to help us leave behind the dust of worldly concerns, the pollutants of our everyday struggles. Ritual purification with water like we see here on the stones is one way to clean away that dust.

What else do you notice?

Theologian: I guess it's kind of odd that so much preparation went into the ceremony, but nobody is here to greet us. The absence is almost uncomfortable. It's like arriving for an important dinner you've been invited to, and the door is open, but you don't even know if your host is there.

Philosopher: I felt that too, but couldn't put it into words.

Guide: It is a bit unsettling, isn't it?

There's something interesting about your observation I'd like to focus on. When I asked you what you noticed, you pointed out the *absence* of a host or someone to welcome us. So, implicitly, you expected the *presence* of someone to greet us.

Theologian: Right, yeah. I thought someone would be here. The absence is quite palpable.

Presence and Absence

Guide: Great. So, we have a subtle yet significant distinction—recognizing something not by what is there, but by what isn't. Let's try to think about your discomfort at this absence. Within the ontological *positive*, we tend to think what is real can be observed, measured, quantified, spoken of and sometimes touched, and for that to be possible, things must be unambiguously present.

If we turn to human action, we might assume that that too can be evaluated purely based on the positive, based on presence—actions too can be seen and measured.

All of that is great, but it means that we're not so good at noticing how someone can act from out of the *negative*, or through *absence*.

Artist: How would we refer to the negative of action? We use the same "non-" negations we've seen?

Guide: Some Daoists do just that. We'll talk about their idea of "non-action" (*wu wei* 無為) now.

But, let me just go back to that feeling we had at the absence of the tea host. We all felt a discomfort as though something was wrong or should be fixed—not that the absence was a deliberate action, but that it was an oversight or a mistake. But, to appreciate some of the subtle aspects of Japanese aesthetics, we have to cultivate a way of seeing this kind of absence, not as an oversight, but as a deliberate aesthetic act. Acting out of the negative is one way that tea masters can considerably elevate their guest's experience.

Let me emphasize this: we can have an effect or be affected from out of the negative.

Theologian: Is this the action of a non-self? Acting out of the negative?

Guide: Yes, but we have to be careful again not to re-invoke absolute positive-negative binaries. Let's bring in some Daoism here. Does anybody know anything about the Daoist idea of action?

Daoism

Artist: You see lots of books about the "way" of different practices—The *way* of archery, the *way* of calligraphy. They're Daoist-inspired, I think. But, now there's a bunch of popular culture books about the "way" of anything: cooking, cleaning, walking.

Guide: Yes, it's good that the idea is getting out there, but that term is being a bit overused, lately. While popular books may not always align with the deeper philosophical roots of Daoism, using the term "way" reflects a recognition that certain practices can embody a flow or harmony—an alignment with something greater than just one's own positive acts.

We'll talk more about the term "dao" or "way", but first, let me say a bit about Daoism itself. It's Chinese in origin and, from our point of view, looks philosophic and religious in different ways. But, even though we use the term "Daoism" as if it refers to some specific philosophic-religious school, it's partly a retroactive construction. There might not have ever been a definite school calling itself "Daoism". Instead, there were many loosely related sects in Zhou Dynasty China following what now look like similar "Daoist" principles.

If you look into Buddhism or Confucianism you'll also find the term "Dao". There might have been hundreds of texts loosely related to what we now call Daoism, but of those that survive, we tend to study two of what we call the "Daoist classics": the *Daodejing* by Laozi and the *Zhuangzi* attributed to Zhuangzi himself. We'll discuss Daoism throughout the course, but at this point, I'd like to focus on the particular brand of non-dualism we find in one of the Daoist classics, the *Daodejing*.

The *Daodejing* isn't non-dualist in the way some Buddhist philosophies are. Its non-dualism actually includes an element of dualism.

Think about this. Whenever we invoke any category, its opposite is already doing some work for us. If we speak of passivity, we're already invoking the meaning of activity. Passivity wouldn't make sense if it weren't opposed to activity. We need the meaning of the opposite. The same applies to binaries like right and wrong, strong and weak, good and bad—these oppositional dualities all need each other. Strength simply wouldn't make sense if we didn't have the corresponding concept of weakness. You couldn't have one end of any of these dualities without the other.

So, here's your first key Daoist principle: *the Dao itself is non-dual*. As non-dual, the Dao is neither large nor small, not good or bad, active or passive. It is non-dual but it is the *source of* duality. Let me read you a few lines from Chapter Forty-Two of the *Daodejing* (2007).

> *The Dao generates oneness*
> *Oneness generates twoness*
> *Twoness generates threeness*
> *Threeness generates the ten thousand things*

The numerology is quite simple. The Dao is "one": it is singular, that is, it is non-dual. But, as non-dual, it is the source of the world of duality. The Dao's oneness generates twoness. "Twoness" is the world of duality. And, this twoness, or duality gives rise to threeness, which are all the things in the phenomenal world we encounter every day, also referred to as the "ten thousand things"—just all the everyday things we experience.

Artist: So, this means that duality is real? It's not an illusion?

Guide: Right. There is indeed high and low, big and small, night and day, summer and winter. Duality is real, but these *dualities arise from a non-dual source*—the Dao.

According to Laozi, the Dao is the source of all things. If the Dao were dualistic, it could not give rise to all the duality we have in the world. If the Dao were *just large*, small things could not emerge in the world. If the Dao were *just hot*, it couldn't give rise to cold things. Likewise, if it were *only passive*, there could be no activity.

Precisely because the Dao is *non-dual*, it can give rise to all the world of duality we experience every day. As non-dual, it encompasses both hot and cold, big and small, good and bad, left and right, top and bottom, activity and passivity and any other binary oppositions we encounter in the phenomenal world.

Philosopher: Is it kind of like the Mahāyāna two-fold truth? Duality is true in a conventional sense, but non-duality in an ultimate sense?

Guide: In a way, we might say that. But, let me just pause here and say that we must always be careful with "is it just like X?" kind of questions, especially when studying foreign traditions.

The difference between the Dao and the ten thousand things does have some superficial similarities to what the two-fold truth evokes, but they wouldn't map perfectly onto each other. To really explore the overlap, we'd have to get deeper into the ideas of *śūnyatā* and see how it compares to the relation between presence and absence in the *Daodejing*. We're likely to find some similarities, but also important differences. "Is it just like" kind of questions often stop at the similarities without digging deeper to find the crucial differences, so just be careful when you feel the instinct to compare philosophies this way. Almost not philosophy or concept is "just like" any other.

For now, let me ask you, can anyone think of a simple and concrete visual symbol in Daoism that makes these questions of duality and non-duality, presence and absence easier to grasp?

Theologian: The *yin yang* symbol?

Yin Yang

Figure 7.2 *Yin yang* symbol (阴阳).

Guide: Yes, that's right. And, now we can get back to the initial topic of this discussion, the non-dual relation between the positive and negative, or presence and absence.

The *yin yang* symbol is likely one of the most widely recognized symbols in the world, and as we'll see, it plays a significant role in the tea ceremony.

Many of the elements within the tearoom and throughout the garden are designed to achieve the kind of dynamic harmony represented in the *yin yang* symbol.

Tea masters viewed the spaces within the garden and hut as microcosms reflecting the macrocosmic structure of the Daoist cosmos. Rikyū, in particular, was known for developing an aesthetic, architecture and a set of disciplines balancing *yin* and *yang* elements.

Although the symbol is quite recognizable, the ontological position it suggests isn't so well understood. Does anyone know what it's supposed to tell us?

Artist: I always thought that it was supposed to represent a kind of movement. Even though it's a static image, it almost looks like it's in motion, or at least suggesting motion, as if the two shapes are following each other around the circle. The whole symbol conveys a sense of perfect circular rhythm and balance.

Guide: Yes, that's a great description. In a concrete sense, the harmonious rhythm depicted in the symbol reflects the movements of nature itself. At the same time, the symbol conveys an ontological point—telling us something about the nature of reality, and in this case, the principle of duality as a relation between presence and absence.

We can think of the two opposing shades as representing this relation. *Yin*, the dark shape, is associated with the feminine, darkness, and obscurity—while *Yang*, the light shape, represents the male principle, brightness, and clarity.

And, in a more abstract sense, the *yin yang* symbol is a visual instantiation of the two ontological valences we've been coming back to—the positive and negative, being and emptiness, presence and absence. But, since the Dao embraces both *yin* and *yang*, the Dao itself is not exclusively one or the other but encompasses both simultaneously.

Philosopher: So, it's almost a representation of a two-fold world?

Guide: In a way yes, but again, be careful of "it's just like" kind of analogies. But, as for what the *yin yang* tells us about Daoism—we can say that the Dao isn't one *thing* or another. It's not the dark part or the light part, but the dynamic harmony they represent.

Theologian: What about those little dots in each shade?

Guide: This is exactly where the *yin yang* symbol becomes nicely complex. If we were to simply take it that the dark *yin* shape represents negativity and the *yang* shape positivity, we can see the role those dots play. Without those dots, then the symbol would suggest a straightforward kind of duality—black against white, *yin* against *yang*, presence against absence. We'd have *pure* positivity against *pure* negativity.

But, those little dots undermine duality. They show, in the simplest visual way, that *nothing is pure—no pure negativity or positivity*.

Each shade, and by extension all things in the world, are always infused with a trace of their opposite: activity always has an element of passivity. Culture is always inflected by nature. Form is complicated by formlessness.

Does that make sense to everyone?

Philosopher: It makes me think of another way of understanding our relation to the eastern world. Just as for Daoism there is no up without down, no forward without backward, no pure white without a tinge of black, similarly, maybe our being in a western or European "worlds" aren't purely "Western".

Guide: Great observation. Yes, it's definitely good to think about this relation beyond simple binaries, and that's what the *yin yang* symbol teaches us. It suggests that even our cultural identities are always intertwined with their supposed opposites, influenced and shaped by what they are not.

Artist: In that sense, it kind of nicely represents my own identity, or lack of stable identity since I grew up between Japanese and western cultures.

Guide: Yes, and it might take a century or two, but it's likely that with continued migration, this kind of in-between identity will become more and more the norm. Even for those of us who aren't Japanese, over the past couple of hundred years our cultural identity as "Westerners" has been built in opposition to what we learned of "other" cultures, including Japan. We don't even become "Western" until there's an "Eastern" or "Asian" world that emerges. Similarly, we don't tend to refer to each other as "earthlings", but if life on other planets were found, we'd see ourselves within the context of new binaries and we might start referring to ourselves as such.

What the *yin yang* symbol teaches us is that there's no ontological realm that is purely what it is: The east is never purely east, west is never only west, the self is never just the self, or to put it in our abstract terms A is never purely A. There's always that not-A dot inside and complicating the A.

And yes, like you said, this is important to keep in mind as we're trying to build bridges between our western world and the world that gave rise to the tea ceremony. If we assume simple un-ambiguous binaries like east vs. west, Orient vs. Occident, *yin* vs. *yang*, then it's difficult to imagine how we overcome one to get to the other. But, if our starting point is the type of dynamic relational ambiguity suggested by the *yin yang* symbol, then the task isn't to build a new bridge, but maybe to expand the one that pre-exists our attempts at "intercultural" encounter.

Theologian: I guess the fact that Buddhism could move from the Indian world into China and Japan is evidence that these kinds of ambiguous, non-dual bridges exist between worlds.

Guide: Yes, exactly. The intercultural progress we observe on a historically large scale offers compelling evidence that our "worlds" aren't dualistic opposites but overlapping, intertwining, and ambiguous shades—much like the *yin yang* symbol suggests.

Now, returning to the situation before us and the question that sparked our discussion of Daoism, presence, and absence: how can we apply this thinking to the tea master, who seems to be absent, acting out of the negative?

Can we truly say the tea master is *purely* absent? Or is there a kind of presence here—just as the black shape holds a trace of white?

Artist: Well, the host's body isn't here, that's for sure.

Guide: Right, but what is here?

Artist: Not sure. Just the half-open door.

Guide: Tell me more about what you think or feel about that door?

Artist: It feels to me like it's not by chance. As if the host is trying to communicate something deliberate to us.

Guide: Great. We can use some of the Daoist tools to interpret this subtle intervention into our expectations.

Our host isn't here, they are absent—but there's still a kind of presence manifesting at this moment. The fact that you've been impacted by their action, shows us that even in their absence, the host can exert a subtle form of presence, much like the little dot of white infuses the darkness of the *yin* shape. In this sense, the particular absence invoked by the half-open door is inflected with a curious and quiet presence of the tea master, and as you've noted, this subtly shapes our experience as we stand here.

Let me repeat what I said earlier now that we've interpreted this experience according to Daoist ideas. The tea host doesn't only operate based on presence or positivity: they *can act, have effects, and be acted upon from the negative*—while absent.

And, that isn't something that is particular to a tea host or the tea ceremony. Nothing in the world acts or has impacts purely through the positive, through presence or being. All positivity is infused with negativity. Seeing this interplay is crucial for appreciating the tea ceremony and most Japanese aesthetic practices especially insofar as they tend to be Zen practices deeply influenced by Daoism.

Philosopher: I think I get how we can understand the host's actions in this Daoist context, but it seems to me that we're definitely highlighting the negative more than the positive.

Guide: Yes, great point. You're definitely right that I've been focusing much more on the negative, but this isn't because the world or reality is more negative than positive. Remember, if that were the case we'd be in a "one-fold" world in Ueda's sense—or only one shade of the *yin yang* symbol would describe reality. I've only emphasized the negative because the western tradition has largely taught us to see the ontological positive. We don't need to cultivate that perspective so much, whereas we do need to do work to learn to understand and see the negative.

But, remember, what we ultimately aim to achieve—philosophically *and* interculturally—is what the *yin yang* symbol shows us: a dynamic and ambiguous relation, or a movement between positivity and negativity, between being and emptiness, form and formlessness, between east and west.

Artist: Can you say a little more about what you meant about acting out of the negative? It sounds fascinating, but I'm not sure I understand.

Non-Action: *Geidō* and *Temae*

Guide: Yes, it's a great time to discuss your question. What we're about to partake in is a highly codified and meticulously choreographed series of rituals. Nearly every movement and gesture, what are called *temae* (点前), adhere to precisely defined rules, varying between schools of tea.

If we think of action and bodies solely in terms of the ontological positive, we risk not only misunderstanding what the host does, we might also have misguided ideas about how our own actions fit into the ceremony. So, including the ontological negative within our understanding of action will help make sure we're aligned with the world in which we'll act and be acted on.

To recap, we noted that the ontological negative helps us understand negations like "non-self". These imply that the self or object is conceived of according to emptiness (*śūnyatā*). An empty self is a relational self. Similarly, with Daoism, terms like "non-action" (*wu wei* 無為) and "non-speaking" (*bù yán*, 不言) instantiate the ontological negative, but with different prefixes denoting the negation, in this case *wu* (無) and *bù* (不). In Daoism, the ontological negative is referred to with *wu* 無 character, but often translated into English as "absence", "non-presence", or sometimes "non-existence".

Let's focus on your question about action now. You asked what it meant for action to be conceived within the ontological negative.

Now, what do we already know about the Dao and duality?

Philosopher: That the Dao is itself non-dual but the source of duality.

Guide: Perfect. And, what would the dualities be regarding action?

Theologian: Movement and stillness?

Guide: Good. But, can we go one step more abstract?

Artist: Activity and passivity?

Guide: Perfect. We know the Dao is non-dual. To be one with the Dao we have to avoid becoming entangled in duality—we need to find a way to move, gesture, perceive or just sit still and listen that is somehow beyond the duality of activity and passivity.

Philosopher: But, when we move we can't help but manifest dualities. Movement involves shifting from here to there, from behind to in front, quickly or slowly. There's no way to move without manifesting these dualities. Acting, by its nature, gives rise to dualities.

Guide: Good point.

Theologian: But, if we just don't move, if we're purely passive, then we wouldn't manifest any dualities, right?

Guide: Let's test the Daoist idea we discussed earlier. Can you give me an example of something you'd say is *purely* active or purely passive?

Philosopher: I suppose walking here today is an example of being active. We wouldn't have gotten here if we had been passive.

Artist: And, maybe meditation is an example of passivity.

Guide: Okay, great examples. With the walking example, remember when we all actively planned how to cross the busy intersection together? We stopped and deliberated on how to coordinate our actions, discussing the traffic lights, agreeing on the appropriate pace and distance to maintain from oncoming pedestrians, all while maintaining a conversation on our philosophic topics?

Theologian: We didn't do that.

Guide: Exactly. That simple act of crossing the street as a group is actually a quite complex set of actions, yet we undertook these highly coordinated movements with perfect harmony, and we didn't have to *actively* think about or discuss any of it. In one sense, we were clearly *active* in that we were moving our bodies, but at the same time, we were *passively* processing what would have been vast calculations and decisions. Actions like that tend to flow more smoothly when there's an element of passivity, where complex movements are coordinated with a natural spontaneity. If we were to *actively* try to execute all the decisions we needed to cross a busy intersection together, that might even impede the natural flow we had. In this sense, our natural spontaneity, so perfect that we didn't even notice it, was achieved by an intertwining of activity *and* passivity. Or, we can put it differently—an element of our actions arose out of the negative. That is, none of the factors that determined our movements had to appear in objective, measurable ways for them to affect us. They remained absent, but nevertheless counted in what was present.

Artist: That's interesting because, when I first arrived in Japan, crossing the street wasn't automatic at all. I actually did have to actively make a bunch of explicit deliberations and decisions before crossing an intersection like that one.

Guide: Great example. You're absolutely right—when we're learning something new, it often takes extra conscious effort and calculation. In these cases, the active–passive binaries might tilt slightly toward the active. We want to bring all the factors to objective presence. But, even then, we're never *purely* active. For instance, we don't actively choose to put one foot in front of the other, and we don't have to consciously think to swing our arms to keep our balance as we stride. There's always an element of passivity in our actions. We might not ever execute any movements with grace if we didn't passively allow the body and environments to inflect our movements.

Theologian: To go back to the idea of "worlds", maybe we could say that when we find ourselves in a new or foreign worlds, we naturally lean more to the active side of the active–passive binary, more towards presence.

Guide: That's an interesting thought.

If what *yin yang* non-duality teaches us is true, then we never find anything in the world—whether in oneself or in nature that is purely active or passive. But yes, different circumstances demand different elements of activity and passivity.

But, let's look at the other example: meditation as purely passive. If you've ever meditated, or even just tried to control your stream of thought, you'll notice how active we are even if our body remains completely still. In one sense, it feels like we're straightforwardly passive when meditating—we're not moving our bodies or traveling from A to B. But, when you begin meditating, you immediately notice how difficult, sometimes excruciating it is to sustain for any length of time. Your body wants to do other things: reach for your phone, get up, have a drink, note down ideas. To resist these impulses, you have to *actively* force yourself to remain still, to *actively be passive*, and doing this can be really exhausting. Sometimes, it feels even more demanding than actions we see as physically strenuous. So, in this sense, trying to sustain passivity actually requires significant activity. Meditation is in no way purely passive.

Philosopher: But what is the goal, then? Is non-action just achieving a balance between activity and passivity?

Geidō

Guide: Good question. Let's explore Japanese aesthetic practices to see how non-action helps illuminate how they learn and refine their arts.

Geidō (芸道) is the Japanese term referring to traditional aesthetic practices. Does anybody notice anything about that term?

~ *All three were silent.*

You might catch what I'm getting at if I tell you that in Japanese, calligraphy is called *shodō* (書道), flower arranging or *ikebana* is called *kadō* (華道), and archery is called *Kyūdō* (弓道). Notice anything?

Artist: There's the repetition of that "*dō*" sound.

Guide: Right, and we spoke earlier about how that "*dō*" is the Japanese transliteration of the Chinese word *Dao*. I think you all probably know where that comes from, right?

Theologian: Is that the same "*dō*" that's in *aikido* and *judo*?

Guide: Exactly. This is the second kanji you might want to try remembering, because aside from its use in *Geidō*, and in Daoism, it's also used more widely—even in Buddhism and Confucianism.

The meaning of *dō* is crucial for *Geidō* practices and the *temae* movement system. All practices ending with "*dō*" are part of what the Japanese call *Geidō* (芸道) practices. *Gei* means "system" or "method" and *dō* or *Dao* is most often translated into English as "way", and sometimes as "route" or "path". The original literal Chinese term *Dao* referred to a "public road" and then later took on the metaphorical sense as a "path" or "way" for attaining a lofty goal.

Particularly Zen Buddhism was significantly influenced by Daoism, and this is where we get the idea of aesthetic practices as a "way". Not just the tea ceremony, which was *sadō* or *chadō*, but also *kyudō* (the way of archery), *shodō* (the way of calligraphy), *budō* (martial arts), and *kōdō* (the way of incense) as well as *judō* and *aikidō* are all systemized according to Daoist principles. They're arts but they pursue the highest aim: spiritual salvation through realizing non-selfhood.

It's worth noting that the tea ceremony existed in Japan before it became systematized according to Daoist principles. Some claim that *Chanoyu* only became a *dō* practice in the eighteenth century, and only then was called *Chadō* and *Sadō*.[4]

Also, beyond the Daoist influence, some have linked *Geidō* practices with Confucian rituals of self-cultivation and others with the samurai code of conduct influenced by Neo-Confucianism.[5] All these influences likely played a role. I'll mostly focus on the Daoist aspect today, but there's an interesting tension in the ceremony due to Daoist and Confucian influence.

Whereas Confucius taught that one should build up the self by acquiring knowledge of the vast rituals that maintained social harmony, Laozi advocated for diminishing the self. Rather than following proscribed ethical dictates, Laozi thought one should be natural and spontaneous, not rule following. He viewed the Confucian concern with knowledge and ritual propriety as obstacles to harmonizing with the Dao.

Rather than mastering endless ethical rules and social rituals, Daoism promoted a natural approach, and this is the term we've been talking about, *Wu wei*, or "non-action". This principle is particularly relevant for understanding tea ceremony *temae*, especially when observing the kind of movements and gestures performed by the tea master.

Artist: If someone wants to learn any of the *Geidō* arts, won't they have to be very active? How can you reach a state of non-action, where an element of passivity enters the practice?

Guide: Thank you—that's a great question. It's interesting, isn't it, that we can all make tea, handwrite, or arrange flowers without being overly active, but for aesthetic practitioners— calligraphers, tea masters, ikebana artists—it takes years, even decades, of disciplined training to achieve a kind of non-action that's a higher order than what most of us experience when we perform these tasks every day.

But, you're right that when they begin learning their arts, they're not likely in a mode of non-action. The goal, however, is to work through the deliberate, highly conscious, calculative efforts to the point of becoming so proficient and natural that, for example, in the case of tea, you achieve a state of natural and harmonious spontaneity, where you're not guided by active cognition, but by, let's say, the flow of an entire environment.

Artist: But, what's the real difference between this Daoist understanding of action underlying *Geidō* practices and our typical European way of learning, which also involves initial periods of directed self-centered activity and learning. I mean, I was also clumsy with a chisel until years of active learning.

Guide: One big difference, I'd say, is that in the west we often see mastering an activity—whether it's an art or any endeavor—as an achievement and a possession of a self.

Philosopher: Maybe because we tend to think of these kinds of things within the ontological positive?

Guide: Yes, I think so. In the west, when we achieve a high level of proficiency, we see this as having elevated, controlled and cultivated the activity of a self. It's an addition to the self. In the Daoist context, while a practitioner also has to go through a long period of deliberate, active learning, the end goal is entirely different: not to build the self up, not to add new things to it, to minimize it. It's a practice of subtracting from the self. This is the essence of Daoist non-action and the *Geidō* practices rooted in the *dō* principle.

And, it might sound abstract but it's something one can verify through experience. We all know it's possible to become familiar enough with a practice that we stop thinking about it and can act spontaneously within a new context. Can anyone think of where we might experience this?

Theologian: I don't have experience with any aesthetic practices, but as you've been explaining non-action and the process of balancing the active and passive elements, I've been thinking a lot about learning to play sports.

Guide: That's a great example—and one many people can relate to. Playing music is another good example. In both cases, when we're first learning, we have to think a lot, we're more in the mode of action than non-action, and that thinking is necessary, but it also obstructs our ability to operate harmoniously with our teams or musical equipment.

But, we become comfortable with our skates, a basketball, the strings of a guitar, or keys of a piano, we can stop *actively* thinking about how to do things, and we can just do them. We stop thinking about dualities like pushing too hard or too soft, striding too long or too short, strumming too fast or too slow—and we just play, and sometimes with the most amazingly beautiful complexity.

In this sense, even elevated forms of non-action aren't entirely foreign to us who haven't been trained as *Geidō* practitioners. So, there is a touchpoint here between cultures, even if the non-action part of our pursuits isn't highlighted so much in a western context.

Philosopher: I think philosophers are starting to catch on to this idea. I've come across this concept of "flow" recently.[6] Scholars are examining highly trained musical improvisers for being in this state of flow, which sounds a lot like non-action.[7]

Guide: And, scientists have become more and more interested in long-term meditators, as well as meditation and mindfulness for high-performance athletes for similar reasons.[8] So yes, even more bridges and touchpoints between east and west.

And, even though these highly trained practitioners are being studied, there's something really important to keep in mind: non-action is the mode we're in most of the time. It's actually the *exception* that we have to think very deliberately about our actions. If you could tally up the minutes during a day we're acting spontaneously without thinking and compare that to the moments we're rationally deliberating upon our actions, I think you'd see that the overwhelming majority of time we're in a mode close to what the Daoists mean by non-action, it's just that the western tradition hasn't focused on these moments or given us much in the way of tools to understand them, that is, until phenomenology.

Non-duality: Partitions—*Kekkai* and *Kire*

Guide: I realize you're all probably very anxious to finally enter the garden, but let's talk about this one last thing before entering. There's actually still a lot of philosophic and aesthetic significance right here with the gate.

We've spoken about the absence we felt here, but let me ask, how does the gate itself appear to you?

Philosopher: I have to say, it seems different now. The simple idea I would have had before was that it's a threshold or a dividing line, separating what's inside from outside. Now, it seems more complex.

Guide: Perfect, yes. Dividing lines like a door or this gate need to be re-thought, since our typical understanding of them relies on unambiguous differences between insides and outsides, internality and externality.

Can you think of any other dualities associated with going through a gate like this?

Artist: The dualities of here and there?

Theologian: Not just spatial but temporal dualities. Having crossed a dividing line implies before and after, past and present binaries.

Philosopher: And of entering and exiting.

Guide: Yes, great. A gate like this one isn't just a metaphor—it's a physical structure that actively cuts space and time into the dualities you've mentioned. Let's focus on this idea of cutting and duality.

If you've been in any traditional Japanese structures—temples, monasteries, ryokan, or even some modern apartments in Japan—you'll notice there's something different about how one goes in and out of rooms.

Artist: Sliding doors, you mean?

Guide: Right. While more and more structures have adopted European-style swinging doors, sliding doors are still very common. Does anyone know why these were used?

Theologian: To save space?

Guide: Yes, but there are some intriguing subtleties of sliding doors and other structures used to divide space in Japan.

We often hear that Japan is such a small and densely populated country and the need to conserve space led to things like sliding doors or standing screens to divide rooms. There's definitely something to that. But, the Japanese use of partitions like doors and gates has deeper significance for the conception of space being employed.

The word for structures used to partition space is *kekkai* (結界). This can refer to sliding doors, standing screens, to the kind of gate we're facing now, but can also refer to sound or even light, which can be used to divide space (Teiji 1982). Once we're inside the tea hut, we'll notice *kekkai* spatial dividers separating the main tearoom from the preparation area.

Kekkai was originally an Indian Buddhist term referring to boundary lines demarcating spaces consecrated for ritual purposes.[9] Dividers were meant to prevent disruption of religious rituals or training within. When the terminology reached Japan by way of China, it integrated with similar conceptions of space and practices of partitioning spaces. One of those conceptions we'll speak about later, is the Japanese conception of space as *"ma"* (間).

Have any of you seen the straw ropes—sometimes very small, sometimes quite large—with the white, lightning-bolt-shaped tassels?

Theologian: Yeah, I've seen those on some of the shrines I've visited.

Artist: I also saw that you can buy them at some markets to use at home.

Guide: Right, those are Shinto and called *shime-nawa* (注連縄). They're another kind of *kekkai* partition, marking a dividing point between the mundane and the spiritual realms.

Philosopher: It sounds like some dualism is creeping in here in that the dividing line maintains binaries like sacred and mundane.

Guide: Good. That brings us to the most important point about *kekkai* dividers. Although we think of gates and doors as dividing, as *kekkai* their function is also to connect.

Kekkai is more like a permeable and ambiguous boundary. Rather than holding binaries apart, they ambiguate dualities like inside–outside, here–there, sacred–secular. One scholar says that "The true beauty of *kekkai* lies in the ability to join rather than divide" (Teiji 1982, p. 57).

Artist: I can see the interesting spatial significance of this kind of dividing, but how is it beautiful, or even aesthetic?

Figure 7.3 *Shimenawa* ropes (しめ縄). R. Loughnane.

Guide: This brings us to a very important Japanese aesthetic principle, known as *kire* (切れ), or cutting. Although cutting suggests duality—cutting *this* from *that*—*kire* too is a connecting kind of cutting.

This is one of my favorite aesthetic principles because once you grasp it, you start noticing it everywhere in Japan—in landscape painting, architecture, flower arranging, Noh drama, even in poetry and cinema. It's relatively easy to recognize the *kire* aesthetic in the visual world. Artists use lines—whether it be with paint or a low-hanging roof—to cut away part of the visual experience. You often see only part of a scene, with another part suggested but not fully revealed. The main subject is partly hidden, divided by a cut. What's revealed and what's concealed coexist in this interplay.

You'll be in an art gallery and notice that the mountains in a landscape painting are partially cut away by mists and clouds. You'll be sitting in a Buddhist monastery and the low-hanging eaves partially cut your view of the autumn maples. Even in haiku poetry, there are literary devices that cut one part of the poem from the other.

Philosopher: Can we think of this in terms of positivity and negativity, presence and absence?

Guide: Definitely. Japanese art often features vibrant, provocative subject matter as the positive element, but a cut divides the work and institutes negative space. And, what do we know about the negative?

Artist: That we can act and be acted on by the negative.

Guide: Exactly. The negative space of an artwork is not meaningless nothingness, it is part of the overall meaningful impact of the work.

But, let's take this half-open door as a case study for this *kire* cutting–connecting idea.

What do you see through the part that's open?

Philosopher: We see a bit of a path, some vegetation and it looks like there's a little hut too.

Guide: Right. And the feeling is that if the door wasn't cutting off the view we'd see more of the garden, right? Our experience would feel fuller.

Artist: That seems obvious. If the door weren't cutting the view we'd definitely see more of the garden. If more were visible, we'd see more.

Guide: Good, yes. More is more, right?

But, what about the negative? What isn't visible, or visually absent. What do you *not* see?

Artist: I suppose we assume there's a whole garden—probably a lot more of the vegetation than what is hinted at through the small opening.

Guide: Good, right. We know it's likely there, but we don't see what's cut away, what constitutes the negative space of our visual field. The door cuts off our ability to experience what we imagine must be a much larger, lusher garden extending beyond the narrow slit we can see through. In that sense, the door keeps a bit of the garden in the negative, let's say. But, do we really experience *nothing* from that negativity?

Philosopher: I guess, like the *yin yang* symbol, there must be some positivity that's part of our experience.

Guide: And, what is that? How can we think of the positivity within this negativity that the door is cutting between?

~ *The three students were silent but visibly pensive.*

Okay, let me ask you this. What if I opened the door and it revealed nothing? What if the big expansive world you expected wasn't there, and opening the door revealed only empty space, or a green screen?

Theologian: I guess I'd be really shocked.

Guide: Why is that?

Artist: Even though we could only see a little portion of the garden through the door, I imagined a whole world overflowing with vegetation, beautiful in that particular Japanese way.

Guide: Right, and even if you weren't consciously aware of it in the moment, didn't that cutting off of the negative create a desire in you to move to shift into a different perspective, a desire to reduce negativity and bring the visual experience more fully into the positive?

Artist: Yeah, I felt that. Since we got here I've had to resist the desire to push the door open to reveal the entire garden. So, yeah, a desire to reduce the negative and increase the positive.

Guide: Let's focus on two things that you mentioned. You said that you *imagined* a whole world, and you said you felt *desire* to open the door. *Imagination* and *desire*. It seems that these feelings were provoked in you.

So, we're getting a bit more detail about how Japanese aesthetic practitioners are able to have an effect *from out of the negative*. In this case, the visually negative, and with a cutting structure.

If the door were fully open, if we had the whole garden in fuller visual positivity, it might not have provoked our imagination or our desire.

So, what we can observe here is that with part of the visual field cut off and remaining in the negative, that cutting isn't just a minus: *something has been added to the experience*—something that might not happen if the entire vista were fully visible in unobstructed positivity.

If we were strictly within a positive substance ontology, if less of a vista is revealed, then we simply see less—"less is less", "more is more", A is A. This kind of thinking might provoke the assumption that cutting away elements of a visual scene, of a poem, or of one's movements results in a diminished experience. You take away, so logically, you end up with less, right?

Artist: Right.

Guide: But, not right.

Just as we'll see that the smaller hut gives us an expansive spatial experience, and the negated self is actually an expanded self, similarly, cutting away part of a scene and allowing negative space to play off of positive space actually enlarges the experience of an art work. The cutting is a plus not a minus.

By leaving this door half open, by obstructing the view of the garden, or of a landscape, a forest or a sky, the Japanese aesthetic practitioner is able to affect us not just from the positive, *but also from out of the negative*.

How do they do that? You've already said it: they bring our *imagination* and *desire* into play. The expansive quality of the interaction of presence and absence enlarges our experience because imagination and desire are drawn into the experience: And, here's a critical point: human imagination and desire are not bound by the limitations of the objective world.

By cutting away part of the visual field in line with the *kire* cutting–connecting aesthetic principle—by provoking one's desire and imagination—the experience isn't *less than*; it's *more than*. When our ontology includes the positive and the negative, the logic is such that *less* can be *more*. Another way for A to be not-A. The interplay between positivity and negativity—because imagination and desire are unbounded by the limits of the physical world—expand the entire experience.

Artist: This is interesting, because I think the typical idea in experiencing the arts is that a subject is revealed better the more is exhibited. We want full unobstructed views. We want the artist, the painter, the filmmaker to give us more, to give us everything they can—full and pure positivity. But, is it possible that by giving us more they actually give us less?

Guide: I think so. By giving us everything, they leave less room for the expansive potential of desire and imagination. The negativity of the non-self is like an opening, if the artwork is likewise open through the negative, we can insert ourselves within the work, and let the work insert itself as part of us, then the experience is a co-creation.

By cutting off part of the experience, whether it is with lines, architectural features, editing cuts, or even words, the Japanese artist augments the aesthetic experience *by giving us a space to be included within the work*, including our desire and imagination. It's another way to think of the relation between a non-self and negated object.

Philosopher: That's really fascinating. But I'm confused. Does this mean that the *cut* is dualistic? Does it create or maintain the duality? Or is the beauty of *kire* in the actual act of cutting, or in overcoming the tension between negativity and positivity?

Guide: Let me give you a complicated technical answer and then a simpler one.

First, the technical response: I need to be a bit more precise about this terminology of presence and absence and the idea of cutting itself. While the structure of the *yin yang* symbolism might suggest that there is positivity in one area and negativity in another area—presence here and absence there—it's actually more subtle. Even the way I've been speaking about the door doesn't entirely capture it.

If I were more careful, I shouldn't say that there is positivity here and negativity in another place. The Daoist *yin yang* symbol represents all of reality, everything is inflected by positivity and negativity. Again, this is why those small dots are so important—they reinforce that negativity and positivity are intertwined *in all places at all times*. Even where we see in plain view, there is a certain inflection of the negative and vice versa. So, for example, when we look at a painting, sometimes we say that an empty space is "negative space" and the parts that are painted are "positive space". But, this doesn't really work for us. We need to grasp that *all* reality—as well as *all* parts of an artwork—are ambiguously positive and negative.

And, the more technical translation of *kire* reinforces this subtle ambiguity. If *kire* were merely a cutting dynamic—as you asked—it would divide things into here and there, left and right, high and low, inside and outside. But, the more subtle understanding of *kire* is that it too is non-dual.

So, what would be the other end of the duality that included cutting.

Artist: Bringing together. Or, connecting?

Guide: That's exactly how *kire* is sometimes translated; not simply as "cutting" but as "cut-continuance" (*kire-tsuzuki* 切れ続き)—highlighting how the division it institutes also connects.

If we had more time we could also talk about Nishida Kitarō's idea of "continuous discontinuity" (*hirenzoku no renzoku* 非連続の連続) because he similarly thinks of relations throughout time and space as both dividing and connecting.[10]

But that's a lot of theory—let's bring it back to what we have here in front of us. We're about to go through that gate, to cross that threshold; about to cross boundaries between outside and inside, here and there. Now that we've learned a bit about the *kire* aesthetic principle, what does that tell us about what's about to happen?

Philosopher: I guess we're about to transform some of the negativity that's fueling our imagination and desire into positivity?

Guide: I hadn't thought of it that way, but that's an excellent observation. Anything else?

Philosopher: Well, I guess, as we go through the gate, we'll shift from one end of the spatial dualities to the other—from the positivity of *here* inflected by the negativity of *there*, to the positivity of *there* with a lingering negativity of having been *here*.

Guide: Nicely put. And, it highlights another reason why I can't take you, as selves, into a tea garden. I can't take you from a purely outside space to a purely inside space, or from an unambiguous before-time to an unambiguous after-time. We were always already a little bit there, and we'll always remain slightly here.

Theologian: Because none of those dualities exist on their own?

Guide: You've got it. And, while it might still sound abstract, keep in mind that ideas in Buddhism and Daoism can almost always be confirmed by what we experience in the real world.

And here, we might have another answer about the challenge of intercultural encounter. If other "worlds," like the world of the Japanese tea ceremony, were unambiguously *cut off* from our own, purely foreign, if there were a simple cultural cut dividing line between east and west, it would be hard to imagine how communication between worlds with no continuity between them could happen. But, the *cultural* partition we face is just like the bamboo one here before us, it divides but also connects.

That doesn't mean that we don't need to do work to have a meaningful encounter with another culture. But when we move away from a strictly positivist ontology to one that embraces both the positive and negative, as Daoism does, the grounds for encountering the other are already woven into the structure of reality itself. Shall we test that for ourselves?

~ *The Guide gestured to his students to follow as he pushed open the gate and moved along the path into the garden.*

Guide: You probably thought we'd never actually get inside.

Artist: Yeah, even though we discussed how we're already part of the everything going on inside here, it's nice to finally go through those gates.

Guide: Yes, part of our task has been to realize how we were already part of the world inside the garden—now that we're in here, we might also reflect on how we're part of the garden's *outside* world.

Theologian: I guess, our entire lives were spent outside the garden, so it's not easy to leave that behind.

Guide: Part of being present in the garden does involve leaving the outside world behind. There's a Buddhist saying often used in tea ceremony, it goes something like "sweeping away the dust of the outside world" (掃去外界之塵,

sōkyo gaikai no jin). Many of the rituals we'll perform are meant to help us achieve this. But, we shouldn't assume we can ever leave the outside world fully behind. It's part of who we are. That outside world is slightly more absent now, but we'll carry it with us throughout the ceremony. We can't get rid of this determination out of the negative any more than *yin* can get rid of *yang*—but the point isn't to get rid of it, but to be as present as we can to what's going on inside the garden.

But, now that we're finally on the path, we're now out of time.

Let's meet back here tomorrow and pick up where we left off.

See you then!

8

Outer Roji

Guide: Welcome back, all!

Follow me inside the garden where we now find ourselves outer again. And, no philosophy humor intended, this time. This first sphere of the garden is called the "outer roji" (*soto-roji* 外露地).

And, we already have some roles to assume, which bring up some philosophic themes. I'll proceed down the path first since I have a kind of seniority by virtue of having the most experience with the tea ceremony. My position is called *Shōkyaku* (正客), or "principal guest" and it comes with several roles and responsibilities. We'll speak later about the Confucian significance of this role.

I'd like to ask our philosopher to assume the role of *otsume* (御詰), the "final guest". You'll also have a few specific roles we'll discuss in more detail as we make our way to the hut. For now, your task is to simply turn around and close the gate behind us by laying that bar horizontally across the door to lock it shut.

~ *The newly appointed Otsume turned, lifted the bar and laid it across the door with a satisfying click.*

Guide: Did you hear that? The sound of the latch dropping signals we've left the outside world behind, stepping into a different "world" here in the tea garden. It also lets the host know we've arrived—one of several acoustic cues in the ceremony.

Our first stop is the *yoritsuki* (寄付), or changing room. As you'll know from your time in Japan, shoes are never worn indoors. Here you'll find *tabi* (足袋) or split-toed socks and sandals. Though it may seem like a simple custom, there's religious-philosophical meaning here. As Okakura Kakuzō writes in *The Book of Tea*, nothing should be brought into the garden "defiled by the soil of the outside world" (1964, p. 34).

As mentioned earlier with the water on the stone path, "dust" or "soil" are Buddhist metaphors for suffering. Enlightenment is often described as casting off that dust—worldly concerns and struggles. As we move closer to the tea hut, we'll engage in a few ritual acts of purification to prepare for the experience. We'll also leave behind personal belongings—wallets, jewelry, watches—symbols of the "dust of the marketplace" (*shijin* 市塵), associated with commerce and its defilements.

Strong perfumes or colognes are also avoided, and mobile phones are strictly forbidden.

Can anyone guess why we would leave our watches behind?

Philosopher: My guess is that if we have a watch, we'll be constantly preoccupied with checking the time and that might take us out of the moment—maybe impede our ability to be present and actually experience the ceremony in a deep way.

Guide: That's definitely part of it. We might think of it more abstractly in terms of further achieving a break with the outside world. There's a Japanese term called *bōki* (忘機), which means "leaving behind everyday concerns".

Outside the tea garden, most of us are constantly measuring time—rushing, staying punctual, avoiding "wasting" time. In this mindset, we rely on a linear, objective sense of time that moves uniformly for everyone. While this is necessary for coordinating daily life, some Buddhist philosophers and phenomenologists emphasize not objective time but the subjective experience of time—something our watches can't capture. Time is felt differently depending on person, place, and circumstance, shaped by our environment and interactions.

Just as we wouldn't bring time-measuring devices into the garden, spatial measuring is likewise forbidden. Later, we'll explore alternative notions of space and time intentionally evoked in the tea ceremony. These will help us understand how the small tea hut can feel experientially vast. Through subtle interventions, the host will shift us away from calculative habits and into a different mode of spatial and temporal awareness—transforming how we experience ourselves in the unique temporality and spatiality of the tea hut.

~ *At this moment the host's assistant (hanto) came in and directed the group towards the kimonos.*

Kimono

Hanto: Welcome to you all.

Guide: Thank you. We're all very happy to be here.

Let me share this with you.

~ The Guide handed the Hanto the water they had collected at Rikyū's Well.

The four of us met earlier this week at Rikyū's Well and wanted to bring this water for our host.

Hanto: Oh, that is most excellent. Your host will be deeply touched to receive such fine water for the ceremony.

Guide: Now, we finally come to one of the most beautiful features of the tea ceremony. I'm sure these need no introduction. They are perhaps one of the most globally recognizable Japanese aesthetic objects—the *kimono* (着物). Countless movies, books and artworks depict pale-faced geisha donning exquisitely designed and embroidered *kimono*. One of my favorite depictions is in the *Ukiyo-e* paintings of Kitagawa Utamaro (喜多川 歌麿 1753–1806). If you ever have a chance to visit major galleries in Japan—or even in London or New York—you'll see some of his masterpiece wood-block paintings depicting geisha wrapped in the most beautiful *kimono*.

Would you mind telling us a little bit more about these garments?

Hanto: Yes, absolutely. Firstly, aside from tea guests such as yourselves, do any of you know who is famous for wearing the *kimono*?

Artist: *Sumo* wrestlers. I've been to a few competitions in Sendai, and the wrestlers all arrived at the event dressed in their *kimono*.

Hanto: Very good. It's not as often these days, but *Sumo* wrestlers are actually required to wear the *kimono* when in public and are permitted slightly more chromatic indulgence than the typical male *kimono* allows.

Men, otherwise, are less likely to wear the *kimono* in public. Aside from ceremonial uses—such as at funerals, weddings, and graduations—you'll mostly see women wearing *kimono* at summer festivals. However, what you might think is a *kimono* is more likely to be the less formal version called a *yukata* (浴衣), which is made from cotton or polyester as opposed to the *kimono*, which is made of different types of silk and sometimes linen or hemp. The *yukata* is lighter, offers greater breathability and freedom of movement, so it's used increasingly for less formal occasions.

Before you put yours on, let me show you something quite remarkable about the *kimono*. Hold it up so that the arms are extended. What do you notice?

Theologian: The arms are really big. And, much more rectangular than I would have expected.

Hanto: Yes, exactly. As a pattern, it is remarkably angular and geometric—simply two square arms and a rectangular body. Despite its angularity, you'll see that when we put them on and cinch them up nicely with this thick band that goes around the waist called an *obi* (帯), the *kimono* transforms.

Yes, it will constrain one's movements due to its stiff and heavy material, but in doing so it creates a constellation of elegant shapes no other garment comes close to replicating. This is very much what Utamaro Kitagawa (喜多川 歌麿, 1753–1806) captures in his depictions—a striking graceful flow emerging from out of constrained angularity.

Traditionally, the *kimono* would feature elaborate seasonal indicators. Different colors and patterns are worn depending on the seasons and possibly even depending on the day or time of day the ceremony takes place. The three main seasons dictating kimono styles are *awase* (袷), a silk-lined kimono worn in the winter; *hitoe* (単衣), an un-lined version for June and September, and *natsumono* (夏物), made of lighter sheer-silk or other more breathable materials for the hottest summer months.

Knowing a little bit about Japan and Japanese aesthetics, you probably won't be surprised to learn that there are detailed calendars[1] and guidebooks dictating the conventions for what colors, patterns, imagery, and embroidery are appropriate during which season and for which occasion. These conventions reflect the deep attention to harmony, seasonal awareness, and detail that is so characteristic of Japanese culture.

Theologian: And, do the designs differ for men's and women's *kimono*?

Hanto: Yes, definitely. As a traditional ritual in a historically conservative culture, kimono design hasn't typically embraced the kind of gender fluidity we see today. But there's now a small movement—some dressmakers and online communities—exploring kimono for transgender individuals. (Copeland 2018)

Our *Flowers in the Sky* group is also experimenting with how to challenge essentialized gender roles in the tea ceremony. Traditionally, men's kimono are limited in color and pattern, while women's allow more expressive detail tied to season or occasion. Fabrics, cuts, and even embroidery can signal things like family, marital status, social rank, or tea school affiliation.

But in *Wabicha*, there's a strong egalitarian ideal—markers of status are deliberately minimized so no guest feels subordinate. Rikyū, the founder of *Wabicha*, took this even further with the use of a muted cotton kimono dyed with ash—what's often called "Rikyū gray"—to erase class or wealth distinctions.

In our practice, we've used Rikyū's neutral palette to question both gender and class aesthetics, while also removing constraints—men can wear any kimono they like. This keeps the ceremony inclusive but rooted in its core philosophy.

Most know the kimono for its beauty, but it's also practical. I'll lend you a few implements—a small folding fan (*sensu* 扇子), paper (*kaishi* 懐紙), cloth (*fukusa* 袱紗), and wallet (*fukusabasami* 袱紗挟み). These will come into play later. For now, as we get dressed, I'll show you how they fit neatly into the kimono's sleeves and pockets. It's customary to return them—along with unused *kaishi*—on your way out.

~ *The Hanto distributed the kimonos and helped the guests put them on.*
The group inspected the implements for a brief moment, wondered about their design and the calligraphed inscription on the kaishi paper.

Artist: What does it say on the paper here?

Guide: I can't read that to you.

Philosopher: Because it's a non-poem?

~ *All three had a good laugh. The Hanto shared a wink with the Guide.*

Guide: You might say it's a sort of non-poem. But, we'll save it until the end, when you're all fully awakened.

~ *. . . he said with a wink back to the Hanto.*

But, I can tell you, it's related to the calligraphy we see on the wall here. Dear Hanto, can you please tell us about this feature of the room before we enter the garden.

Hanto: Gladly.

Notice this recessed space in the wall? That's an alcove, or *Tokonoma* (床の間) and in there is a hanging scroll, called a *kakemono* (掛物). It's the first of two you'll see today and one of the most significant aesthetic features of the *Wabicha* ceremony as formalized by Rikyū. It's very much the aesthetic starting point of our journey. Or, let's not say a "starting point"—as though a tea ceremony starts and ends at some point in time—let's say, it's a sort of aesthetic nexus among all of the vast relations that are without beginning or end.

While it might look like it's been hanging there for years, in keeping with the *ichigo ichie* principle—"one time, one meeting"—this has been specifically selected for this one day and for your particular group. If you were a different group or arrived on a different day or season, we might have selected a different scroll. With this selection, we introduce you to the central themes of the ceremony.

Now, look closely—we can discern hints at the many small, deliberate decisions the tea host has made to weave a thematically appropriate and consistent experience.

The calligraphy is a fragment from the "Dream of the Butterfly" passage from the Daoist text the *Zhuangzi*. It reads "Once Zhuang Zhou dreamt he was a butterfly, fluttering about joyfully just as a butterfly would." (2009 p. 21).

~ The group lingered for a moment to appreciate the poem and its fine calligraphy.

Before we move on to our next station, notice this detail of the changing room—a smoking set (*tobako bon* 煙草盆). This indicates that we're still in the informal part of the ceremony where light conversation is permitted, and strict observance of tea etiquette is not yet expected.

The smoking set is followed with cups of hot water (*osayu* お白湯), which can be plain or lightly flavored with salted cherry blossom or sometimes seaweed. These small but meaningful gestures reflect the intentional pacing of the ceremony; easing us into the more formal stages to come.

Guide: Okay, now that we're suited up and ready to exit the changing room, let's all please bow to our Hanto to show her our appreciation.

~ The group bowed to the Hanto and sipped their water. They then slowly exited the changing room, and the full vista of the garden opened before them.

The three meandered for a short span, exploring the garden's mineral and vegetal worlds. They stepped across the broad, flat stones and their eyes were drawn towards the beautiful sights, their noses catching the subtle fragrances emanating from the garden's outer perimeter. After a short while, they returned to a seating area where their Guide was waiting.

Roji

Guide: Let me tell you about where we are now. As I mentioned, this is the outer garden or *soto-roji* (外露地), as opposed to the second garden where the hut is, the inner garden, or *uchi-roji* (内露地).[2]

Gardens like this weren't always part of the tea ceremony. They only became prominent in the early Edo period, around 1600, when they began springing up around medieval Japan at the residences of wealthy merchants, aristocrats, military lords, and Buddhist temples (Keane 2014).

As for the etymology, it's a bit more complex than simply referring to a garden. *Roji* translates as something like "dewy ground" and it actually has deeper significance within Buddhist lore. The name comes from a scene in one of the most important Buddhist texts, the Lotus Sutra. The quote goes:

> *escaping from the fire-stricken habitations of the Three Phenomenal Worlds (desire, form, and formlessness) they take their seats on the dewy ground.*
>
> (Sadler, 1962, p. 19).

The story depicts children trapped in "the burning house of the three worlds" (*sangai no kataku* 三界の火宅), which symbolizes the suffering caused by earthly passions. The parents outside the house—representing Buddhist elders—convince the children to leave the house and to take refuge on the "dewy ground", or "*roji*" outside. The movement from the burning house into the garden serves as an allegory for the Buddhist path towards enlightenment. Rikyū, in his *Nampōroku*, invokes this metaphor in a verse:

> *Since the roji*
> *Is the path*
> *Leading out of the "floating world,"*
> *Why should we scatter*
> *The dust of our minds.*

Let's stroll over in this direction now and take a short pause at the waiting arbor.

Confucianism and *Koshikake Machiai*

Guide: This is the next stage of the ceremony, the outer waiting arbor, or *koshikake machiai* (腰掛待合). As you see, it's a modest structure, not much larger than your average bus shelter. And like this, it typically has bamboo and straw walls on three sides, leaving it open to the garden.

You'll often see low-hanging rooves like this one, which perform the *kire* function by cutting away some of the upper canopy of vegetation around the garden's outer perimeter. Take note at this structure, because this little hut serves as a symbolic mediator between a normal house and the tea hut we'll encounter later. You'll later notice that some of the aesthetic features of this arbor echo those in the tea hut.

Let's have a seat and see what you notice?

Artist: The garden is beautiful and so lush, but I'm a little surprised that there isn't more color. It feels like the garden designer must have chosen to cultivate a very constrained palette.

Guide: Yes, very good. You actually won't notice many vibrant colors here or in the tea hut—though there will be a few small exceptions we'll see later. This stands in contrast to other kinds of Japanese gardens, especially strolling gardens associated with courtly culture, where vibrant colors, flowers, and flowering trees would have been more prominent.

In the *Wabicha* garden and ceremony, color is mostly absent. Likewise, any shapes that would call attention to themselves—oddly formed tree trunks, comical stones, or eye-catching shrubbery—are avoided as they distract the tea guest. A Japanese scholar Okuda Shōzō says that the tea garden was "for purification of the mind, not the delight of the eye" (Okuda 1990, 18).

Theologian: What about this straw broom here. Are we supposed to use that?

Guide: You can use it, but it's mostly symbolic. It reminds us to continue the process of sweeping away the dust of the world as we prepare for the ceremony.

And, here's a small Confucian detail—right underfoot. Notice how the stones beneath us are slightly uneven? You three share that single long, flat stone, and I have this larger round stone just for myself. That's not accidental. Does anyone know anything about Confucianism?

Theologian: I know that it was the state religion or philosophy of China for many centuries. And, it was based on the teachings of an actual person, Confucius.

Philosopher: I've read a little bit of the main text of Confucianism—I think it's called the *Analects*. If I remember, Confucius emphasized the importance of social rituals that one must learn to become a proper Confucian gentleman.

Guide: That's right. Confucianism was the state religion in China until quite recently. While *Chanoyu* is most often linked with Buddhism and Daoism, it also includes important Confucian elements. Rikyū references Confucian principles in his *Nampōroku*, and several Confucian thinkers deeply influenced the ceremony's development.[3]

Confucianism dominated as state doctrine for over 2,000 years, whereas Daoism never held comparable political sway. Think of Confucianism as embodied by the scholar-official, upholding strict social norms—Confucius himself being the model. Daoism, by contrast, aligns with the reclusive poet-philosopher, dwelling outside society in nature. These archetypes—Confucian order and Daoist withdrawal—interact subtly in the tea ceremony, blending ritual precision with simplicity and natural flow.

Confucius, whose birth name was Kǒng Qiū, is known through the honorific Kǒng Fūzǐ (孔夫子), or "Master Kong"—a title given long after his death. Born in 551 BCE in Lu (now near Nanjing), he came from modest means and studied in a school for commoners. He rose to public office but was exiled after a failed revolt aimed at restoring centralized authority. He continued to develop and teach his ethics until his death at age seventy-one.

Though he didn't find success in his lifetime, Confucius's legacy is enormous. His teachings were adopted as official doctrine after the Qin dynasty's fall in 206 BCE and remained dominant until the early twentieth century—making Confucianism arguably one of the most influential philosophic-religious systems in history.

Some call it religion, others philosophy, virtue ethics, or secular morality—it contains elements of all but defies any single category. Unlike in western traditions, Confucianism is more integrated and hybrid.

The main text linked to him is the *Analects* (*Lunyu* 論語), not written by Confucius himself but compiled by his disciples after his death—much like Socrates and Plato. The *Analects* doesn't aim to present metaphysics or ethical theory. Instead, it offers brief accounts of conversations between Confucius, his students, and others, focusing on everyday ethics.

The emphasis isn't on theorizing, or speculating about the nature of reality or knowledge, but on exemplification—Confucius as a moral exemplar. Being a good Confucian wasn't about knowing a theory, but emulating the master's actions. While often seen as rule-based, Confucian ethics actually stress contextual judgment over rigid rule-following.

It's also about self-cultivation, but not knowledge for its own sake—rather, knowledge of rituals that promote social harmony. Core virtues include benevolence (*ren* 仁), ritual propriety (*li* 礼), righteousness (*yi* 义), wisdom (*zhi* 智), and fidelity (*xin* 信).

And returning to where we began: filial piety (*xiào* 孝) is perhaps the most central Confucian virtue—governing not just how we sit, but even the stones beneath our feet.

Anyone know anything about filial piety?

Theologian: Yeah, I think that means having respect and following the rules set down by one's superiors—primarily your parents but also elders, like an older sibling, your boss, or political leaders.

Guide: Filial piety means respecting and following the example of elders or superiors. The elder is seen as the moral exemplar. But there's also a duty called "remonstrance" (Jiànzhèng 諫諍)—to question or advise an elder when needed. Still, the elder holds final authority and must ensure their actions align with virtue.

To maintain authority, a superior must act virtuously. If they don't, they lose the moral right to their title—they can't "rectify" their name, whether as elder, father, or ruler.

Filial piety isn't just about obeying the eldest. There's also a cosmological dimension. In Confucius' time—similar to ancient Greece—people saw heavenly movement (*tian* 天) as perfectly ordered, unlike the chaos of earthly life. Confucius imagined filial piety as a way to bring earthly life into harmony with the heavens. Just as smaller stars orbit larger ones without straying, children or subordinates should align with the "moral gravity" of their superior.

And that's what we're doing now. I'm not much older than you, but I'm seated here with my own stone because I'm the eldest and serve as *Shōkyaku*—the first guest. I entered first, will move into the inner *roji* and tea hut first, and will be served tea first.

That said, being second or third doesn't mean lesser. For example, the *otsume*, the last guest who closed the gate, plays a key role in completing certain parts of the ceremony.

Guide: We have a bit of time before moving to the next stage. Let's take a short stroll through the *soto roji* before we're called in by our host to the *uchi roji* where the tea hut is.

As I mentioned, this garden is slightly bigger than typical gardens, so we have a little extra room to explore, and a few more paths to meander down. Let's meet in 10 or 15 minutes over there at the next stage, the outer waiting bench (*soto koshikake* 外腰掛). We'll pause there until our host calls us into the inner garden.

> ~ *The group dispersed, exploring the various garden paths. After some time, the three naturally found their way to the outer waiting bench and sat alongside their Guide, waiting for the tea master to call them in.*

The Un-named Artist Copying Copies

Mimesis Copy/Original

Guide: Welcome back. Any thoughts about what you saw during your meanderings?

Artist: I kept thinking about whether the ceremony is art, an artwork, or if it's something different.

Guide: And, what did you come up with?

Artist: The main thing that came to mind is that the tea ceremony doesn't seem to be about something else. It's not like a painting of a person or a landscape, or even a movie, where the artist is trying to make a likeness of some person, object or event.

Guide: I'm glad you brought this up. It's a very important question, so find a comfortable spot because we're going to go on a deep dive into some advanced topics here—probably the longest talk on philosophic topics—so if you prefer to skip this content, feel free to wander around and join us for the next talk.

The question of the status of the tea ceremony as art is fascinating but complicated. It seems to have *elements* of art—sculpture, painting, poetry, while also resembling performance, ritual and even religion. But, is the tea ceremony itself art, is the host an artist, these are difficult questions.

You made a great observation in noting how the aspects of the garden we've seen so far don't seem to directly be *about* anything, unlike a great deal of European art history—and lots of Asian art—which in one way or another aims to imitate, symbolize or let's say *represent* something. And, this brings us to a vast set of issues that cut across art and philosophy, that is, regarding the concept of *mimesis*.

Western philosophy began with an account of reality that was fundamentally mimetic. One of the deepest and mostly un-noticed ways that we carry forth this tradition—one of the ways many of us are "westerners" or "European" without even realizing it—is in how we carry mimetic assumptions and expectations not only when thinking about art or philosophy, but in our everyday lives.

Artist: Can I ask, where does this word *mimesis* come from? What exactly does it mean?

Guide: Does anyone know?

Theologian: It sounds like there's a connection to the word "mime".

Guide: Indeed, there is. "Mimesis" (μίμησις) is the Greek word referring to imitation or copying. The basic idea is quite simple, but it has many metaphysical assumptions loaded with meaning—and also loaded with problems, the main one being the often quite strict binary distinction between what is real and what is un-real, or relatedly, many other binaries, like original vs. copy; reality vs. illusion ; nature vs. artifice; original vs. reproduction; authentic vs. imitation.

These distinctions might seem un-controversial, but thinking based on these binaries has profoundly determined how we as westerners think about and act in the world. Does our philosopher know where this comes up?

Philosopher: Yeah, Plato is known for dividing the world into two realms: the real world and the less-real copy of that world. For him, the real world was the world of forms and the one we perceive with our senses is an imperfect copy, an illusion.

According to Plato, sensory perception gives us access only to the copy, but this isn't a source of reliable knowledge. To be a philosopher is to see the universal forms with the intellect not particular material things with the eyes.

Guide: Can you give us an example?

Philosopher: The example my professors always gave was the relation between a chair and the form of a chair. The physical chair we see and sit on is an imperfect, less-real copy of the form or the essence of all chairs. I think that word you used, "representational" is usually used to describe that relation. Perceptions are thought to be less-real *representations* of real things. Philosophies following this "Platonist" assumption typically devalue sensory perception.

Artist: If perception is devalued, then we can guess that artworks are devalued as well.

Guide: One quick point. Plato didn't use a term exactly corresponding to our term "representation". But yes, as you suggested, the strong division he makes between forms and copies of forms sets our tradition on a trajectory of valuing artworks within a copy–original framework, where artworks have been construed as copies of more real objects.

And, since the "real" world was elevated, the artwork copying that world was demoted to a lower value—the painting *is less real* than the thing it represents. Whether it's the Mona Lisa, a Monet or even a Michelangelo, the artwork remains a *less-real* copy of a *more real* world.

Have any of you read Plato's *Republic*? Does anyone remember why Plato wanted to ban the poets from his ideal state?

Theologian: I think it was something about their inability to tell the truth.

Artist: I read about this in an art theory book. He said paintings were not just copies; they were *copies of copies*. They're twice removed from the original. When the artist paints a chair, or the poet writes about a chair, they're copying the physical chair, which is itself already a copy of the original form or essence of a chair.

Guide: Yes, exactly. For Plato, a painting of a chair is in a mimetic relation with the chair—not with the real form of a chair—but with its *less-real* physical instance. So, as a copy of a copy, an artwork is of an even lower order of reality than the thing it represents. For this reason, Plato believed that the artist offers no opportunity for the kind of knowledge the philosopher wants. He thought that this was so dangerous for the pursuit of truth that he even proposed banning poets from his Republic.

When we turn to his student Aristotle, we find a different stance on mimesis. In his *Poetics*, Aristotle appreciated the positive aspects of mimesis and disagreed with Plato on some key points. There are even several interesting studies placing Aristotle in dialogue with Japanese thinking on imitation, particularly on the topic of drama and theater.[1] However, even in Aristotle's philosophy, the metaphysics of copy and original remained central.

From these Greek beginnings—and with very few exceptions—western thinking about art continues to revolve around mimetic, or what we now call a "representational" framework. A strong opposition between what is real and what is a copy, an imitation or illusion still shapes how we think about reality in the most fundamental way.

Mimetic assumptions remained dominant in European art for centuries, enduring until historically quite recently. Until around the nineteenth century, most artists still worked under the assumption that an artwork was better in proportion to how closely it imitated the "real" world. Artists would even compete to see which medium was better at representing reality.

Does our artist know the story of the competition between Zeuxis and Parrhasios.[2]

Artist: Yes, I remember this one—it's from Pliny. Zeuxis apparently painted grapes so realistic that birds flew down to peck at them. But, Parrhasios went one step further. He presented a painting covered in a sheet. When Zeuxis attempted to uncover the painting, he found that it wasn't a sheet after all, but such a remarkably perfect copy that nobody could tell the difference between the painted copy and a real sheet.

Guide: What this story nicely illustrates is something a former professor of mine once pointed out, that within a mimetic framework, "art is more perfect the more deceptive it is" (Moeller 2004, p. 140). This way of thinking persisted well into the Renaissance. At this time, scholars debated, and artists held competitions called *paragone* to determine which medium—sculpture or painting—provided the most faithful representation of reality.

Artist: I'm not a specialist in Japanese art history, but I've seen enough to know that a lot of Japanese art also represents the world. There are many depictions of nature and humans, landscapes, birds and other animals. Aren't these artworks also mimetic?

Guide: Yes, there are absolutely representational structures in Japanese art. And maybe there are even implicit original–copy types of binaries at play. It's not that the Japanese didn't think about or have concepts similar to the western notion of mimesis, they certainly did.[3]

The crucial difference is that in the Japanese context, the underlying metaphysics didn't *cast the copy as less real than the original*. This is the decisive difference. Plato demoted the copy to a lower metaphysical status. This made a painting less real than the thing it depicts. No matter how realistic as an artwork might be, it could never equal the reality of the object it represents.

The Chinese, and by extension the Japanese, didn't share this assumption. Even when trying to render the world or objects as accurately as possible, they didn't assume that the resulting painting or drawing was of a lesser degree of reality. The *painting of the landscape wasn't less real than the landscape*—no less natural. Likewise, a drawing of pears, a cat, or cherry blossoms, these are just as real, just as natural as what they depict.

Philosopher: Did Japanese philosophies also repudiate mimetic and representational assumptions?

Artist: I was wondering the same thing. *Geidō* art practices like the tea ceremony, archery or flower arranging don't seem to be, at least not primarily, about copying something more real, but what about the practice of learning these arts.

Aren't they based on prolonged imitation of a master? Is learning a practice like the tea ceremony not deeply mimetic in this sense?

Guide: Another great question. The answer is yes and no. And, let me repeat, it's not that there are *no* mimesis-like aspects in tea gardens or throughout the ceremony, or as you've rightly observed, in *geidō* training.

Many garden designers, for example, arrange stones, shrubs and mosses deliberately to represent "places of scenic beauty" (*meishō*, 名勝) or famous scenes from Japanese literature or poetry. You might find several stones arranged to invoke images of disciples sitting around the Buddha as he gives a sermon, or a reference to a well-known scene from *The Tale of Genji*, or a haiku of Bashō's. There's an element of copying or mimesis here. One eminent scholar of Japanese aesthetics, Yuriko Saito has a great article detailing the different representational features of the tea garden.[4]

So remember, it's not that some form of copying or representation is completely absent from the tea ceremony. The crucial difference lies in the underlying metaphysical assumptions.

The philosophies that came to determine Japanese thinking about art—Buddhism, Daoism, Shinto and Confucianism—weren't "mimetic" in the sense of dividing reality into the real and the less real.

To illustrate how different the Japanese thought about artworks or artistic production, let's consider the landscape painting tradition Japan inherited from China. For a substantial part of its history, this tradition was mostly a studio practice.[5] Artists would often spend substantial parts of their careers indoors, not painting landscapes directly from nature, but copying masterpiece landscapes of other great artists.

Theologian: Great artists copied other artists' works? And, were these considered their own?

Guide: Yes, they were.

Artist: But, if they're copying other painting and not real landscapes, wouldn't that mean that they're almost *more* mimetic than Greek painters were?

Philosopher: Plato would say they're copying copies of copies of copies of the real landscape.

Guide: Yes, Plato might say that. His metaphysics basically disallowed him from seeing that a painting could be just as real as the landscape it depicts, perhaps more real.

Artist: Can a painting really be just as real as the landscape it depicts? Even if we don't hold the original–copy binary so strongly, one is still natural and the other is derived from it.

Guide: It is surprising to learn that great artists worked indoors, copying paintings. Aside from the metaphysical issues, it clashes with the common image of the Japanese being a nature-loving people.

Most of us would imagine a Japanese landscape painter out in the open air, breathing in the fresh mountain breeze, and gazing over expansive vistas with the sun rising and setting over the horizon, birds chirping, and trees swaying in the wind. Few would imagine an artist working away in a small studio, vistas constrained by four walls, painting a two-dimensional copy of a landscape they might have never seen.

But this practice is worth thinking about, because it reveals some of the deeply held assumptions we carry about what is real, "natural" and what we think isn't. Even I was quite shocked when I first learned that great Japanese artists worked this way. Looking back, I can see how much my thinking was shaped by a western mimetic bias.

What if I said that what these painters were doing in their studios, emulating the great works wasn't really copying? And that what they produced was no less real than what we consider a "real" landscape.

Philosopher: I can maybe understand that a painting isn't necessarily less real. It's obviously a real thing. I mean, it exists as a thing. But, isn't it still a copy? The painting isn't the landscape? I can't walk around in a landscape painting the way I can in the actual landscape.

Guide: Let me share with you another example of artistic competitions in China where ideas of copying come up. Even more than Renaissance Italy, ancient China had a highly organized world of artistic learning, regulation, codification, commentary, and criticism. The Chinese produced hundreds of state-sanctioned manuals, extraordinarily detailed, dictating conventions and styles of different schools of art.

Let's consider Wu Daozi (吳道子), an eighth-century painter famed for his ability to depict the world with extraordinary precision. Legend has it that, after painting a landscape on one of the imperial palace walls, he walked into the scene and disappeared.

Obviously, pure fantasy, right?

Theologian: Obviously, he doesn't disappear. A painting isn't something you can stroll into.

Philosopher: I know what you're going to say. *You* can't stroll into it because you're a *self*.

Artist: And, you'll say that Daozi's painting doesn't depict a place, and it isn't an object. But, I still don't see how that redeems the story as anything other than fantasy.

Guide: Let me ask you this, what were some of the binaries being invoked here regarding space when we take it that one cannot walk into a painting?

Philosopher: The internal–external binary we already spoke about at the gates.

Guide: Can you say a little more about that?

Philosopher: Part of why it feels absurd to say someone walked into a painting is because we assume a clear separation between the inside and outside of a work of art. Humans either stand outside and create an artwork, or they appear depicted within one, but they can't cross from the external world into the internal space of the artwork, or the other way around.

Guide: If we tried loosening that binary, how might we rethink this legend?

Artist: I'm not sure. I get it about holding binaries more loosely, but I can't see how it applies here. Even a non-self couldn't step into the internal space of a painting.

Guide: Remember when we talked about the concept "world" earlier? One aspect of our present western world—something that wouldn't hold true for all worlds—is our specific conception of space. It wasn't until the Renaissance that we began depicting the world in art using geometric perspective. That's become second nature to us, right?

Artist: Yes, of course.

Guide: But when artists such as Leonardo, Michelangelo, and Brunelleschi began depicting the world using the principles of geometric perspective, their works shocked audiences and fundamentally altered how people thought about space. These innovations were so transformative that we can say the western "world" itself was reshaped by them. People began experiencing space—and their bodies within it—in new ways. As part of an emerging scientific worldview, concepts of self, space, and objects shifted—maybe only slightly—but these artists had some impact on the western "world".

The French phenomenologist Merleau-Ponty writes about this kind of shift in our visual world in great detail. He shows how the Renaissance innovations profoundly influenced not just the artworld, but they were so profound, so impactful that they actually changed the way the westerners experienced themselves as bodies in space.

He comments on how this shift brought about by artists has led us to conceive of space only according to its positivity,[6] as though we are objects in a container, but this doesn't capture our full experience of space. He criticizes Descartes for this kind of positivist conception of space, claiming that we do not experience space as "a geometer looking over it and reconstructing it from outside", but instead, "I live it from the inside; I am immersed in it. After all, the world is around me, not in front of me." (1993, p. 138)

Merleau-Ponty is trying to show us that after almost two millennia of "representational" and mimetic philosophies, and around half a millennia since Renaissance art, we've come to understand our relation to the visual world—including our relation to visual art—almost as though we're visual mechanisms, or cameras—as though we're fundamentally at a remove from the world we see: we are subjects *here* and the things we see are objects out *there* in space.

But, for him, vision is a way we're immersed, or to use his term, "intertwined" (*entrelacs*) with the world. There's no dividing line between our perceptual bodies and the world. Vision isn't a way of standing back from the world to represent it like an object at a distance, it's a way our body is able to go outside of itself, to be out there among the things in the perceptual field.

And, interestingly, even though we can't go into these details, like many Asian philosophies, Merleau-Ponty also thinks of the relations between things as a kind of negation (Loughnane 2019).

Artist: I don't get it. The body is still in here, even if I see the world out there.

Guide: The typical phenomenological response would be that, objectively speaking, yes, the body is limited to its outer edges. In here not out there. But, perceptual experience isn't *merely* objective. If we could somehow get beyond the reduction of perceptual experience to the objective or positive, what we might come to see is that the "in here–out there" binary doesn't hold. With every perception we're experiencing beyond the body–world binary. We're intertwining with the world, not representing it. And, as intertwined, there's no way to perfectly demarcate where the body ends and the things the body perceives begin.

Philosopher: Difficult to scribe the circumference or graph the perimeter?

Guide: Yes, good. But, let's think about that for a minute. If we're "intertwined" with the world through perception, then upholding the binary between the space inside and outside of the body is problematic.

So, we come back to the original question. What about the space we think is simply "out there" in the paintings we perceive? We also have to rethink that. What do we do?

Philosopher: I'm totally stumped.

Guide: It's a tricky thought but let's return to the original binary we began with—the space internal to the painting versus the space external.

What did the Renaissance painters do? They didn't just show us new ways of painting, they changed our experience of space. What that means is that, "out here", what we think of as the space *outside of* paintings, this has somehow been shaped by what's going on *inside* the paintings.

Theologian: . . . wait, can you say that again?

Guide: We've already said that artists, with their paintings, were able to change the way people experience space, right?

Theologian: Yes.

Guide: Then, this means that the space depicted *inside* their paintings, changed how we experience space outside their paintings.

Theologian: Okay, I see.

Guide: So, it sounds like, how we experience space is an odd mix, where "out here" is determined by "in there".

So, we have to ask, on what grounds do we uphold a strict internal–external binary in terms of space?

This is what Merleau-Ponty is trying to help us see. If artists can depict space internal to an artwork and change our experience of space in what we think is outside the artwork, then it becomes difficult to hold that binary so strongly. He has a great line invoking this idea, he says "the artist changes the world into painting" (1993, p. 123).

Artist: But, didn't those artists just give a more accurate depiction of space. It wasn't so much that our "world" was *created* with a new space as much as those artistic innovations uncovered the space we were always living in?

Guide: That really gets at the crux of Merleau-Ponty's phenomenological conception of space and vision, and another way we can think about getting over this obsession with dividing the more real from the less real, the copy from the original, or subjective from objective space.

For him, the innovations of the Renaissance painters didn't give us a more "real" conception of space. Let me read this to you:

> *painters knew from experience that no technique of perspective is an exact solution and that there is no projection of the existing world which respects it in all aspects and deserves to become the fundamental law of painting . . . . The perspective of the Renaissance is no infallible "gimmick." It is only one particular case, a date, a moment in a poetic information of the world which continues after it.*
>
> (Merleau-Ponty 1993, p. 135)

Renaissance perspective may have offered a more accurate objective framework for representing measurable space. Architects and engineers likely find this conception of space very useful. However, for most phenomenologists, the key idea would be that *objective* space isn't inherently *more real* than our *subjective* experience of space.

But, as westerners, taught to chop the world up into the more real and less real, we tend to think that an objective account of space—space that is always the same whenever or wherever we measure—is more real.

Theologian: Because our metaphysics has been mostly obsessed with permanence.

Guide: Yes, and because subjective experience of space is variable—differing between people and changing depending on states of mind or body, and ultimately less permanent—this is *less real*, so it goes.

But, here's a funny question: how often are you actually measuring space objectively compared to experiencing it subjectively? Most of us don't spend our time analysing space as a scientist or engineer would—dividing space into objective measures, meters and millimeters, hectares and volumes. By far our experience of space is predominantly subjective.

Instead, most of our experience of space is closer to a feeling than a measurement. We feel the pain of the space that divides us from loved ones, the safety of space between ourselves and unsafe parts of the world, or the frustration at the space remaining between us and the finish line of a marathon. Of all of our experiences of space, these are much more common.

This is why Merleau-Ponty and other phenomenologists pay close attention to artists. Painters like Cézanne, Matisse or Gericault don't give us a depiction of space that would be very useful for those who have to measure space like the builder or engineer, but they remind us of our embodied, subjective experience of space.

Philosopher: Aren't we re-invoking binaries by speaking of subjective and objective space?

Guide: Yes, thank you. To be more precise, I should say that phenomenologists—and Merleau-Ponty especially—are mostly concerned with experience beyond subjective–objective binaries. Merleau-Ponty isn't worried about arguing that either our subjective experience of space or objective account of space is *more real*. They're both real. He's more concerned with what reality must be such that those two perspectives seem to always be possible.

But, because of the enormous power of the scientific worldview—and with the division Plato's instituted between the more and less real—our western world has propped the objective up as what is most real and demoted the subjective to a lower metaphysical status. So, to level the playing field and overcome the over-objectification of space, we often have to push from the other side, which might make it seem like we're promoting a subjective account. The aim should be to get over that binary if we want to capture what it is to experience space.

Artist: I guess that why we often hear people say, "that's just subjective", the implication being that it's less real.

Guide: Right. But, the idea of phenomenology isn't to all of a sudden make the subjective more real, but to problematize the subject–object binary altogether.

Generally, we don't need the subject–object distinction. And, if we explore most of our experience of space, we're not arriving at it from a series of thoughts or deductions. It's "lived" space, not "thought about" space. It's pre- or non-reflective. We find ourselves always already immersed, or "intertwined" in space and before we reflect on it, the binaries like here and there, inside and outside—these aren't so much in play, not shaping how we experience the world. It's when we analyse space, reflect on it that these binaries like subjective–objective appear.

But, how often have you had to analyse space to ride your bike or go up a set of stairs?

~ *The three pondered for a moment and shook their heads.*

Okay, let's bring this down to earth. We were talking about Daozi. How can we use these phenomenological ideas of space to reconsider how he might walk into his own painting?

Artist: Maybe Daozi didn't walk from the outside to the inside of the painting. Maybe, just in walking, he was already in an experiential world somehow ambiguously between the space internal to the painting and external to it.

Guide: That's a really great way to put it. Of course, the scientist will argue that objective, measurable space is more real, and incommensurable with the kind of space Daozi is evoking.

But, when we speak of our "world", we're not talking about what we get when we measure things objectively, we're talking about the *meanings* associated with experiences, which are always partly subjective, partly objective. It's this moment of experience, which is most of our experience, where our experience of space can be shaped by art works.

If we're speaking in that register, we can read the Daozi story in a different light. Sure, still as quite fanciful, but nevertheless pointing to something that is true about how we experience space when we're not thinking about it or measuring it. Again, remember, our "world" shapes how we experience things without our having to think about it, it shapes experience "pre-reflectively".

Philosopher: So maybe it's not about us entering the frame of the artwork, but rather the spatiality of the artwork pervading our own spatiality. If we can imagine that idea, then perhaps it's not so hard to see how we're already walking within the space of paintings and artworks.

Artist: Probably, we're all walking still in the space of Renaissance artists, aren't we?

Guide: That's a perfect way to put it. Even though the artists from that period tended towards an objective depiction of space, which doesn't capture our "lived" experience of space so well, I think you're right that it is the spatiality developed in that period that has determined how our present "world" shapes our experience of space.

Merleau-Ponty paid a lot of attention to Cézanne's paintings because he thought those works shifted our focus to how we experience space in pre-reflective experience. But unfortunately, it doesn't seem that Cézanne's innovations have been as determinative of our "world". So yes, I think you're right that we're still very much in the space of Renaissance paintings.

In either case, we can keep in mind that as we move around *out here*, we're always already in a space instituted *in there*, by paintings and art. So, why not loosen our grip on those internal–external, subjective–objective binaries?

Artist: It definitely should expand our experience of artworks.

Philosopher: In that way, the representational framework seems really limiting for appreciating art. I mean, it's probably simpler to think of two different spatialities—one in the painting and the other one we live in—but, that doesn't seem to actually capture what's actually going on in our lived experience of space. But, I'll have to think more about this idea of "intertwinement".

Guide: These are not easy ideas, but I think you're getting the hang of thinking phenomenologically.

(Negated) Creativity: (un-)Originality and (non-)Selfhood

Guide: So, I realize this is a lot of dense and abstract material. Is everybody still with me? Still up for some more philosophy?

~ *All three nodded.*

Okay, then. Let's return to the question about artists copying other's paintings. There's more interesting philosophical insights we can draw out that highlight significantly different ideas about artistic creativity and originality in Japanese and western art worlds.

Let me ask you, what about that detail where Daozi *disappears* into his painting?

Artist: Maybe it suggests that the artist is so small in comparison to nature that they become almost imperceptible.

Guide: That's a nice twist on what I was thinking. Yes, it's often the case that humans are depicted as dwarfed by the landscape in Japanese art. You'll often first see an expansive landscape and then upon inspecting tiny details you might spy a monk, a few fishermen, or maybe just their footsteps leading through a path to an almost imperceptible hermitage. In the face of nature, humans are often rendered as exceedingly diminutive.

This reflects more than just how the artist conceives of humanity—it also speaks to how they perceive themselves. Daozi disappearing into his own painting aligns with a Japanese artistic tendency to minimize the self, making it almost imperceptible, working towards its disappearance.

Philosopher: Art practice as a negation of the self.

Guide: Exactly. That's why I find the Daozi story so compelling. It narrativizes the act of creating a great artwork as one leading to the disappearance of the self.

In our western world, creating a great artwork tends to have the opposite aim; not to minimize the self, but to aggrandise it. Our great artists don't disappear in their works, they're made ever more visible, larger than life. Leonardo didn't disappear in creating the Mona Lisa. He constructed a self that lives on long after his own death.

Especially in our present art world, creating great works becomes a scaffold for the self and the ego. But, Daozi's disappearance reminds us that, historically, in the Asian art world, aesthetic practice sought to diminish the self, to negate it rather than aggrandize it. Practices like those in the *Geidō* tradition we'll be experiencing today were a highly disciplined attempt to negate the self.

Let me ask, what makes a great artist in the tradition that arose in Europe? What provides the foundation for their self?

Artist: Creating something beautiful?

Guide: Yes, but what if an artist today created something beautiful just like DaVinci did, or Picasso?

Artist: Then it wouldn't be as valuable because it's already been done.

Guide: Exactly. And, what does one need to do if they want to be recognized as a famous artist-self?

Artist: They have to be original. Obviously not make copies of other artists, but there has to be the "shock of the new" in order for an artwork to be valuable.

Guide: Precisely. We can see that Plato is back: the mimetic copy–original binary is at work here again. Originality has been one of the overriding principles determining the value of art works in the west. To secure a place in the textbooks, art galleries or collections, you must show us something importantly new, "original". With very little exception, if an artwork doesn't give us something demonstrably new, we have little need for it.[7]

This means that in European art history, it's usually easy to tell which artworks belong to which periods. It's unlikely that an art historian would confuse a Leonardo with a Monet, or a Raphael with a Turner.

Now, turn to China, and we see nearly the opposite. Especially with the landscape painting tradition, it's often extremely difficult, sometimes impossible to locate an un-identified painting even in a broad historical period let alone attribute it to a specific painter.

This is because, rather than pursuing originality, Chinese culture has been oriented towards *preserving* culture rather than *innovating*. Where the tradition did evolve, advances were often minute and imperceptible. Without a strong drive towards originality or a mimetic metaphysics that devalued "copying", we don't see strong marks of originality even on the order of centuries.

Let me share a note I brought from Fritz van Briessen, the art historian shedding light on this idea.

> *Whenever in the history of Chinese art a new style emerged, it was usually without any conscious idea of breaking away from tradition. Innovations in style were sometimes made so gradually—deriving as they did from the conditions of the period and education—that neither the age nor the individual painters were aware of them. It was not until later that these developments could be recognized in their proper perspective.*
>
> (2011, p. 34)

We see here again the connection between philosophy and aesthetics. Because Asian philosophies, for the most part, haven't created stories about a more perfect world of which our world was a less-real copy, the copy–original binary hasn't influenced thinking about art to the extent it has in the western mimetic tradition. Copying doesn't have the strongly negative connotation it does in the west, and, on the other side of the coin, originality and creativity also lose some of their value.

This isn't to say that Japanese artists didn't seek to innovate—they certainly did, and Rikyū is a prime example. But, the underlying metaphysics—ideas about what is real and not real, what is a copy and what is original, as well as ideas of the selfhood based thereupon—differed significantly between aesthetic traditions east and west.

All of this shapes how we think selfhood is grasped in the art world. Rather than striving to be the "artistic genius" based on one's individual super-human originality, the great Japanese artist is still human, they might also want to be a great painter, but they might achieve that by copying other's artworks. Rather than seeking to distinguish themselves *as selves* or individual creative geniuses, they might have sought to diminish the ego, part of a practice seeking non-selfhood.

Artist: This seems to answer my earlier question about the lack of representation in the garden. I guess, walking through a garden is not like going through a museum where we see a Warhol here, a Vermeer there and a Pollock around the next corner. The artist is absent, but that's how it's supposed to be, right? Like Daozi, the tea master isn't trying to make their creativity conspicuous, or trying to exhibit their originality, but seek to disappear in their art work?

Guide: *sō desu ne.*

Theologian: Is it true that many Japanese and Chinese artists wouldn't sign their works?

Guide: Yes, that's a great example showing another side of selfhood in the Asian art world. In the west, being an artist is often a way to enlarge the self—to solidify identity and gain recognition, not just for the art but for the artist as a creative genius. That's clearest in the act of signing a work with a personal seal.

In the art market, people often ask, "Is it an original?" If it's just a copy, it loses value—sometimes entirely. In today's contemporary art scene, with its celebrity culture, this western focus on the self is taken to the extreme. The cult of the artist only makes sense in a tradition that's built a metaphysical framework around the idea of the self and the meaning of signing an "original."

Compare that to Japanese art traditions, where artists often didn't sign their work. Or they practiced arts like archery or flower arranging, where signing isn't even possible. This connects to the idea of the "un-named" Japanese artist or craftsperson (Yanagi 1989). Even more radically, a work might be stamped not by the artist, but by the owner—sometimes multiple times as it changed hands.

Philosopher: Is that what those square-shaped red stamps on Chinese and Japanese paintings are?

Guide: Yes, it was the owner claiming ownership of the work. This would be nearly inconceivable in European art history, an affront to the artist, which reflects a different conception of creativity and selfhood in the Japanese art world.

Artist: There are actually many western artists who didn't sign their works. Van Gogh, Leonardo, DaVinci, Vermeer, Michelangelo.

Theologian: . . . there are also cases where owners or patrons would sign or put their seal on the works of artists. Jan van Eyck's *Ghent Altarpiece* (1432), is inscribed by his patron, and I'm pretty sure the Medici's also put their seal on any works they commissioned.

Guide: Okay, I actually didn't know this. So, this is a great example of where we have to always be careful about making generalizations that rely on strong east–west binaries. When we do that, we almost always find exceptions.

Artist: Wouldn't you also say that in the twentieth and twenty-first century there has been an explosion of non-mimetic artforms in the west? And with the art world becoming so international, isn't it much harder to draw sharp distinctions between artistic practices?

Guide: Yes, absolutely. The twentieth century saw major shifts in western art. Non-mimetic forms like abstract expressionism, conceptual art, and Dadaism challenged traditional ideas of representation and originality. With globalization, artistic traditions now mix more freely, making clear distinctions harder to sustain.

That said, we're speaking in broad historical terms. At that level, differences between western and east Asian art traditions have persisted for centuries. But you're right—we have to be careful. The more examples we consider, the harder it is to talk about fixed "eastern" or "western" art histories. And today, even the contemporary Japanese art world often mirrors the western model of the artist as individual genius, complete with celebrity culture.

But let's pause and return to the original question—whether the tea ceremony and its practices count as art. We're now in a better position to see the problem may lie in our assumptions about what art is. If we can move beyond mimetic ideals and the metaphysics behind them, we can recognize practices like archery, calligraphy, flower arranging, and the tea ceremony as art forms in their own right.

Artist: Maybe "art practices" rather than "art works"?

Theologian: . . . or, non-art forms?

Philosopher: . . . or, art formlessness?

Guide: If any of you actually existed, I'd say you've got the idea.

Creating and Copying: *Utsushi—Sha-i* and *Sakui*

Guide: If you're up for one last topic, I'll share with you another particularity about how creativity has been understood in Japanese art history.

In the west—again, speaking historically very broadly—creativity has been elevated to almost a godly status. It seems that there's nothing better than being a "creative" person. And, it's not that there isn't a certain idea of creativity in Japan, indeed, there is a term called *sakui* (作意), used in the Japanese art world referring to something similar to our idea of creativity. But, let me suggest that we might be careful about our western obsession with creativity and the type of selfhood that comes along.

Artist: This was why I asked earlier about the training we learned about at the Urasenke Institute. If tea practitioners spend years learning to imitate their teacher's movements and gestures, are they actually learning to be creative?

Guide: There are two key points to keep in mind. First, you're absolutely right: in the tea ceremony and other *geidō* arts, students spend years imitating their masters. But the aim isn't blind copying. There's a concept in Japanese art training called *shu-ha-ri* (守破離): *shu* means obeying the forms (*kata*), *ha* means breaking them, and *ri* means transcending them.[8]

Even in *ri*, though, we shouldn't assume it's the same as western creativity. A Japanese artist might still copy a landscape, or a tea student copy a master's movement, and even at the level of "transcendence", the result may look nearly identical. The goal isn't shocking originality, as in the European art tradition, but a deep internalization of form. Only a trained eye might detect what's changed.

This ties into Koga Kenzo's essay "Utsushi: The Aesthetics of Imitation" in *Chanoyu Quarterly*, which I wanted to share. While the dictionary definition refers to duplicating an original text, making a certified copy, or a work patterned on an original,—these being more directly applicable to the tradition of sutra copying and copying of Chinese tea utensils[9]—but in art practice, there's an important additional aspect in the deployment of copying as *utsushi* (写).

By the late nineteenth century, a distinction emerged: *shasei* (写生), meaning realistic representation, (à la mimesis), and *sha-i* (写意),[10] which aimed to capture the spirit or inner essence of a thing. Some painters even signed their names with the character *sha* (写) to show their goal wasn't likeness, but resonance between artist and landscape (Kenzo 1991).

Artist: But how did they understand this artistic activity? Did they see it as creation or creativity the way it's understood in European art history and aesthetics?

Guide: Now we're getting to some important points. Kenzo explains how creativity does demand some element of copying, but one must go further: He says,

> only when the creator of a work has gone through each step of this progression is imitation transformed into creativity. Otherwise, the final product remains mere forgery of the lowest order.

(1991, p. 8)

There's a similar concept called "allusive variation" (*honka-dori* 本歌取り), used by the great Noh dramatist Zeami. It emphasizes that, despite the great degree of formalization and imitation in Noh training, one must surpass realistic imitation to create new variations on the forms being emulated.

You've probably heard the cliché that in any art, you must first learn the rules before breaking them. Yes, there's a high degree of conformity—like how our tea host adheres strictly to Urasenke conventions—but the idea is that once someone masters the art, they can express a spontaneous effortlessness that transcends rule-following or imitation.

Philosopher: Can we think of this along the lines of non-action?

Guide: Yes, absolutely. *Chadō* is a *Geidō* practice, and that *dō* character indicates that part of the goal is a natural spontaneity aligning with nature, or what we've been referring to as non-action. If there is a type of creativity here, it doesn't arise from asserting the self, but from negating it. Originality is more like a side-effect of this negation rather than the goal. Let me read another passage from Rikyū's *Nampōroku*. The key point is that, once one reaches a level of proficiency, they operate beyond mere imitation. He writes,

> *Transmission from the masters regarding the placement of utensils and the performance of tea-preparation include a vast number of details, and it is impossible to escape them. But once you have learned them fully and thoroughly, down to the fundamental rules of measurements and the secret matters of yin and yang, you are free and unrestricted amid a thousand changes and a myriad variations.*
>
> (Jakuan, 1995, p. 276)

And we have several instances of great tea masters urging practitioners to move beyond mere copying. Shinkei, the poet we discussed earlier who inspired Shukō, strongly opposed slavish imitation. In the "Ten Points of Attention for the Practitioner of Tea", (*Chanoyu-sha Kakugo Jittei* 茶湯者覚悟十躰), a section in the "Record of Yamanoue Sōji" (*Yamanoue Sōji Ki* 山上宗二記)—a compendium of tea utensils, teachings and traditions compiled in the late sixteenth century—the author writes;

> *Concerning tea manner, in training, depend solely on that which is old. In personal inventiveness, all should be new. Consider how one can accord with one's own times . . . one must not, however, imitate another's inventiveness.*
>
> (Hirota, 1995, p. 206)

And, a seventeenth-century Daimyō and tea master, Katagiri Sekishu says "be vigilant not to perform another's chanoyu" (p. 291).

The concept of creativity as *sakui* was especially prominent in tea-related texts from the late sixteenth and early seventeenth centuries. There was a deep respect for tradition, grounded in devotion to a master, where a disciple emulated the master's practice but was ultimately expected to transcend imitation. As Tanikawa (1979, p. 46) writes, quoting the *Yamanoue Soji-ki*,

> *one should learn the techniques for the procedures of tea from tradition, but sakui (creativity) should be something wholly new.*

In the *Sōshun-ō chadō kikigaki* (1956), the unknown author says

> *chanoyu without sakui is stiff, lacks variation, and remains dull. The key to chanoyu is to approach it with a new conception while using old utensils.*
>
> (Tetsuzo, 1970, p. 46)

One last point before we move on—just to complicate the east–west comparison a bit more. While we've been framing Japanese art as an alternative to western individualism, it's worth noting that even before contact with the west, Japan's art world was already a competitive space. Artists, poets, tea masters—even monastery heads—actively built reputations, often centered on personality and prestige. Many fought for recognition, patronage, government commissions, and inclusion in official art catalogues. Artistic schools competed fiercely, and personal ambition was very much part of the scene.

More specifically regarding selfhood, Japanese artists engaged in different aspects of self-mythologizing to establish their reputations as venerable painters or poets.

Philosopher: Then how is this different from traditions where unrestrained self-construction, creative originality, and self-assertion are explicitly sanctioned?

Guide: Sure, we could just say that everyone's human—even poet-monks and painter-priests still had egos. That's true. But there may still be a difference in how art celebrity functioned across cultures.

In Japan, artists often gained recognition not by amplifying the self, but by diminishing it. Many framed their work as Buddhist ritual, so the "cult" of the artist-self often became a competition in self-negation.

One example is the ideal of the "untrammelled" (*yipin* 逸品) artist, from Tang and Song China and later Japan. This figure embodied non-selfhood—drifting with impermanence, detached from worldly concerns. It meant avoiding social approval, petty disputes, and empty conventions.

Theologian: It seems a bit paradoxical, doesn't it? Japanese artists worked to distinguish them*selves* by undermining the self.

Artist: Distinguishing them*selves* as undistinguished non-artists.

Guide: Yes, it does sound a bit comical, but I think that captures it perfectly. It's akin to the familiar paradox you often hear about Buddhism and the cessation of desire. In Buddhism, desire is seen as the root of suffering. But if one strives to eliminate desire, the paradox emerges: you're *desiring* to end desire, which seems self-defeating. Similarly, artists gaining fame for their "untrammeled" persona were, paradoxically, seeking notoriety for a self they were trying to erase.

But, remember what we spoke about earlier. Our western tradition avoids contradictions, thinks they're a mistake demanding fixing. In Buddhist logic, where A can equal not-A, paradoxes aren't a problem. Just as a Buddhist practitioner can make progress in desiring to reduce desire, so too can the artist gain recognition for their self as artist pursuing non-selfhood.

> ~ *The group sat together quietly in the waiting arbor. Virtually noiseless movements filtered in from the inner garden. Their collective anticipation grew for soon nearing the tea hut.*

Guide: I think we're going to be called into the inner garden soon.

10

Inner Roji

Shintoism and Ritual Purification

Guide: Can you see through the azaleas? That's our host. She's just come out of the tea hut and must have the water we brought.

Theologian: Our host is a woman?

Guide: You expected otherwise?

Theologian: I guess I did, yes.

Guide: That's not an uncommon assumption, and it raises an interesting topic in the history of the tea ceremony. But I want to focus on what she's doing now, so let's come back to the gender question later.

She's now initiating an important ritual to complete the preparations for the ceremony. If we could see her now, we'd notice that she's carrying a bucket containing the *Rikyū no I* water we brought—she'll amble over to a small stone basin not far from the hut where more water was poured at dawn.

Philosopher: Why was the water put there so early?

Guide: Although the ritual she's about to perform is a Shinto one, the collecting and handling of water follows Daoist principles. A ceremony might start as early as 6:00 a.m. for "dawn tea ceremony" (*Akatsuki-no-chaji* 暁の茶事) or can begin as late as 5:00 or 6 p.m. with "winter evening tea" (*Yobanashi-no-chaji* 夜咄の茶事). But, regardless of the timing, the water is always drawn from the well at dawn.

That water, called "the flower of the well" is favored because, in Daoist cosmology water is associated with the *yang* principle, like the morning. Later times are associated with *yin*, and it was believed water drawn later might have lost its spirit—or worse, would be poison.

The small well she's visiting is called the *tsukubai* (蹲踞). If you listen carefully, you can hear her pausing there and sprinkling some of the water around the stones surrounding the basin. Next, she'll wash her hands and rinse her mouth, pouring the rest of the water she collected into the *tsukubai* until it overflows slightly and wets the surrounding stones.

That sound is an important and deliberate aural gesture. The sound of water spilling over is our signal that she'll soon greet us. Before that, she'll carefully place a ladle (*hishaku* 柄杓) over the basin for us to use when we enter the inner garden.

> ~ *A moment later, the host passes through the middle gate (chūmon 中門) and approaches the group at the waiting arbor. The Guide signals to the three to stand, stepping forward to offer a long, deep bow to the host. Without a word, the host pivots silently and returns through the middle gate. The group follows into the inner garden (uchi roji 内露地). The host disappears back into the teahouse as the Guide leads the group to the freshly filled water basin.*

Here at the *tsukubai*, we'll perform a Shinto purification by rinsing our mouths and hands. Earlier, we passed through several stages of cleansing in the outer garden. Now, entering the inner garden near the tea hut, purification deepens—we're no longer just clearing the dust of the external world, but bringing the elements onto our skin and inside our bodies. It's a move from symbolic to physical purification.

One scholar describes this intensified purification as shifting from our "conventional social roles to that of [our] ritual personae" (Anderson 1991). That shift will continue, echoed in the symbols and actions we encounter from here on.

As for the basin itself, *tsukubai* comes from *tsukubau*, meaning to crouch or lower oneself. Earlier basins were higher, but Rikyū lowered them deliberately—to provoke a humble gesture as we bow toward the water. You'll feel that same bodily humility again as we enter the tearoom.

Let's rinse. Any guesses about the meaning of the objects you see here?

Theologian: I've seen these wells and ladles at other temples around Japan. I think they were Buddhist temples, though.

Philosopher: I've seen a smaller version of these along the roadside when I was walking to a bus stop in Osaka.

Guide: That's right. You'll often see purification basins outside Buddhist temples or even in random roadside locations throughout Japan. However, this ritual isn't Buddhist—it's Shinto. Does anyone know anything about Shintoism?

Artist: I don't know much, but I went to a fire festival last summer in a place outside of Kyoto called Sakyo. It was incredible. The monks carried enormous torches through the village. You could smell the burning pine and cedar traveling through the valley long before we arrived. Monks had enormous torches, probably three meters long and twice as thick as telephone poles, carrying them on their shoulders through the crowd and then piled them on an altar in the village center to make a massive bonfire. It was one of my favorite and most surreal experiences in Japan so far.

Guide: It sounds like you attended a *himatsuri* (火祭り), a Shinto fire festival. There are many seasonal Shinto festivals. Any idea what the purpose of the fire might have been?

Artist: I think it also had something to do with ritual purification.

Guide: Exactly. Ritual purification is central to Shinto, and that's the idea behind the water we're using now. One of Rikyū's four tea principles was *sei*—purity—and the lowered *tsukubai* draws directly from Shinto practice. When rinsing the mouth, we're not just cleaning the body but purifying the heart-mind.

Shinto uses all the elements for *harai* (祓い)—not just water and fire, but also salt, wood, and paper. You'll often see Shinto purification basins at Buddhist temples, which shows how smoothly these traditions coexist in Japan.

Aside from a brief period during the Meiji era, when Buddhism was suppressed to promote Shinto as a national religion, they've largely coexisted in harmony.[1] Even today, people don't feel the need to choose—they often identify as both Buddhist and Shinto. You can see this in life rituals too: births and weddings are usually Shinto, while funerals follow Buddhist rites.

Theologian: Was there really no conflict when Buddhism or Daoism first came to Japan and began coexisting with native Shintoism? It's quite rare, isn't it, that foreign religions can move into a new territory or nation and assimilate so peacefully.

Guide: Yes, good point. Let me share some background on Shinto to explain how this kind of peaceful coexistence became possible.

Shinto is considered Japan's only indigenous religion.[2] Its origins are unclear, but scholars suggest various sects may have come together during the Yayoi period, around 300 BCE. Today, it's the largest religious group in Japan, with over 100,000 shrines across the country and a few in East Asia.

Buddhism, Daoism, and Confucianism were brought from China or Korea by missionaries and travelers. Shinto, by contrast, developed entirely within Japan. Like the others, it resists being neatly defined as religion or philosophy—it's often described as a nature or folk religion,[3] or as a "way", similar to Dao.[4]

What makes Shinto especially hard to define is its lack of central organization or hierarchy. Unlike most major religions, it has no founder, sacred text, or official doctrine. Practices vary by region, and there's no single authority overseeing them.[5]

While there's a high degree of regional variation, one thread binding most Shinto sects is their "animism". Rather than worshipping a central figure like Buddha or Christ, Shinto honors nature itself. Nature is seen as alive, animated by spirits called *kami* (神).[6] These can be natural forces, ancestors,ced clan leaders, national heroes, or members of the Imperial family.

While *kami* are sometimes called deities, they're not like western gods. There's no single divine figure—Shinto recognizes hundreds of *kami*, each with their own role, like guarding roads or presiding over ceremonies.[7] Even when *kami* take on human traits—as they sometimes do in modern practice—they aren't outside nature, like a transcendent god. Instead, they're the animating force within nature itself.

And, *kami* are said to be channels of *musubi* (結び), the energy that binds all things. Though invisible, *kami* are felt in nature's movements and rhythms. That's why Shinto holds natural places in special reverence—they're seen as rich with *kami*.

As we discussed with Geidō, the idea of the "way" appears here too. Shinto followers seek harmony with the *kami* through *kannagara no michi* (惟神の道)—the "way of the *kami*". It's a version of *Dao*, but here it's called *michi*, like in *Tetsugaku no michi*.

Philosopher: How exactly does ritual purification fit into animism? Are we more in touch with *kami* spirits if we've been purified with water or fire?

Guide: One reason for purification is to attune ourselves to *kami*—not to see them directly, but to sense their presence in nature. Physical cleanliness is believed to foster spiritual clarity, making us more receptive to *kami* activity.

Kami are thought to have dual aspects: one loving and harmonious the other chaotic and destructive. They animate not just nature but also the social and political world. Most Shinto followers seek the peaceful side, but we shouldn't project western moral frameworks onto this. Shinto doesn't divide actions into good or evil the way many ethical systems do. Even violent forces in nature aren't seen as morally wrong—they're just part of how the world works.

Still, purification is often done to gain the favor of *kami* and avoid their destructive aspects. By washing before entering the tea hut, we aim to clear away physical and spiritual defilements so they don't interfere with the ritual ahead.

Philosopher: Is there a relation at all between this act of cleaning with water and the later act of drinking we'll undertake?

Guide: Yes, absolutely. As I've mentioned, we've undergone several progressive stages of purification—some symbolic, others involving physical actions by the host or ourselves. Until now, these acts have occurred outside the body. By rinsing our hands and mouth, we expand the ritual field to include our corporeity.

Artist: In a way, we're breaking down the internal–external spatial binary, this time with our bodies, aren't we?

Guide: Beautifully put. Yes, our bodies are now vessels where the internal and external are traversed by the ritual elements.

Imagine this, if you can. If you were faced with the task of bringing out the deep existential potential of drinking tea together, if we simply arrived, sat down and drank tea without any preparation, the profound significance of that first sip would be drastically diminished—perhaps lost entirely.

So, we must ask, what do you do if you want to fully actualize the human potential of sharing this ritual together? Would it be enough to brew the tastiest tea possible? Is it a lack of flavor that disallows us from appreciating tea? Probably not. The question becomes: how do we transform such a mundane experience into one of the most philosophically and religiously profound experiences humans can have, while also being the most mundane? How can sharing a cup of tea be a ritual every bit as profound as other rituals, like receiving the body and blood of Christ, a pilgrimage to Mecca, or ayahuasca ceremonies? How do we awaken the immeasurable beauty of our shared humanity in a simple cup of tea?

Theologian: I guess, when we make tea, we don't often take into account so many things that can seem un-related to the tea itself.

Artist: It seems like here, nothing is *un*-related to tea. Everything we do is kind of accumulating.

Philosopher: This is the relational ontological aspect, right? The tea isn't just tea, isn't just an object. It's everything that's not-Tea. It's a relational nexus. A world, not an object.

Guide: Thinking of a cup of tea as a "world"—rather than an object—is perfect. The tea master orchestrates every possible relation to infuse our cups not just with hot water and tea leaves, but with the full presence of everything that can be brought into relation with this simple act: the garden, precisely crafted rituals, architecture, food, dress, scrolls, flowers—all augment the elements of that cup-as-world. So, at the moment we take our first sip, we are, in a literal sense, sipping the entire shared world that has been activated and elevated along the way to the hut.

Artist: I wish I would have been thinking this way from the very beginning.

Theologian: Yes, going all the way back to when we collected water in one of our first meetings.

Guide: Yes, but we shouldn't think too hard. We have to be careful how we frame that eventual experience of drinking the tea. If we expect it to be like moments depicted in other religions—apotheosis or rapture where we transcend this world into some realm of tea bliss—we'll be sadly disappointed. Drinking the tea will be the most normal experience: fully and completely mundane and fully within *this* world. You're even likely to find the astringent taste surprisingly off-putting and the whole experience disappointingly unexciting. The first time I tried the thick tea we'll soon taste, I wanted to spit it out, it was so bitter.

Philosopher: But then you were tasting it as an object, weren't you?

Guide: Good point. Yes. It was so unexpected that my experience was contracted, and I only tasted the tea-as-object. The only relation activated was between molecules and my tongue, not between myself and the entire constellation of aesthetic elements constituting a world.

So, our important question is: how do we shift from a *self* tasting a *thing* to a non-self immersed in tea-as-world?

The difficulty is that it's definitely supposed to be an elevated experience, especially relative to our typical cup of tea, but—we have to be vigilant with this particular point—*it's elevated not by adding to the experience, but by stripping away from it.*

If you're worried about not having enough of the right information to invoke at the moment of drinking the tea, that itself might impede your experience. It's good to understand everything that has gone into putting together such a ritual, but we're not going to have a better experience or transcend into some higher realm by knowing more or thinking better. In fact, it might be better to expect nothing at all.

Artist: Expecting nothing *to happen,* or expecting *nothing* to happen?

Guide: Oh, nice one. I can only say *both-and* to that.

~ *All three smile in mutual unspoken understanding.*

Okay, let's now undertake this next stage of purification. As you can probably imagine, there are specific ways to carry out this ritual. Let me show you.

~ The Guide held the ladle in his right hand, pouring water into his left, then reversing the motion, pouring it into his open right palm. To clean his mouth, he avoids drinking directly from the ladle, instead forms a small basin with his left hand to hold the remaining water, which he then drinks. Finally, he tilts the scoop ninety degrees, allowing the remaining water to rinse the inside of its chamber in preparation for the next guest. Each of the three performs the ritual in turn.

Drinking Philosophy and/or Religion

Philosopher: These ritual movements are really interesting. Can we say these are actually philosophic acts? Or, non-acts?

Theologian: They seem more like religious acts, to me.

Guide: How so?

Theologian: When I think about ritualized ways of drinking or eating, I think about the Christian sacrament of Eucharist or the Muslim Iftar, which are religious. I'm not sure if any of these rituals are considered philosophical, though. I realize that Buddhism and Daoism are in a different category—not strictly philosophy or religion—but, I'm having a hard time imagining how this act of purifying oneself with water can be a philosophical act.

Artist: Or, how drinking tea will be philosophical.

Guide: Yes, these ritual aspects of the tea ceremony do seem more religious than philosophic. And, many great tea figures have described *Chanoyu* as a religious ceremony. Sen Sōshitsu XV himself, says that "Tea is the practice of realization of religious faith," but with the important qualification that it is religious faith "no matter what you believe" (1978).

Others have been more explicit. Okakura Kakuzo who wrote the "The Book of Tea" (1964) had many ways of referring to this aspect of *Chanoyu*, including a "religion of aestheticism", "a religion of the art of life", and "a sacred function at which the host and guest join to produce for that occasion the utmost beatitude of the mundane."

More recently, both native and non-native scholars have analysed the tea ceremony as a religious cosmology.[8] Some have claimed that *Chanoyu* is precisely the kind of ritual that makes it impossible to distinguish between the sacred and the secular (Di Berardino 2018).

There is, however, an important counter voice on this topic. Ueda Makoto claimed "In the tea ceremony man remains within a human world, and in that sense it is not religious . . . The closeness of the tea ceremony to Zen is often exaggerated" (1967, p. 95), His position is based on the belief that the binary between art and religion was never overcome in the medieval arts.

Theologian: But, what about the ritual side of things, specifically. It seems like every inch and every action of the tea ceremony is ritualized. I just don't see anything like that in philosophy.

Guide: If someone watched this ceremony and compared it to what philosophers do, they probably wouldn't see much in common—or anything obviously philosophical. That's partly because academic philosophy today rarely reflects on its own rituals, even though we do have them. They've just become invisible to us.

We tend to assume the way we study philosophy now is the only way—that it's neutral, natural, and non-ritualized. But there have been many different systems for teaching and studying philosophy across cultures and history. Our current western model is just one among many.

If we stick to a narrow, modern definition of philosophy, it's hard to see the tea ceremony as philosophical. But the way we do philosophy today is quite new. Even in the west, philosophy once involved ritual.

Greek scholars used elaborate memory techniques, and Stoics practiced ritual meditations and recitations to prepare for study (Kalmanson 2023). Dialectic itself—the Q&A method—was highly ritualized. Philosophical reading also varied: sometimes done through interpreters or by copying and annotating texts. Outside the west, Indian logic schools held structured debate competitions with judges, and early Buddhist schools used rapid-fire Q&A rituals between teachers and students.

Publishing original research, going to academic conferences, and lecture-style teaching are only a very recent set of rituals we now think are *the only* way of doing philosophy.

And, you might have noticed that becoming part of a university, carrying out one's studies, and concluding them all involve commencement and convocation rituals. Can anyone think of any others?

Artist: Where I did my undergraduate degree, we had very elaborate rituals to mark the beginning and end of our degrees. Our induction and graduation ceremonies were even conducted in Latin.

Guide: If you pursue advanced philosophy or become an academic, you'll encounter plenty of rituals—how to run conferences, introduce speakers, give keynotes, structure talks, or handle criticism.

Unlike the tea ceremony, where rituals are taught explicitly over a lifetime, academic philosophy relies on unwritten rules. You learn by observing and adapting, but the rituals are still there—just rarely named.

So while it may seem different from something like the tea ceremony, the contrast may lie more in how rituals are learned and passed on, not in their absence.

Philosopher: What about the fact that the entire ceremony revolves around a drink? Surely philosophy can't be based on that kind of activity. Maybe a *rational analysis* of the ceremony can be "philosophical", but drinking tea itself can't be philosophy.

Guide: Right, and as just mentioned, ritual drinking tends to be associated with religions—wine in the Christian holy communion, or *kiddush* in Judaism, or the use of *Kapala* in Buddhist ceremonies or sake in Shinto rituals.[9]

But, even within our western philosophic tradition we have a moment where philosophic activity intersects with the act of drinking, don't we?

Philosopher: Oh yes. I think I remember one of Plato's dialogues where a bunch of Athenians gather at a drinking party to talk about beauty or love.

Guide: Right, that's Plato's *Symposium*—the speeches were in praise of *Eros*, the god of love and desire. Events like this are rare in European philosophy,[10] but they followed ritual conventions in ancient Greece and Rome. Learned men gathered for formal meals with structured philosophical discussion.

Like the tea ceremony, everything was regulated—the room size, seating, and utensils. Special pottery was used, postures were prescribed, and food and drink were served in a set order. The offerings, like the speeches, honored gods or the dead. One shared cup, like in *Wabicha*, was passed among guests. The goal was to cultivate virtues like moderation and generosity, all within a strong guest ethic—just like in the tea tradition.

Theologian: Sounds like it's philosophy in practice, and through ritual.

Guide: Yes, very much so.

Like the tea ceremony, the symposium was led by one person—the symposiarch—usually the host. They chose the aesthetic details and guided the ceremony through its stages.

Drinking wasn't as tightly regulated as in tea practice, but it followed ritual rules. You might recall Alcibiades being scolded for disrupting the proper order of speeches and breaking the norms of decorum and moderation.

This shows that ritual can be sacred or secular, religious or philosophical. While religion tends to highlight its rituals, philosophy has its own—spoken and unspoken—that shape how we work. It's also worth asking what academic rituals leave out, since that reveals how the institution shapes our practices.

As for rituals and drinking, there's nothing that necessarily excludes them from the realm of philosophic practice. If the tea ceremony cultivates a guest ethic or embodies principles like emptiness or non-self, then it clearly serves a philosophical function. It may not be "academic", but if we limit our definition of philosophy to the academic definition, then we exclude a big part of that tradition's history, not to mention many of the world's traditions.

Can anyone think of any other differences between philosophy and religion and the tea ceremony?

Philosopher: It seems that in both philosophy and religion, there are typically specific figures we study or worship. Whether it's Plato or Jesus Christ, there's always someone—and they're usually men.

Theologian: Men and the texts they've written.

Guide: Yes, exactly. Unlike many religions, the tea ceremony doesn't require belief in a transcendent deity. When Sōshitsu calls it a form of religious faith, he doesn't mean faith in a transcendent god.

And you're right to mention texts. Unlike most religions, the tea ceremony has no central scriptures. It follows Zen Buddhist pedagogy, focusing on direct master-to-student transmission rather than text-based instruction.

Rikyū is often seen as the "great man" of *Wabicha*, but like Socrates, he left no writings. What we know comes from his students' records and detailed records of his ceremonies.

One of his key innovations was separating the tea ceremony from temple settings. He also made the tea hut *aniconistic*—free of images or icons of the Buddha.

In the end, we shouldn't settle for labeling the tea ceremony simply religion or philosophy, sacred or secular. These categories aren't wrong, but they weren't used in Japan the way we use them. One of the great benefits of engaging with Buddhism, Daoism, or the tea ceremony is how they challenge our western habit of forcing practices into neat, predefined categories.

Why don't we take a short break from our discussions and stroll around the inner garden?

~ The group paused for a moment, then one by one, dispersed and wandered through the garden.

Garden Stroll: Stone and *chi*

Guide: And, how was your stroll? Anything caught your eye?

Artist: I was actually kind of struck by the stone itself. I found myself, at a couple of points, admiring some of the formations throughout the garden.

Guide: The mineral world of the tea garden offers lots to talk about. To appreciate the Japanese aesthetics and even metaphysics associated with stone, we need to challenge some of the ways we've been taught to think about the mineral world. If we can do that, we can really appreciate the deep aesthetic significance of stone and how it might have impacted all of you in the last half hour of meandering, without your realizing.

How do we think about stone in our European intellectual tradition, or "world"?

Theologian: I'm not sure we think about it so much. Unless you're a geologist, the mineral world doesn't seem that important to us.

Guide: Yes, I think you're right. Does anybody know why that might be?

Theologian: Well, maybe because the kind of stones we have here aren't that special. We love the mineral world when it's turned into crystals and precious stones, but these ones in the garden don't have that kind of beauty.

Philosopher: And, stones don't really do anything.

Guide: Don't do anything?

Philosopher: They're inert. Not animated like animal bodies are.

Guide: Okay, let's start there. In our metaphysical tradition—or perhaps our dismissal of certain things—we tend to see anything not alive as just "matter". We're sentient; stone is inert. If it moves, it's only because something else made it move.

Even when we admire stones in a garden, we don't usually see them as meaningful for beings like us—who think, feel, and perceive. Without needing to study metaphysics, we place stone low on the metaphysical scale—as passive, lifeless material.

So let me show you a different way of thinking about stone. For that, we return to China.

Qi

Guide: In early Chinese views of nature, there wasn't a division between two realities or substances—one animate and the other inanimate. All things were understood as being pervaded by a vital energy called *qi* (気).

Has anyone heard of this concept?

Artist: I often hear it in the context of martial arts.

Philosopher: and practices like Tai Chi.

Guide: Yes, exactly. *Qi* was one of the most basic metaphysical concepts in traditional Chinese thought, appearing across art, philosophy, science, and medicine. Many martial arts—like Kung Fu, Aikido, and Kendo—are based on *qi*. You'll also see it in acupuncture, where Traditional Chinese Medicine seeks to balance the body's *qi* flow. Practices like Tai Chi and Qi Gong are movement exercises designed for the same purpose.

Like many Chinese terms, *qi* has a broad range of meanings—breath, air, vapor, energy, or vital force—depending on context. Though some link it to Buddhism, it predates Buddhism in China, appearing in ancient cosmologies as early as the fifth century BCE. It later comes up in Confucianism, Daoism, Chinese Buddhism, and later in Neo-Confucianism.

Artist: Isn't it also related to the art of arranging living spaces?

Guide: You're probably thinking of Feng Shui, a type of geomancy based on *yin-yang* principles. Though popularized recently, it's actually a complex system for arranging spaces to balance *qi* energy.

But, let me tell you a little bit about *qi* itself, so that we can understand how these stones are perceived, and handled within the Japanese garden.

Rather than a division between two separate substances, or any kind of ontological dualism, *qi* energy was thought to be a continuum underlying all reality—stone, minds, and everything in between.

Traditional Chinese thinkers didn't ignore the differences between mind and matter, but unlike western metaphysics, they didn't treat them as separate realities. Instead, they saw one metaphysical continuum—spanning the densest concentration of *qi*—typically stone—and the most rarefied concentration—mind.

So while stone and mind are different, they're not different substances, and one isn't more real than the other. In the west, we've split reality up like this and then have spent a few thousand years trying to put it back together. In *qi* metaphysics, there's no such problem—mind and matter are already part of the same reality.

This helps explain the deep respect Chinese and Japanese traditions had for the mineral world, especially the carefully chosen stones in important gardens. As dense forms of *qi*, stones were thought to help balance bodily energy. This also relates to the cultural reverence for nature and sacred mountains. It may sound mythical to us, but within *qi* metaphysics, it makes perfect sense.

Landscape painters were especially sensitive to *qi* flowing through nature. While geophysical energy usually moves too slowly to notice—except in earthquakes or eruptions—Chinese and Japanese painters developed nomenclature to depict how *qi* moves through the land.

If you've flown over mountain ranges, you've seen their ripple-like patterns. Chinese painters developed a visual grammar for these, with names like "emerging dragon" (出龍), "receding dragon" (退龍), "crouching dragon" (伏龍), and "prosperity dragon" (旺龍). Each came with rules on how to depict them, depending on the painting school.

The ridges and peaks were called "dragon veins" (龙脉, *lung mo*). When a landscape was complete, artists would say, "the dragon veins have been stretched properly." So—with all that in mind, how do you now see the stones in the garden?

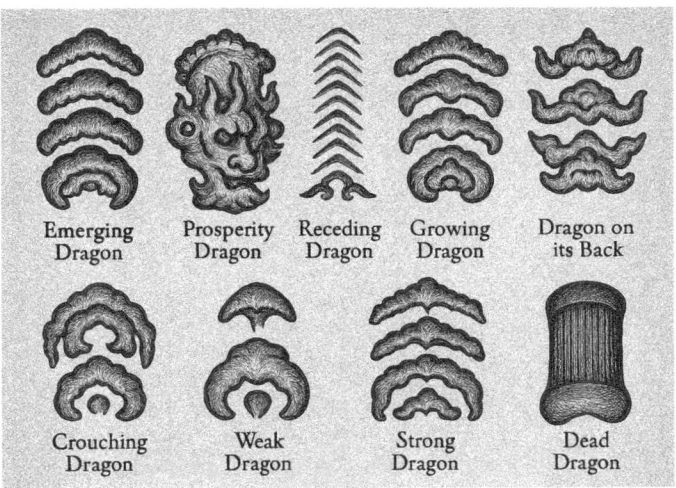

Figure 10.1 *Qi* energy patterns in mountain landscape. R. Loughnane.

Philosopher: It's still quite hard to imagine having anything in common with a stone or the mineral world. I think I'd like to walk around some more with this in mind.

Theologian: . . . me too. That's a good idea.

~ *The group dispersed again and wandered throughout the garden paths.*

Guide: So, what did you notice?

Philosopher: I noticed a stone over there on the path leading to the *tsukubai* had what looked like some kind of twine tied around it.

Guide: Oh yes, that's a *sekimori ishi* (関守石),[11] or a *"keeper of the barrier"*. Any idea what that might be for?

Philosopher: I'm not sure exactly what it meant, but it gave me the feeling that I shouldn't go around it.

Guide: You're maybe more tuned in to the pre-reflective mode of experience than you realized. It seems like you're saying that before you rationally

Figure 10.2 Barrier Stone. (*sekimori ishi*, 関守石) R. Loughnane.

understood or could define the object, you already felt that the stone placed you in a particular orientation, maybe subtly directing your body and motion.

Philosopher: I didn't think of it that way at the time, but maybe, yes.

Guide: See, you're already feeling a sort of continuity with the mineral world. It's nothing particularly unusual—it's just that we don't tend to focus on this aspect of our experience.

There's another aspect to keep in mind: this is one way the tea master can act on our bodies in her absence, through the negative. Your intuition was correct that we shouldn't wander beyond those stones. The *sekimori ishi* is used by the tea master to indicate where we should and should not go. It's one way that she can shape the thematic whole of the ceremony.

Artist: I don't get it. The stone helps her determine the thematic?

Guide: Imagine it's late fall and the early afternoon sun is hitting the maple trees, illuminating their branches and casting long shadows on the leaves scattered below. Perhaps this particular vista reinforces some aesthetic dimension of the day's ceremony, so the tea master would want to gently direct you to increase the chances you'd see it, and away from other areas that might not contribute to the theme.

Or, perhaps in the hut's alcove there's a famous Bashō poem about Mount Fuji in the winter. The host could use the stones to direct you towards a lookout where you glimpse the snowy mountain peaks beyond the garden walls, thus placing you into a visual relation before the linguistic relation you would enjoy within the hut.

If it were another season, and another group with their own particularities, it could be that the host wouldn't have used the stone, or she might have used it somewhere else to direct that group to a different part of the garden.

Artist: When I think back, there was another moment where I found that the stones seemed to pattern my body below the level of my rational reflection. I didn't think about it the first time, but in this last wander through the paths, I could feel that the arrangement of the stones in the path kept me slightly off balance—but not so much that it was uncomfortable.

Guide: That's a great observation. What you described is exactly what the tea garden designer wants to achieve. Throughout the garden, the different patterns of stone are meant to subtly influence how bodies move.

As you noticed, the stones are spread out such that we feel in our body the appropriate speed to walk across them. Unlike a paved road or sidewalk, which don't inherently communicate anything about our movement, the paths in the tea garden clearly suggest limitations on how fast we can move. Those stones, "stepping stones" *tobi ishi* (飛石), are deliberately arranged and spaced out to communicate to us that we should follow them at a moderate or slow speed. We don't have to think about it or reflect on this body–stone relation: Pre-reflectively, we already know what the stones require of our bodies, and we walk the way they demand.

And, sometimes stones are arranged differently to enable us to move with great ease. With hardly a glance, they communicate to us that we need not look down to see where we're stepping, thus freeing our attention to take in the surrounding garden. In contrast, the others are deliberately unevenly arranged, and in this case, they compel us to slow down, focus on every step, and turn our attention inward, away from the broader landscape.

Did anyone encounter a few large flat stones?

Artist: Yes, I do remember one of those. I didn't think about it, but I stood there for quite some time because there was an amazing view of some vines draped over the garden walls.

Guide: Right, these are called "lingering stones" and they're meant to do just that—invite you to pause. Their larger, flat surface offers a sense of stability and comfort, encouraging you to linger and take in the surroundings without worrying about balance.

There are slightly elevated stones, (*Gakumi ishi*)[12] also inviting us to linger a while. You step up onto them and you have the subtle maybe unconscious feeling—or what we called a pre-reflective apprehension—that you've arrived somewhere, so you have the inclination to look around and take in the view from that spot.

The garden designer places these lingering stones where there's something especially captivating—a beautiful sunset, or the first glimpse of the tea hut, perhaps. That's how they use stone to guide guests to see and feel aspects of the garden that reinforce the ceremony's thematics.

The stones are far from incidental or merely decorative—they're a fundamental part of the mineral–body interaction. They don't simply determine *where* we walk, and not even just *how* we walk, they place us into a chosen set of relations to enhance the ceremony's theme. This influence goes deeper than simply directing us along one direction or another. In this sense, the *tobi ishi* paths carry a Buddhist meaning. They symbolize the garden designer's care for our salvation and represent what they believe to be the best spiritual path.

Philosopher: It's interesting to think about how the stone arrangements provoke different bodily movements, but I'm not sure about the idea that it's actually the stones and the paths themselves that change our body and movement. Isn't it simply that we see the stone, cognize the features of the terrain and then decide how to move? It's not that the stone is actually determining our bodily movements—we do.

Guide: Of course, we can observe the surface of a stone walkway, stop to think about how to walk, and then consciously decide and implement those considerations. But if you think about it, we almost never move this way. Once we've learned to walk, we become pre-reflectively intertwined with our environments.

Theologian: Is this another case of *wu wei*? We're neither completely active nor passive?

Guide: There's an element, yes. Obviously, if we're walking across a stone pathway, we're actively propelling our bodies. But, there's also a passivity where we're giving in to what the terrain demands of our body and its movements. As you've noted, below the level of reflection, we can feel how the stones provoke something from our body and its movements without our having to actively calculate or decide.

The Japanese even have a term for this phenomenon: *kowan ni shitagau*, which refers to the "requesting mood of the stone". The stones ask something of us—not through commands that we cognize, not through linguistic positivity—but by gently shaping how we move and orient ourselves in the environment.

Following the Request of Stone

Guide: I realize the idea that a stone "requests" anything might sound absurd, but if we move away from typical western metaphysical dualism—where stone and mind are considered different realities—and instead adopt a psycho-physical continuum like *qi* metaphysics offers, we no longer need to assume such a stark division between our movements and the movements provoked by stones.

The idea of stone having a "requesting mood" is found in one of the more famous texts on Japanese garden design, the eleventh century *Sakuteiki* (作庭記). *Kowan ni shitagau* (乞はんに従う), or "following the requesting mood" of stone, describes not only how we move in a garden but also how a garden designer selects and positions stones to build a garden.

Most people don't realize how complex stone placement in a Japanese garden really is—it takes years to master (Keane 2002). Unlike the western idea of a subject placing an object, the concept of *kōwan ni shitagau* reflects an attunement between a non-self and a non-object. The designer doesn't impose their will but listens to what the stones suggest.

In a Japanese dry landscape garden, the process starts with selecting the "master stone" (*shuseki* 主石), which sets the orientation for all others. Once it is placed, it orients the space in ways that call for the alignment of other minor stones. In this context, stones aren't merely objects, and their placement isn't determined by a subject or self imposing pre-decided plans. The garden designer doesn't make a free choice in the conventional sense of deciding upon a certain placement before constructing the garden, which is then imposed on the materials. Rather, the designer enters into a kind of dialogue with the stone and space, becoming so attuned that they can sense and measure the stone's "mood"—its particular character, weight, texture, and its orientation within the wider relational setting. This attunement allows the stone's own qualities to guide the arrangement, helping the designer discover rather than dictate how the mineral constellations within the garden should unfold. The process reflects a collaborative relationship between designer and material, where human intention and natural form work together rather than one dominating the other.

Artist: But, in the end, the garden design isn't purely natural, right? We can't completely negate or ignore *our own* "requesting mood" as animate beings, can we? Whether when designing a garden or wandering through it.

Guide: Yes, absolutely. Although the Japanese do venerate nature, the stone garden surrounding the tea hut has a high degree of human artifice. The mineral elements, the greenery, and even the trees and shrubs are often meticulously pruned.

However, the principles underlying their design differ greatly from those guiding the gardens around European palaces. The goal isn't to highlight the gardener's self as a great artist but to assist the natural beauty of the stone or tree in *expressing itself*.

Yuriko Saito (1996) offers a helpful contrast with European aesthetics, which often emphasize an "aesthetics of expression"—where the artist uses materials to express themselves, highlighting creativity and originality. She contrasts this with an "aesthetics of discovery", where the artist lets the materials express themselves. In Japanese garden design, this approach is central—nature becomes, if not the only, then at least one of the artists. Individual originality isn't so much in play here.

Philosopher: This is really far away from how western artists understand their relations to their materials.

Theologian: Yeah, we definitely don't tend to think of the material world as wanting to express itself.

Phenomenological body – Tools and "Inter-expression"

Guide: There are, actually, some interesting European and North American art movements that emphasize the "agency of materials"[13], but these are historically speaking very recent. Otherwise, western ontology has largely conceived of matter as inert, making the idea of materials possessing agency, or "requesting" something, more or less inconceivable. The artist has traditionally been the expressive agent, not their materials.

Artist: Some art movements—Process Art, Postminimalism, Arte Povera— have explored material agency in different ways.

Guide: Right, but I don't know of any that offer an ontology explaining how materials can demand something of us or express themselves. Artists may not need one, but since that's our focus, it's worth noting—especially since phenomenology does offer such an ontology. It also creates an intercultural bridge, as both Merleau-Ponty and Nishida, to thinkers subject to comparative research,[14] describe the world as inherently expressive, often using mountains and landscapes as examples. Merleau-Ponty says, "it is the mountain itself which from out there makes itself seen by the painter" (1993, p. 128). Nishida similarly writes, "the mountains and rivers must also be expressive" (1970, p. 35).

Artist: I can see how a landscape *inspires* a painter, but I'm not sure how it has agency. In the end, the artist has to move their bodies to express themselves.

Guide: A good way to approach this is by examining how Merleau-Ponty and Nishida conceive of the artist's body in relation to their tools. Typically, we imagine the body and tools as separate, but both thinkers challenge that division.

Let me read you some quotes. Nishida says that "when painting our body becomes the tip of the brush, when sculpting, the grip of the chisel" (2003, p. 177). And in a later work, "there is an eye at the tip of the artist's brush or the sculptor's chisel" (1973, p. 156).

It might sound like poetic embellishment rather than a literal description of body-tool relations, but this idea aligns with what phenomenology calls the "ecstatic" account of the body.

Do any of you recognize that term?

Theologian: Yeah, it comes up in religious contexts—the idea of being outside of oneself.

Guide: Right. *Ek*, is the Greek for "out" or "outside" and "*stasis*" refers to "standing". So, *ek-stasis*—standing outside of oneself.

Artist: Is this another way of talking about a non-self? The not-A part being the aspect outside of oneself?

Philosopher: The opposite of the circumscribed body—no *perigraptos*.

Guide: In a way, we might say that. Although neither Merleau-Ponty nor Nishida used the term "non-self", they both sought to move beyond subject–object metaphysics, defining the body through its relationships rather than as an isolated entity.

Theologian: Sure, but how can a paintbrush be part of the body? It's always external in some way.

Guide: Let's turn to Merleau-Ponty's account of tool use to answer that. According to him, when we stop reflecting on a tool and instead perceive the world through it—for him, that's when we should include it within our definition of the body.

His key example is the blind person's cane. At first, the cane feels like an awkward object. At this point, the blind person is focused on the contact between the hand and the cane. At this stage, the subject–object binary might seem appropriate to describe the relation. But over time, as the body *intertwines*—to use that term of Merleau-Ponty's again—the focus shifts: the sensitivity no longer obtains between the hand and the cane but between the end of the cane and the ground. He writes, "The blind man's stick has ceased to be an object for him, and is no longer perceived for itself; its point has become an area of sensitivity" (2002, p. 165).

We've all experienced this transition. Initially, a tool demands our attention, but once we become proficient, it moves to the background of awareness, and once it does, it extends our body's capabilities. As Merleau-Ponty puts it, "extend[ing] the scope and active radius of touch" (ibid.)

Artist: That describes my experience with tools, but I don't know—I still feel like there's a dividing point between my body and my tools, even if I'm completely used to them.

Guide: Of course. From one perspective, the subject–object divide can always appear, especially when we revert to the reflective stance. But phenomenologists distinguish between two ways of viewing the body, using the German terms *Leib* and *Körper*. *Körper* refers to the body as an object, while *Leib* is the lived body—the body from a first-person perspective, within experience. From that perspective, oppositions like subject–object or body–tool become mostly irrelevant. When we step outside and reflect on experience we get those binaries, but they aren't part of lived experience itself.

Philosopher: So, the ecstatic body is the body extending itself through tools? It sounds like another way not-A becomes part of A. Do Merleau-Ponty and Nishida also have a negative ontology?

Guide: With Nishida, yes. With Merleau-Ponty, he's less explicit early on, but in his later writings, he increasingly invokes the language of the negative.[15]

Philosopher: But we're talking about the body extending through tools. What about landscapes being expressive?

Guide: Let's take one more step to get there.

We now have the ecstatic body, but not yet in terms of its moving or expressive aspect. The challenge is overcoming the idea that the artist is the sole expressive agent, the active element, while the world remains passive.

Artist: When I think about my artistic work, I do feel, at first, that I'm highly volitional—I have to put in all the work, do the research, deliberate, make decisions. I feel like a self. But when a work gains momentum, it seems to take on a life of its own. Of course, I'm still moving my body, but it often feels like my efforts are about keeping up with something compelling me forward, channeling something beyond myself, rather than directing the work strictly on my own. There's a kind of non-action—or maybe something like *kōwan ni shitagau*.

Guide: I think you're perfectly in line with Merleau-Ponty and Nishida on this. Nishida's term for what you're describing is "Inter-expression" (*hyōgen-teki kankei* 表現的関係).[16] Instead of the artist being the sole expressive agent, he writes, "In artistic activity, we neither structure things conceptually nor imitate things merely passively. Things beckon and move us. Things become the self and vice versa" (1970, p. 179).

Let me read you a longer passage from his essay "The Historical Body":

> *An artwork combines both—subjective activity and objective result.... If one speaks of an opposition of subject and object, the artist acts out of his subjectivity and at the same time he is acted upon from the side of the object. The artwork is realized from a mutual interaction—or reciprocal transaction—of subjectivity and objectivity.*
>
> (1998, p. 40).

We see this same reciprocal expression in Merleau-Ponty. He writes that every artistic act is "moved by some impact of the world which [they] then restore to the visible through the traces of a hand" (1993, p. 127). In any simple movement, the artist is "receiving and giving in the same gesture" (1973, p. 11).

The artist isn't the sole agent—they "lend [their] body to the world" he says, to reveal what it wants to show. Merleau-Ponty says it's "impossible to distinguish between who sees and who is seen, who paints and what is painted" (1993, p. 129).

And here's one final passage from my notebook—Merleau-Ponty writes that Cézanne didn't impose his vision on the world but rather "released that meaning" which was already present. As he puts it, "it was the objects and the faces themselves as he saw them that demanded to be painted, and Cézanne simply expressed what they wanted to say." The painter becomes one who listens to what the world wishes to communicate.

So, we can see that Merleau-Ponty and Nishida are very much aligned in their views on artistic action and expression. Both challenge the very European idea of the artist as the sole creative or expressive agent. They don't have the exact concept *kōwan ni shitagau*, but their concepts of expression share the basic idea of artistic activity where the material world isn't simply inert matter but expresses itself through the artist's body.

Theologian: If we take this idea back to our first meeting, maybe we could say that *you* can't design a garden: a garden is always a co-creation with nature.

Guide: Yes, exactly. A self can't design a Japanese tea garden. It's not an object a subject creates.

Unlike grand western gardens, often designed to control nature and showcase the designer's artistic brilliance, Japanese gardens are about submitting to nature—a way of practicing non-self. Zen priests created them not just for meditation, but to cultivate this very attitude.

Whereas a western gardener might start with a plan and impose it on the land, the Japanese gardener works in dialogue with nature. One begins with reason, the other with observation. Saito writes—

> *The measure of artistic excellence in Japanese gardens can only be phrased in a paradoxical way: they are successful to the extent that human artifice seems absent, that is, the ideal gardener lets nature be the guide in determining the particular design, instead of imposing an overall scheme on individual materials and forcing them to conform to the preconceived plan, irrespective of their own characteristics.*

(1996 p. 59)

Guide: She further explains that this approach to garden design means that "the garden looks as if it simply 'became' rather than was 'made into' one." This is the paradox: intervening in nature to bring it to a higher expression of itself, rather than an expression of the artist.

What about our Theologian, any observations on your stroll through the garden?

Theologian: I was kind of surprised how little time seemed to pass. When we first set out from the waiting arbor, I thought I would only walk around for a few minutes before I had seen everything. But, what must have been a very short departure seemed to last quite a long time, and felt somewhat separate from my prior experience here in the garden.

Philosopher: I was a little surprised too, but not so much about how much time had passed, but how vast this small space felt. It actually looked very minuscule from my earlier perspective on the bench, but now, having returned, it doesn't feel like there were any boundaries limiting it.

Guide: Thanks for those observations. This brings up some important questions about space and time, but perhaps we'll pause things for now and return tomorrow to resume our discussion of those topics.

But, that's about all the time we have today. We'll pick things up tomorrow, but we won't meet here. We're going to discuss one of the most important and well-known Japanese aesthetic principles, which I'm sure you've all heard of; that is, *wabi-sabi*. Since this principle is most beautifully embodied in Japanese pottery, we'll meet at the Raku Museum and workshop and discuss *wabi-sabi* and Raku pottery there.

Meet you there tomorrow!

11

Wabi-Sabi, Raku and Zen

Pottery

Guide: Welcome back! We're now at one of Japan's most important cultural heritage sites. As you know, this is the Raku Museum, and the Raku workshop, built on these very grounds in the Momoyama period, almost 400 years ago, and rebuilt in 1855. The tradition and techniques of making Raku pottery have been passed down almost unchanged throughout the family's lineage. The museum was set up by Raku Kichizaemon (*Kakunyū* XIV, 1918–80)—a fourteenth-generation descendant of the Raku family—and houses many of the family's masterpieces.

Let's step inside and meet our guide. He's a seventeenth-generation descendant of the *Raku* clan, so you'll notice he goes by the name honorific, *Raku*.

Raku Oie: Welcome! Great to see you again!

Guide: Great to see you, Raku Oie! *Ohisashiburi*!

These are our students. They're very eager to learn about the *Raku* tradition.

Can you tell us a little bit about the history of pottery in Japan?

Raku Oie: Yes, absolutely. Follow me and I'll take you into the museum.

While some tea-related pottery was inspired by Chinese ceramics brought to Japan during the Tang Dynasty (eighth century), Japan also has a long-standing pottery tradition going back to the Neolithic Jōmon period, over 10,000 years ago.

In the west, pottery has often been seen as craft rather than fine art. In Japan, it's highly esteemed—some teaware are considered national treasures, on par with major works of painting, calligraphy, or sculpture.[1]

Japanese ceramics include many styles, some with bold designs and vivid glazes. But *Raku* ware (楽焼, *raku-yaki*) stands apart. As you can see, these bowls are unglazed, with subdued earthy tones, rough and uneven—prized in *Wabicha* for their simplicity and natural beauty.

Figure 11.1 Raku Pottery. (*raku-yaki*, 楽焼). R. Loughnane.

Guide: Can you tell us a little bit more about the history of the *Raku* style? How it came to be so intimately related to *Wabicha*.

Raku Oie: This brings us back to the sixteenth century and Sen no Rikyū. Have you discussed him?

Guide: Yes, Sanada-san gave us a great lecture on Rikyū a few days ago when we visited the Urasenke Institute.

Raku Oie: Perfect, as you know, he was instrumental in popularizing the tea ceremony. Part of that involved seeking out ceramicists to create new designs aligned with the *Wabicha* aesthetic he was creating. This led him to a collaboration with the potter Sasaki or "Raku" Chōjirō (長次郎).[2]

As an alternative to the highly sophisticated Chinese porcelain that had long been admired, Rikyū favored rustic, hand-made Japanese-style earthenware and pottery. As you can see, rather than being crafted according to the aesthetic expectations of the nobility, Raku works were more utilitarian in design—designed for everyday use—more for the farmer than for an aristocrat or high-ranking dignitary.

Let's go into the workshop and I can show you the materials and techniques my family has been using for centuries.

~ The group followed Raku Oie from the museum to the workshop.

This is where my family's descendants and some apprentices work. If you take a close look at the materials we use, you can see that the clay is quite crude—not the silky smooth kind you might have seen potters use. We fire finished pieces at lower temperatures than most ceramicists would, using techniques more akin to how rooftiles would have been fired in medieval times.

As for the form, notice that the cups and bowls come out with these broad bottoms, which make them perfect for kneading tea and thick walls to insulate and keep the liquid warm.

Artist: Is their un-evenness deliberate, or is that just this particular bowl?

Raku Oie: Oh yes, it's absolutely deliberate. That irregularity is one of the most distinctive features of the style. *Raku* pieces are hand-rolled, not on a potter's wheel, which delivers greater consistency of form and uniformity across pieces. In contrast, the shape of *Raku* ware can't be fully predicted until it emerges from the kiln. Each piece has some irregularities, is never symmetrical, and when glazes are used, they're generally applied unevenly. Look here—you can see the rough and porous clay shows through in certain spots.

These intentional imperfections are key to the style. They make the pieces feel unfinished, inviting hosts and guests to complete them through use over time. This aligns with Rikyū's philosophy of yielding to nature rather than imposing control.

When *Raku* spread to the west, a new practice was added: placing the hot piece into a container with combustible materials like paper or animal hair. The resulting smoke and ash patterns emerge naturally, reflecting the materials' own dynamics—very much in line with Japanese and *geidō* aesthetics.

Wabi-Sabi

Guide: Oie-san, we're all very eager to learn about the *wabi-sabi* aesthetic. Can you explain how this principle relates to *Raku* pottery, and how it evolved alongside *Wabicha*?

Raku Oie: Yes, it is really one of the most important aesthetic principles binding the *Raku* lineage with the tea ceremony.

At its core, *wabi-sabi* evokes solitude and a deep melancholy for impermanence. Hermits and farmers lived with a strict economy of humble possessions—

nothing shiny or new. Their way of life and surroundings shaped the ethos of *wabi-sabi*.

Out of this austerity grew an appreciation for simple objects that showed the passage of time—not just through human use, but how nature had shaped them, rounding edges, smoothing surfaces, or making them rough and worn.

Part of the *wabi-sabi* aesthetic is finding beauty in the imperfections that emerge over time through human use. It's not the bold beauty of something new or flashy, but a quiet, subtle presence that blends into its surroundings—revealing itself as powerfully evocative only to those who take the time to really see it.

More broadly, *wabi-sabi* refers to an aesthetic tied to raw materials shaped by time and weather. These aren't glossy tea utensils, but objects that bear traces of long use—wood worn by footsteps, bowls darkened by hands, teapots bound with decade's old frayed twine, monastery walls weathered by wind and rain. Objects worn down, softened by the elements, material bodies disclosing nature as an expressive force.

A *wabi-sabi* object isn't fully formed when it leaves the kiln. Its beauty emerges through a slow collaboration between user, item, and nature. With time, edges soften, colors fade, and simple, natural lines appear. Beauty resides in the absence of embellishment or ostentation. No ornamentation or excess.

These items serve their function, and their beauty comes from that. A spoon, rake, or sandal is made with the bare minimum. Instead of showing off the artistry of human effort through polish or decoration, effort was made to appear effortless—revealing the quiet beauty of the materials themselves: wood, stone, bamboo, grass, or clay.

While these are the aesthetic features discernible, especially in *Wabicha*, they aren't merely aesthetic but have deep philosophical and soteriological significance, resonating with principles of impermanence, simplicity, and harmony with nature.

A key feature of *wabi-sabi* is the patina that builds up over time. The most valued tea bowls develop subtle, uneven shades through years of use. Take this one—it started with a uniform surface, but after nearly 300 years, the touch of many tea masters has left behind oils and airborne particles that shaped its texture and tone.

The same bowl would look differently if it would have been in different air, not so close to the sea, if it would have been held for decades in the hands of a tea master with different body chemistry, or a different manner or rhythm of moving in tandem with tea implements. A bowl's appearance would vary depending on how it was cleaned and whether it was air-dried in the sun or tucked away in the darkness of a cupboard. What we might instinctively try to wipe away from our own teacups is, in fact, this record of relationality accumulating on the objects we use.

Guide: That's fascinating, Oie-san.

My Japanese isn't so great. Maybe you can share with us some of the etymological details surrounding *wabi-sabi*?

Raku Oie: Yes, as for the term itself, *wabi* has been translated in many different ways. Originally, the verb *wabu* expressed a sentiment of discouragement, whereas the adjective *wabishi* implied "helplessness and an inconsolable emotional state and . . . the dreariness of life in wretched surroundings, being reduced to a threadbare condition" (Hirota 1995). As the term evolved into an aesthetic principle, it came to signify something along the lines of a rustic or austere beauty rooted in insufficiency.

Before becoming associated with the tea ceremony, *wabi* was more of a cultural ideal associated with love, but eventually shifted, around the end of the fifteenth century, towards an emphasis on the aesthetics associated with the poverty of the reclusive hermit. This semantic shift was largely influence by the tea masters you might have already discussed, Takeno Jō'ō, who, in turn, drew inspiration from the poet Sōgi. In his seventies, Sōgi began interpreting *wabi* in new ways in his writings.[3]

In his "Letter on Wabi" (詫びの文 1956), Jō'ō promotes an unassuming attitude of "open straightforwardness" (*shōjiki*), described as "deeply modest and considerate, and free of arrogance". He also associates *wabi* with the quiet sadness of approaching winter, reflecting its connection to simplicity and transience.

As *wabi* evolves, it increasingly accentuates sadness as a melancholy form of beauty. Through things like old worn tea utensils, it evokes the bitter loneliness of living alone in nature—the melancholy associated with a lack of human contact and paucity of materials connected to the ideal of the reclusive monk.[4]

However, the more subtle nuance the term has accrued is psychological, rather than material. It wasn't simply the lack of human contact, belongings, or wealth that were the most definitive of *wabi*, but the state of mind such absences provoked. The *wabi* aesthetic was cherished because the general insufficiency allowed the farmer or the hermit to reflect on suffering and impermanence in a way not possible amidst the distractions associated with pursuing abundance and wealth. In this sense, it is a profoundly spiritual aesthetic, aiming to guide the practitioner to a freedom beyond the material world.

Daisetsu Suzuki encapsulates this idea, explaining that *wabi* is

> *to be poor and yet to feel inwardly the presence of something of the highest value, above time and social position: this is what essentially constitutes wabi.*
>
> (1973, p. 22)

Guide: There's also an element of quiet political protest in the *wabi* aesthetic, isn't there?

Raku Oie: There very much is. It was an attempt to counter the otherwise ostentatious style associated with the *Shoin* tea ceremony and its displays of wealth and power. The integration of *wabi* into the tea ceremony aimed to displace and shift the power of aristocratic aesthetics, which venerated expensive and rare imported Chinese utensils.

The poverty of *wabi* also sensitizes one to the sorrow of the present and the longing for a real or imagined past when times were better. Authors such as Kenkō developed an entire aesthetics based on recognizing that the true beauty of things are recognized only when they are gone. The moon, obscured by the clouds is more beautiful than the full moon in a previously clear sky. In his *Tsurezuregusa* he writes "Cherry blossoms are better after they scatter, the moon is better on nights when it rains."[5]

Guide: We've spoken about how the small hut has great spatiality, and we'll later discuss how the tiny *haiku* is the most expansive poetic form. What about *wabi?* Is it strictly an aesthetic of poverty and privation, a "less than" kind of aesthetic?

Raku Oie: I think your intuition is right. In poverty lie great expansive worlds. Let me read you a quote from a scholar of the tea ceremony, Hirota:

> *even amid insufficiency, one is moved by no feeling of want. . . if you lament insufficiency as privation, if you complain that things have been ill-disposed—this is not wabi. Then you are indeed destitute.*
>
> (1995, p. 275)

Artist: What about the second part? You're talking about *wabi*, but does *sabi* convey similar aesthetic ideas?

Raku Oie: The *sabi* aesthetic is related to *wabi* but emphasizes different qualities. Literally meaning "rust" or "to become desolate" (*sabireru* 寂れる), *sabi* refers to the patina objects gain from contact with other things and from time spent in certain environments. It's also tied to the image of the solitary monk in harmony with nature.

Sabi often describes weathered, spare, even cold-looking objects or spaces—like the desolate landscapes in Japanese painting. Because these patinas form slowly, *sabi* values the aged, used, and time-worn, linking objects to the past.

Have any of you come across the Japanese aesthetician and art historian Tanizaki Jun'ichiro?

Artist: Yes, we studied one of his books in a Japanese Studies class—*In Praise of Shadows*.

Raku Oie: It's really one of the masterpieces of writing on Japanese aesthetics. There's a great quote here which evokes *sabi* aesthetics.

> We do not dislike everything that shines, but we do prefer a pensive luster to a shallow brilliance, a murky light that, whether in a stone or an artifact, bespeaks a sheen of antiquity. . . . We love things that bear the marks of grime, soot, and weather, and we love the colors and the sheen that call to mind the past that made them.
>
> (Tanizaki 1977, p. 11)

Taken together, the meanings of *wabi* and *sabi* are quite broad, actually. And, you'll find many authors popularizing these principles lately. Some other terms you might come across in relation are: *Fukinsei* (不均斉, asymmetry, irregularity), *Kanso* (簡素, simplicity), *Shizen* (自然, without pretense, natural), *Datsuzoku* (脱俗, unbounded by convention, free), and *Seijaku* (静寂, tranquility). Each is distinct, but in one way or another *Raku* pottery embraces almost all of these within its *wabi* ideal.

Guide: Oie-san, thank you for your great generosity! This has been a real blessing for us. It will illuminate so much of what lies ahead.

Raku Oie: You're very welcome. I hope the rest of your learning and the ceremony goes very well.

> ~ *The group left the workshop and wander through the city streets, eventually arriving on the grounds outside Daitoku-ji temple.*

Guide: Okay, let's go into the garden here and have a seat under these black pines.

Theologian: Is this a Buddhist temple?

Guide: It is indeed, and perhaps one of the most relevant for us.

It's called Daitoku-ji temple (大徳寺), or "Temple of Great virtue" and it is the cradle of the *Wabicha* aesthetic and deeply intertwined with the Way of Tea. Murata Jukō, the "founder" of *Wabicha* we spoke of trained here. And Rikyū was closely associated with Daitoku-ji, having helped design the gardens and tea huts of several of its subtemples.

Overall, Daitoku-ji embodies the *wabi-sabi* spirit: imperfection, humility, impermanence, and rustic simplicity.

Furthermore, it is one of the more important temples in Kyoto for the Zen lineage of Buddhism, which is what I'd like to speak to you more about now.

Philosopher: Is this where the Buddhist monk we spoke of practiced?

Guide: You mean Dōgen? No, although he was a Zen practitioner, he was part of the Sōtō lineage, whereas this is a Rinzai temple, in fact, the head temple of the Rinzai sect.

But, let's not worry too much about the details regarding the various sects. Can anyone tell me anything about Zen in general?

Zen Buddhism

Artist: I don't know much, but Zen does seem to have a very particular aesthetic—very minimal. Their robes are gray and black rather than the saffron and gold colors worn by other Buddhist monks.

Theologian: And, I think meditation is a really big part of that tradition. Don't they meditate facing a wall?

Guide: Yes, you're both right. Zen does have a unique aesthetic and is deeply rooted in practice and meditation. Most schools of Buddhism stress meditative practices rather than speculative inquiry, but Zen puts even greater emphasis on practice. The Japanese term Zen (禅) is a transliteration of the Chinese term *Chán* (禪), which itself is a transliteration of the Sanskrit word *dhyāna* (ध्यान), meaning meditation.

Seated meditation, or "zazen" (座禅) is at the core of all Zen schools, yet other meditative techniques play significant roles—*kinhin* (経行) or walking meditation, along with other linguistic and sutra recitational practices (*nenju* 念誦), mantra recitation, chanting (*dhāranī*), and in some cases fasting, ritual prostrations (*raihai* 礼拝), martial arts (*budō* 武道), long group practice (*sesshin* 接心), and of course the aesthetic practices, or *Geidō* we've been discussing—these are all part of various Zen traditions.

Zen claims to be a "a special transmission outside the scriptures."[6] Some have interpreted this as anti-intellectual, but as you can imagine, things are never so simple. While Zen prioritizes meditation and claims to reject textual learning, it nonetheless endorses studies, and adheres to a substantial body of canonical texts. As part of the Mahāyāna tradition, Zen follows many foundational sutras—the Platform Sutra, Heart Sutra, Lotus Sutra, Laṅkāvatāra Sutra, Avatamsaka Sutra, Dhyāna Sutras, Tathāgatagarbha Sutras, and Prajñāpāramitā Sutras, all conveying the teachings of the Buddha.

And this brings us to what is probably the second most recognizable aspect of Zen Buddhism—*kōan* practice. Does anyone know anything about this? It's made its way into popular culture recently.

Philosopher: When a teacher asks something like "What is the sound of one hand clapping" or "What did your face look like before you were born?"

Guide: That's right. Those are two of the most well-known examples. In fact, there are extensive collections of *kōans*, such as the *Blue Cliff Record* (*Hekiganroku* 碧巌録). Kōan practice became a central feature of the Rinzai school of Zen. But what do you think is the purpose of engaging with questions that seem absurd or paradoxical?

Philosopher: I can't imagine what the right answer would be to one of these kinds of questions.

Guide: That's exactly the point. Attempting to answer *kōans* is ultimately futile because there really is no rational or even correct answer. The point is to try to break our attachment to rationality itself. Zen masters were even said to use shock tactics or sometimes even violence to jolt practitioners free from their reliance on logical thinking.

Ultimately, the goal is a non-conceptual wisdom (*prajñā*) arising from direct insight rather than conceptualization or memorized sutra passages. There's a funny saying in Zen—*yako-zen* (野狐禅), or "wild fox Zen"—which refers to intellectual understanding not supported by direct experience. But, there's another side to the coin: the Zen *temma* (禅天魔) or "Zen devil" is someone with experience but no intellectual capacity to grasp it (Hori 2000).

There are many schools of Japanese Zen Buddhism and even more in Chan. There's Sōtō and Rinzai we already spoke about, but there's also a few small sects such as Obaku, and Fuke-shū, and the esoteric school of Kwan Um School.

While tea isn't the only Zen-related aesthetic practice, it has deep roots in Zen history, reaching back to China and India. Chan monks were the first to develop ceremonial tea drinking, sharing a single bowl before images of the Buddha (Kumarasuriyar 2011). By the thirteenth century, tea rituals were mostly confined to Zen temples. When the tea ceremony took its definitive form, key figures like Shukō, Jō'ō, and Rikyū had all trained in Zen monasteries.

Throughout history, many key figures in the tea tradition have understood it as a Zen practice. Sōtan, Rikyū's grandson and author of "The Record of Zen Tea" (*Zencharoku* 禅茶録) puts it most famously when he wrote "Tea and Zen are of one taste (*cha zen ichimi*)" (Hirota 1995). He further claims that

> the mind of tea is precisely the mind of Zen. Whoever puts aside the mind of Zen does not have the mind of tea, and whoever does not know the flavor of Zen does not know the flavor of tea.
>
> (Ludwig 1981, p. 368)

Others have echoed this sentiment,[7] most notably Sen Sōshitsu XV, who stated that "Chanoyu is a popular expression of Zen" (1970, p. 8). Even western commentators such as Steve Odin writes that

> *chanoyu* is the Zen experience of a calm and clear mind culminating in *muga*, or ecstatic selflessness, through meditation upon those arts and crafts which manifest the aesthetic ideal of *wabi*.
>
> (1988, p. 35)

Two final points to slightly complicate this story. Firstly, although Zen is typically treated as the primary—or even sole—influence on the Japanese tea ceremony, elements of the Pure Land sect of Buddhism also play a role (Porcu 2008). Some scholars note that both Shukō and Jō'ō make references to Pure Land, but the most striking example is the "One Page Testament of Rikyū" (*Rikyū ichimai kishōmon* 利休一枚起請文) attributed to but likely not written by Rikyū, is modeled on the main proponent of Pure Land, Hōnen's "One Page Testament" (*Ichimai Kishōmon* 一枚起請文). In this text, Rikyū urges practitioners to abandon contemporary obsessions with tea conventions and return to Hōnen's teachings, which had inspired him. With this, Rikyū re-invokes the religious sentiment of Pure Land Buddhism Hōnen promoted, and *suki* as a way of life of the hermit—seeking Amida Buddha's Pure Land through an attunement to the impermanence of all things.[8]

Philosopher: Maybe it's similar to the first line of the *Daodejing*. The Zen that is called Zen is not the permanent Zen.

Guide: Dōgen would definitely agree. In his *Butsudō* fascicle, he wrote,

> *Those who randomly call themselves by the name "Zen sect," which has never existed in India in the west or in the eastern Lands, from the past to the present, are demons out to destroy the Buddha's truth. They are the Buddhist patriarchs' uninvited enemies.*
>
> (2008, p. 88)

Guide: Unless you have any questions, let's take a walk and see a few of the temple's sites.

~ *The group wandered together to one of the temple's tea huts.*

Guide: Here's one of the main tea huts on the Daitoku-ji grounds. This is the Jukō-in (聚光院) subtemple and aside from this beautiful tea hut, Rikyū is actually buried here. It's considered the spiritual home of the Urasenke school. It was patronized by the Sen family throughout centuries and contains artifacts and architectural features aligned with Rikyū's ideals.

Artist: This seems like the perfect place to do our ceremony. Why didn't you organize it here?

Guide: I can't take you to a tea ceremony here.

Philosopher: . . . but you couldn't take us to the other garden either, but we were there.

Guide: Yes, in this case, it's just that it's not open to the public.

You're right, though. It is perhaps the most historically significant for our purposes, let me take you to a lesser-known subtemple,

~ *The group strolled together to the Zuihō-in subtemple.*

Theologian: That's odd. Why is there a statue of the Virgin Mary in a Zen temple?

Guide: Yes, good that you noticed that. This is actually a rare touchpoint in the Japanese tea world between east and west. This hut was founded in 1535 by Ōtomo Sōrin, a daimyō and tea practitioner who was baptized into the Jesuit order.

As we can see, the garden and hut have several elements of cross-cultural symbolism with a fusion of Christian and Zen elements, most prominently that statue you noticed.

And, Sōrin wasn't the only powerful daimyō to convert to Christianity who participated in and impacted the tea ceremony. Before the Tokugawa period when Christians were persecuted, there was a brief window in the late 1500s where tea practice evolved in dialogue with Europe. Jesuit missionaries in particular were drawn to the refined and spiritual character of tea practice, seeing it as a correlate to Christian asceticism, and a bridge between cultures.

Although the impact on the ceremony was not substantial, this short moment in *Wabicha* history shows us that tea can be a site of inter-cultural encounter.

But, that's it for today. There's many more subtemples with their own tea huts here, so feel free to wander around and check them out. Otherwise, that's all for today. See you back at our tea garden tomorrow!

12
Space and Time

Phenomenological Space and Time: *Ma* and Betweenness

Guide: Welcome back to the garden. I hope you had a good rest. Let's head into the inner *roji* again and pick up on the topic we left off with the day before yesterday.

If you'll recall, one of you commented on how little time passed in what seemed like a quite substantial stroll, and another made a similar comment, but about space, and how you were surprised that such a small garden could feel so expansive.

Do these observations remind you of anything we've spoken about?

Artist: About how the small hut is so expansive.

Philosopher: . . . how the smallest poem is the biggest.

Theologian: . . . about the garden not being a place you can take us to.

Guide: Good, yes. With little exception, western philosophers have conceived of time and space, mostly implicitly, within the law of non-contradiction. Spaces are either large or small; times are either short or long.

But, within a relational context, in the formlessness of the Buddhist notion of *śūnyatā* or emptiness, when we consider things like poems or tea huts as "worlds", then small can be big, and short, very long.

Why should this way of thinking still strike us as somewhat odd regarding space and time?

Philosopher: Space is an objective dimension—it might *feel* smaller or vaster, but ultimately it is an objective magnitude. Maybe what explains our different experiences is that there's a subjective element involved, since feeling it as larger or smaller depends on our individual perceptions.

Guide: Yes, that's what our western philosophic and scientific tradition have taught us about space and time. They're absolute, objective facts of the world that exist outside of our minds or independent of subjectivity. Space is thought of almost like a container within which other things exist, and time is just a series of "now" points, one after the other. As you noted, an *objective* magnitude cannot be both A and not-A, it can't be both a long *and* short time or distance.

In this sense, despite innovations in twentieth-century physics, our "world" remains mostly Newtonian when it comes to space and time. We continue to think of them as "absolute", and this is despite over a century of thinking about space and time that have challenged this model.

Theologian: If there have been innovations in our conceptions of space and time, why haven't these become part of our "world"?

Guide: That's a great question—and honestly, I'm not sure. While Einstein and quantum theory radically changed how physicists understand space and time, I don't think those ideas have reshaped our everyday sense of the world the way Newtonian physics has.

And, it's not about knowing or not knowing these newer theories. Remember, ideas shape our world not because we think about them, but because we don't. As Husserl put it, the lifeworld isn't something we add to experience—it's the pre-reflective background we think from.

My only conjecture—and I haven't worked this out yet—is that shifting our current background might require a type of practice, an active pursuit of different ways of experiencing. Perhaps moving beyond the Newtonian idea of space-as-container-of-objects, seeing things as non-objects, as empty, relational objects requires the type of meditative practices Buddhists engage in. Or, maybe we can derive a new conception of space from experience within the tea ceremony.

Okakura, for example, described the tearoom as presenting a "theory of the non-existence of space to the truly enlightened" (1964, p. 37). And, enlightenment takes dedicated practice. Although we're not going to engage in meditative practice today, we can think of this highly orchestrated environment as being designed to enable us to experience emptiness. If that might be possible, we should expect that our experience of space and time should go beyond absolute, objective magnitudes.

This is another reason why instruments to measure space or time are strictly prohibited within the tea hut, and why we left our watches in the changing room. Our host is trying to help us have an experience beyond objective time and space and those instruments might fool us into thinking that quantifiable time or space are the only versions, or the more real versions.

Light within the tearoom is carefully modulated so as to shape the experience of time. The typical progression from light to dark is somewhat reversed: It's preferable to have a slightly darker start to the ceremony and more lighting in the latter half (Keisen 2019). Tea huts are oriented, window openings are designed, and materials chosen to either block or allow sunlight, all to provoke different experiences of time and space. This use of light is another innovation associated with Rikyū's *Wabicha*.

Space as *Ma*

Theologian: Can you say a little bit more about how space or time are empty, or don't exist?

Guide: Remember, for something not to exist, for it to be empty, negated, it's *not* for it to exist *in no way at all*, but for it to exist in a different way, a non-objective, non-essential way. As a thing constituted by its relations, not a circumscribed object or absolute dimension.

Theologian: Okay, so space and time as relational. That seems intuitively to make sense.

Guide: It is objects that are typically thought to be real, but what's between them doesn't tend to have the same status. But, in a relational ontology, it's what's between that is most real. Relations are what make things what they are. So, it shouldn't be surprising that even when thinking of space or time, the Japanese focus not only on specific points *in space*, or moments *in time*, but on the significance of the spatially and temporally "between".

The Japanese term for space and time as "betweenness" or relationality, is "*ma*" (間), and it has several key features distinguishing it from the conceptions dominating our western world.[1]

Ma is translated as "interval", "gap", "pause", "between", or "the space between two parts". The kanji combines the radical for doorway (門) with the sun (日), invoking the image of the sun shining through gates.

In the western tradition, space and time are usually treated as abstract and separate from other aspects of existence, thinkable as *just space* or *just time*. In contrast, the Japanese concept of *ma* sees them as relational and contextual—for example, as the interval between people, as the rest in music, silence between lines in a poem, the negative space between objects in paintings or calligraphy, and also timing within Japanese *noh* or *rakugo* performances. In all these cases, space and time are not abstracted away from, but are deeply entangled with human existence.

Ma is so foundational that the character appears in the name we give human beings, *ningen* (人間), signaling that the Japanese understanding of existence itself is relational, not based on one's circumscribable *internal* essence, but what is *between* us and others. We are not objects but intervals. Sen Sōshitsu XV writes that "one becomes truly human through interaction with another", which is particularly important for *Chanoyu*, where "host and guest are in harmony . . . merg[ing] into a single entity that transcends their respective roles" (1979, p. 40).

To grasp *ma*, we need to move beyond abstract ideas of space and time and see it as a "cultural paradigm as a fundamental way of 'seeing' things—within the culture of Japan." (Pilgrim 1986, p. 32). As such, *ma* has an even broader range of meanings, referring to a pause or silence, or the act of listening to the other. A good conversation, for example, needs *ma* (Kondo 1985).

Let me see if I can find a quote from another scholar of Japanese aesthetics, Marcello Ghilardi who puts it very much in line with the dividing–connecting aspect of the *kire* aesthetic principle and Nishida. Oh yes, here it is:

> *Ma is a sort of aesthetic perceptive and emotional awareness coming up from a fissure, and implies a cut, a discontinuity . . . yet it involves or creates a link, a passage, a gateway or continuity, otherwise there would not be any recognition of this difference. So, ma allows the appearing of a continuity of discontinuity, in Nishida's words.*
>
> (2015, p. 81)

Nishida: Space–Time

Since we're talking about space and time, it's a good moment to bring in some phenomenological theories that can deepen our understanding of the tea ceremony. As we've seen, the experience the tea master creates contrasts sharply with dominant notions of space and time in our world—another place where phenomenology can act as an intercultural bridge.

From its inception, phenomenology focused on re-thinking space and time beyond absolute dimensions and objective measures. We could focus on Husserl, Heidegger or later thinkers like Merleau-Ponty, but as this European tradition was reaching Asia in the early twentieth century, phenomenological conceptions of space and time began to emerge in Japan.

Let's now turn to Nishida Kitarō (西田幾多郎, 1870–1945), one of Japan's most important philosophers. He developed a conception of space we can consider within a phenomenological framework.[2]

Late in his philosophical career, when his ontology had matured over a lifetime of writing, he developed a concept called *Basho* (場所). We'll explore this concept of space as I think it can help us understand tea garden spatiality and temporality, and the observations you reported after your stroll the other day.

Before diving into these ideas, does anybody know anything about Nishida?

Philosopher: Yeah, I've heard of him. He was the first Japanese philosopher, I think. Didn't he found the Kyoto School?

Guide: Whether he was *the* first Japanese philosopher isn't so straightforward,[3] but we can say he was the first to gain substantial prominence, and with him the Kyoto School first gained recognition as a distinct philosophical movement.

Specifically, with his first major work, *An Inquiry into the Good* (*Zen no Kenkyū*, 善の研究) Nishida caused a great sensation in the Japanese intellectual world. This wasn't merely a huge *academic* success; the book's popularity spilled out into Japanese culture. It stood as a statement on behalf of the Japanese nation that it too had a great intellectual tradition capable of standing shoulder to shoulder with the other major traditions.

It was an immense source of pride for the Japanese public and the momentum of Nishida's work shaped what we now know as the Kyoto School of philosophy, which began with him and then continued with his student Nishitani Keiji (西谷啓治, 1900–90) Tanabe Hajime (田辺元, 1885–1962), Watsuji Tetsuro (和辻哲郎, 1889–1960) and Ueda Shizuteru (上田閑照, 1926–2019). Despite their vastly different approaches, one common element uniting these diverse Kyoto School philosophers was their shared ambition to build a philosophy embracing both eastern and western traditions, often seeking to reconcile religion, philosophy, and science.

Phenomenological Spatiality

Let's get back to the question of space and see what Nishida can tell us about our experience here in the tea garden.

Despite its great success, Nishida actually came to repudiate his earlier writings as being overly subjectivistic. Over time, he evolved his own thought, passing through several phases of critical revision before developing what became his mature philosophy: the ontology and logic of *Basho*.

Basho (場所) is sometimes left un-translated, other times rendered in English as "place", "*topoi*", and even as "*chōra*" (χώρα), a reference to Plato's idea of the "receptacle", which some scholars have explored for its similarity to Buddhist notions of emptiness.[4] We might consider his theory, not an objective, but a phenomenological conception of space.

Let's consider your earlier comments about your experience walking through the garden. You highlighted this tension between objective measures and subjective experiences of space and time. To begin, we should remind ourselves that, while you might have been walking faster or slower, wandering from one place to another, and shifting between passivity and activity, it's unlikely that any of your movements involved consciously invoking such binaries or making deliberate decisions based on them. Nor, I imagine, were you calculating objective measures and contrasting them with subjective impressions of space and time, right?

Philosopher: No, all that would have been before or below reflective intellection—pre-reflective.

Guide: Right. We don't need to measure, theorize or reflect about space or time to navigate a city, our homes, offices, or this garden. This is the starting point for Nishida's *Basho* theory: its focus is not on what space is *when we think of it*, but in the moment of lived experience—space as experienced, not as an abstract object of thought. Space as lived, as it unfolds before we invoke binaries of subjectivity and objectivity. It wasn't that Nishida wanted to deny the reality of these binaries so much as to understand our experience of space before they arise in our thinking or experience.

What Nishida sought to understand was how entities, bodies and beings interact and inter-determine each other in this field he conceived of as an all-inclusive field of non-differentiation. He called this field a "place of true nothing" (*shin no mu no basho* 真の無の場所) and also "place of absolute nothing" (*zettai mu no basho* 絶対無の場所). We don't need to go into the particularities of those ideas, but does anybody recognize any of the terminology?

Philosopher: Yeah, that character *mu* (無).

Guide: And, what do you remember about that character?

Philosopher: It refers to emptiness. *Śūnyatā*.

Theologian: Emptiness as a kind of relationality. Not a "less than", but a "more than" definition.

Guide: Yes, exactly. With *Basho* as a "place of nothingness," Nishida rethinks space relationally—a major shift from Newtonian notions of absolute space. In that framework, space is a neutral container, unaffected by the relations among things *in space*. The garden, then simply holds objects and the person performing the ceremony.

Basho, by contrast, sees space as inseparable from the relations between things. It is a field of relationality, not a fixed background. As relations shift, space itself changes—space is not absolute.

And remember how I mentioned earlier that our default ideas of space tend to carry Aristotelian logic, even though our conceptions of space have evolved beyond that? Nishida, in developing *Basho*, also worked out an alternative logic to account for what happens within this relational field.

Rather than the Aristotelian A ≠ not-A, Nishida developed several versions of logic where A is intimately related to not-A. Throughout his career he had several terms invoking different aspects of this contradictory logic, including "logic of absolutely contradictory self-identity", "self-identity of opposites", "affirmation of absolute negation", and "absolute negation-qua-affirmation".

So why does this matter as we move through the stages of the tea ceremony, the garden, and engage with the objects and rituals?

Philosopher: Because we have to try to get beyond subject–object metaphysics?

Guide: Right, yes. Without having to consciously think about space or time in these terms, our "world" often leads us to think of things in space as objects within a neutral container, even though our actual experience often feels quite different.

Science has advanced by treating space and time as objective, uniform fields unaffected by what happens within them. But this view says little about the intimate, embodied experience central to the tea ceremony—so it's of limited use here.

Nishida, by focusing on the experience of space before the split between subject and object, allows us to see experience not as "merely subjective" but as fundamental. In his view, the subjective–objective divide hasn't yet emerged, so our experience of space and time is direct and unmediated.

This shift has profound implications for experiencing every aspect of the garden. If we simply see ourselves as objects in a container-like space, we reduce our interactions to the causal, mechanical kind—a series of billiard-ball interactions between ourselves and the objects we encounter. But, when we conceive of space as one of the ways that we're actually constituted by other objects, and when these relations are elevated to what is *most* real, then our interactions with materials like stones, raw wood, or water basins take on profound existential significance. The entire field we're moving in becomes activated, metaphysically expanded, and soteriologically elevated, because we're no longer separate from space, but woven into its fabric: *who* we are because of *how* we are *where* we are.

And, this is yet another reason I couldn't bring *you* to a tea garden. That phrasing already assumes you're an outside subject entering into a container-like, objective spatial realm.

Philosopher: . . . and also assumes that who we were as selves before we arrived at the garden is the same person we would be once woven into the garden's world.

Guide: Yes, exactly.

But, if we can focus on a phenomenological conception, which I believe Nishida's *Basho* theory qualifies as, we have the possibility of a much deeper and more intimate experience, especially within the spatial peculiarities of the tiny-but-expansive tea hut we're soon to enter.

Artist: So, if I understand correctly, you can't take us as selves to a place *in* space. But, as non-selves, as relational selves, you can help us see how we're already woven into a relational field, like *Basho*.

Guide: I think Nishida helps us see that. The ways we're already deeply intertwined before you have to think about it.

Philosopher: . . . then maybe, the problem we started with, about our inability to experience the tea ceremony, maybe it's the same thing. We don't necessarily have to *add* things to our knowledge or ourselves to overcome the east–west divide, but subtract things away to see how we're already intertwined with enough elements to enable a true and non-self defeating intercultural encounter.

Guide: I like it.

Artist: Can you give us an example of how this changes our experience? How we experience the tea ceremony differently if we're within space-time of emptiness or *Basho*?

Water and Non-Self

Guide: I can try.

Well, why don't we think about the spatiality of the body conceived of as an object. That body is circumscribable; it ends at the outer edge of the skin. Things come in and go out, but spatially speaking, your body remains confined within its objective spatiality. Now, let's think of the non-self, as an empty, a relational self within the ontological negative.

Let me ask you: what is the main thing we're seeking to come into relation with in the ceremony?

Artist: Tea?

Guide: Exactly. All this effort—the meticulous design, the rituals, the paintings, the stonework, architecture, you tolerating my endless lectures—all to consume a liquid in a specific way. And, temporally speaking, while that consumption still lies in the future, it has been governing everything we've been doing for days. But, where did we begin this adventure?

Theologian: At the Rikyū's well.

Guide: Temporally that relation with water lies in the past, and in a different spatial location, but we still began the course in relation to liquid, to water.

Where else did we notice water?

Philosopher: The water splashed on the stone entryway.

Artist: . . . and when we cleansed ourselves with water at the *tsukubai*.

Guide: Good. And let's not forget how our movements have been shaped by needing to pause and drink, or return water to the earth at the privy. We can reflect on all the appearances of water—the well, the moisture in plants and sky, sweat on our bodies, and eventually the tea. Objectively, these are just instances of water-as-object. But they also shape our experience beneath reflection. Before we identify each one, they're already part of a non-differentiated field—what Nishida calls *Basho*—where the self is relational, spatially extended, and no longer bound by the skin as its outer edge.

This water aspect of our experience won't be reached through a series of deductions. But, if we choose to focus on it now, we can see that there's a dimension of our experience that is a nexus of liquid relations, among other constellations we could highlight if we chose.

The entire ceremony is a sophisticated aesthetic world designed to highlight one key relation unfolding in its final moments. It's not just an experience *of* tea, but of the self *as* tea. The non-self, sustained throughout, culminates in this moment of relation.

If space is abstract and indifferent, then spatial relations are incidental. But if *Basho* truly captures our experience, then space is always relational. The garden, in particular, is crafted to reveal this—to help us feel the body's spatiality. If we only grasp this through reflection, we miss the deeper, pre-reflective continuity where the self is already spread through things like the various recurring punctuations of water in our spatial field of relations, in *Basho*.

Rather than thinking of our arrival into and movement through the garden as objects traversing a container and encountering indifferent objects, we can understand the tea garden spatiality as a carefully constructed field of existential relationality.

Artist: So, tea ceremony as liquid-expanded non-self?

Theologian: . . . then, couldn't we say that gardening and *ikebana* gives us a vegetal-expanded non-self?

Philosopher: . . . and, the stone work, a mineral-expanded non-self?

Guide: Absolutely. I chose the water element as an example, but we could examine the orchestration of the mineral and vegetal worlds, also through air, fire, or history, language and aesthetics, all relational strands running through the ceremony, all meticulously orchestrated relations that obtain at these levels enabling the self to expand in these ways you're rightly suggesting.

But, one thing to keep in mind is that it's not just particular events or rituals that offer opportunities for an expanded self. As relational beings in a relational world, it's simply the structure of reality that *we are* the things we're related to. It's not just aesthetic or religious rituals that provide this expansion—it's everything: the air we breathe, the food we eat, relations with friends and family, even gravity and light—all ways in which we exist beyond the circumscribable boundaries of our objective, positive body.

A ritual like the tea ceremony is meant to help us be this expanded non-self, but like Zen practice it's based on, the idea is that the everyday mundane world always holds the possibility for such experience.

But, that will be a topic for tomorrow's meeting. We'll see you back here then!

13

The Tea Hut

Women and Tea

Guide: Welcome back, everyone. A few days ago, upon first encountering our tea host, you expressed some surprise that she was a woman. Did any of you assume that a tea master had to be a man?

Theologian: Yes, when you showed us the invitation and repeatedly referred to our "tea master", I had always imagined that it would be a man.

Artist: I'm embarrassed to admit, but even as a committed feminist, so did I.

Philosopher: Maybe it's understandable given that the history of *Chanoyu* seems to have been exclusively male.

Guide: Yes, that history definitely would lead us to assume that tea masters are men. Certainly, all of the *iemotos* (家元) of the Urasenke lineage have, so far, been men. And, before the late nineteenth century, tea practitioners were almost exclusively male. But as Japan entered the twentieth century and sought to model itself on the globalized nation-state, women were increasingly permitted to partake and eventually to enroll in training to become a host.

Interestingly, today, the gender imbalance has reversed. Women now vastly outnumber men, making up over 90 percent of registered tea practitioners.[1]

But, we should also recognize that even historical accounts might not fully reflect the important role women played in the tea ceremony. Some scholars have noted how, specifically in Sōtō Zen tea practice, women were vital for preserving the ceremony, both in terms of *chadō* itself, but also the related arts of flower arrangement, calligraphy, and poetry (Porcu 2008).

Artist: Are there any feminist interpretations of *Chanoyu*, either its history or its present day form?

Guide: Difficult question. While it's often said that there has been a "feminization" of the tea ceremony, we might be careful to claim that feminism has really prevailed here, or in Japan in general.

Firstly, bringing women into *Chanoyu* was driven not so much by a spirit of inclusion or equality between the sexes, so much as a fear of institutional decline. During the Meiji Restoration, tea schools lost their wealthy patrons, and Japanese traditional arts were in sharp decline due to the push for westernization. Including women was more of an effort to sustain a faltering institution rather than an effort to promote ideals like gender equality.

Even when women were incorporated into training, it was mostly framed as bridal training—teaching young women how to manage the domestic sphere and be "good" housewives, which normally meant submissive wives (Kato 2015). In this sense, the ceremony remained a strongly gendered institution, and inclusion was conceived of according to the ideal for women to be what was called *ryōsai kenbo* (良妻賢母), a very *un*-feminist term translated as "good wife and wise mother".

Inclusion was mostly a continuation of a set of gender expectations that denied women autonomy by seeing them in merely domestic and supporting roles for male breadwinners.

Women were largely excluded from the status and power flowing through the ceremony. Even today, under the hereditary system, school heads remain male, despite women vastly outnumbering men as practitioners. Women are still often confined to roles of caretakers or householders, while the minority of men gain more recognition and social capital across a broader range of roles (Carriger 2021).

Theologian: Wasn't gender equality enshrined in the constitution in 1947?

Guide: Yes, though, progress toward gender equality in Japan has been slow, with patriarchy still strongly shaping women's lives compared to other developed nations. Some argue this is beginning to shift, with women gaining more agency through training and participation in the tea ceremony.[2]

The idea is that, within the tea hut's egalitarian setting, women can connect across social and political lines (Kato 2004). Whether this leads to real change is unclear, but it may offer space for further progress—as Japan moves, however gradually, toward a level of equality other developed nations claim to have reached long ago.

Let me now show you another station of ritual purification we should consider before entering the hut.

Dust hole

The last stop before entering the tea hut is here at the "dust hole" (*chiriana* 塵穴). You'll notice the small twigs and leaves, these represent the dust we've referred to several times. The *chiriana* serves as the receptacle for that dust, and while we won't set fire to the scraps in the hole, its original use evokes fire as a purifying element in Shinto. This is the final step to cleanse oneself of the dust that has accumulated on the body and mind through everyday concerns and struggles.

As tea guests, we're now prepared, through the progressive stages of ritual purification, to enter a new domain—transformed from everyday affairs and their physical and spiritual impurities. But, it's important to keep in mind that we don't leave the world of dust by transcending into another realm transcending this one. Everything in the tea ceremony is rooted in *this life*, and *this world*, tied to the immanent and mundane. Yet, it's an immanent world purified and expanded by the rituals we've undertaken on our approach to the hut.

~ The group wandered over to another waiting bench, where they had a view of the tea hut they had been anticipating for days.

Mutual-Containment of finite and infinite

Guide: We're now seated at the inner waiting bench, the *uchi koshikake* (内腰掛). We can finally see the hut.

First impressions?

Theologian: We had spoken about its objectively small dimensions, but I still thought it would be bigger than that.

Philosopher: Yeah, it's remarkable how much effort goes into constructing such a specific experience with the orchestration of all the aesthetic elements throughout the garden, and then the hut is so diminutive.

Guide: And this isn't even a version of the smallest huts that were built. Rikyū was known for first having drastically reduced the size down to 4.5 mats, then to two, and later even built a 1.5 tatami hut.

But, before we proceed, I want to return to the point I made on the first day while at the Urasenke Foundation. Does anyone remember?

Artist: You said something along the lines of the small size of the *sōan*-style tea hut being what makes it so large.

Guide: Right, very good. From a disengaged spectatorial vantage point—treating the hut as an object in objective space—small is simply small. A is A. But, from a phenomenological perspective, and in line with the conception of space we've been discussing, I want to now try to help you see that the hut's small structure affords a spatially expansive experience.

Keep this in mind because we'll also discuss later how the small poem—the modest *haiku*—is tiny but linguistically expansive.

The idea is that the infinite is within the finite. Does that idea ring a bell to anyone?

Theologian: That poem by William Blake comes to mind—the one where he says something about "a world in a grain of sand".

Guide: Yes, great. That's William Blake's "Auguries of Innocence". It's a longer poem, but the part you're referring to is:

To see a world in a grain of sand
And a heaven in a wild flower
Hold infinity in the palm of your hand
And eternity in an hour.

This way of thinking about the relativity of the large and small, the finite and the eternal, is quite rare in our western tradition. But, there's intriguing speculation that Blake might have been inspired by his readings of the Bhagavad Gītā, in which case, the origins of this very non-western thinking might be Asian, after all.[3]

If we were to extract the metaphysics from Blake's poem, we would arrive at what in Buddhism is called *sōsoku* (相即), which translates as **"interpenetration"** or sometimes "mutual-containment". It is also sometimes referred to as a "holographic" conception of reality, and specifically of space. This means that the whole (*holo*) is inscribed (*graphic*) in all parts.

This view of the structure of reality surfaces in several Zen koans that refer to a mountain contained within a poppy seed. Shokin also invokes the same logic regarding the spatiality of the tea hut, asserting that "Rikyū's was just such an achievement: the containing of the infinite within the finite" and further, "it was he who first realized that the greatest spaciousness was to be achieved in the smallest room" (Shokin 1989, p. 13).

But, the question remains: how does such a small room, phenomenologically-speaking, possess such expansive spatiality.

To begin answering that, let's talk a bit more about the *sukiya* style of tea hut.

> ~ *The group leaves the waiting bench and follows their Guide to their last waiting station under the eaves of the tea hut, a small bench known as the sheltered waiting bench. They sit and the Guide recalls their earlier discussion of the sukiya from their Urasenke Foundation visit.*

Sukiya

Guide: Before getting back to the topic of holographic metaphysics, let me tell you a little bit more about the history and structure of the *sukiya* tea hut.

Tea house design and construction flourished during the tumultuous Sengoku period (mid-fifteenth to early seventeenth century), a time when Japan's weakened central government allowed Samurai and wealthy landowners (*Daimyo*)—many of whom were Zen Buddhist practitioners—to accumulate and wield significant power. Seeking refuge from the chaos surrounding them, they turned to the tea ceremony as a space carved out to cultivate Zen ideals of peace, tranquility, and simplicity.

From the outside, the tea hut resembles the most modest grass hut you can imagine. As you know from our discussion with Sanada-sensei, this style is referred to as *sōan* (草庵). It reflects the rustic aesthetics of small hermitages or farmhouses in feudal Japan. The structure typically consists of bamboo frames and walls plastered with clay. The bamboo is left unfinished, and the timber posts and beams are left with their bark still intact.

The most striking feature of the *sōan* style— the one that distinguishes it from other Japanese and Chinese structures—is the grass roof. Unlike thatched tile or wood shingles, the grass invokes the poverty of the farmers' and hermits' abodes in medieval Japan. The windows (*shitaji mado* 下地窓) are also modeled on the small houses of farmers who couldn't afford glass windows so they improvised by leaving an opening in the bamboo frame unplastered. As you can see here, they are covered with lattice, which serves to dim the light inside. Combined with the wide, overhanging eaves, the openings provide a dim and contemplative illumination within the tearoom, even on sunny days.

There's an additional historical point about this rustic aesthetic that is interesting because of its subversive nature. As we learned from our teacher at the Urasenke

Foundation, during the sixteenth century, with the dominant *shoin* style, tearooms were meant to showcase wealth and power. At that time, the merchant class—previously the lowest rung within the strict social hierarchy—was accumulating great wealth. However, social dictates prohibited them from openly displaying that wealth.

It was these merchants from Sakai who propelled *Wabicha* and the *sōan* style into prominence as a way for them to counter the opulence of the Samurai class and their lavishly decorated tearooms. The *sōan*-style hut and *Wabicha* ceremonial principles became ways for the merchant class to challenge the social barriers they otherwise were forced to observe. Even in the architecture itself, medieval tea masters sought to undermine the hierarchies of their time and create a space of equality among all people (Kumarasuriyar 2011).

It was also thought that Rikyū adopted these aesthetic principles in part as a critique of the indulgent tendencies of the emperor Hideyoshi, who famously had Rikyū design and build a solid gold tea hut, which was meant to accompany him not just on his travels but even into battle.

Ironically, while Rikyū's vision sought to level the social hierarchy and the extravagant displays of wealth inherent to the *shoin* style, *sōan* tea huts were often incredibly costly to design and to build. Sourcing the best materials and employing the most skilled craftspeople required significant expense, highlighting a paradox within this otherwise egalitarian vision.

Now, let me tell you a little bit about the inside of the tearoom, or the *chashitsu* (茶室). What we'll see today is the specific style called *sukiya* (数奇屋),[4] which Sanada-sensei mentioned was referred to as the "abode of fancy", "the abode of the asymmetrical" or the "abode of the void".

Returning to the earlier question about the size of the tea hut, and how the small size makes the structure bigger, let's address this in the first and more straightforward sense. Rikyū designed his hut with specific elements to evoke a visual and even bodily experience of an expansiveness despite the confined space.

For instance, the compression one feels when going through the very tiny entrance was supposed to make the room feel more voluminous than it would if we entered through a normal human-size door. Furthermore, Rikyū rounded the edges of the walls, making it visually harder to perceive fixed boundaries, giving the impression of limitless dimensions.

We might think of these as visual tricks or illusions, intended to make the small *appear* large. However, later we'll discuss how, in a more metaphysical sense, the small is not merely *perceived* as large but is actually rendered expansive, perhaps even unlimited, in its spatiality (Masao 1995).

~ Shortly after their discussion of the Sukiya, the tea host came out to invite them in. She then disappeared around the corner to enter the hut from the tea master's entrance.

Nijiriguchi

Guide: Now, we're finally ready to enter the hut. Any idea how we get in?

~ The students were slightly perplexed. They had admired the fine details of the hut from a distance, and now up close, but they hadn't noticed any door to enter through. They looked around, searching for any sign of an entryway, but found none.

Guide: There, that's where we'll go in.

~ The Guide pointed to a small sliding panel located in the bottom corner of one of the walls. The students laughed in astonishment.

Artist: I figured it would be small, to match the hut's dimensions, but that almost looks like you couldn't get through.

Guide: Before Rikyū's time, there was, in some cases, an alternate larger door called a *kinin guchi* (貴人口) reserved for nobility, who were not expected to humble themselves before the tea master. But, in line with his egalitarian ideals, Rikyū is known for having done away with that door, which had reinforced class divisions.

This *nijiriguchi* (躙り口) thus has an equalizing effect on tea guests. Translated roughly as "crawl in space" or "wriggle in space"[5] and measuring around 60cm x 60cm (2ft x 2ft) it was a sliding panel rather than a swinging door. It's so small that it serves to eliminate other signs of class—preventing Samurai from entering with their two swords,[6] and disallowing the aristocracy or courtiers entering with their signs of rank, such as large top hats. By requiring all guests, regardless of station, to enter through the same humble opening, the *nijiriguchi* created a space not striated by the various signs of social hierarchies otherwise dividing the social realm in medieval Japan.

Furthermore, the *nijiriguchi* served to sever the space between the outside world— where conversation and figures of speech could invoke aspects of the social hierarchy, from the inside where no such language was permitted. In the *Wabicha* tearoom, any reference to one's societal position, including mentions of

Figure 13.1 "Crawling in space" (*nijiriguchi*, 躙り口). R. Loughnane.

employment, income, wealth, or power were strictly prohibited (Nishihara 1968).

It's thought that Rikyū got the idea for the *nijiriguchi* from the tiny portals sailors used to enter and exit ships, which he observed in the harbors of Sakai. Or, it may have been inspired by similar miniature apertures in theaters called "mouse wickets" (*nezumikido*, 鼠木戸) where actors crossed over from the everyday world into the theatrical world. Some have also speculated that moving through such tiny openings re-enacts our original entrance into the world at birth.

We'll discuss later how the *nijiriguchi* shapes an experience of space crucial to the overall tea ceremony. But for now, in terms of what we're about to undertake, the meaning of this entryway and our movement through it comes from another source. Can anyone guess?

Theologian: Maybe the movement is a way of humbling oneself out of a Confucian respect for the tea master.

Guide: That's a good guess. There's definitely a sense of humility involved, but the idea is more aligned with Buddhism. If you can imagine that by compressing oneself to pass through, you are symbolically squeezing the self—or the ego—out of yourself. There's literally no room for the ego to fit. Only a minimized self, a non-self can enter the tea hut.

Philosopher: Is there a specific way we should enter the hut?

Guide: Yes, as you expected, there is. This stage is called *seki-iri* (席入り), or "entering into one's seat". First, you remove your sandals and prop them up against the outer wall of the hut. But, you don't then launch yourself head first through the aperture. Typically, the guest first bends down and kneels on one knee. The entry is a kind of lateral motion. You lower your head under the lintel and slide in sideways in one smooth movement.

Now, one last detail. Again, as we're entering a new stage of the ceremony, crossing over into a new space, Confucian role ethics govern the order of our entry. As we discussed at the outer gate and at the waiting benches, I am in the position of *Shōkyaku*, so I'll go in first. As *otsume* (御詰) our philosopher will be the last to enter, and it will be your job to close the *nijiriguchi* behind us.

You might have the instinct to not disturb the silence inside the tea hut, but you should resist that inclination and give the sliding door a good firm push to close it. This is another case where the acoustics are important. That clicking sound will signal to the host that we've all entered the room. Be attentive to what follows, as this isn't the only moment where sound—particularly percussion—plays a role in orchestrating a choreographed set of interactions in the absence of speech.

> ~ *The Guide kneels down and enters, followed by the Artist, the Theologian, and lastly the Philosopher, who slides the nijiriguchi closed with the requisite click. With all three now inside the hut, the Guide leads them across the room to the alcove.*

14

Alcove and Hanging Scroll

Guide: Now, at long last, we're finally inside. We'll pause at a few points to discuss what's going on, but this is not typically allowed inside the tea hut, nor is the excessive amount of talking we'll be doing. There are, in fact, conventions about speaking we would normally follow. It's not that we have to be strictly silent—there are moments when speech is expected—but in general, we employ a restrained economy of words and a humble use of language, which you might imagine, has some philosophic-religious significance.

There are many details to keep in mind beyond this point, we'll pause as needed, and I'll explain everything you need to know. Please follow me over here.

~ *The students were visibly amused because they're accustomed to a slight bit of locomotion when somebody says we'll go "over there". In this case, it only required a small turn and a shuffle, and they were already at the other end of the hut.*

The first stage takes place in the absence of the tea master here at the alcove or *tokonoma* (床の間). Remember we first encountered an alcove in the changing room?[1] And, as in the first, there is another scroll here—this one is meant to recall and advance the theme introduced in the first.

There is also a flower arrangement today. On other days, there might be a writing box or some other objects accentuating the themes the host has developed.

Now, let me test some of the knowledge you've gained so far. The two main objects we have here are calligraphy and the flower arrangement, the Japanese terms for these are *shodō* and *kadō*. Do those names mean anything to anybody?

Theologian: Yeah, they both have that "*dō*" syllable we spoke about the other day.

Guide: That's right. And, what does that mean?

Philosopher: Those are the transliteration of the Chinese "Dao" and must be part of the *geidō* practices we spoke about earlier.

Figure 14.1 Alcove. (*tokonoma*, 床の間). R. Loughnane.

Guide: Yes, that's exactly right. *Shodō* (書道) and *kadō* (華道) are two of the central *geidō* practices, and the "*dō*" (道) character indicates that they're also practiced according to Daoist principles.

Although it looks like a relatively modest arrangement, we could spend all day here discussing the practices and principles informing each piece and the relations accruing between them. But, recall that the hanging scroll was made the thematic centerpiece of Rikyū's version of *Wabicha*.

Artist: What would have been the centerpiece before Rikyū?

Guide: Tea utensils—specifically Chinese utensils. And, as we discussed earlier, in the *Shoin-Daisu* period, the central aesthetic element was the tea caddy, the *Daisu*.

Theologian: But, was there no alcove or scroll before Rikyū?

Guide: Yes and no. The alcove and scroll draw on earlier Chinese rituals of drinking powdered tea in front of pictorial works depicting Buddhist patriarchs—a custom adopted by Japanese monks who spent time in Chan monasteries of Song China. However, as a structural element housing art, the alcove wasn't part of the early days of *Chadō* in Japan (Fukutaro 1983).

Notice, too, that this scroll is calligraphed. In the formative years of *Chanoyu*, scrolls were mostly pictorial. Some, for instance, depicted landscapes such as the famous Xiao and Xiang rivers.

It is thought that the alcove came into the ceremony in the Momoyama period (1568-1600), inspired by the Buddhist tradition of hanging images for worship below which flowers and candles would be placed on a table. If you look closely, you'll notice a slight rise in the floor within the alcove, signaling that it's a sacred area.

Remember Murata Shukō? It was his innovation to begin hanging calligraphy in the alcove—as it reinforced the Zen sensibilities he wanted to infuse into *Chanoyu*—but it wasn't until much later that this became the norm. While Rikyū shifted the focus from Chinese utensils to the hanging scroll,[2] there's some debate as to whether Rikyū favored pictographic or calligraphic works in the alcove.[3]

Although Rikyū avoided representations of Buddhist figures, he did allow some as long as it served spiritual edification and avoided becoming a Buddhist altar (Shokin 1989). Yet, from around this time the tradition moved increasingly away from images and towards calligraphy. For example, *Zenkiga* (禅機画)—paintings depicting Zen activities or legendary encounters drawn from sutras—became rare in alcoves after the medieval period.[4]

From around the mid-sixteenth century, wealthy merchants of Sakai developed a taste for *bokuseki* (墨跡 "ink trace") calligraphy—calligraphy scribed by Japanese Buddhists. Rikyū's significant innovation in this regard was his elevation of *bokuseki* over Chinese pictorial and calligraphic works.[5]

We now have a new ritual procedure to observe.

~ *The Guide reaches into his kimono and pulls out his fan, holding it vertically and un-opened in front of his chest.*

Please, take your fans out from your kimono, and hold them as I'm doing. You might be surprised that the fan should never be open within the hut. Its main purpose isn't to keep us cool, but to mark a symbolic frontier between oneself and the various ritual objects, such as this hanging scroll, or sometimes as a sign of respect between teacher and student.

Artist: It sounds somewhat at odds with the relational ontology, to mark boundaries and divide us from them.

Guide: You're right.

Theologian: . . . maybe it's a division that elevates continuity, like we spoke about with *kire* aesthetic.

Guide: I don't know if the fan is thought of in the context of *kire*, but that would be in line with the ethos of Rikyū's ceremony. But, we also shouldn't expect that every single element of the ceremony is reducible even to the main aesthetic principles. We'll see a few more exceptions in the coming stages.

Now, as we pause before this hanging scroll, a moment of deep significance, we should read it for the resonance it evokes with the first hanging scroll in the changing room and for further themes and symbols it invokes. In this case, the connection is quite clear since it's another fragment in the *Zhuangzi's* known as the "Dream of the Butterfly". This time, it reads;

> *Suddenly he awoke . . . He did not know if Zhou had been dreaming he was a butterfly, or if a butterfly was now dreaming it was Zhou.*
>
> (p. 21)

~ The group paused for a few moments to appreciate the scroll and allow the resonance to embrace all they had experienced between this scroll and the first.

Guide: We'll have a chance to discuss this passage later in the day. For now, you might not notice, but what the script is calligraphed on is a very special Japanese paper called *washi* (和紙), typically made by hand from locally sourced fibers of the gampi tree, mitsumata shrub, or the mulberry bush. This particular method of making paper is so unique and so significant to Japanese culture that UNESCO has granted it intangible cultural heritage status.

Before the medieval period, scrolls like this were highly prized and exceedingly rare, usually scribed by Chinese Buddhist monks. One of Rikyū's innovations was to commission Japanese Buddhists to craft them. The calligraphy can quote a Buddhist or Daoist sutra or famous saying, a *haiku* poem, or phrases more specifically tied to the tea ceremony, often invoking the four virtues—harmony, respect, purity and tranquility—or the *ichigo ichie* saying we've discussed.

Shodō Calligraphy

Guide: Let's take a moment and consider the inscription.

We already spoke about how the smallness of the tea hut makes it the most spatially expansive, now I'm going to propose that, likewise, the small poem known as the *haiku* is the largest poem.

But, before we delve deeper, let me give you some background on Japanese calligraphy and poetry. Does anybody know about or practice calligraphy?

Artist: Yes, I've actually been taking a calligraphy course through the Kobe International Community Centre. They offer six months of free lessons to any foreigner interested in learning.

Guide: I did the same thing when I first arrived in Japan. So, what have you learned about Japanese calligraphy?

Artist: Well, I guess the first thing is that the characters are actually Chinese.

Guide: Yes, exactly. The Japanese didn't formalize a writing system until around the fifth century. Instead of creating their own to suit their various local oral cultures, they adopted the Chinese system. As you know, *kanji* (漢字) literally means "Chinese character". It's a great example of Japan's openness to foreign influence—but the adoption wasn't without its challenges. Any thoughts?

Theologian: Yeah, the problem was that they incorporated the written language but not the spoken language. They had to figure out how to adapt their spoken language to fit the Chinese system, which is why they created the *kana* system.

Guide: Can you say a bit about that?

Theologian: *Kana* are two syllabaries, *hiragana* and *katakana*, which were developed to add flexibility so the written language could fit the spoken language.

Guide: Right, and unlike kanji, kana aren't pictographic. They didn't start as visual representations of things like many Chinese characters did. Kana are much simpler, and it's easy to spot the difference: Chinese uses only characters, while Japanese includes these more abstract, simplified shapes from the kana syllabaries.

Figure 14.2 *Kana* (仮名).

Here's a bit of Japanese philosophic-linguistic trivia for you: the syllabaries were partly developed by one of the figures considered Japan's earliest philosophers: Kōbō Daishi, or Kukai (空海, 774–835). While philosophy and religion existed in Japan before Kukai, they had been almost entirely imported from China. Kukai is often regarded as the starting point of philosophy and a form of Buddhism that was uniquely Japanese in character.

Like most Japanese aesthetic practices, calligraphy was first practiced in China and later brought to Japan, in this case around 600 CE. Over time, Japanese calligraphy evolved and distinguished itself from the Chinese tradition, particularly within the context of Zen Buddhism.

Unlike how we tend to think about handwriting—as a tool for communicating information—as a Buddhist practice, it was one of many disciplines that fit into an overarching pursuit of enlightenment.

Nishida was actually a calligrapher himself, and viewed the practice as an effort to achieve "no-mind" (*mushin* 無心) (2017). Similarly for us, appreciating a scroll or great calligraphy can serve as a way to clear our own minds, preparing us for the stages of the ceremony to come.

Philosopher: How could that work, though? Is it just that the images evoked in the poetry are supposed to have a calming effect on us?

Guide: This brings us back to some metaphysical ideas we've discussed. We don't usually think this way about our own handwriting, but to truly engage with calligraphy—and let it prepare us for the ceremony—we need to shift in new ways from western metaphysics and aesthetics. That includes the concept of *qi* energy.

To appreciate both the act of writing and how it affects us, we have to challenge another key western binary: the split between mind and matter.

In calligraphy, the character for "mountain" is seen as sharing the same *qi* energy as actual mountains. The calligrapher isn't working mimetically, treating the character as an abstract symbol "representing" something existing in a different metaphysical state. Instead, through *qi*, there's an energetic continuity between the mountain and the brushstrokes. Writing the kanji for "mountain" is meant to connect with and evoke the same energy animating the mountain.

Philosopher: I find this language of "energy" is so over-used and vague. Everybody talks of the "energy" of this and "energy" of that.

Guide: It is terribly over-used to the extent it becomes almost meaningless. We could probably use another term. Let's just keep in mind that *qi* is a continuity, and if we're not calling it "energetic", we should just keep in mind that it is a moving force. Maybe that's the better term, "force". There are actually many terms, depending on what context *qi* is referred to, including: vital breath, primordial vapor, earth current, dynamic flow, regenerative essence, vital circulation, and so on.

Artist: But, what about us viewing the calligraphy? Do we also participate in that energetic continuity?

Guide: That's exactly what I was getting at. In Japanese aesthetics, the distinction between creator and viewer isn't as strict as it tends to be in western aesthetics. In European art history, until quite recently, the act of viewing works didn't hold much importance relative to the status of creating works. So, we have another binary separating those who make works and those who merely experience and appreciate them.

But, if we can sidestep some of the assumptions sustaining these kinds of divisions, even as we sit here admiring this piece of calligraphy, we might be able to notice how we too are part of the energetic continuity the calligrapher engaged with in inscribing the characters. Recognizing this might feel difficult because we're so deeply entrenched in mimetic ways of thinking, which break the experience into distinct parts—mountain "out there", perception of mountain "in here".

But, it's not so hard, or even foreign to our ways of thinking. If we try to focus on a different valence of our experience, we can actually sense a really simple and basic continuity with the work. Can anyone think of how that might be possible?

Theologian: We did see some mountain peaks just over the crest of the south wall. Maybe the same way we discussed that within space understood as *Basho*, there's a continuity between the different instances of water, maybe there's a continuity now between our experiences of mountains.

Guide: Yes, excellent. Let me ask you, what did you feel when you saw the mountains?

Theologian: I remember feeling a desire to overcome that enormous distance, to actually get up to the snowy peaks and look down on the garden from there.

Artist: I felt something similar. Maybe not sadness, but a tinge of suffering at that vast distance—how enormous the mountains were and how small I am.

Philosopher: For me, it was a bit different. I climbed Mt. Fuji a few years ago, and it was the last adventure I had with someone very important to me. Seeing the peaks reminded me of that day. It made me quite sad.

Guide: Thank you all for sharing. We've already talked about the sadness associated with *mono no aware*, where objects evoke a sense of pathos, sometimes associated with their impermanence. But, let's consider the sadness you've expressed in different ways.

Yes, from one perspective, the one Ueda called "actuality", those mountains are simply objects, collections of minerals and vegetation. Nothing inherently emotional about them. But, when you look back, you don't remember their objective features, their magnitudes, or measurements. Before thinking about it, you're already in an energetic continuity with them. They're shaping your experience, mood, feelings, and ultimately, your perceptual experience, how you feel in your body.

Now we're in the tea hut, we might say that those mountains are now simply absent. But, let's sit with that for a second. As we take in the calligraphed characters for "mountain" here, isn't there some resonance, at least an element of this experience tinged by the earlier viewing of the mountain peaks, inflected by the emotional response you had?

Artist: I don't know if I would have noticed it explicitly, but now that you mention it, yes, I can definitely feel that I carried something with me from that earlier experience that colored the appearance of the mountain character here with the scroll.

Guide: This is another way that the tea master is able to intervene in the energetic continuity of the entire ceremony, and bring us in relation to different elements to augment our experience. If she would have chosen a different scroll, with a poem invoking the morning fog, or falling azalea leaves, perhaps she might have chosen another scroll to reiterate an aspect of that experience from outside the hut, to animate the aesthetic elements within the hut. The sadness we felt earlier now has a focal point in the tearoom, and even without deliberate reflection on our part, a relation is born—a presence of the mountains resonating throughout the space.

Philosopher: Wow, it's amazingly complex. I'm trying to think of the other different relations that might have been woven throughout the experience so far.

Guide: Yes, from one vantage point it looks like nothing could be more simple than a modest hut in a modest garden. But from another perspective—it's enormously complex.

And yes, we can try to imagine all the other connections that might be subtly impinging upon our experience. We can note having seen certain plants or stone arrangements earlier and appreciate the tea master having reinvoked that experience by choosing particular calligraphy, or tea utensils. She might have anticipated those mountain peaks would be perfectly visible in today's weather conditions, and known that the maple trees would only have enough leaves to only partially obstruct the view of their peaks.

Philosopher: I wouldn't have thought of that, but I wonder if it would be better not to think about it, not to make these relations an object of reflection.

Guide: Although we all experienced different emotional inflections upon seeing the mountains and feeling their echo with the calligraphy in the hut, the key point is that we were drawn into an energetic continuity *before* needing to think about or reflect on what the mountains meant to us. The characters aren't primarily meant to provoke a *less-real* mental representation of *more-real* mountains, but rather to help us feel that energetic continuity, to be patterned by those relations, or let's say, "attuned" by those experiences.

This is a way of thinking about emotions that is rare but not completely absent from western philosophies, so there's a bit of an inter-cultural bridge I can share with you on this topic.

There's lots of philosophic approaches for inquiring into human emotions, but phenomenology began with a slightly different approach. Rather than looking at the emotions that we can identify, analyse, and represent, they were more interested in the background of un-represented emotions, feelings, or what has come to be called "affect" recently.

We owe much of this way of thinking to Heidegger. His notion of *Stimmung*—often translated as "mood" or "attunement"—differs from emotions we can represent or even think of, such as anger or excitement, for example, which are clearly directed toward specific objects. Heidegger focused instead on how the world is inflected by *Stimmung* below or before we represent any particular emotions, and before emotions attach to particular objects.

We might think of the tea master's goal, not necessarily to have you focus on specific, strong emotions that are representable—which might only distract you from the ceremony—but rather to evoke non-representational attunements or *Stimmungen*, and to do so in a way that they accumulate into a beautifully animating force, or *qi*, woven into an aesthetic, emotional and existential field—*Basho*, perhaps—where the tea will eventually bind the entire nexus of aesthetic relationality that has been activated at different stages of the ceremony.

Theologian: It's almost like she's curating our world below the level of conscious reflection.

Philosopher: . . . or orchestrating our non-selves.

~ *The Guide said nothing and bowed slowly.*

Haiku

Guide: Let's go back to the holographic aspect of the poem. Does anybody know anything about *haiku* (俳句) poetry?

Artist: The only thing I know is that it's a very short poem. I think it has specific rules for how they're written—something to do with a certain amount of syllables in each line, I think.

Guide: Yes, it does have a limited amount of syllables—seventeen, divided into three phrases of five, seven and five syllables. Those syllables are called "on" (音) but they're slightly different from what we consider a syllable, but close enough for our purposes today.[6]

Maybe you know that *haiku* wasn't always an independent poetic form. The *hokku* (発句), the verse later called the haiku, originally served as the first stanza of a longer poem called *Renku* (連句) or *Renga* (連歌), which was a collaborative poem written by several poets and calligraphers. It was only in the seventeenth century that Matsuo Bashō (松尾芭蕉, 1644–94), the most famous of all Japanese poets, popularized the *haiku* as an independent poetic form.[7]

An interesting connection is how *Renga* was, in some ways, a precursor to elements of *Wabicha*. Composing poems together in groups became an elaborate ceremony in Muromachi Japan with hosts even constructing purpose-built huts in gardens, separate from their main residences, which contributed to the *sōan* style we've already spoken of (Bullen 2016).

Renga gatherings became increasingly sophisticated and ritualized to high aesthetic standards. It could be that the *Chanoyu* minimalism and austerity emerged in this context.[8] There's also speculation that a convention of non-repetition began within these *Renga* gatherings (Decreux 2014).

Another clear influence of *Renga* on *Chanoyu* was the centrality of nature. In fact, one formal constraint of *Renga*'s first stanza, the *haiku*, was the inclusion of a seasonal reference, called *kigo*.

Kigo

Guide: A seasonal word in *haiku* is called a *kigo* (季語). It doesn't have to name a season directly. It can refer to markers like falling leaves, budding branches, or animals linked to a time of year. It might also evoke a season through festivals or seasonal kimono colors and patterns.

You may have noticed this during your time here—the Japanese take great pride in their sensitivity to nature and subtle seasonal changes. Japanese literature often contains beautiful depictions of these transitions. They frequently emphasize that they enjoy four distinct seasons, especially in contrast to places where changes feel less marked—like Ireland.

In culturally rich times like the Heian period or Bashō's time, poets could rely on a readership attuned to seasonal subtleties. The cultural elite would have known key works in literature, painting, or poetry often celebrating the seasons. There were even books called *saijiki* (歳時記), or "year-time chronicles", cataloging the main *kigo* and their appropriate use in different poetic forms. Today, as a modern-day *saijiki*, there's even a *kigo* database with over 6,000 seasonal references, symbols, and themes (*kidai* 季題).[9]

Theologian: But, what about your claim that *haiku* is both the smallest and the largest poetic form?

Guide: Yes, let's get back to that. Remember the distinction between the ontological positive and negative? If we were to remain within the positive, the poem is simply a small poem.

Artist: Small is small.

Philosopher: So, in that case, we're treating it like an object, right? Circumscribed—not physically or spatially—but linguistically.

Theologian: . . . then, the poem begins with the first word and ends with the last. Everything happens in between those two words.

Guide: Right. From a strictly positivist perspective, the poem is seen only based on its objective features—only the syllables and ink on paper. But, we all know better than to remain confined to the positive. The *kigo* word is a clear example of how *haiku* transcends a simple large–small binary.

That small reference can evoke an immense range of cultural allusions, appealing to the reader's seasonal sensitivity, to their emotions and deepest longings, thereby summoning an entire relational world.

Of course, we don't perceive that world in the marks on paper, but here's the crucial point: we don't see the entirety of the relational world because that aspect of the poem remains in the negative—illegible yet present. Just like the tea master who can act through the negative, likewise the *haiku* poet can harness the power of language by activating the linguistic negative.

So yes, objectively speaking the positive aspect of the poem—the marks on paper—is simply small. But, because of the ability to call on the negative—what Ueda called "hollowness"—the poem is potentially as big as a world.

Artist: But, wouldn't more words evoke more meaning, make the world even more vast?

Guide: You might think so, but not necessarily. Let's consider the masterpieces of Chinese and Japanese landscape paintings. Think of the landscapes by Sesshū, with their evocative negative spaces. When you look at his work such as "Splashed Ink Landscape", do you feel that *more* ink on paper would augment the impact of his painting?

Artist: No, definitely not. They wouldn't be more impactful with less negative space. That's what's so distinctive about them.

Guide: Exactly. And why was that?

Artist: Because the negative space allows for our imagination to participate in the co-creating of the artwork. Through the negative. And, our imagination is

Figure 14.3 Sesshū Tōyō. "Splashed Ink Landscape" (破墨山水図, *Haboku-sansui*), 1495. Ink on paper. Tokyo National Museum.

more expansive than the objective features of artwork can be, which is constrained—in its positive valence at least—by its frame.

Guide: Exactly, and likewise with poetry. A wordy poem might seem impressive due to its linguistic complexity, but it risks closing off the reader's imaginative engagement. The more the poem asserts itself with positive presence—through elaborate language and densely packed ideas—the less room there is for the reader's own interpretive play, which enters by way of the negative.

Take hyperrealist painting as an example. It's quite amazing to see these works, but in a sense, they overwhelm us with positivity, and they might minimize our ability to intertwine with them through the negative—so full of themselves in an A=A kind of way that they leave no space for us to meet them halfway. They limit us to only representing their objective features rather than intertwining and entering into their definition, and them into ours.

So, consider this: in the case of such paintings, *more* might actually be *less*. Too much positivity could actually mean a smaller, diminished aesthetic experience.

And, if that's the case with a hyperrealist visual artwork, what about the correlate in poetry?

Artist: I suppose, it could be that too many words would likewise be too much positivity, and no negative linguistic space for us to participate in as readers.

Guide: One way *haiku* has been understood is exactly along those lines. It reduces positivity to its absolute minimum. So, from an objective point of view, only accounting for positivity, it is simply a tiny poem. But, from the point of view that grasps the interplay of linguistic positivity and negativity, we get the opposite view. By reducing the positive to its bare minimum the *haiku*'s negativity can be most expansive; the maximum opportunity for the reader can bring their own world into the poem.

Philosopher: This seems to raise a paradox: the highly elaborate, sophisticated poems, despite their abundance, might actually be more constrained in their capacity to evoke.

Guide: Quite possibly. Overly wordy poems might be *small* because they're *large*, whereas *haiku* is *large* because it's *small*. Of course, there is beautiful poetry striving for verbal sophistication. It can be amazing to be overwhelmed with the positivity of history's greatest writers like Shakespeare or Melville, but in the end, this might mean that we're not invited in to co-constitute the work—rather than an inter-expressive relation, it's simply a self expressing itself. And, in this case, the reader is more in the position of observer rather than co-creators.

We can deeply appreciate these works—some of them are amazing artistic works—but it's not so much an invitation into an experience of co-constitution as much as an appreciation of *someone else's experience*. *Haiku*, by contrast, doesn't rely on many words or sophisticated references because *they're not written for you to appreciate someone else's experience*: the aim of *haiku* is to provoke an experience in the reader. The poet steps aside, avoiding language that explains the feelings or experience.

This is another way the creator–viewer binary dissolves. Just as calligraphy offers a shared energetic continuity between artist and viewer, the openness of *haiku* through its negativity allows the reader a much more substantial constituting role—beyond simply being a consumer of some other self's art object.

Kireji

Guide: Okay, let's talk about another structural feature of the *haiku*, the *kireji* (切れ字). Does that term remind you of anything we've already discussed?

Theologian: It has that "*kire*" sound. Is it related to the *kire* aesthetic?

Guide: Yes, precisely. *Kire* is the cutting aesthetic we discussed and *kireji* means "cutting word". It's a structural necessity within *haiku* but also appears in other poetic forms, such as the opening verses (*hokku* 発句) in classical *renga* and *renku*.

The *kireji*—sometimes a single word, sometimes a combination—is meant to achieve a subtle interruption in the reader's expectations. It can manifest as a grammatical or punctuation irregularity, like an ellipsis or an exclamatory particle, and in such cases, clearly visible to the reader's eyes. But it can also be merely auditory with no visible trace in the lexical aspect of the poem. More subtly, the *kireji* can simply intervene in the meaning or the logic established in earlier parts of the poem.

The cutting effect comes not from a sharp turn, but a subtle or oblique shift—just off from where the reader expected the poem to go. The *kireji* isn't meant to surprise or shock. It gently disrupts the rhythm, inviting a new angle of perception rather than a dramatic twist.

The aim isn't to evoke an entirely new emotion or conjure an image not previously evoked. Rather, the *kireji* cuts to tease out un-activated complexity inherent to the work, drawing attention to a slightly different valence of emotion or imagery that was already there but unnoticed. It's less like adding a brand-new flavor, but maybe more like the faintest seasoning that draws out a taste that was already there but hidden.

Philosopher: It's like the *kire* aesthetic in that it's not a cut that divides things absolutely, but a cut-continuance?

Guide: Right. Some scholars have noted this exact point (Shirane 2002). It's not a division but a subtle reorientation, a pause or shift that doesn't sever but reshapes. Like the *kire* aesthetic principle, there is a cut but also a continuity. The emotion might shift from happy to sad, or from pessimistic to optimistic, but in such a case, it shouldn't be a transition from one emotion replaced by another: the poet coaxes the reader to see how the new emotional valence was already present in the earlier part of the poem—imperceptible, perhaps, but latent.

It's relatively simple to provoke a reaction by juxtaposing something happy with something sad, but far more challenging to remain within a happy emotion while revealing its hidden valence of sadness. This sadness doesn't negate the happiness; it inflects it, adding depth and complexity without breaking the continuity.

Non-Speaking

Artist: I love this understanding of poetry, but it's hard to imagine how an author can observe all of these constraints in such a tiny poem.

Guide: Okay, but remember we discussed how the tea master aims at a natural spontaneity, a "way" of moving beyond active–passive binaries, as expressed in the Daoist idea of non-action, or *wu wei*. We're now facing a similar case, but with language.

Yes, a *haiku* poet needs extensive training and must observe many rules, but in the end, they too are aiming at a natural linguistic spontaneity, beyond *active speech* and *passive silence*. Let's build on what we know of Daoist "non-action" and discuss another major principle in the *Daodejing*, "non-speaking" (*bù yán*, 不言). In the second chapter of the *Daodejing*, Laozi writes

> *Therefore the sage resides with the task of non-action, practices the teaching of non-speaking.*

Theologian: How is it that someone could be in a state of not-speaking and write a poem?

Guide: The essential point to keep in mind here is that non-speaking is non-dual; in this case, it doesn't abide the *speaking–silence* binary. So, non-speaking isn't silence. Remember, the Dao is the non-dual source from out of which duality arises? Non-speaking is a way of using language attuned to the Dao, and such an attunement makes both silence *and* speech possible.

The important thing to keep in mind for your concern is that, for *Geidō* practices based on Daoist principles, the type of effort cultivated is, paradoxically, a kind of effortlessness. If the *haiku* poet feels like they're over-exerting themselves, they might not be in a state of non-speaking.

Becoming a poet—or any Japanese aesthetic practitioner—requires years of disciplined training and deep knowledge. These practices are famously rigorous, with strict codes and long-term dedication. But the ultimate aim is unity with the Dao, whether in action or language—and the Dao moves with simple, spontaneous naturalness. Language, too, should follow this natural, non-forced flow.

Nature doesn't need to think or exert its will to do the beautiful things it does—it is effortless and spontaneous. Likewise, a haiku poet has enormous constraints imposed upon their expression, but ultimately, the aim is to let go of all deliberation and volition, and allow language to occur naturally, effortlessly, to be taken by the world and allow it to express itself through one's own linguistic negativity, or absence.

But, let me emphasize, non-speaking isn't a go-with-the-flow kind of passivity. Non-speaking is neither actively speaking nor passively remaining silent, it's simply a type of language that is attuned to the natural world, attuned to the Dao, and thus beyond the dualities of speech and silence, activity or passivity.

Artist: But, we can all speak effortlessly in many situations. I don't imagine I could ever compose a good *haiku*.

Guide: This is emblematic of Japanese aesthetic practices: many are highly sophisticated practices of simple things we all do in everyday life—arranging flowers, handwriting, making tea—but after a lifetime of dedication, these practitioners infuse them with the most profound depths of humanity and existence. Importantly, the practitioners don't reach some elevated state divorced from the mundane. Even those who achieve the utmost levels of aesthetic mastery remain immersed in the everyday. This, in many ways, captures the essence of Zen Buddhism and the *Geidō* aesthetic practices based thereupon.

Philosopher: But, I still don't understand. How can you use language but remain between speaking and silence? If I write something, or say something, aren't I on one end of that binary? Speaking and not being silent?

Guide: This is an important question not just for Japanese aesthetics or the tea ceremony, but also for phenomenology, as several of its major proponents also invoke this idea of silence.[10] But, let's go back to Daoism for one more minute.

The Chinese word for non-speaking is *Bù yán*, (不言). Don't worry about the character for now, but note that "*bu*" is another way to form a negation in Chinese. So, once again, we're alerted to think about language not just in terms of positivity, but also negativity.

Earlier, we spoke about how the Dao is non-binary. How did that relate to how the Dao is visualized? Does anyone remember?

Theologian: Yeah, with the *yin yang* symbol.

Guide: Right, and that symbol shows what? In the most abstract sense?

Theologian: Non-duality.

Guide: Yes, and in the case of that symbol, what is the non-duality between?

Theologian: The non-duality of presence and absence, positivity and negativity.

Guide: Perfect, yes. The *yin yang* symbol illustrates the mutual interpenetration of presence and absence, positivity and negativity. If non-speaking is a way of using language aligning with the Dao, then we should imagine that non-speaking also has this ambiguous dynamic of absence and presence.

Remember, too, the other key point about the *yin yang* symbol: neither *yin* nor *yang* is ever purely what it is. There's always an element of the opposite inflecting what seems otherwise present or absent. The same holds true for speech and silence. You don't have speech at one time and silence at another: speech depends on silence, and all silence is punctuated by speech, deriving its specific meaning from the language surrounding it.

Artist: I guess it's similar to that point you made about the Japanese landscape paintings. There's no negative space "here' and positive space "there". Negativity and positivity pervade the entire painting.

Guide: Precisely

Philosopher: So, when we're saying things or not saying anything, speech and silence are both part of these linguistic expressions?

Guide: Always. And, let me pick up on this other term you just used, "expression". Even that term is perhaps slightly inappropriate for describing what the *haiku* poet does with language.

The Latin roots—*ex* ("outward") and *primere* ("to push")—reflect the western idea of expression as subject pushing inner thoughts into the external objective world. This reinforces familiar dualities: inner vs. outer, active creator vs. passive world.

For the *haiku* poet, though, the goal isn't to express internal desire, but to let the world speak through the poet's silence—through their linguistic negativity. Just as we engage with the negative space of a haiku or painting, nature can speak through the poet's quiet.

But, let me repeat, we must not think that the poet's non-speaking as merely passive silence. Of course, there's still some linguistic activity, otherwise a poem would never be written. Or, we might say, there would be no linguistic positivity at all. But, we know from the dots in the *yin yang* symbol that there's always an element of positivity inflecting the negative, and vice versa—never pure positivity or pure negativity. And, by extension, never pure speech or silence.

For a negated self, at the moment of artistic action, everything is let go. The goal is to empty the self, so that a much greater artistic agent can implicate itself in the expression: nature itself.

If the artist were to rely only on what *they* thought or what *they* wanted to express, this would constrain expression to the realm of the positive, leaving less room for nature to speak and express itself. This is a crucial aspect of Japanese aesthetic practice: nature is regarded as the greatest aesthetic force. By emptying the self and embracing the interplay of positivity and negativity, the artist makes space for nature to participate in the creative act.

This is why some theoreticians have described the "haiku attitude" not as an ability, skill, or capacity, but as a "readiness" (Yusada 1995). If we were selves, we might believe that we can dictate when and how things will happen—when we will speak and when we'll remain silent. But, as a negated self, calligraphy, archery, or flower arranging issue not just out of one's own positivity but out of the vast realm of relations emerging through the negativity of the self. So, there's no guarantee that you can choose the moment a poem will come into being. You can't choose when or how to write a poem, but you can cultivate a "readiness" for relations to coalesce such that one comes into being.

In this sense, the *haiku* poet doesn't see a tree, form a mental representation, deliberate on it, and then decide out of their individual cognitive and linguistic resources the best way to depict that tree in a poem. That would be an act of self-driven expression, not poetry as non-speaking.

In the case of the "haiku attitude" or readiness, it would be more as if, in the presence of the tree the poet doesn't so much choose to write a poem as they find themself already compelled to do so. Through its negativity—its relationality—the poet herself is constituted by the tree, echoing the Chinese saying that if one wishes to paint bamboo they "must learn to grow bamboo inside oneself." It's not a case of the self acting upon something external, or "expressing" itself, but rather the tree, already a part of and acting through the poet who becomes the site through which nature expresses itself.

This is one way of understanding the unique task of the Japanese aesthetic practitioner: to empty the self and cultivate readiness so that art emerges not as an act of individual volition but as a collaboration with the vast relationality of nature.

Artist: Okay, I can see now how we all have an effortless way of doing mundane things, but to elevate that, to make handwriting or tea serving into an art this is substantially more demanding.

Guide: Yes, and even though, according to Buddhist thought, we're all non-selves—that is our reality—we're deluded about this reality by attachments, desires and ignorance.

Philosopher: . . . and substance ontology.

Guide: Right, and just as the practice aiming at Zen realization is a lifelong endeavor, so too is the path of becoming effortlessly spontaneous as a *haiku* or calligraphy artist.

We can all write a description of a tree, but few can do that with seventeen syllables in a way that reaches so deep throughout the negative that it remains open for centuries for others to enter into relation with.

So, in the most abstract sense, the difference between us and a highly trained Japanese aesthetic practitioners comes down to our ability to modulate the linguistic positive and negative.

Theologian: I think I get it. When I speak of the tree, as someone untrained, not a poet, I use words—positivity—to describe the tree, but I invoke very little beyond the positive, only the minimum negativity inherent to language itself. A highly trained poet, on the other hand, when moved to write about the tree, they can use fewer words, the minimum *positivity*, but they can evoke vast worlds *in the negative*.

Guide: I'm going to write that down. The *haiku* poet minimizes the positive and maximizes the negative. That's perfect. And, another way of expressing the idea that artists can affect us from out of the negative. And, a perfect explanation of how the smallest poem can be the largest.

What then about the tea host herself?

Tea of no Guest, no Host

Philosopher: What host?

Guide: Our host.

Philosopher: There's no host.

Guide: Ah, I see. Nice. You've turned the table on me.

Artist: So, if we've done away with the host, I guess there are no guests either.

Guide: There's actually a tea saying from medieval times, *mu-hin-shu* (無賓主), that conveyed that idea.

Anybody recognize anything in this phrase, "*mu-hin-shu*"?

Theologian: The *mu* (無). It must indicate that we're speaking of emptiness. So, along the lines of relational ontology and co-dependent origination.

Guide: Great that you recognized the *mu* character. The other parts of the phrase, the *hin* (賓) and *shu* (主) refer to host and guest, respectively, or sometimes to teacher and student, master and disciple. Put them together, and we have "the non-existence of guest and host" (Sen Sōshitsu XV, 1971, p. 1).

And, what do you remember about negation?

Theologian: That it's not *less than*. It's ontologically *more than*.

Guide: Exactly. By each striving towards negation, host and guest enable something bigger than the sum of their parts. Let me read you what Sen Sōshitsu XV says:

> *when host and guest are in harmony at a tea gathering, they merge into a single entity that transcends their respective roles.*
>
> (1979, p. 40)

There's an interesting twist here, though. The terms host and guest, master and disciple all seem to suggest a power imbalance where the master is superior to the disciple. In Zen, particularly in the Rinzai sect, it's the *disciple* who leads the master (Sen Sōshitsu XV, 1971). Rikyū followed this logic in his tea ceremony, according an elevated status to the disciple over the master, and the guest over the host.

It's getting late. Let's break now and come back tomorrow to speak about some other elements here in the alcove.

15

Flowers for Tea

Ikebana / Chabana / Kadō

Guide: Welcome back non-guests!

~ *All three smile as they bow.*

Let's head back into the hut and talk about the flower arrangement, shall we?

~ *Without saying a word, the group arrange themselves in a line and one-by-one slide through the nijiriguchi into the hut.*

Does anyone know anything about this?

Artist: That's *ikebana*, right?

Guide: Close. *Ikebana* (生け花) translates as "arranging flowers", but there are two more specific terms worth learning. First, there is *kadō* (華道), which, as you'll know by the "*dō*" sound, refers to the practice of flower arranging as a "way"—a Daoist practice.

But, more specifically for our purposes, these flowers we have here would be referred to as *Chabana* (茶花), or "tea flowers", a distinct style that developed within the tea ceremony.

Relative to *ikebana*, *chabana* inclines more towards an augmented simplicity, to use a bit of a contradiction. There's even less color here than you're probably used to seeing in an *ikebana* arrangement.

Chabana also inspired an interesting convention called "throw-in flowers" (*nageirebana* 投入花), which became one of the dominant styles throughout the twentieth century and is now almost synonymous with *chabana*.

Chabana is often considered a more "naturalistic" style—not manipulating or contorting stems as is the norm with *ikebana*. As "thrown-in", flowers are meant to spontaneously arrange themselves with minimal human intervention.[1] Unlike *ikebana*, where there are many schools with their own elaborate codes and rules, *chabana* is said to have almost no rules other than looking as natural as possible, free from human expression (Davidson 1970).

The idea is to discard as many flowers as possible to create an arrangement that feels incomplete (Amagasaki 2017), and to invite the guests to engage their imagination—something unnecessary in an arrangement bursting with flowers with obvious marks of human intervention. Further in line with these aesthetic preferences, buds or early-blooming flowers should not be overly fragrant to avoid their scent pervading the hut.

You'll notice that the vase is made with a single piece of bamboo. This is a direct reference to Rikyū, but it need not always be this specific vessel, it can be made of pottery, metal or woven reeds fashioned into a basket. Depending on the season and the themes the host is exploring, the flower arrangement can also hang from the ceiling or be affixed to the back wall of the alcove.

There's one moment in tea lore that beautifully illustrates this *chabana* principle. White camellias, highly cherished by tea masters, were preferred not as fully bloomed, but as buds on the verge of unfurling. The story goes that Hideyoshi (豊臣 秀吉, 1537–98), the great ruler and unifier of Japan, specifically requested an abundance of camellias to decorate a ceremony he attended. Upon arrival, he was shocked to find none in sight. Rikyū had cleverly played on Hideyoshi's expectations, deliberately excluding all flowers from the garden, with only one single camellia in the alcove.

Can anyone think what his aim might have been?

Artist: Hideyoshi had assumed that more would have been more. He couldn't see that less is more.

Theologian: . . . he could only see the positive absence of the flowers, not their negative presence.

Guide: Very nicely put. Rikyū, though, did understand that if the camellias filled the garden, they would make a strong impact in the positive valence, in "actuality", but the overall experience would be, as you said, "less than". He knew that excessive positivity can actually reduce the impact of things.

If flowers can have an impact, they do so through the positive *and* the negative, in two-worlds, "actuality" and "hollowness". Rikyū might not have used such terminology, but seems to have intuitively grasped these aesthetic principles. Rather than diluting the effect of the flowers with an indulgent display of blossoms throughout the garden, he chose to amplify their significance through absence, elevating the experience with a single flower.

There's a Japanese principle called *isshin tokudo* (一心得道), which Rikyū reinterprets as meaning the full beauty of camellias manifesting through a single flower.[2]

Philosopher: It sounds like another instance of the holographic logic we already encountered.

Guide: Yes, good observation.

Let me share more about the religious and philosophical significance of flowers in Japan. As I mentioned earlier, *kadō* reflects Daoist influence. Flowers are also deeply significant in Buddhism, as seen in the naming of some of its most important sutras, such as the *Flower Garland Sutra* (*Kegon-kyō* 華厳経) and, of course, the *Lotus Sutra*.[3]

Can anyone think how flowers might play a role in Shintoism?

Theologian: Maybe it was a way of invoking *kami*, of appeasing them so they assist with the ceremony?

Guide: That's right. In ceremonies or rituals at temples or sacred events, flower arrangements often serve as a means of appealing to the *kami* spirits, inviting them to dwell in the space and bring good fortune. This practice is tied to invocations called *yorishiro* (依り代).

Many Shinto objects, such as gates, large hemp ropes (*shimenawa*, 注連縄), and paper tassels (*shide*, 紙垂) shaped like lightning bolts, are thought to be *yorishiro*. These can also be large sacred rocks or trees, and in some cases, flower arrangements like this one. Some even describe the stems and branches of flowers as resembling lightning rods, channeling the presence of the *kami* into the ceremony (Tamura 2000).

Those are some of the philosophical and religious principles guiding a *Chabana* artist. Let's now consider the practice itself, as it shares similarities with and differences from other *Geidō* practices.

Like many Japanese aesthetic traditions, flower arranging originated in China and arrived in Japan with Buddhism in the early sixth century. After its introduction, the practice became highly systematized and took on distinctive Japanese qualities, especially during the Heian period (794–1185). If you're interested in early texts or manuals that systematize the practice, let me know, and I can send you some references.[4]

As I mentioned, the Japanese are deeply attuned to nature, and their artists have developed refined ways of portraying seasonal change in literature and visual art. In *kadō*, flower arrangements reflect the seasons, with living plants making seasonal harmony essential. Japanese arts often include detailed flower descriptions to evoke seasonal particularities.[5]

Originally, flower arranging was used in various ceremonies to adorn altars, ancestral shrines, and alcoves like this one, common in traditional Japanese homes. It became popular and systematized alongside the rise of the tea ceremony in the sixteenth century. Since then, many styles[6] have developed, each with detailed rules we can't fully cover today. If you're interested, I'd recommend visiting Rokkaku-dō (六角堂), a Kyoto temple linked to traditional Japanese flower-arranging arts.

Nishitani – Cutting between Life and Death

Artist: In Japan, is flower arranging itself considered an art form?

Guide: What do you think?

Artist: It's probably considered more of a craft in the western world, isn't it? Definitely not one of the fine arts.

Philosopher: It's interesting that flower arranging can be considered an art. I can't think of any other art form where the object is living at one point and dead in another.

Guide: If you remember back to our earlier conversation, about *mono no aware*, we discussed how the western art world has venerated permanence and has gone to amazing lengths to maintain and restore great artworks, hoping to preserve them for as long as possible, thus trying to deny time. But, the main principle underlying *ikebana* or *chabana* were impermanence rather than permanence, so flower arrangements are meant to be part of the flow of time rather than denying it.

Theologian: If the goal is to be truly mimetic, shouldn't they embrace impermanence instead of denying it? Wouldn't it make more sense to use a living substance to represent a living being?

Guide: That observation leads to an interesting etymological point. Although I agree completely with what you're saying, we might be reifying another binary, this time between life and death.

It might seem contradictory, but another translation of *ikebana* (活け花) is "giving flowers life".

Philosopher: But, it's the other way around? Cutting flowers takes life, it doesn't give life?

Guide: Can anyone think of any problems with this thinking?

Theologian: It's hard to imagine how there might be a middle way between life and death. With that binary, it seems pretty straightforward—you're either one or the other.

Guide: Yes, it's challenging to think about life and death outside strict binaries, but that's precisely what both eastern and even some western philosophers have done—particularly in Buddhist philosophy but also in phenomenology (Loy 1990).

Let me introduce a Japanese philosopher who engages deeply with these questions of life and death in his writings. I have a few quotes from Nishitani Keiji (西谷啓治, 1900–90), a Kyoto School philosopher, that speak directly to these questions of permanence and impermanence, life and death in the context of *ikebana*.

Does anybody know anything about Nishitani?

Philosopher: I think he was alive until not that long ago, wasn't he?

Theologian: He's written about often in a religious context. I seem to remember that he studied in Europe, right?

Guide: Yes, that's right. Nishitani was in Germany from 1937 to 1939, and this is one of the early east–west touchpoints between the Kyoto School and Phenomenology: he actually attended some of Heidegger's lectures on Nietzsche in Freiburg.

Nishitani completed his PhD with Nishida at Kyoto Imperial University and later became the Chair of Philosophy and Religion, holding that position from 1943 to 1964.

His dissertation explored several European philosophers, and he continued writing on the likes of Bergson, Kant, Schelling, Kierkegaard, Pascal, Augustine, and especially Nietzsche, frequently placing them in dialogue with Buddhist philosophers and concepts we've discussed—such as emptiness, non-self, and co-dependent origination. One of his abiding concerns was with the question of nihilism in Europe and Japan. He also commented on aesthetics, specifically addressing life and death in the context of *ikebana*. Let me tell you a bit about how this interest of his came about.

After returning to Japan from Germany, where he had the chance to see many of the great works of European art history, he had an epiphany upon seeing *ikebana* with new eyes. This led him to write an article entitled "The Japanese Art of Arranged Flowers" where he remarked on how he felt European art seemed to "ignore the change wrought by time and desir[ed] to remain no matter what, these works of art manifest a will to endure." European art, he thought, "seeks eternity by denying temporality", whereas *ikebana* "tries to unveil eternity by being thoroughly temporal."

Let me read you a little bit more of where he elaborates on this idea.

> *the beauty expressed in ikebana is created to last only for a short time. Such art changes with the season and reveals its beauty only for the few days after the flowers and branches have been cut. It is, by its very nature, something temporary and improvised... It is a beauty which embraces time, a beauty which appears out of the impermanency of time itself... Instead of trying to deny time while in the midst of it, ikebana moves along in time without the slightest gap.*
>
> (Nishitani 1995, p. 23)

Artist: Fascinating. Greek sculpture seems to deny time and strive for permanence, and *ikebana* artists actively provoke the flower's impermanence.

Guide: Yes, exactly. This idea of denying time or mortality brings us to some fascinating intersections of Buddhist philosophy and phenomenology.

To go back to the earlier question about the non-duality of life and death, Heidegger is perhaps most well known in the west for having complicated this binary.

Of course, in an everyday sense, what Heidegger called the "ontic", death is simply death, and it happens at the end of life when your vital signs go flat. In the ontic sense, life and death are mutually exclusive and can't exist in one being at the same time. A *cannot* equal not-A. But, in what Heidegger called the "ontological" sense, life and death are more nuanced and profound.

Philosopher: Is this ontic-ontological distinction like Ueda's "two-fold" world idea?

Guide: Hmm, there might be some basic similarities, but we would have to be careful with making too easy of a comparison here. Whereas Ueda's "hollowness" and "actuality" might line up with positivity and negativity, that's not necessarily the case with what's called Heidegger's "ontological difference". That's not to say that we couldn't find some similarities, but again, we have to be careful with "is it just like?" kind of comparisons. It could be that Ueda had Heidegger's "ontological difference" in mind when constructing his theory of a "two-fold" world, but we would definitely find aspects of Ueda's theory that aren't in Heidegger's.

In any case, what's important is that for Heidegger, death is *part of* existence. Even while alive, we are, what he calls "being towards death" (*Sein zum Tode*). Death isn't only an event at the end of one's life. Instead, the entire structure of human existence—our everyday activities, goals, even how we relate to others—are oriented by the inevitability of our mortality.

Theologian: Even if we don't ever think about death, how is it part of the structure of existence when alive?

Guide: Remember what we've already said about the phenomenological concept of "world"? Our world shapes us not just through conscious reflection but in the pre-reflective ways it imposes on thinking and acting. Even if the thought of death doesn't explicitly enter our minds, it still permeates our existence in an *ontological* sense. In fact, it might shape us even more because we *don't* think about it directly.

Heidegger isn't so concerned with the moment when we think about or reflect on ourselves as mortal beings. His point is that the "world" is only disclosed to us insofar as we are being-towards-death. Despite this inescapable aspect of our existence, Heidegger believed that we often act in ways that deny or ignore this ontological reality. For him, such denial leads to an "inauthentic" existence. To live inauthentically is to deny how we exist in time, to avoid acknowledging that every moment of our lives is shaped by the fact that we're finite beings.

His masterwork, *Being and Time* (*Sein und Zeit*, 1927), centers on embracing time and our *being-towards-death*, rather than denying it.

Can anyone think how this might relate to Nishitani and *ikebana*?

Philosopher: It seems like Nishitani is saying that western art, particularly the instances that sought permanence, are denying time—ignoring death and impermanence. Maybe Heidegger would have also felt that *ikebana* and its artists affirmed time more authentically by embracing impermanence as finite existence.

Guide: Of course, Heidegger didn't write about *ikebana*, but I think he would be predisposed to your interpretation. As we've discussed, he had a keen interest in Asian philosophies. He even wrote *"A Dialogue on Language between a Japanese and an Inquirer,"* (Heidegger 1982) where Heidegger cast himself as the "Inquirer." The "Japanese" in the dialogue, named "Count Kuki", almost certainly refers to the Japanese aesthetician Kuki Shūzō (九鬼 周造, 1888–1941) who was also visiting Europe and meeting important intellectuals during the time Heidegger was lecturing.[7] You'll find many scholars commenting on the fascinating similarities between Heidegger and Asian philosophies.[8]

Theologian: But what about the question of the life-death duality? How can cutting flowers actually give them life?

Guide: Maybe the issue lies in how we interpret "gives them life". We might instinctively think it refers to "more" life—an increased *quantity* of life—which, of course, sounds unlikely. But perhaps what Nishitani means is that it gives them augmented *quality* of life.

Philosopher: Since the nature of reality is impermanence, maybe the act of cutting flowers accelerates their eventual death, but it is still an act aligned with their reality as impermanent.

Guide: I think you've hit on Nishitani's essential point. And, to put that in the context of our concern with aesthetics, in his "The Japanese Art of Arranged Flowers", he highlights a special kind of beauty that emerges from embracing, rather than concealing, the impermanence of flowers.

> *Such beauty is momentary and yet it is as if that momentariness is transformed into a beauty of a higher order. The essence of the plant being turned into art lies in the aforementioned activity of cutting the plant.*
>
> (1995, p. 26)

His point is quite simple, yet profound. Essentially, as you've already mentioned, the nature of all things, including flowers is impermanence. He argues that all beings—flowers and humans alike—are constantly striving to maintain their existence, constantly trying to deny our inevitable impermanence—running from our being-towards-death, Heidegger might say.

To cut a flower does indeed hasten its death, but in those few days when it remains alive, severed from its source of life—what Nishitani calls its "rootedness"—the flower reveals its nature. It discloses its impermanence, and perhaps even the existential nature of time itself. This act of cutting and arranging intensifies their aesthetic impact, suggesting that there is a realm—both existential and aesthetic—where life and death are non-dual.

Let me read to you more from Nishitani's piece:

> *The flower is thus made to stand poised in its hidden essence, to reveal that essence. From the perspective of their fundamental nature, all things in the world are rootless blades of grass. Such grass, however, having put roots down into the ground, itself hides its fundamental rootlessness. Through having been cut from their roots, they are, for the first time, made to thoroughly manifest their fundamental nature—their rootlessness.*
>
> (p. 25)

How can we connect this metaphor of "rootlessness" to the language we've been discussing?

Theologian: It sounds like another term for Ueda's "hollowness".

Philosopher: Or, "emptiness".

Guide: Yes, great. Nishitani makes this exact connection. By cutting the flower, he writes that "the *emptiness* (*kū*) which lies hidden in the depths of the plant is unveiled." And he places this unveiling firmly within the context of time.

> *It can even be said that the plant itself, in being empty, is the appearance of eternity in time. This momentariness of a higher order expresses eternity. Time itself, in being completely temporal, becomes an eternal moment.*
>
> (p. 26)

As you said, the *quantity* of time the flower exists might be shortened by the act of cutting, but it is in embracing time—embracing impermanence and aligning with emptiness—that binaries of short and long, permanent and impermanent, life and death are overcome. Even in a fleeting encounter with emptiness, as flowers can reveal, there is the possibility of an experience beyond life and death—an experience where eternity is disclosed. As Nishitani writes, "With the activity of cutting, emptiness is unveiled in the depths of existence, and the eternal moment is realized." (p. 26)

Theologian: You mentioned earlier that we'd discuss flower arranging in terms of non-action and non-speaking. I can see how the "thrown-in" style has an element of non-action, but what about non-speaking? How are we supposed to think about *Chabana* in terms of language?

Non-speaking, *Hanakotoba* and Mimesis

Guide: You might be surprised to hear that even here, with these flowers—seemingly mute entities—there is a linguistic aspect.

As you might expect, there's an elaborate system of codification surrounding what certain elements of an arrangement communicate, it's known as *hanakotoba* (花言葉), which translates roughly as "flower language".

While this may seem quintessentially Japanese, many cultures have practiced "Floriography", linking flower types and colors to emotions, virtues, sins, historical events, war, and religion. It appears in religious, secular, and folkloric contexts across Europe, Asia, and Africa—and in the works of writers like Shakespeare, Austen, Brontë, and Steinbeck.

In Victorian England, floral dictionaries[9] enabled readers to decipher hidden codes that flowers could communicate—often emotions or desires social conventions prohibited from vocalizing.

While *ikebana* conveys meaning, we shouldn't see it as encoding hidden messages or simply symbolizing something beyond itself. Once again, we need to set aside representational thinking and strict binaries between linguistic and non-linguistic forms.

In most western cases, whether religious or secular, flowers *convey* human language, but they aren't themselves considered linguistic. A person giving a specific flower as a symbol of their love, for example, is merely using the flowers as a medium to convey their own human language. The flower itself isn't linguistic, it's merely a vessel *representing* what humans can put into words.

You might be asking: how is *ikebana* different, since it also conveys information or communicates messages to us, like the details of a season.[10] But, the difference is crucial, and brings us back to our broader attempt to distance Japanese arts from our western mimetic assumptions.

In *ikebana*, flowers invoking a particular season are not meant to *represent* or communicate information about that season. The idea is that summer or autumn are *actually* made present—the season is *there* in the flowers, twigs, and leaves. *Hanakotoba* does not function as a symbol, standing in for something it is not. The flower does not *represent* autumn. The flower *is* autumn. And, the point is not to think about the qualities of a season when seeing an arrangement, but to *feel* the fall, to experience it.

Take these budding leaves on this Japanese Andromeda shrub, for example. We don't need to consciously reflect on them or deliberately contemplate what they symbolize—how they might gesture toward the garden's awakening from winter, or foreshadow the warm summer days ahead. Before any of that enters our thoughts, those budding branches are already shaping our experience at a level below conscious awareness. They don't *represent* summer, or heat, or longer days; rather, they pattern our bodies in a kind of silent attunement. And now, that world of pre-reflective sensation is being invoked—echoed in this flower arrangement. Those sensations from *outside* the hut have been brought into the relational context *inside* the hut, permeating this space through the few dried twigs and leaves the tea master has deliberately retained.

Using our earlier terms, we might say the flowers are linguistic—much like how the tea host acted through absence. When language is understood ontologically, including both presence and absence, the line between speech and silence softens. This lets us see flowers as part of a broader linguistic continuum shared by all of phenomenal reality.

Philosopher: I'm still having a hard time understanding how flowers are actually *linguistic*.

Artist: . . . then, wouldn't all reality be linguistic?

Dōgen—Language beyond Anthropocentrism

Guide: The western philosophical tradition has largely seen language as a dividing line between humans and the rest of existence: we're linguistic beings and the rest of the world isn't, so it goes. In this sense, our ideas about language are un-apologetically anthropocentric. Essentially, *language is something that divides us away from the world*—we are in a *dis*continuity with the rest of existence, insofar as we are linguistic beings.

But let's return to the Japanese Zen Buddhist philosopher we spoke about a few days ago, Dōgen, to see how language constitutes a *continuity* among all existence—not a way that we're divided from reality, but something binding all things.

Artist: I think I might have visited one of Dōgen's temples, *Eihei-ji* was it?

Guide: Yes, Dōgen founded *Eihei-ji* (永平寺) and served as its head during the last decade of his life, between 1243 and 1252. He moved outside Kyoto to establish training grounds, in part to distance himself from the rivalries with Rinzai Buddhism.

An interesting intercultural note is that several scholars have drawn comparisons between Dōgen and European thinkers, noting how his ideas prefigured phenomenological approaches to time, ontology, existentialism, and language—in some cases by as much as 800 years (Heine 1985).

But for our purposes, what's most important is Dōgen's understanding of language. His view helps us shift from our anthropocentric assumptions to an understanding of language that includes all phenomenal reality—hopefully giving us an appreciation of *hanakotoba* beyond mimesis or symbolism.

For Dōgen, it wasn't only humans, but all phenomenal reality was constantly communicating the Buddha's teaching. In his *Bukkyō* (仏教) fascicle, he writes

> [N]ot to proclaim those sutras—that is how they are proclaimed. "Proclaimed" means the entire universe, and the entire universe proclaims. . . . This world and other worlds also proclaim those sutras. . . . We must know that the vast and unlimited Buddhist teaching is not separate from the shippei or fly whisk. The vastness of the Buddhist teaching is revealed in a staff and fist.
>
> (Kim 1985)

Dōgen revised an earlier position of Kūkai's (空海; 774–835), whose theory "*hosshin seppō*" (法身説法) asserted that all *sentient* beings proclaim the Buddha's dharma. Dōgen took this another step further, proposing *mujō seppō* (無情説法), claiming that not only all sentient beings, but *all beings*—sentient and *insentient* alike—proclaim the dharma.

Artist: I'm not sure I get it. I can see how other sentient beings, animals for instance, might have language, but insentient beings? Clearly, they don't articulate themselves the way humans do.

Guide: Of course, we shouldn't assume that human language and the language of the landscape or stones are the same. As Dōgen writes,

> *The manner in which "the insentient preach the Dharma" must necessarily be as in the case of the sentient.*
>
> (2009b, p. 157)

And, he gives a subtle warning of our anthropocentric views of language when he says

> *to wrest voices from the sentient world and to liken them to the voices of the insentient world, is not Buddhism.*
>
> (p. 157).

Dōgen is urging us to move beyond the expectation that the rest of the world must have a verbal form of language like ours—with alphabets, grammatical structures, and punctuation. His point is that just because our language is different, this doesn't necessarily mean that we are linguistically *discontinuous* with the world. Yes, we express ourselves differently, but all phenomenal reality is constantly expressing itself.[11]

Theologian: Okay, so he wouldn't say that all reality has language the way humans do.

Guide: No, definitely not. A typical reaction to this idea is to resist what appears to be an attempt to *elevate* insentient phenomenal reality up to the linguistic level of humans. But it's more useful to think of it the other way around. *Mujō seppō* isn't about raising insentient beings to a higher level, it's more like he's lowering us down to see the most basic fact of human language, that it is expressive: at this level we find a continuity with all beings.

Philosopher: Okay, I see. So the point isn't to erase differences in how all phenomenal reality expresses itself but to recognize that this expressive nature is something we share rather than something that sets us apart as different and special.

Guide: Right. Dōgen is particularly concerned about how we suffer and harm the world because of anthropocentric views, seeing the world only from a human perspective. He promotes a way of seeing things as they appear for all beings, which is referred to as his "polycentric perspectivism".

And, for our purposes, we can adopt this way of thinking about language as a means of overcoming the mimetic and representational assumptions we would normally use to interpret the various details within the ceremony—flowers, stones and otherwise.[12]

While we can discuss those details and analyse them in lectures like this, the point isn't to be interpreting a set of symbols throughout the day. All of the aesthetic details—the half-open door, the stepping stones, the hanging scroll, and the tea itself—these aren't symbolic, they're not primarily meant to be reflected upon but to be experienced. And not experienced as objects, but as a non-self extending throughout its environment. Everything we encounter serves as conduits into a different experience of selfhood, and while studying can help us understand how that can happen, or even elevate our experience, you don't need any specialized knowledge. All you need to do is drink a cup of tea.

Likewise, the tea master arranges each element—from water on the path to stone placement—not as information or symbols, but as invitations into an expanded self and experience. These elements gently tune the non-selves who enter the garden, helping us feel the deep relationality that shapes who we are—or who we can become at our most expansive.

The beauty of this practice is that it doesn't aim to transport us elsewhere or reveal a deity, but draws us closer to what's already here—in the plants, minerals, raw wood, and withered flowers of the *chabana*. In this simplicity, we feel how we're made of the same everyday elements and expressive forces that shape the world around us. This is the heart of the tea ceremony and of Zen-inspired *Geidō* practices.

And after spending two days discussing the objects here in the alcove, it may seem excessive that we have not yet begun the tea ceremony. And it is. But, as I mentioned, Rikyū made this space the aesthetic heart of *Wabicha*, and we could spend many more days discussing just this *ikebana* arrangement.

Artist: I think I'll never look at flowers the same again.

Guide: Well, if that's the case, it might be a good sign that you're genuinely engaged in this aesthetic world. These are things—flowers, handwriting, tea— that go completely un-noticed in our day-to-day lives, but the Zen arts mean to bring our attention to the depths of these everyday things, and the soteriological potential of the everyday itself.

Zen—Phenomenology of the *Alltäglich*

Guide: Unlike most fine arts originating in Europe, where painters and sculptors work with materials to produce objects most people never touch, housed in churches or museums none of us live in, *Geidō* practitioners do things almost everyone does: calligraphy is just writing, tea drinking is just tea drinking, and arranging flowers is just arranging flowers. We do these anywhere—in the homes we live in—no need for sophisticated tools or materials.

Theologian: They're certainly not seen as spiritual practices.

Guide: Exactly. One of Zen Buddhism's most fundamental tenets is the soteriological potential of everyday existence. That might sound complicated, which is completely against Zen ethos, but it's very simple—the simplest, perhaps. It means we don't need to do anything special to practice Zen. No church, no sacred texts or eminent teachers are necessary. The fabric of existence itself, always here, always now, perpetually offers the opportunity for spiritual exercise, and ultimately, realization. Just in the act of writing, sitting, arranging flowers, or drinking tea—everything we need is always right here, in the mundane everyday.

This quote by Haga Koshiro sums it up when it describes Zen as

> *single-minded attention to the task at hand; when sitting, just sit; when writing, just write; when making tea, just make tea. Completely merged with the here and now of any activity, on experiences the state of single-minded attention which is the heart of Zen practice and the origin of true Zen art.*

(1983, p. 11)

Zen places the greatest importance on what's always already right in front of you. Zen is always underfoot, is a common saying expressing its ethos. Unlike other religions or philosophies that speculate about transcendent realms, rely on complex methodologies, or require elaborate institutions, Zen believes that the highest philosophic or religious potential lies within the world we're ever surrounded with.

One of my favorite expressions of this comes from Dōgen:

> *the real aspect is all things. All things are this aspect, this character, this body, this mind, this world, this wind and this rain, this sequence of daily going, living, sitting, and lying down, this series of melancholy, joy, action, and inaction, this stick and wand, this Buddha's smile, this transmission and reception of the doctrine, this study and practice, this evergreen pine and ever unbreakable bamboo.*
>
> (1969, p. 365)

As I mentioned, Dōgen has been widely discussed in relation to phenomenology, especially for his views on time, being, and poetic language. He doesn't just value the mundane—he dissolves dualities like nirvana and samsara, meditation and realization, showing the soteriological power of this very moment. Zazen isn't a method for reaching a higher state. As Dōgen says, it is "practice-realization, one and the same" (*shushō-ichinyo*, 修証一如)—meditation is enlightenment itself.

Many philosophical traditions are divided into specialized fields—epistemology, ethics, metaphysics, aesthetics—each suited to certain contexts, but rarely applicable in *this* moment. Epistemology tells you how you know things; Ethics considers what is right, good, or just; Metaphysics explores the nature of reality; and Aesthetics defines beauty. But how often do we actually engage in epistemological debates? When was the last time you needed a well-reasoned argument about the metaphysical structure of reality? Have you recently invoked ethical theories to justify your actions or critique others? These moments do happen, and it's important to have philosophical tools when they arise—but they are rare, aren't they?

Knowledge of these domains of philosophy is certainly valuable, but they function more like specialized tools for special situations—but, situations rarely arising for most of us. Existentialism, by contrast, is the situation every one of us is in *all of the time*—from the moment we awake until we shut our eyes at night, our existence is at stake. Zen is "existential" in the sense that its practices are applicable *in all moments*, wherever one might find oneself.

When it comes to our existential well-being—how we suffer, and how we might strive to modify that suffering—this question is always present, not just when we debate or write philosophy. Our suffering is an issue in *every single moment* of our existence, woven into everything and everybody we encounter—the objects we use, the environments we navigate and the people we meet along the way.

Zen, as a philosophy-religion, insists that it is precisely in these moments—in *every moment*—that we need a practice of self-cultivation. But it's a different kind of self-cultivation than we're used to, which we typically associate with higher or advanced knowledge, whereas in Japan, the term for self-cultivation is *shugyō* (修行), which is associated in general with craftspeople (*shokunin* 職人), but is also used to describe *Geidō* aesthetic practices. Rather than elevated or sophisticated pursuits, *shugyō* refers to what we can learn by doing everyday mundane things, but—most crucially—doing them with care and single-minded attention.

This is why seemingly ordinary acts such as drinking tea, arranging flowers, or handwriting can express profound philosophical or religious value. We practice these activities with the greatest of care precisely because the great majority of our time—indeed, most of life itself—is spent immersed in such mundane pursuits. If we can cultivate deep, life-giving connections with others through serving them tea, arranging a few flowers, or scribing beautiful handwriting, then we discover a far greater source of salvation than any found in rare or elevated moments. This salvation is one that's always right underfoot, perpetually available in the fabric of everyday existence itself. By bringing sustained attention and care to these simple, repetitive acts that fill our days, we transform the ordinary into a continuous practice of spiritual cultivation, finding transcendence not by escaping the mundane but by fully inhabiting it.

Philosopher: Is this another east–west touchpoint, between the existential aspect of Zen and western existential philosophy?

Theologian: There are definitely some differences that make them hard to reconcile, but yes, there are many similarities scholars have noted over the years.

One point I find interesting is that among several of the existential philosophers, such as with Pascal, Kierkegaard, Tillich, Bultmann, Marcel, Jaspers, Ricoeur, Marion, and Heidegger, there is a strong engagement with religious themes. Many also invoke ideas relating to negation, nothingness, the void and notions of anxiety and existential angst that have a similar focus on the everyday mundane source of suffering.

Regarding Zen's focus on everyday, mundane existence, existential phenomenology is particularly relevant. Heidegger is the philosopher known to have made phenomenology existential. In calibrating his methodology, he realized very early on that human existence (*Dasein*) is best revealed not in moments of elevated philosophical speculation, or scientific analysis, but in the everyday world we're always immersed within before reflecting on it—what he called the *Alltäglich*, the "everyday".

The entirety of the first division of his magnum opus *Being and Time* is dedicated to revealing the structures within Dasein's everyday modes—how we experience and exist before or independent of moments of epistemological, ethical, metaphysical or logical analysis. This stands in contrast to the western tradition culminating in Descartes' methodology, which prioritizes detachment from worldly involvement. By contrast, Heidegger prefers to explore Dasein in its everyday "absorption" (*Aufgehen*) in the world of involvements. Maurice Merleau-Ponty is also part of this existential phenomenological movement, and likewise seeks to uncover the structures of everyday perceptual absorption.

Together, these two among many philosophers advancing their project, give us some beautifully complex ways to view our everyday experience that are crucial at this moment—highlighting some aspects that resonate with but might not be articulated this exact way in Zen.

We're getting closer to finally immersing our bodies in a very elaborate environment, with many aesthetic objects, utensils, rituals, precisely choreographed movements, highly aestheticized food—entering the ceremony assuming that we are subjects immersed in space containing a bunch of objects would be a bit tragic. So, let's talk a little bit more about how existential phenomenology gives us some interesting tools for experiencing the tea world we're about to enter.

Phenomenology and the Non-Object

Theologian: Does what you said about the tea garden not being a thing relate in any way to how we encounter things in this *Alltäglich* mode?

Guide: Oh yes. Good question. Yes, as a matter of fact, there is a connection there.

Although not many of us are scientists, many of our ideas of thinghood stem from a scientific metaphysics. And, it's not that the idea of thinghood as objectivity is necessarily problematic. When we need to deliberately analyse things, reflect upon them, seek knowledge about them, treating things objectively might be an appropriate enough way of dealing with them. However, we should recognize that in day-to-day existence, we interact with many—perhaps most—

things without reflecting on them or attempting to gain knowledge about them. Imagine having to reflect on your shoes, glasses or bike every time you used them. To reinvoke the phenomenological term, most of our experience remains in the "pre-reflective", and in this moment, the subject–object binary doesn't structure our engagement. We function better with our everyday things precisely when experience isn't divided up this way.

Until existential phenomenology, our western tradition largely overlooked the philosophical significance of the pre-reflective mode of engagement, focusing instead on moments when we, as subjects, deliberately engage with objects, trying to gain knowledge or exert control over them. That might be why the scientist has been more of an exemplar for western philosophy, not the artist.

Artist: But don't tea practitioners have to reflect deeply for many years to gain knowledge of all the tea implements, rituals, and body movements? Wouldn't that mean they're treating everything like an object?

Guide: Prolonged practice is necessary precisely to move beyond treating things as objects. A Japanese aesthetic practitioner, like our tea host, undergoes a much longer period of learning with tools like teapots and teacups than most people ever would. Yet, even though they take extreme care in every movement, the goal isn't to grasp their tools as objects but to transcend the subject–object division and intertwine with their tea bowls, whisks and ladles in a way that negates objecthood itself.

Philosopher: But, isn't the tea master kind of absorption in his world foreign to our world?

Guide: Maybe, but the innovations in phenomenology, which have spread quite rapidly across many philosophical domains—even across the analytic-Continental divide, which typically polarizes the discipline—suggests that there might be some latent overlap between east and west.

Achieving a non-objective relation to the tea world might seem nearly impossible if the only path requires a lifetime's dedication to Zen, grounded in Buddhist notions of *śūnyatā* and *pratītyasamutpāda*. But this is precisely why phenomenology serves as such a valuable intercultural bridge. From within our own tradition, we can uncover bridges into a world that, in many ways, aligns with Asian philosophical heritage.

So, let's return to Heidegger and Merleau-Ponty—both of whom conceive of a negated object from within the western tradition. And to give you a hint, both accomplish this by shifting slightly away from substance ontology and slightly in the direction of relational ontology.

Heidegger—*"Equipmentality"*

Guide: Broadly speaking, Heidegger redefines what it means to be a self—or rather, he dispenses with the terminology surrounding selfhood altogether, replacing it with his own term, *Dasein*. *Dasein* isn't a self-contained subject locked inside its own head or body and divided away from the world. Instead, *Dasein* is what Heidegger calls "being-in-the-world" (*In-der-Welt-sein*) and "being-with-one-another" (*Miteinandersein*). He foregoes the typical western ways of defining what we are by isolating us from the things we're related to. Instead, his starting point is the way that we're related to the world and to each other. And, although we can't go into the details, for Heidegger being "in" the world isn't about a being, a thing inside a container—the "in" isn't a spatial location but a way of what he calls "dwelling", where we're always embedded in meaningful relations.[13]

Although he doesn't highlight this term "relational", his way of conceiving of *Dasein* is radical precisely because it is a relational account of human existence.

Philosopher: So, *Dasein* is Heidegger's version of a non-self? How is it that it deals with negated objects?

Guide: Yes and no. Again, always be careful with "is it just like?" kind of questions when doing intercultural philosophy. These kinds of comparisons almost always overlook something crucial. If two ideas were "just like" one another, there would be no need for the two ideas, just the one would suffice. And, given the many conceptions of non-selfhood across schools of Buddhism, we have to be careful there too. Heidegger and other phenomenologists are responding mostly to their own tradition, so their innovations and interventions are in response to figures in that tradition.

That said, could we find similarities between the general idea of non-selfhood and Heidegger's notion of *Dasein*. Possibly. At that level of generality, we could definitely say that Heidegger and Buddhist philosophers shared a serious apprehension with describing humans as self-contained, circumscribable objects.

Nevertheless, Heidegger is responding to terminology from his western tradition. The German word for "object", *Gegenstand*, which means "standing against" emphasizes a division from and even an opposition to the self. And, the Latin *obicere (from ob + iacere)* refers to something "thrown against", so you can see that oppositional meaning and implicit duality.

In both cases, these western terms reinforce a division between things the kind of beings we are and the things we encounter. So, while "object" seems like a completely innocuous term, it's actually one of the most philosophically loaded terms shaping how we understand human existence and experience. Heidegger gave us this term *Dasein* so we could move away from this structure altogether and see a completely different valence of experience where we're not divided away, but existentially absorbed in the world.

Theologian: If he gets rid of the terminology of selfhood and subjectivity and replaces it with *Dasein*, does he also replace the terminology associated with thinghood or objecthood?

Guide: He absolutely does. Throughout the entirety of his long philosophical career, he's attempting to give us new language for "thinghood"—seeking to bring us beyond descriptions of self-contained objects towards seeing relational contexts we're embedded within.

We could spend all day on this aspect of his philosophy, but let's focus on one of his earliest concepts, since the imagery he uses helps us think about the relational context inside the tea hut.

One of Heidegger's terms meant to replace the nomenclature surrounding objectivity is "equipment". Some scholars find this to be an unsatisfying translation of the German *Zeughaftigkeit*. In fact, most German speakers wouldn't immediately recognize its meaning. Other translators render it as "useful thing", which has its own problems but avoids common connotations associating "equipment" with specialized tools one needs specialized know-how to use. So, we should set aside the idea of specialized tools and instead think of familiar everyday things like your shoes, a bike, or, let's say, a teapot.

To grasp how radical this concept is, particularly in how it moves toward relational thinking, let's look at some key details of "equipmentality". Firstly, with objects, we can speak of *an* object, an isolated self-subsisting entity—a shoe, a phone, a hat. But Heidegger writes, "There 'is' no such thing as *an* equipment" (2008, p. 97). For him, equipment doesn't exist in isolated units—*equipment is always relational, it is a context, not a single object*. He writes that "Equipment – in accordance with its equipmentality – always is in terms of its belonging to other equipment" (p. 97).

Instead of defining objects by characteristics like extension, size, or weight, Heidegger considers "availability" (*Zuhandenheit*) to be one of the main qualities of equipment. Equipment is never simply "available" as a singular object but always encountered within a network of "assignments" or "references" (*Verweisung*).

Even though Heidegger doesn't emphasize the terms "relationality" or "relational ontology", his way of defining things not by their internal essences but through their "references" to other things is fundamentally relational thinking.

One of Heidegger's main examples in *Being and Time* illustrating the relational nexus of "equipmentality" is the craftsman's workshop, but I'm going to pretend it was a tea hut.

Think of the tea pot. Of course, we can admire it on its own and analyse it as an object, the way a scientist would, or *qua* teapot as philosophers would. We can measure it and determine its objective qualities, or try to define its essence. Most of these modes of engagement are those of a subject "standing against" an object, treating it as what Heidegger called "present-at-hand", i.e., as an object.

But, we almost never encounter a tea pot this way. When we want to use it for what it is, we get wrapped up in a series of "references" extending beyond the pot itself. A pot wouldn't be a meaningful or useful tool unless it had a "reference" to a heating element, to hot water, to the act of pouring, to the contours of the hand, and to human beings preparing a drink.

Philosopher: It seems like we have another instance of thinking beyond the law of non-contradiction, don't we?

Guide: How so?

Philosopher: When we engage with the pot, or A, leads us to related things—not-A—that give it its meaning and use.

Guide: Somebody has trained you well.

~ . . . *he said with a wink.*

I don't know that he breaks it down in those logical terms, but I think you're right. When he speaks of a pen, A, he finds "assignments" to "ink-stand, pen, ink, paper, blotting pad, table, lamps, furniture, windows, doors, room", these are all not-pens, so not-A routes to A.

And, we can do the same thing for the tea hut. Rather than seeking an internal essence, we can focus on its "references" to tea, water, tea pot, brazier, tea bowl, tea host, tea guest, tearoom, and on and on. If we really tried to isolate any of these, we'd see that we lose their meaning. They would not even have been invented if they weren't part of a broader context of equipment. And, as opposed to substance ontological thinking where a thing's essence or definition is internal, equipment is only meaningful and useful as a network of assignments and relations beyond itself.

This system of external references, where A refers us on to not-A, is the existential structure of equipment. Again, we could analyse it scientifically as an object—examining the molecular structure of the clay, the lacquer's chemicals, or the thermal properties of the tea pot—but, this mode of analysis isn't how equipment is meaningful to us in an everyday sense, in the *alltäglich*, or in the pre-reflective mode of engagement. In the everyday, I don't grasp the pot to analyse it scientifically like an object, I use it "in order to" (*um zu*) achieve other ends beyond the pot itself. This "in order to" is another structure of equipment Heidegger identifies—another vector external to the object, a relation to some task defining what the thing is.

Artist: I'm curious—if you include all the references constituting something like a tea pot, it seems like you have a drastically more complex picture. How could you ever take into account all of its relations when using it?

Guide: You don't.

In fact, Heidegger says that things must "withdraw in order to be available quite authentically".

Theologian: Withdraw?

Guide: Yes, think about anything you use in an everyday context. When you first learned how to hold a guitar, ride a bike, or pour tea from a pot, you had to pay attention to them as objects. But once you're proficient with that tool, they "withdraw" into the background. As withdrawn, they enable you to focus with an expanded scope—you don't focus on the guitar, but on playing a song; not on the bike, but on visiting a friend down the street; not on the tea pot, but on sharing a drink.

And, here's Heidegger's great insight: it's only when equipment is broken or malfunctions that it announces itself, sticks out from the background relational context demanding attention as an object, demanding reflective intellection to repair. But, once repaired, it "withdraws" again into the background and becomes transparent within its equipmental context.

Artist: I see, so grasping the relational totality of the tearoom isn't the goal, in fact, it should be avoided.

Guide: And you couldn't really grasp all the relations anyway, since the tearoom's "references" have no outer edge to hold. Even limiting it to that room and everything in it would still involve "assignments" extending to the weather, the history of tea, Buddhist philosophy, and Japanese literature.

Heidegger actually elaborates equipmentality in terms of our experience of residing in rooms. "What we encounter as closest to us . . . is the room" (2008, p. 98). And he writes that we "encounter [the room] not as something 'between four walls' in a geometrical spatial sense, but as equipment for residing" (p. 98).

This is another sense in which the tea hut is not a place I can take you to, but that's a good thing. If I could take you to an objective space, it would be much more restricted, limited to its objective dimensions, its four walls. But, if Heidegger's right, our experience of space extends out beyond its "geometrical space" through its "references".

Theologian: So, another way to think about the small room being large?

Guide: I suppose so. We could measure the space of the tea hut, determine its square meterage, but that wouldn't reveal much about the lived experience of the space, because that experience extends far beyond objective or geometrical spatiality, which is tiny.

Artist: But, is there no end to the tea hut's "references"?

Guide: What could this be?

Theologian: The tea garden?

Guide: Think slightly wider.

Theologian: Japan?

Guide: Almost.

Philosopher: The "world"?

Guide: Exactly. Or, we might even say *śūnyatā*, emptiness.

In phenomenology, "world" is typically referred to as the widest horizon of meaning-giving relationality. But, we have to avoid thinking about "world" as an objective ground, and more like a relational nexus.

Now that we've viewed the alcove, we're ready to proceed to the next stage of the ceremony, where we'll examine the tea utensils and the charcoal fire. And, before we do that, there's one last ritual detail to observe.

The alcove and the hanging scroll hold such significance that, upon departing from this station, one should never turn one's back. Since this level of respect is typically reserved for humans, especially ritual practitioners of the highest rank, our gesture confers an almost human reverence onto the alcove, elevating it to the highest significance within the tea hut (Decreux 2014).

In fact, some have observed that these objects—including the scroll, the brazier, and the tea implements—are considered extensions of the tea host. In viewing them and expressing appreciation, guests engage in an opportunity for heightened connection with the host (Kondo 1985).

16

Sitting

First Charcoal Ceremony

Guide: Let's make our way over to the serving area. Before sitting, we'll want to view the brazier and charcoal arrangement the Host has prepared. This is the *shozumi* (初炭) or first charcoal ceremony—the first of two.

The Host has arranged the brazier before our arrival so that, as you might have noticed, the coals were already glowing, and the kettle had just begun to steam as we entered the hut.

Figure 16.1 First Charcoal Ceremony. (*shozumi*, 初炭). R. Loughnane.

Because this is a late spring ceremony, the charcoal fire was prepared in the portable brazier you see, called a *furo* (風炉). In winter, the fire would be built in a recessed hearth below the floor, called a *ro* (炉), positioned between guests and host.

Now, let's take our seats. You might not realize it, but our seating positions are organized for us in a particular way. If you recall, we sat in the outer waiting arbor according to Confucian principles; this time, Daoism will determine our orientation within the tearoom.

You'll notice the flooring appears divided into sections. These are called *iatami* (畳) mats, which I imagine you've seen before. Made of straw and cut into standard sizes depending on their region or origin, they are typically twice as long as wide, measuring approximately three by six feet. However, the tea hut itself is never measured in reference to feet—only in terms of the number of tatami mats.

What we have here is the most traditional orientation for *Wabicha*: four and a half mats, known as *yojohan* (四畳半). This arrangement is said to reflect the small room in which Vimalakirti preached to his 84,000 disciples—a story we discussed earlier, which poetically evokes the relativity of the large and small. Beyond the 4.5 tatami *yojohan*, there are some different set ups, from up to 16 mats to as few as two, or even 1.5 mats.

This division of space using the tatami mats also carries Daoist significance. In Daoist cosmology, the cosmos has a directional, cardinal structure. Early Daoists were passionate about a directional form of divination and this became significant in Japanese culture around the time that the tea ceremony took root in medieval Japan. Following Rikyū's modifications, the tea hut was oriented along the north–south axis, with the windows and entrance placed on the south side.[1]

Beyond the cardinal directions, spatial divisions carry additional meanings. Notice how four full-sized *tatami* mats surround the half mat in the middle. If we divide each mat in half, we arrive at nine equally sized sections, each corresponding to a trigram (*bagua* 八卦).

Does anyone know where those trigrams come from?

Theologian: Yes, I know these well. They're from the *I Ching*. They're those three-line symbols with two different kinds of lines: unbroken *yang* and broken *yin* lines with a gap in the center. Each trigram carries its own meaning and is used for predicting the future and guiding decision making.

Guide: Right. And, here in the tearoom, each of the nine tatami quadrants is associated with a trigram, and an element such as water, wind or fire, and a virtue such as strength, generosity or pleasure.

Here, I have an image here so you can see.

When we entered the hut, we landed on the section associated with flexibility and penetration.

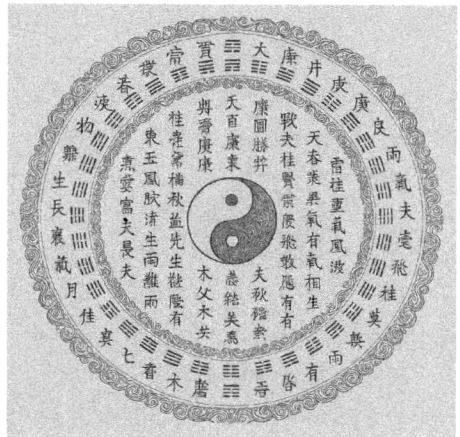

Figure 16.2 *Book of Changes.* (*I Ching*, 易经). R. Loughnane.

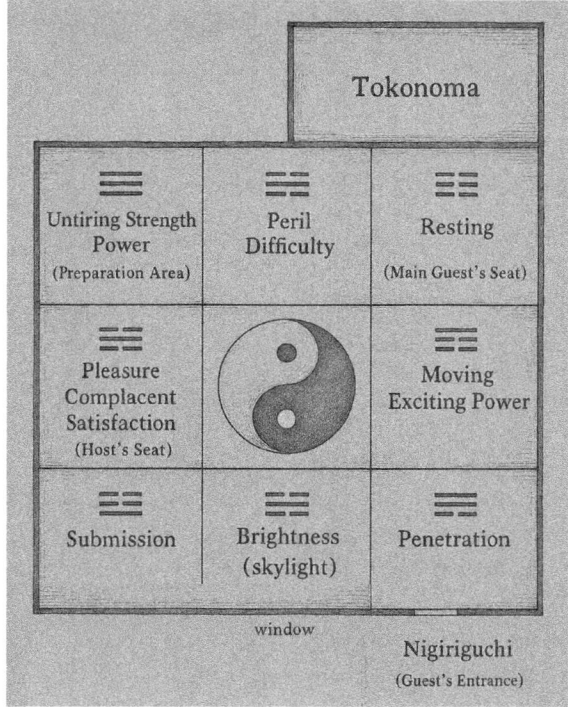

Figure 16.3 Tearoom Floor Plan. R. Loughnane

The central half-mat is associated with the Dao, serving as the energetic center of the room—where the tea is prepared. To the west of this central mat lies the area associated with pleasure, occupied by the tea master, who orchestrates the particular kind of pleasure we'll be enjoying.

Just above that mat, in the north-west corner is the area linked to strength and power—where tea preparation takes place. All utensils, pottery, and the tea itself will first be positioned here. One section to the right, the northern area is associated with danger or peril, so that spot remains vacant throughout.

Adjacent to that, in the north-east corner, is the segment associated with rest and repose. This is where I'll sit as the main guest, in the *kamiza* (上座), or "upper seat" which is typically as close to the alcove and as far away from the *nijiriguchi* as possible.

Moving clockwise to the south-west, we pass through trigrams representing moving power, penetration, and brightness, where a window or skylight is usually found. Finally, the last space in the south-west corner is associated with submission, where the Host enters.

Now, with that in mind, at long last, the ceremony is about to begin. Remember everything we've discussed—every detail, every aesthetic principle, every philosophical theory—and just let them all drift away. If they arise in your mind, just acknowledge them like clouds and let them float by.

> ~ *The guests follow their guide to the seating area, taking their designated places on the tatami mats.*
>
> *In the opposite corner, a large door slides open. The tea Host kneels on the floor, and all four guests bow in unison with her. She remains in place until invited in by the main guest.*

Guide: Please, join us.

> ~ *The Host rises to her feet and slowly makes her way to the pleasure quadrant, carrying the first round of tea implements: the tea bowl, tea caddy, and ladle.*
>
> *The Guide gently removes his fan from his kimono and carefully places it on the ground with all three following suit.*
>
> *The Host settles slowly and deliberately into her seating area and proceeds to exchange formal greetings with each of the guests, one by one.*
>
> *As the main guest, the Shōkyaku returns greetings, offering a few light comments about the garden, the hanging scroll, and flower arrangement.*
>
> *The Host ritually purifies the tea bowl, tea scoop, and teapot before bowing to the guests and announcing that she has prepared a meal, which she will now retrieve.*

Rising to her feet, she leaves the room, returning in a moment with the ladle for scooping water, and the rinse-water container.
Once seated, all bow in unison.

Food: *kaiseki*

Guide: Now, we're about to be served a small bite to eat before two separate servings of tea.

~ *The Host returns with the Kaiseki meal and chopsticks for each guest.*
Lowering herself slowly back to her area on the tatami, she places the tray of food in front of the Guide.
Remaining on his knees, the Guide slides forward to receive his meal, bowing first to the Host, then to the other guests.
The Host leaves once more and returns with meals for the remaining guests. She bows and invites them to begin.

Guide: We will begin.

~ *The guests slowly eat their first course.*

Guide: Normally, our Host would exit while we eat, but this is a practice run, so we'll take this opportunity to have her tell us a little bit about the food she's shared with us?

Host: Yes, of course. First of all, I want to welcome you all to the *Flowers in the Sky* tea hut. It's my deepest honor to have you here and to serve you tea today. Please go ahead and start while I share with you some details about the food you are enjoying.

What you have before you is called *kaiseki* (懐石), or *cha-kaiseki* (茶懐石) when prepared specifically for the tea ceremony.

Kaiseki is particularly renowned here in Kyoto, to the extent that it is sometimes referred to as "Kyoto cooking" (*kyō-ryōri* 京料理). It is served in many traditional restaurants (*ryōtei* 料亭) and sometimes in traditional inns (*ryokan* 旅館), where it reaches the highest levels of delicacy and refinement—on par with what we might call *haute cuisine* in the European culinary tradition.

Guide: Can you say anything about the term *Kaiseki*?

Host: Oh, yes. *Kaiseki* has an interesting Buddhist etymology. *Kai* (懐) refers to the inside of one's clothing, while *seki* (石) means stone. The literal translation is something like "breast-pocket stone," referring to the small, heated stones Zen monks would place inside their robes near their stomachs to fend off hunger at night.

The different courses you'll enjoy all have their own codification.[2] A typical serving, as you see here, consists of rice along with "one soup and three side dishes" (*ichijū sansai* 一汁三菜). The meal comprises numerous small dishes, served with rice, miso soup, vegetables, and cooked fish, all presented on a single platter.

Of course, the small meal will be delicious, but it is as much a feast for the eyes as it is for the mouth and stomach (Parkes 1995). Notice how carefully the modest portions are arranged, each morsel individually, with each selected and presented in harmony with the season. The theme on the serving dishes reflects the time of year and can even evoke details from the guests' lives. Whenever possible, the food is locally sourced and foraged for maximum freshness.

Now, we will proceed to the next stage of the ceremony with drink.

> ~ *The Host rises gracefully to her feet, bows to the group, and exits the room.*
> *Moments later, she reappears at the door, repeating her bow before entering with sake and cups for drinking.*

Sake

Guide: Now comes a significant moment in the ceremony—the drinking of Japanese rice wine, or *sake* (酒). This is another Shinto ritual.[3] *Sake* is considered the essence of rice and is traditionally offered to *kami* in various ceremonies. It carries important social meanings, symbolizing camaraderie and friendship. In keeping with this spirit, *sake* is an exception in the tea ceremony in that the Host partakes in drinking alongside guests.

> ~ *The main guest picks up the sake and cups, bows in appreciation, and passes them to the other guests.*
> *The Host pours sake for the main guest, then moves to the others, bowing before and after filling each cup.*
> *All four drink together.*
> *The Host asks if the guests would like a second serving, to which the main guest responds with the customary assent, adding the slight modification that they will serve themselves.*
> *The guests bow and enjoy a second round of sake.*

The Guide takes a sheet of kaishi paper from the pad in their kimono, using it to clean the insides of his cup.

The Host departs once more, returning with a bowl of delicacies in broth, gently encouraging the guests to enjoy.

Host: Please, eat before it gets cold.

~ *The Host leaves again and returns with a serving of broiled fish. As before, she places it in front of herself on the floor. The main guest slides forward to receive the food with a bow before passing it to the other guests, bowing to each in turn.*

The Host inquires if anyone would like a third serving of sake, to which the customary response is a polite decline.

The Host bows and leaves the room once again.

Host: I will have my meal in the preparation room.

~ *The main guest offers a customary invitation for the Host to join them, to which she graciously declines and leaves the room with a bow.*

Once the meal is finished, the last guest gathers all the implements and neatly stacks them beside the door to the preparation room.

Hearing the rattle of dishes being stacked, the Host is cued to slide open the door, momentarily enter to collect the dishes, and bow before exiting once more in what appears to be one swift gesture.

The Host re-enters with hot broth.

Host: Please have your soup.

~ *The Host leaves the room.*

Next comes a round of delicacies from the ocean, accompanied by more sake.

The second guest serves sake to the Host.

After enjoying her own drink, the Host leaves the room and returns with delicacies foraged from the mountains.

The Host borrows the main guest's cup to enjoy one last drink of sake.

She leaves and returns with a container of crisp browned rice, hot water, a ladle, Japanese pickles, and bamboo chopsticks.

The Host exits once more, allowing the guests to eat.

When finished, they clean their dishes and chopsticks using another sheet of kaishi paper from their pads.

Guide: Now, we have another intriguing acoustic intervention within the ceremony. As we finish this last part of the meal, we collect our dishes and place our chopsticks on top of our bowls, but positioned slightly askew so that, with a gentle shake, they fall onto the tray, creating a distinct *click* sound; another percussive cue signaling to our Host that we have finished our meal.

~ *The Guide gives his chopsticks the requisite nudge, and with the click, the Host enters the room once more, collects the dishes, and leaves—as always, with a deep bow.*

Guide: The Host is now in the preparation room. We can't see her because of the dividers you see there, the *tsuitate* (衝立), another example of *kekkai* partitions.

~ *The Host slides the door open with one delicate movement, places both hands on the tatami in front of her, and takes a deep bow before returning to her seated position.*
  She carries a small ash container, a spoon, and metal chopsticks for arranging the charcoal.

Second Charcoal Ceremony

Guide: This is what's known as *gozumi* (後炭), or the second charcoal ceremony. Watch how she places the charcoal. The pieces are arranged to maximize ventilation while also maintaining aesthetic harmony. Typically, three pieces of charcoal (*shitabi*, 下火) are pre-lit in the preparation room, then carried in and placed on the brazier.

~ *The Host spoons a small amount of white ash from the container onto the charcoal. On the floor in front of her, she arranges all utensils, including a feather, paper, the incense container (kōgo 香合), and the metal rings, before placing the lid on the kettle.*

Guide: The teapot will now be placed on the brazier, but notice that she doesn't simply lift it with her hands. See those large protruding lugs on either side of the kettle? Watch as she takes the two metal rings and slides them through the openings in the lugs.

~ *The Host removes another sheet of paper from her kimono, places it gently on the tatami, and lifts the kettle to rest on the paper. She uses the feather to lightly dust the kettle in a gesture of ritual purification.*
  Next, she picks up the chopsticks, arranges the charcoal for optimal ventilation, adding more ash. She places a small amount of sandalwood incense from the incense container onto the coals.

Guide: Do you see that stick of sandalwood, that's referred to as "the scent of Buddha's paradise".

At this point, we should ask if we can view the incense container.

This incense container has a quiet presence. May I ask about its origin?

Host: It was made here in our province, by a potter who shapes the clay with little adornment. The container's rounded form is meant to suggest a lotus bud—closed, but already hinting at its unfolding.

Guide: I see. The surface is soft, almost like stone smoothed by water.

Host: Yes, the glaze was drawn from ash of local pine. Nothing exotic.

Guide: And the fragrance—there is a faint bitterness, yet also something sweet.

Host: It is blended to recall the smoke of temple incense: a reminder of impermanence. Inhaling it, one might remember the Buddha's words—that all things are like a dream.

> *~ While the other guests examine the container, the Host lifts the kettle onto the brazier and departs once again for the preparation area.*
>
> *Upon returning, the Host kneels and removes the feather from her kimono again, lightly dusting the brazier and the surrounding area before leaving again. Moments later, she re-enters, now carrying a silk wiping cloth, used to clean and purify both the brazier and the kettle.*
>
> *The guests are attuning to the rhythm and intention of her understated gestures.*
>
> *The Host rises and exits the tearoom, returning with the first round of sweets in lacquered boxes.*

Sweets: *Higashi, Omogashi*

Guide: Please, can you tell us a little bit about the sweets?

Host: Yes, absolutely. Let me first open the door to air the room.

> *~ The garden's cool breeze, laden with the subtle scent of damp earth and growing things, softly flows through the chashitsu, subtly rejuvenating the guests.*

These are called *Wagashi* (和菓子) and there are two sorts, *higashi* (干菓子), which are dry sweets, and *omogashi* (主菓子), which are moist sweets. Typically, we would have *higashi* with thin tea (*usucha*), and *omogashi* with thick tea, (*koicha*).

As you can see, these small sweets are typically arranged in groups of three to seven and carefully aestheticized. They reflect nature's beauty and contrast with the tea's bitterness to enhance its flavor—often drawing motifs from classical poetry or painting.

Like all the other aesthetic elements you have encountered—from the garden to the tearoom—these too fluctuate with the seasons. Their texture, colors, shapes, and aromas depend on what nature gives us at any time, as the ingredients are foraged locally.

Figure 16.4 Traditional Japanese Confections (*wagashi*, 和菓子). R. Loughnane.

As you can see, they are remarkably colorful, though not due to overly vibrant hues. Even the greens and pinks are somewhat muted, yet within the otherwise monochrome, earth-toned environment of the hut, they create a striking contrast.

Wagashi are traditionally plant-based, often made with *anko* (azuki bean paste) and mochi from glutinous rice. Though some modern versions use wheat flour, this isn't traditional. Local fruits or berries are sometimes added to enhance flavor and reflect the season.

Theologian: How did this come to be a part of the tea ceremony?

Host: The idea is simple: tea-goers often become so absorbed in the ceremony they forget to eat. To prevent hunger from distracting guests during the ceremony's latter stages, these mildly sweet treats offer a gentle blood-sugar boost—enough to sustain alertness as the gathering enters its third or fourth hour.

Artist: The dishes the sweets are served on look quite different from the rest of the aesthetic elements in the hut.

Host: Well observed. This is one instance where there is a slight departure from the *wabi* aesthetic, which typically avoids objects that appear overly refined. The plate with raised edges is called *fuchidaka* (縁高), chosen to reflect the season and featuring a substantial lacquer finish.

The selection and presentation of sweets—along with their serving ware—can be quite elaborate, varying across tea schools. Some serve one type, others use bowls instead of plates, and sometimes chopsticks are provided. Despite these differences, the core idea remains: the sweets express the season within the hut.

Guide: If we think back to our earlier discussion of mimetic aesthetics, this is a perfect example to challenge that framework. Representation typically involves a subject positioned over-against a separate object. Here, something beautiful goes into our bodies, negating that subject–object division.

Philosopher: And we're not just ingesting an object—we're ingesting a world, aren't we? Taking in all the *not-A* relations: the soil, the climate, the rain and sun, even the pollination of bees—everything that came together to grow the ingredients used to make these exquisite non-objects.

Guide: Beautifully put. Within the mimetic framework, we wouldn't likely recognize that we are actually incorporating the landscape, the environment, the climate, and the soil into our bodies, blurring the boundaries between self and environment, between the inside and outside of our bodies.

Now, we will leave the tearoom and take a short break outside in the waiting area while the tea is prepared.

~ *All four stand, one by one, leaving the tea hut out through the in door.*

Kintsugi

Guide: Any thoughts on how things are going so far? Any questions, or have you noticed anything interesting?

Theologian: I noticed that the tea bowl had a crack in it. Is that also part of the *wabi-sabi* aesthetic?

Guide: Good that you noticed that. We might say it reflects the general idea of *wabi-sabi*, but it's actually part of a distinct practice. Does anyone know what it's called?

Artist: I've heard of it—it's called *kintsugi* (金継ぎ). When an object breaks, it is repaired with gold. From what I understand, the process of mending it is meant to enhance its beauty and even its value.

Guide: That's right. The term translates as "golden joinery" or sometimes "golden repair". The most brilliant examples use gold or even platinum to fill the cracks to reconstruct a tea bowl or pot.

According to legend, in the fifteenth century, the Ashikaga Shōgun sent a damaged Chinese bowl back to China for repair. From here, two stories emerge. One recounts that the bowl was returned with large, irregular metal staples holding it together—too unsightly for the shogun's tastes—so he instructed his potters to develop a more beautiful means of repair, giving rise to *kintsugi*. The other version suggests that those metal staples themselves were admired as beautiful, and the piece was named *Bakōhan* (馬蝗絆), or "large locust clamp," since the staples resembled insect legs. From that point, the practice evolved from individual staples to the smooth yet visibly filled cracks you saw in that piece.

Sound

Philosopher: I'm not sure if I misheard, but it sounded like something was clicking inside the kettle.

Guide: No, you didn't mishear. Tea masters sometimes place small stones or iron beads at the bottom of the kettle, creating that ringing sound.

Philosopher: Is this to let you know when the water is boiled?

Guide: That's likely part of it, but if you reflect on our journey so far, you might notice how different objects, rituals, and events have engaged different senses.

Our visual sense has been continuously stimulated—the garden design, the stones, flowers, and paths, the hanging scroll and of course, the tea hut itself, all arranged to create specific visual impressions.

You've also experienced tactile engagement—feeling the stones underfoot, the textures of the surfaces we sat on, the rawness of the tea hut's walls and timber, and the materials of the ladle and tea bowls. Even though we haven't yet had tea, our sense of taste has already been activated through the water purification, the *kaiseki* meal, and the sweets.

Then there is scent—subtle fragrances from the garden, the wetness rising off the stones, the bushes coming to life after a long winter, the burning sandalwood incense, which, along with tea and flowers, completes what is known as the "three ways" (*san-dō* 三道 or sometimes also *cha-ka-kō* 茶花香). In this way, all the guest's sensory modalities are drawn into the relational fabric of the tea garden and ceremony.

The inclusion of small iron beads in the kettle serves a similar purpose, ensuring that aural perception also plays a role in this immersive experience.

Artist: Ah, okay. Interesting. Is it the only instance of deliberate aural stimulation?

Guide: Did anybody else notice anything?

Theologian: I remember that when the Host came out to get the water from the *tsukubai*, although she wasn't visibly present, we knew she was there by the sound of water pouring.

Philosopher: And we were told that clicking the door of the *nijiriguchi* would signal that we had all entered the tearoom.

Guide: Yes, very good. You're right—these subtle acoustic punctuations signal different stages and even create a rhythmic structure for the ceremony. You'll notice this pattern recurring at various points. Some scholars have even highlighted the percussive aspect as crucial to the ceremony's overall experience (Kondo 1985).

Now, we're entering the part of the ceremony where tea will be served. Let me explain how the next stages will unfold so that we're all well prepared for the cup of tea we've been working toward since we began our class several days ago back at *Rikyū no I*.

The full *Wabicha* ceremony, called *Cha-ji* (茶事) actually includes two tea servings.[4] The first, known as *Koicha* (濃茶) or "thick tea" is the most formal serving and represents the culmination of the ceremony. This tea will be quite thick, and its bitterness can sometimes be striking. If you've had *matcha* before, it shouldn't be too difficult to drink, but for someone experiencing it for the first time, it can be quite off-putting.

Upon returning to our seats, we will have a second serving of sweets—this time the dry *higashi* (干菓子) variety—in preparation for the second serving of tea, known as *usucha* (薄茶), or "thin tea," which is the less formal stage of the ceremony.[5] The intention being to create a more relaxed atmosphere, or what Zen calls "downward training". The tea will be much lighter and easier to drink.

At this stage, conversation is slightly less constrained. We may comment on the tea, ask about the provenance of the *matcha* powder, or inquire further about the tea utensils and other aesthetic objects we have encountered.

> ~ *Meanwhile, the Host steps into the garden, removes the ladle from the water basin, arranges the cushions, puts away the smoking utensils, and lowers the bamboo blinds from the tearoom window, allowing the late-afternoon light to filter throughout the hut. She returns to the preparation area and sounds a gong, signaling the guests to return.*
>
> *The guests purify hands and mouth again at the tsukubai before re-entering the tearoom, once again clicking the nijiriguchi door to signal their return.*
>
> *After taking their seats once more, they observe the newly arranged kettle, fire, brazier, water container, and the container for thick tea, along with its silk bag, commenting on each in turn.*

Guide: At this point, it is my role as the main guest to offer comments regarding the host's selection of tea implements. Of greatest significance is the tea bowl (*chawan* 茶碗). We should inquire about the name of the craftsperson who made it, the geographic region in which they worked, the object's history, and whether it may have been passed down from previous tea masters.

Beyond these objective features, we should also express the subjective impression the implements have on us as guests, appreciating how they contribute to the overall aesthetic constellation the host has so carefully orchestrated.

Of particular importance are the tea scoop (*chashaku* 茶杓), the tea kettle (*chagama* 茶釜), the waste water container (*kensui* 建水), and especially the silk bag (*shifuku* 仕服) used to carry the thick *matcha* tea caddy (*chaire* 茶入).

We are now moving to the next stage, where the host will clean and purify the kettle with a cloth.

> ~ *The host enters with a bow, takes her seat, and carefully arranges the culminating tea implements around her on the tatami in the quadrant associated with pleasure.*

Guide: Now, remember the water we collected when we first met at the *Rikyū no I* well? That is what you see here.

> ~ *The host uses a bamboo ladle to scoop the collected water and pour it into the pot for boiling.*

Guide: As the water boils, guests may comment on the teaware—the bowls, utensils, and kettle—as many are artworks in their own right. But remarks should be modest, not displays of knowledge or sophistication. The aim is quiet praise, in keeping with the teaware's restrained beauty and the host's thoughtful choices.

Koicha (濃茶)

Guide: Our host is about to begin the most formal moment of the ceremony. Let's pay close attention as she undertakes her ritual movements—these are some of the most solemn and the most beautifully intricate gestures we'll see.

~ *The Host inspects the whisk before placing it in the first tea bowl. She then performs delicate, precise whisking motions, blending the water and matcha powder into a frothy mix.*

Once the surface of the tea displays a thick froth with bubbles of the correct magnitude—indicating a perfectly mixed bowl—without standing, she shifts slightly toward the Guide, bows, and turns the bowl so that its most beautiful side faces him.

She gently sets the bowl halfway between herself and the Guide, in the central quadrant representing the position of the Dao.

The Guide slides forward, carefully takes the bowl in his hands, and returns to his position before a deep and prolonged bow of gratitude, which the Host returns.

The Guide slowly turns the bowl so that its most elegant side faces the Host, tips it slightly as a sign of respect, and proceeds to drink the tea in three and a half sips.

The Host asks how the tea was, to which the Guide responds "It is delicious."

The Guide places the bowl down in front of himself, removes a sheet of kaishi paper from his kimono, and wipes the rim before turning 180 degrees to pass the bowl to the next guest, the Artist, who has a sip, passing it to the Theologian and then the Philosopher.

Once all the guests have had their turn to sip the thick tea, the bowl is passed back to the Guide for viewing and further appreciative commentary. He places the bowl on the tatami in front of himself, ensuring that its front faces the Host. At this moment, all bow in unison.

The Host raises the bowl and ladles hot water into it for rinsing. As the main guest, the Guide enquires about the tea bowl—its origin, materials, the craftsperson who made it, and the seasonal references it evokes.

After a brief response, the Host wipes the tea scoop with a silk cloth, at which point the Guide requests to view the koicha container, the scoop, and the silk bag used for holding the tea container. The Host consents, setting these items out for viewing.

All four bow in unison.

The Host returns the remaining implements to the preparation room while the guests examine the utensils more closely, with particular attention to the matcha scoop (chashaku 茶杓*).*

After this brief exchange, the Host bows to the group once again and leaves the room.

Upon returning, the Host reaches for the water scoop, gently lifts it in front of herself, and holds it upright, with the scoop facing up and the handle pointing downward, for inspection. She shifts the matcha container and the first tea bowl into the space directly in front of her. Next, she removes her silk wiping cloth (fukusa) from her obi and carefully inspects its four edges.

Guide: Perhaps you wouldn't mind explaining the cloth and its purpose?

Host: Yes, I would be happy to. This is called a *fukusa* (袱紗), a special silk cloth used to clean and purify tea implements. Historically, this small cloth was also used to wrap gifts.

Traditionally, male hosts use a purple *fukusa*, while female hosts choose red or orange. Some are plain, others embroidered with seasonal motifs, family crests, local deities, auspicious animals, or Buddhist and Daoist themes.

This is one of the few moments where bright colors punctuate the atmosphere, which is otherwise pervaded by muted shades and earth tones.

Earlier, I folded and tucked the *fukusa* into my *obi*, the large sash wrapped around my midriff.

Guide: As the *fukusa* appears from out the *obi*, this is our cue to place our fans on the floor behind us, symbolically removing a barrier between guests and host.

Now begins one of the most intricate and beautifully precise manual rituals leading up to the serving of tea.

See if you can discern a subtle rhythm of her movements. You'll observe something quite remarkable—what's called the *jo-ha-kyū* (序破急) progression. *Jo* refers to a slow, almost hesitant and slightly extended prelude to a movement, followed by *ha*, the movement itself, and finishing with *kyū*, a brisk concluding gesture.

This rhythm is seen in other *geidō* practices too. Whether it's the completion of a calligraphic brushstroke or a *judo* throw, gestures in various Japanese arts follow this structured *jo-ha-kyū* progression, but it is particularly evident in the *fukusa* ritual, where she will perform a deliberate sequence of folding movements with the *fukusa* to prepare it for the ritual purification of the utensils and tea bowls.

> *~ The Host removes the cloth from her obi and unfolds it into a single triangular shape. Holding it vertically along its longer side, with her right hand on top and left hand on the bottom, she folds it back once, then, using her fingertips, folds again from back to front. She then places the fukusa in her left palm, facing up.*
>
> *With her right hand, she takes the left side and folds it in half to the right. Now, with a subtle yet decisive gesture, she points her index finger at the outer edge of the fukusa, her gaze fixed at the point where her finger meets silk, slowly tracing a line across the cloth with that finger then folding the right side under the left hand.*
>
> *Holding the fukusa with her right hand, she gently extracts her left hand from the layered folds. The left hand then moves under the right, forming the final shape, preparing the fukusa for purifying the tea implements.*

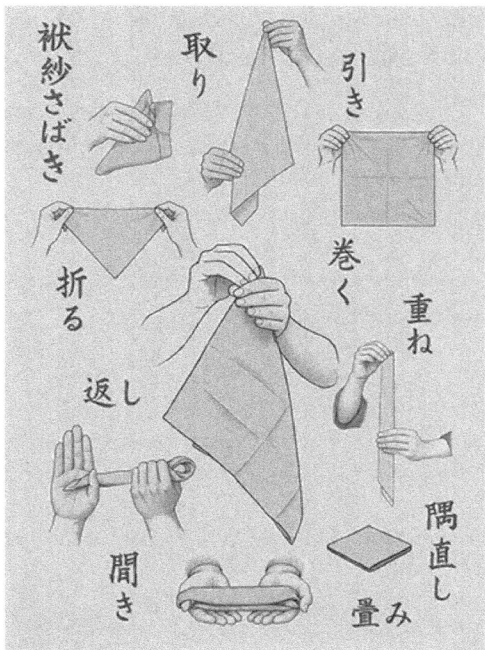

Figure 16.5 *Fukusa* Folding Ritual. R. Loughnane.

All five remain still for a moment, allowing the Host's intricate movements still reverberating throughout the room to settle.

Guide: Can you tell us about the symbolism of the *fukusa*?

Host: Like everything in the ceremony, the *fukusa* has a simple, functional purpose, but it also evokes deeper philosophical and religious principles. In this case, it brings Daoist and Buddhist symbolism into the tearoom.

Like all elements of the ceremony, the *fukusa* reflects *yin–yang* harmony: its outer side symbolizes heaven (*yang*), the inner earth (*yin*). Folded in fourths, the layers correspond to the four Daoist directions, ritually purified during utensil cleansing. These corners also represent the Four Heavenly Kings (*Shitennō* 四天王). Folded into eighths, the *fukusa* signifies entry into enlightenment.

Please allow me to demonstrate.

~ *The Host refolds the cloth and gently strokes the thick tea container, then the bamboo tea scoop, before placing it back atop the thick tea container. She lifts the water ladle, scoops hot water from the kettle into the tea bowl, and returns the ladle with one graceful movement.*

Guide: This movement is known as *oki-bishaku* (置き柄杓), which is meant to resemble an archer fitting an arrow to the bow.

~ *Placing the whisk in the bowl, the host empties the water into the rinse-water container, and wipes the bowl with her linen cloth (chakin 茶巾). She then opens the thick tea container and carefully scoops the powdered tea into the bowl.*

Now, her gestures follow a complex set of movements referred to as the hiki-bishaku.

Guide: This first movement, *hiki-bishaku* (引き柄杓), evokes the moment an archer's bow is drawn to full extension before release.

~ *The Host taps the scoop on the edge of the bowl—another percussive moment that seems to resonate far beyond the confines of the small space—and then closes the matcha container.*

With the ladle, she scoops water from the kettle into the bowl with a slightly elongated and measured movement, returning the ladle to rest atop the thick tea container.

Guide: Now the *kiri-bishaku* (切り柄杓) movement, the archer releases the arrow.

~ *Lifting the water scoop, she holds it upright once again, and carefully cleans it from top to bottom. She then uses the fukusa to open the kettle. Holding the water scoop in her left hand, she transfers it to her right, scoops water, and pours it into the first tea bowl before resting the scoop atop the kettle's opening.*

The whisk is slowly lowered into the tea bowl when the host begins the delicate, precise whisking motions blending the water and matcha powder into a frothy mix.

With the matcha now dissolving in the hot water, the host takes the whisk in hand and begins kneading the tea within the bowl until it reaches the perfect consistency, signaled by a thin layer of tiny bubbles forming at the surface, creating a light froth partly concealing the deep green tea beneath.

Once the tea is properly blended, she shifts slightly toward the guest, bows, setting the bowl down halfway between herself and the main guest, turning the bowl so that its most beautiful side once more faces the guest.

Without rising, the main guest slides forward on his knees, takes the bowl in hand, and slides back to his position. He turns slowly and bows to the other guests, apologizing for taking priority, before picking up the bowl and turning it twice to avoid his lips touching the front of the bowl.

Now, he has his drink.

He pauses for a second before turning and gestures to pass the bowl on.

The three guests, readying for their final drinks are on the verge of full absorption into the entirety of the tea world surrounding them, when they hear—

"CUT!!"

17

As if in a Dream

Theologian: What just happened?

Philosopher: . . . where did the tea hut go?

Guide: You assumed it would remain?

Philosopher: I did, yes.

Guide: Expectations for permanence can be quite tenacious that way.

Artist: I feel like our world just dissolved.

Philosopher: . . . was the garden, the hut never real?

Guide: Do they feel unreal now?

Theologian: I'm not sure what's real now.

Artist: I can't tell if I'm dreaming now or if everything before the walls falling down was the dream. Where did the tea hut go?

Guide: Well, this might be a dream too, but I'll explain that later.

> ~ When the group heard "Cut", the lighting in the tearoom had shifted in an instant as the walls of the hut fell away. Flood lamps clicked on, illuminating the full expanse of the set, flanked by rigging, lights, and microphones. What seemed like a film crew stood at the perimeter, surrounded by a massive green screen that, just a moment ago, had displayed the tea garden. In an instant, the entire world they had inhabited disappeared before their eyes.
>
> The three guests sat motionless, visibly shaken, anticipating some explanation for this unforeseen transformation. The Guide, unfazed, gestured for them to join him in seats behind one of the monitors, where their entire journey within the garden and hut had been displayed.
>
> The group settled into their chairs, their breath slowing as they collected themselves, waiting for their nerves to steady.

Philosopher: So, this is what you meant by not being able to take us to a tea ceremony.

Guide: Yes, that question we began with—how we, as foreigners, might have an authentic experience of the tea ceremony—this is more complicated than we originally thought.

Artist: "We"? Are you part of this project?

Guide: Of the *Flowers in the Sky* project? I am, yes.

As I mentioned before, our group has been experimenting with the tea ceremony, exploring what might be possible in this moment of history, nearly 500 years after the period that gave us *Wabicha*. We take very seriously the question as to whether the tea ceremony is alive and thriving, dead and stagnating, or possibly in a moment of re-birth and re-animation.

Artist: How would it be dead if we can still undertake tea ceremonies?

Guide: Maybe it's dead when there's no way to experience it other than as a tourist. Or, as a subject experiencing objects. It's a vexing question whether we, inside our present "world", east or west, can really engage with this tradition. Perhaps we can't. But, this is a real danger with cultural practices like the tea ceremony, which are threatened in our present globalized, highly-materialist world. Simply repeating the glorious past won't keep any tradition alive.

Philosopher: So, this project is doing what Hisamatsu said, "killing the ancestors"?

Guide: You might put it that way.

One might assume that the gravest danger would be the loss of the practice itself, that the ceremony would cease being performed. While that would indeed be tragic, we believe the greater danger is that it persists but becomes a locus of attachment to a fixed and very old idea of what *Chanoyu* is. This is a real risk, and it was one of Rikyū's main concerns in his own time. He was well aware of the possibility that *Wabicha* could become rigid, adulterated by formalization.

Despite his having written in his death poem that "with this treasured sword, I slay both ancestors and Buddhas"[1] sadly, *Wabicha* did become overly formalized after his death, degenerating into what some later referred to as a self-indulgent *fūryū* style of tea.

A later master of *Wabicha*, Jakuan Sōtaku, wrote in greater detail about the dangers of attachment in his *Zen Tea Record*, he says,

> *By performing a mode of chanoyu that has agitating and exciting the mind as its moving force, people give themselves up to an utter inversion of original Zen tea. All proclivities and inclinations, even toward chanoyu, are movements of mind based on attachment to things; they are exercises of thought and will. Thus, when the mind is agitated by the concept of "wabi," extravagance is born. When agitated by utensils, rules of measurement are born. When agitated by "suki,"*

personal preference is born. When agitated by "naturalness," artifice is born. When agitated by "contentment," discontent is born. When agitated by "the way of Zen," heretical teachings are born.

(1995, p. 270).

If the tea ceremony can only be experienced as an artifact of a past age, not a living, breathing practice, then it *will* become an object of attachment. And, if I bring you to this version of tea, it's questionable whether I'm actually bringing you to a tea ceremony.

This isn't unique to the tea ceremony. Any practice with a strong historical legacy risks becoming fixed and rigid. When we cling to a static version, we stop innovating and simply reproduce the past. The tradition freezes—no longer a living response to the present. Once an art becomes an object packaged for subjects, the chance for authentic experience may already be lost.

This is one reason why the tea ceremony holds such significance for philosophy and religion. The threats faced by aesthetic practices and rituals are the same threats that philosophies and religions confront; soteriological philosophy-religions like Buddhism and Daoism.

Theologian: You have to not just kill the Buddha, but perpetually kill him, I guess.

Guide: That's one way to think about it, yes.

We have mostly spoken about the history of *Wabicha*, but to take it seriously in the present moment—in a world it fits into very awkwardly—we must ask: as this world continues to evolve at an unprecedented pace, shaped by the proliferation of media, the internet, virtual reality, and cinema, how can *Wabicha* continue to evolve?

Artist: How can it avoid resting on an identity? *Wabicha* as *Wabicha*.

Guide: Exactly. Once it's attached to its own identity, it risks becoming a cultural artifact, a museum piece, an object that simply *represents* an earlier time.

Of course, *Chanoyu* holds immeasurable value as part of Japan's cultural heritage. At a time when so many traditions are disappearing, it must be preserved. But if it remains static, if practitioners don't risk evolving along with the rapidly changing conditions outside the tea garden, it will contradict the Zen principles on which it is based.

Killing Buddhas at a pizza restaurant, performing the ceremony on a movie set, or even someday engaging in *Chanoyu* through virtual reality might seem like distortions of a practice that should remain *pure*, but we already know from our study of Daoism that there is no purity, and the attempt to maintain purity is a struggle against nature itself.

Perhaps, then, in searching for *Wabicha*, we should not be looking at what it *is*, not just for what it *is not*—but we have to also ask what it could be. This is what we've been experimenting with in our *Flowers in the Sky* tea group.

Theologian: But, why bring us into the cinematic world?

Guide: It didn't have to be cinema. Maybe next time it will be something else. But, when trying to answer the question about what the tea ceremony can mean today, in the contemporary world, we can't ignore how that world has been radically impacted by media.

And, cinema is a crucial part of the contemporary Japanese aesthetic world. We couldn't conduct a course on Japanese aesthetics without discussing it.

But, let me ask all of you what you experienced in that moment of drinking tea before we heard the "Cut".

Artist: The anticipation was overwhelming at that point. I've never prepared so much for such a simple act. Leading up to the last serving of tea, I wasn't sure exactly what to do or how to act. But then I recalled our discussion of the *Dao* and the idea of *non-action*. I don't know if I succeeded, but I tried not to be overly active, nor passively going with the flow.

Philosopher: . . . I was also really overwhelmed in that moment, but I thought back to the concept of emptiness and how it describes a field of relations. I tried to let myself sink into all the relations that had accumulated through the various contexts we had encountered and focused them on the tea at the moment that last sip was approaching. I suppose I was trying to be empty—trying to be a *non-self* drinking a *non-object*, but also conscious that trying too hard, or even *trying not to try* was going to take me out of the moment.

Theologian: . . . I was thinking a lot about our original question—how to have an authentic experience as a foreigner undertaking a Japanese tea ceremony. But I have to admit, at the moment where I received the bowl, I felt a profound inauthenticity. Despite all the learning we've done, I felt my foreignness acutely, as though I didn't belong in this world, that I was just pretending.

Guide: Let me address some of your reflections, because each of you touches on how the philosophies and religions we've studied have tried to find an antidote for this very danger—the danger of attachment and reification.

Regarding Laozi, he was highly aware of the risks involved in striving too rigidly for philosophical or religious goals. In Chapter 29 of the *Daodejing*, Laozi writes:

> *The world is a sacred vessel,*
> *And not something that can be acted on.*
> *Those who act on things will be defeated by them.*
> *Those who take things in their hands will lose them.*

And later, he adds,

> *Therefore the sage*
> *Will not act and thus not be defeated,*
> *Will not hold on and thus not lose.*

Artist: I can see now that even in trying to have a Daoist *non-acting* experience, I was still holding onto the experience, trying to grasp it as an object.

Guide: It could almost not have been otherwise. The point was never to *overcome* our tendency to grasp our world or the things in it. Whether it is even possible to have a fully non-objectifying experience—one in which we do not "hold on"—is a question in itself. For centuries, our world has shaped us into selves who can do little else *but* hold onto objects, and when we encounter philosophies, ceremonies, or rituals, we tend to do the same.

Being able to enact *non-action* is something practitioners pursue for an entire lifetime, but it is deeply paradoxical—it requires trying *not* to try, willing *not* to will. Laozi recognized this contradiction and understood that it could be self-defeating.

Interestingly, some of our western philosophies—particularly phenomenology—have also identified this problem. Heidegger (2001) was deeply concerned with the destructive tendencies of western metaphysics, which he saw as an unrestrained "will to will". He wrestled with a version of a question Laozi did. He asks,

> *can there, however, be a heightening of this willing beyond the absolute of purposeful self-assertion?*

and his answer is "no". His claim is that

> *those, then, who are at times more venturesome can will more strongly only if their willing is different in nature.*

To achieve a willing of a "different nature" he tells us that we must will "non-willing". But, again like Laozi—who influenced Heidegger a great deal—

non-willing doesn't mean passivity, "non-willing means, therefore: willingly to renounce willing." (1966)

We could spend hours unpacking the fascinating implications of these questions, but let's turn to another of Heidegger's ideas.

Let me ask our Theologian—you said you were trying to have an *authentic* experience?

Theologian: Yes, that's right.

Guide: You wanted to overcome inauthenticity?

Theologian: I thought any lingering western philosophical, religious, or even artistic attachments would somehow pollute my experience, making it inauthentic.

Guide: That's very understandable. We tend to imagine that we're either in a state of authenticity or inauthenticity, and that one excludes the other.

Theologian: But, yes, I remember that point from our discussions about Daoism. How the *yin yang* symbol shows us that nothing is purely what it is, that the negative is always permeated by the positive, and vice versa.

Guide: No matter how much we might learn about the Japanese world, we shouldn't expect to ever avoid having our western dot complicating the purity of the eastern shape, or vice versa.

But, let's go back to what you said about authenticity. For Heidegger, authenticity is not the binary opposite of inauthenticity but a *modification* of it. We are never in a state of pure authenticity. In fact, *Dasein*'s basic existential condition is *inauthenticity*.

We exist inauthentically insofar as, in an *everyday* mode of being, our thoughts, actions, expectations, and desires are dictated by our world. We think and act according to an anonymous *"they"*, what Heidegger calls *"das Man"*—the impersonal, collective way things are done.

However, in exceptional circumstances—what Heidegger (2008) refers to as *limit situations* (*Grenzsituationen*)—we rise above this, confront our own finitude, grapple with guilt, and exist authentically. But even then, it is questionable whether Heidegger believed we could sustain such a state. He called it an *"outlandish imposition"* (*phantastische Zumutung*) to expect oneself to remain in a constant state of authenticity.

Despite all of our learning, to uncover and go beyond the assumptions of our western "world", it might be equally outlandish to assume we could have a *purely* authentic experience of a complex Japanese ritual.

But, you also mentioned feeling like you didn't belong in *this* world.

Theologian: Yes, as the moment came to drink that last sip, I felt my surroundings becoming increasingly foreign, and myself increasingly out of place.

Guide: That might actually suggest you were tending more toward an *authentic* experience. To follow Heidegger some more: when we take for granted how "*they*" live—when we are fully absorbed in the everyday world—*that's* when we feel comfortable and at home.

But when we begin to question this world, that's when we find it unsettling—a feeling Heidegger calls *Unheimlichkeit*, a sense of being *not at home* in the world. If any of you felt this, it isn't necessarily a bad thing. Given our efforts to uncover and grapple with our western world and step into another, this discomfort is likely inevitable. If someone didn't feel some element of discomfort, it might signal that the issues of intercultural encounter aren't real questions for them.

Theologian: So, regarding our original question about having an authentic experience, in the end, it's not possible?

Guide: It's a bit more complicated than that. Heidegger says authenticity is the "possibility of the *im*-possibility of existence".

Heidegger can be slightly enigmatic sometimes. Let's just say, it's possible, but it's rare, and it's unlikely that we're going to bring it about from a heightening of our individual will. In his later works he explores the idea of "waiting", such that an event "appropriates" us, rather than us trying to make something happen.

But, let me ask our philosopher; you said you were trying to manifest emptiness? As non-self?

Philosopher: I think so, yes.

Guide: What emptiness?

Philosopher: The notion of emptiness we were talking about—*śūnyatā*.

Guide: There's no *śūnyatā*.

Philosopher: Okay, I remember how this goes. If there's no emptiness, then there must be non-emptiness?

Guide: Sort of.

Philosopher: We had the negative of the self. Can't we have the negative of emptiness?

Guide: Closer.

Philosopher: Wouldn't the negative of emptiness be like the negative of negation?

Guide: Emptiness as the negative of negation—I think you have it.

If you recall the Mādhyamika philosopher Nāgārjuna, he had another way of describing what you're referring to: *śūnyatāyāh śūnyatā*, or the "emptiness of emptiness."

This is one of the foundational principles of our *Flowers in the Sky* project. But, we also know that adhering to a foundational principle can be dangerous—insofar as we become attached to it.

Nāgārjuna recognized this tendency toward objectification and attachment is so strong that even philosophies advocating negativity and non-attachment can themselves become objects of attachment. Just as we can objectify the self or things, we can also turn *emptiness* itself into an object of attachment. We can *reify* it. Become attached even to non-attachment.

The danger is that if we become attached to emptiness as a *principle*, then we are no longer treating it as *empty* but as a fixed thing, a concept to cling to—essentially, like an object. To counter this, his idea of the "emptiness of emptiness" stresses that even the most foundational philosophical principle—*emptiness itself*—is empty. Basically, he makes it so that there's nothing to hold onto. No final ground for attachment.

Philosopher: So, the foundation is kind of like a reminder not to have foundations.

Guide: That's a good way to put it.

Theologian: But, don't we need something real, some foundation for *some* real world?

Guide: Are we in the real world now?

Theologian: It seems like we're in a different world than we thought we were.

Guide: When did it become another world?

Theologian: When the director yelled "Cut!".

Guide: What do we know about cutting?

Philosopher: Ah, right. The *kire* idea. So, there's a division but also some continuity between these two worlds we've just cut between?

Guide: Right. It's not that the previous world wasn't real. Even though we're in a cinematic version of the tea ceremony, there is still a continuity with the previous world.

Artist: I still feel like we've gone from something that appeared real, to something less real, in cinema, I mean. Wasn't this all just a copy of the real ceremony?

Guide: Is an actual tea ceremony more real just because it happens in what we think is real life and not in a movie or a great book?

In this case, we're turning to cinema because, in a simple sense, we can't have a complete discussion of Japanese aesthetics without Japanese cinema.

Let me give you a bit of background and then we can discuss how a few pieces of great Japanese cinema help us sort out the question of what "real world" we're in.

Japanese Cinema

Guide: Japanese cinema—*Nihon eiga* (日本映画) or *hōga* (邦画, "domestic cinema")—is one of the world's oldest and most celebrated film traditions. Like other arts we've studied, filmmaking came from abroad and, some say, was perfected in Japan. It began in 1897, and by 1909, Japan already had journals critically analysing its cinema.

Since then, Japan has produced the fourth-highest number of films of any country. While not many make their way outside of Japan, some of the best film critics consistently rank several among the greatest of all time. Akira Kurosawa's *Seven Samurai* (*Shichinin no Samurai* 七人の侍, 1954) has often been voted the greatest foreign-language film[2] and Yasujirō Ozu's *Tokyo Story* (1953) appears in the top five of many of the most highly-regarded lists.

Though not a classical aesthetic discipline, Japanese cinema draws heavily from theatrical traditions like Kabuki, Noh, and Bunraku. The tea ceremony often features in films, especially those of Yasujirō Ozu (小津　安二郎, 1903–63), notably *Early Spring* (*Sōshun* 早春, 1956), a film often ranked among the greatest ever made.

And this brings us back once again to the *kire* principle. *Cutting* plays an essential role in cinema. Can anyone think of how?

Artist: Through editing. They actually call it "cutting" a film.

Guide: Right, exactly. Like the *kire* aesthetic—where a cut creates continuity—film editing connects through cuts. Without some element of continuity in nearly every scene, the narrative couldn't build. It's so essential that film sets have dedicated continuity specialists. At its core, cinema is the art of cutting and maintaining continuity.

One of my own philosophy teachers, the great scholar of Japanese philosophy and cinema, Graham Parkes wrote about the *kire* principle in relation to Ozu. "For each cut Ozu makes," Parkes notes, "he has arranged for at least one formal element to provide continuity (*kire-tsuzuki*) between the adjacent scenes." He calls Ozu's the "kindest cut of all" in world cinema. (2024),

Theologian: If we've *cut* between worlds, even if they're connected, one has to be more real, doesn't it?

Guide: Let's take two steps to answer this question. First, following Parkes some more, let's consider Akira Kurosawa's *Rashōmon* (羅生門, 1950), and a kind of multi-perspectivism we see in this movie?

Artist: Yeah, that's a great movie. I've seen it several times.

Guide: *Rashomon* is a psychological thriller renowned for its pioneering use of a multi-perspective narrative.

And, we have another nice inter-cultural connection here: Heidegger, who was otherwise quiet about cinema, makes one single reference to a movie in all of his thousands of pages of writing.

Philosopher: . . . to *Rashomon*?

Guide: You guessed it. In a moment when he is contemplating the ills of "Europeanization", through the voice of a Japanese interlocutor, he proposes that there is something redeeming about Kurosawa's film.[3]

Theologian: And, what's the "multi-perspectivism" you mentioned?

Guide: The production is set in Heian-period Japan in the town of Rashomon, where a murder and rape occur. Three suspects and the wife of the victim each give their account of the crime. Throughout the film, we are taken into three different "worlds", each reflecting the perspective of a different character.

Kurosawa developed innovative cinematographic techniques to overlap and juxtapose these worlds. In the end, rather than resolving the contradictions by making one world more real than another, he allows the "worlds" to coexist. There's no resolution where one becomes more real and the others turn out to be illusions.

Though it's a cinematic technique, this kind of perspectivism has profound philosophical and religious implications.

Has anyone heard of the philosophical principle called *perspectivism*?

Philosopher: In Nietzsche, right?

Guide: Yes, but long before that in Zhuangzi and Dōgen. Dōgen developed his "polycentric perspectivism", which we've already mentioned. It challenges our tendency to see the world only from a *human* perspective. He asks,

> are there many ways to see one thing, or is it a mistake to see many forms as one thing?
>
> (2009a, p. 89)

And his answer is unambiguous—*yes*, it is a mistake to see many forms as *one* thing.

He calls this a "conditioned view", an error that is like "looking through a bamboo tube at the corner of the sky" and mistaking what we see for the whole world.

By contrast, Dōgen insists that "the ultimate realm has one thousand kinds and ten thousand ways." Thus, we should not "judge mountains by human standards". Let me read you a longer passage on this topic from his "Mountains and Waters as Sutras".

> *Do not foolishly suppose that what we see as water is used as water by all other beings. You who study with Buddhas should not be limited to human views when you are studying water.*
>
> *Some beings see water as a jeweled ornament, but they do not regard jeweled ornaments as water. What in the human realms corresponds to their water? We only see their jeweled ornaments as water. Some beings see water as wondrous blossoms, but they do not use blossoms as water. . . . Some see it as the Dharma nature of pure liberation, the true human body, or as the form of body and essence of mind. Human beings see water as water.*
>
> (p. 90)

Artist: How far can we take this? Are all perspectives real? Is there nothing *unreal* or *less real*?

Guide: Can you imagine how the tea ceremony could be fully *un*real?

Philosopher: If it were a hallucination.

Artist: . . . or a dream.

Guide: But, can we ever be sure we're not in a dream?

~ *The three paused for a moment.*

Can anyone recall what the scroll in the alcove said?

Artist: Something from *Zhuangzi* about butterflies.

Guide: Right. This is the second point for answering your question.

Each scroll had a quote from the "dream of the Butterfly" passage from the *Zhuangzi*.

In that story, Zhuang Zhou dreams he is a butterfly. Then, suddenly, he wakes up and is Zhuang Zhou again. But now he is uncertain—was he Zhuang Zhou dreaming he was a butterfly, or is he a butterfly now dreaming he's Zhuang Zhou?

And then there are two decisive lines where Zhuangzi elaborates these ideas about dreaming: He says, "While dreaming you don't know it's a dream. You might even interpret a dream in your dream—and then you wake up and realize it was all a dream" (p. 19).

Let's say that Zhuang Zhou is experiencing a "world shift", from a state he thought was real, to one that appears less real. We also underwent a similar world shift when our tea world fell away.

Once we undergo any world shift like this, our instinct is to say that *that* world was a dream and that *this* is the real world. But Zhuangzi warns us: "fools imagine they are already awake—how clearly and certainly they understand it all!" (p. 19)

Maybe you feel a sense of safety, security, or certainty in this world now that it appears stable, permanent, and fully real. You think you know what this world is and where your self fits within it. You're now a subject in relation to a new set of objects, probably already forming attachments to this world.

But how do you *know* you are not still in a dream?

Artist: On another film set.

Philosopher: . . . inside virtual reality.

Theologian: . . . or some kind of simulation.

Guide: To put this in the context of Nāgārjuna's efforts to avoid attachment—even to philosophical principles—we can ask ourselves: *What if the philosophical principles we're trying to derive from our wakeful state reveal themselves as dreams?*

Zhuangzi pushes the implications of such questions to this extreme with one decisive line, and this is why we chose him for our scrolls. He says: "when I say you're dreaming, I'm dreaming too!" (p. 19)

Think of it this way: it would be very easy to accept Zhuangzi's teaching and say, "Yes, you're right Master Zhuang. Everything appears to be a dream. I'll just stick to this idea and then I'll be safe with *this* as my philosophical foundation."

But if you were to do this, you would, in a sense, be saying that everything is a dream—*except for one thing*: except for *this* philosophical principle.

You would have gone very far, philosophically speaking, toward perspectivism, but you would still be holding on to one last certainty—the certainty that everything is a dream. You would have turned that idea into an object, an attachment. The idea that everything is a dream is no longer itself a dream.

But Zhuangzi thwarts this when he says, *"I'm dreaming too."* He undoes even that foundation. If the one telling you that everything is a dream is also dreaming, then *everything* becomes ambiguous—there is no firm ground left, no final philosophical foundation to grasp.

And with nothing to hold onto, there is nothing left to be attached to. No reason to prioritize one world over another, to say that one is real and another unreal. No need to decide between Zhuang Zhou and the butterfly.

Theologian: Do you think this is what Kurosawa had in mind with *Rashomon*, to blur the distinction between dreams and reality?

Guide: It's a tendency apparent in many of his films. Nearly forty years after *Rashomon*, he made *Dreams*, another series of vignettes—this time even more multi-perspectival. Like the "dream of the Butterfly," almost every one of the eight stories features a character slipping into dreamlike visions. And since all eight are drawn from Kurosawa's own dreams, the film mirrors the dream-within-a-dream structure found in Zhuangzi.

And, remember last week's discussion of Wu Daozi and his having walked into his painting and disappeared? In the fifth sequence of the film entitled "Crows" (鴉), Kurosawa brings that concept to life: the unnamed dreamer actually wanders throughout several of Van Gogh's colorful landscapes.

Another intriguing piece of east–west trivia—Van Gogh is played by American director Martin Scorsese, who was deeply influenced by Kurosawa's films.

Artist: Is there some way for us to experience the tea ceremony by treating it like a dream, or a dream-within-a-dream, but without it being less real?

Guide: You're touching on something central to our group. It's why we chose the name *Flowers in the Sky*, or *Kuge* (空華) in Japanese. *Kuge* is a Buddhist term often translated as "empty flowers", originally with negative connotations—referring to illusions or hallucinations. Just as someone with an eye disorder sees floating spots, deluded beings mistake empty phenomena for something real and substantial.

It's not a void, but a blossoming reality. In this sense, dreams and illusions become paths to realization.

We don't use the orthodox meaning, though—we follow Dōgen, who reclaims *kuge* in a positive light. The *ku* (空) syllable is crucial. It's the Japanese rendering of *śūnyatā*, or *emptiness*. For Dōgen, *ku* isn't a symbol of illusion or deception. He re-reads *kuge* as *"flowers of emptiness"*, reminding us that emptiness is not a deficiency. A lack of foundations is not *less than*—it is, in fact, *radically more than*. Emptiness is not an illusion or a meaningless abyss but an expansive, blossoming reality. In this sense of *kuge*, dreams and illusions—all perspectives are a pathway to realization.

Artist: So, we can use the perspectivism inherent to the dream-within-a-dream structure to help us answer our question about experiencing the tea ceremony?

Philosopher: Our *selves* can't be brought to a tea ceremony, but maybe our dream selves in a dream world can somehow overlap with the world of the tea ceremony?

Guide: I think you've got it.

Let's go back to some of the other questions we shared at the very beginning. Does anyone remember?

Artist: I wanted to know if the tea ceremony could be considered art.

Theologian: . . . and whether it was philosophy.

Philosopher: . . . or religion.

Guide: It's completely understandable these questions come up in the context of foreigners taking part in a tea ceremony. They inevitably arise, at least in part, because we've inherited a tradition that demands that when we find real things, they aren't ambiguous, empty or dreamlike. We've been taught to assume that the real corresponds to one single perspective yielding one single definition of something permanent, and when we find this perspective, we won't ever wake up to find anything different.

Yet, if we can cultivate a way of sustaining multiple perspectives, what emerges is something else: from various perspectives—philosophical, religious, *and* artistic—diverse aspects of the tea ceremony can come into view. And crucially, these perspectives don't need to be ranked as *more real* than the others, nor do they demand that we cordon off the practice as strictly religious, philosophical, or artistic. These domains are all dreams appearing rather permanent now, and although we might not be around to see it, our world eventually transitions away from them just as Zhuang Zhou transitioned into a butterfly.

The *expansive nature* of the tea ceremony comes through precisely by embracing *all* of these perspectives at once, without having to argue for what is more or less real, or discarding what is *unreal*. And, this form of perspectivism affords a much more expansive space to consider how the tradition might live on in other mediums.

Experiencing tea rituals doesn't depend on whether one is more or less "real": It doesn't require achieving some kind of *world-transcending* state of authenticity: Nor does it depend on it being a *traditional* tea ceremony rather than a *cinematic* version.

And future experiences of the tea ceremony? They may not even be limited to what we can even dream. Where and how the tea ceremony might be *real* will not depend on it being a fixed thing—an object with an unchanging identity, remaining the same as worlds themselves go through the radical transformations we're seeing lately. Our worlds are changing so rapidly, if the tea ceremony remains A, if it doesn't find out how to kill its ancestors, it's unlikely to remain a living tradition. But, maybe it will die, but be born again, in virtual reality, in a dream, in someone else's dream, maybe it lives on in cinema, in poetry, or in a book about the tea ceremony.

> ~ *On the teahouse veranda, the group paused, suspended in a moment that defied the ordinary measure of time – neither fleeting nor drawn-out. A scattering of pleasantries culminated in the final, graceful bows of gratitude to their Host and Guide before quietly departing the garden.*
>
> *As they gathered their personal belongings, a collective remembrance surfaced: the Hanto's polite request to return their tea implements at the yoritsuki.*

Philosopher: Oh yeah, what about this poem on the *kaishi* paper? You said you'd read it to us on the way out.

Hanto: That's Rikyū's death poem. He wrote that for his last ceremony and read it just before taking his own life.

Artist: What does it say?

Hanto:

> *"Like dewdrops fall, like dewdrops vanish*
> *such is my life.*
> *Even the affairs of Naniwa*
> *are but a dream within a dream."*

Notes

1 What is (not) Tea?

1. In his "Introduction to the Aestheticism of Chanoyu" (1970, p. 311) Dan Ino explains that, despite being widely sanctioned terminology, "tea ceremony" is a slight misnomer arising from a western guide in Yokohama who mistakenly associated the etiquette employed for "ceremonial" rituals, whereas "*Chanoyu*" simply refers to "heating water for making tea."

2 Water for Tea

1. The *Chanoyu Hyorin* (茶湯評林) is a seventeenth century, nine-volume compendium on the tea ceremony authored by Endō Genkan (遠藤元閑), which lists the fourteen famous water collecting sources in Kyoto. Also, the *Yoshu Fushi* ("Topography of Yoshu", Ogura 2005) lists many sources. See also, *Miyako Meisho Zue* (都名所図会) "An Illustrated Guide to Famous Places in the Capital [Kyoto], 1780), and *Kyoto Bo-moku Shi* (京都某目誌) (Kyoto Sectional Survey", Kyōto-fu 1916).
2. Sencha tea, or the practices surrounding it, *sencha-dō*, involve different ways of preparing tea, which evolved through a slightly separate history and lineage going back to Tang dynasty China. Sencha also first comes into the written record around the seventeenth century as associated with a lesser known Zen sect, the Ōbaku. Murase Kōtei (1764–1818) wrote that "*matcha* is for the mind, *sencha* for the spirit". See Graham (1993).
3. There are over twenty kinds of *chaji*, the main forms being: 1) *Shogo* 正午-, noon tea; 2) *Yobanashi* 夜 (夕) 咄- sunset tea (4: 30-5pm); 3) *Asacha* 朝茶- sunrise; 4) *Hango* 飯後 a.k.a. *Kashi-cha* 菓子茶- just after another meal; 5) *Rinji* 臨時 a.k.a. *Buji* 不時- spontaneous, not "timed"; 6) *Atomi* 跡見- Guest invite self(ves) to view previous chaji; 7) *Akatsuki* 暁- pre-dawn.
4. Some conjectured that if you drink tea, you will sprout feathers enabling flight, or become a wizard (*sennin*). See. Hisamatsu (1993)
5. The earliest reference to tea drinking in Japan involves Emperor Shōmu inviting a hundred monks to the Imperial palace in 729 where he gave a lecture on the Great Wisdom Sutra followed by serving tea. See Hisamatsu (1993)

6. Some have conjectured that it was with Shingon Buddhist monk Kūkai that tea drinking began in Japan. Upon returning from China in 804 he is said to have brought Buddhist artworks, scripture and tea. (mentioned in his *Shōryōshū* collection of writings) See Anderson (1991).
7. *Cha awase* were part of a broader category of *mono awase* games that were popular in Heian Japan involving matching objects in various categories, including plants, birds, insects, and eventually teaware and utensils, or *ko awase*, the identification of incense. These were detailed in a book of tea drinking conventions know as the *Kissa Ōrai*. See Viswanathan (2017), Kenzo (1991).
8. Among the ailments that tea was said to treat included; healing fistula, boils, promoting urination, reducing thirst, fever, helping digestion, reducing need for sleep, strengthening the will, invigorating the heart, harmonizing the five organs as well as eliminating fatigue and promoting longevity. Hisamatsu (1993)
9. See Heine (1985), Parkes (1992), Loughnane (2023).
10. Works from the period describing the *fūryū* movement, include the *Kissa Ōrai* ("Letters on drinking tea", 1971), and for *fūryū* culture in general, *see Taiheiki* ("Chronicle of the Great Peace". 1992).

3 Urasenke Institute

1. He was known to have used the *bokuseki* (墨跡) style for hanging scrolls, making these the focal point of the tearoom.
2. In his "Record of Yamanoue Soji" (*Yamanoue Sōji ki* 山上宗二記) Yamanoue (1995) credits Shukō with the establishment of grass-hut tea and the initiator of the movement away from earlier warrior-dominated tea culture and practice.
3. Shukō is said to have studied with Ikkyū Sōjun of Daitokuji, who taught that "the Buddha dharma is also in the way of tea". Ikkyū rejected monastic and authoritarian norms, emphasizing enlightenment in the everyday (Ludwig 1981). Some scholars question whether Shukō had direct contact with Ikkyū or others like Yoshimasa, Nōami, or Shinkei (Slusser 2013).
4. The term was first used by the servants of Ashikaga shoguns (*dōbōshū*) who learned the specific movements required to handle treasured utensils and serve tea gracefully. See Di Berardino (2018)
5. See Masao (1995). Mark Keane (2014) also elaborates on the intermediate stage in the evolution of the tearoom, known as *Kakoi*; a hut of five or six tatami mats not yet in a separate structure, partitioned by standing screens, which was between the *Shoin*-style gatherings and the later reduced *sukiya*.
6. Some have read Shukō's "Letter on Heart's Mastery" (1980) as remaining concerned with promoting the interests of the wealthy merchant class seeking to

define a new way of tea to counter the warrior-aristocracy. Rather than a purely aesthetic document, it has been interpreted as an "attempt to change the contour of the field to express their social position and interests" and can be read as a "statement of the merchant's strategy to establish themselves within the field" (Slusser 2013, p. 44).
7 See Hayakawa (1995), Hirota (1995) where the author analyses Rikyū's own etymology of this term. See also Masao (1995).
8 The full title, *Kissa Nampōroku* (喫茶南方録) is thought to have been authored by a disciple of Rikyū's Nambō Sōkei. The text has various translations depending on whether the character *bō* is substituted for *hō*, changing the translation from "The Southern Record" or "Record on Tea Drinking, which comes from the South" to "The Record of Nambō"). See Hirota (1995)
9 Hideyoshi was a patron of *Chanoyu* but manipulated the ceremony for his own political aims, including dictating aesthetic choices to leading tea masters, practicing *Chanoyu* on the battlefield and holding strategy meetings in tearooms.

4 Tetsugaku Michi

1 Norinaga develops his interpretation of *mono no aware* in his annotations to the text of the *Tale of Genji*.
2 See Watsuji Tetsuro (1996) for understanding the mechanics of an aesthetic death in the name of the nation.
3 Before reaching enlightenment and becoming the Buddha, Prince Siddhartha was said to have had four "sights" of human suffering upon first leaving his family's palace grounds, including old age, sickness, death and a wandering ascetic who had devoted his life to uncovering the root of human suffering.

5 Kyoto Daigaku I

1 Some of those include: Nishi Amane (1829–97), Fukuzawa Yukichi (1835–1901), Nakae Chōmin (1847–1901), Inoue Tetsujirō (1855–1944), Inoue Enryō (1858–1919), Ōnishi Hajime (1864–1900).
2 Another construal of his, is "I am I, precisely because I am not I". Ueda (1991).
3 Both depict a holographic cosmology where each part reflects the whole, but while Leibniz's God-preharmonized monads stress theological determinism, Indra's Net, grounded in Buddhist thought, emphasizes interdependence and emptiness without a divine creator. Indra's Net points to ethical responsibility through interconnectedness, whereas Leibniz prioritizes metaphysical coherence over ethics.

4 Aristotle uses the term "choriston" (χωριστόν, "separate" or "separable") primarily in discussions about forms, substances, and universals, particularly in his critique of Platonic Forms. In Metaphysics (Book A, 991a20-30), Aristotle challenges Plato's notion of separated forms (*chorista eidē*, χωριστὰ εἴδη). "For they make the Forms separate (*choriston*), but the essence of a thing is identical with its form." (Metaphysics 991a20)
5 Some have argued that the religious cosmology implicit to the tea ceremony was uniquely Japanese. (Carriger 2012, Kondo 1985, Anderson 1987, Colby 1991, Surak 2012, Suzuki 1999). For a discussion on the notions of "invented tradition" and "imagined communities" in relation to the tea ceremony, see Tanaka (2007), Kumakura (1980).
6 See Hobsbawn (1983), Plutschow (1999), Surak (2013) and Cross (2009).
7 The most controversial Kyoto School debates occurred in three *Chūō Kōron* (中央公論) symposia in the early 1940s, where second-generation thinkers Nishitani, Kōyama, Kōsaka, and Suzuki discussed Japan's wartime stance and the Great East Asia Co-Prosperity Sphere. Some (Najita, Harootunian) view these as supporting Japanese fascism, while others (Williams 2014; Heisig, Maraldo 1995; Parkes 1997) see them as flawed attempts to resist western imperialism. In 1942 leading Japanese intellectuals came together in Tokyo for the so-called "Overcoming Modernity" symposium (近代の超克 *kindai no chōkoku*), where they discussed alternatives to the western project of modernity. Proceedings were published in the *Bungakkai* journal (文学会). See Krummel (2021).
8 See Loughnane (2022).
9 *Chanoyu Quarterly*, published by the Urasenke Foundation (裏千家) put out 100 volumes from 1965–2007. It was an English-language journal dedicated to the study and promotion of *Chanoyu*, and one of the most important international publications on the subject, covering a wide range of topics related to tea practice, history, aesthetics, and philosophy.
10 www.urasenke.or.jp/texte/uac/midori/index.html

6 Kyoto Daigaku II

1 See Chiba (2011); Corbett (2009, 2014, 2018); Kato (2002a, 2004, 2015)
2 Harris (1986), Taiichi (1970), Kanazawa et al. (2015, 2016), Keisen et al. (2019), Garcia Villarreal (2017),
3 Abe, Heine (1997), Benesch (1997), Burik (2010), Deutsch (1975), Goto-Jones (2013), Jung (2011), Larson, Deutsch (2014), Lau (2016), Ma, v Brakel (2016), Loy (2012)

4 This term (*Vorläufigkeit*) refers to the anticipatory structure of understanding. Heidegger argues that our understanding of the world always involves a forestructure (*Vorhabe, Vorsicht, Vorgriff*) operating prior to deliberate reflection.

5 In his *Kriegnotsemester* lectures, Heidegger responds to Natorp's critique of Husserl by rejecting the idea that reflection "stills the stream" of experience. He introduces "formal indication" to describe a non-objective way of encountering experience, where all experience is already interpreted and expressive. Rather than imposing language on a formless flux, Heidegger sees immediate experience as already structured with meaning. Formal indication thus points to phenomena with radical openness—general, indifferent, and contentless—allowing interpretation without fixed standpoint (Kisiel 1995).

6 Merleau-Ponty is a rare exception to western philosophy's demotion of the artist to a lower status than the philosopher. In many ways he elevates artists, stating that especially the painter "draw[s] upon this fabric of brute meaning," and "only art does so in full innocence." The "writer and philosopher is hindered because from them we want opinions and advice. We will not allow them to hold the world suspended. We want them to take a stand . . . . Only the painter is entitled to look at everything without being obliged to appraise what he sees." (1993a, 1993b). Nishida writes that "just as art demands philosophy, so, too, does philosophy demands art." (1973, p.97)

7 While silence hasn't been a much employed concept in western philosophy, it does show up in medieval philosophy, particularly in the apophatic traditions of negative theology including de Cusa, Eckhart, Eriugena, and also has a little-recognized impact on later concepts of silence in Heidegger and Derrida.

8 The main Zen sutras include; Lankavatara Sutra, the Vimalakirti Sutra, the Avatamsaka Sutra, Platform Sutra, and the Lotus Sutra.

9 See Heidegger (1982, 2001).

7 Tea Garden

1 Nishitani (2011) is invoking Nietzsche's *Gay Science* (1974)

2 Prior to the nineteenth century there was no single calendar for all regional Shinto denominations. The calendar was based on different rituals, feasts and festivals which would vary based on the need to honor deities of particular locales. Since the late nineteenth century, major shrines have coordinated their calendars.

3 The characters in the Buddhist term for "dust" (塵坌) is also used to refer to "objects" (塵事), "defilement" (塵垢), "falsity"/"impurity" (塵妄).

4 See Ino (1970) However, there are earlier references, such as in the writings of the Yoshida Kenkō (吉田兼好, 1283–1350). See also Kasoku (1982)

5 Anesaki, Barrow (1964), Brinkley (1901), Ludwig (1974, 1981)
6 The Hungarian psychologist, Mihály Csíkszentmihályi (1991) was the first to introduce the term "flow".
7 See Beaty (2014, 2015), Bengtsson (2007), Berkowitz (2010), Dietrich (2004), Limb (2008), McPherson (2013), Norgaard (2011), Pinho (2014).
8 See Aherne et al. (2011); Bernier et al. (2009); Gardner (2007); Luders et al. (2009, 2011); Lutz et al. (2004); Sacchet et al. (2024); Tang et al. (2015)
9 The Sanskrit term *sīmā-bandha* (सीमाबाध), meaning "binding the boundary" (*sīmā*=boundary, *bandha*= binding), referred to ritual boundaries in Indian Buddhism, marking areas for monastic practices like ordination or confession. This concept was key to delineating between sacred and mundane space. Transmitted to Japan, it influenced the term *kekkai* (結界), meaning "binding boundaries," used in esoteric Buddhism and Shinto to protect ritual space with physical or spiritual markers (e.g., *shimenawa* ropes). A related term, *kṣetra* (क्षेत्र), meaning consecrated field or Buddha-field, also shaped East Asian practices of sacred space in esoteric Buddhism (密教, Mikkyō) and Shinto.
10 While Nishida uses this term mostly regarding time, Krummel and Nagatomo read it more broadly as a general ontological principle arrived at through self-negation. They write: "self-negation (*jiko hitei*), which [Nishida] also considers a 'continuity of discontinuity' (*hirenzoku no renzoku*) . . . . We find that this dialectic [of self-negation] involves a chiasma of vertical and horizontal interrelations manifest in various types of relations—such as individual-environment, person-person, subject-object, etc." Nishida (2012).

8 Outer Roji

1 The *nijūshisekki* (二十四節気) calendar, which charts the seasons during one solar year was virtually lost around the nineteenth century but still remains active within the tea ceremony to dictate different aesthetic choices, including the seasonality of the kimono.
2 The tea garden did not begin as bifurcated between the inner (*uchiroji*) and outer (*sotoroji*). Originally, it was a single garden known as *ichijū-roji*, or "single tea garden", which later developed into the "double tea garden" or *nijū-roji*, separated by a "middle gate" (*chūmon*). Di Berardino (2018).
3 Important Confucian practitioners of tea include; Kobori Enshū (1579–1647) a disciple of Furuta Oribewho founded the Enshū school of *Daimyō* tea. Matsudaira Sadanobu (1758–1829), a famous daimyo wrote several texts on tea and saw *Chanoyu* as a means for achieving Confucian forms of social harmony. See Porcu (2008).

9 The Un-named Artist Copying Copies

1 Cseh (2017), Sata (1999), Ward Lott (1993), Parkin (1993), Smethurst (1989, 2013).
2 A second version of the story by Pliny depicts Zeuxis again painting grapes but this time in the hands of a young boy. But, the artist is disappointed because when the birds come to peck at the fruit he takes it as indication that he hasn't rendered the boy with as much realism, since that would have scared off the birds. From Moeller (2004).
3 In Japanese thought, the concept closest to western *mimesis* is *monomane* (物真似), though philosophical and aesthetic discourse more often used *modoki* (擬き) or *modoku* (擬く). Tracing back to the Heian period, these terms often implied inferiority or inauthenticity—like "pseudo-" or "quasi-" in English—suggesting imitation that falls short (Megumi 2002; Lucken 2016). Viswanathan (2017) notes that during the Heian period, notions like *nazurae* (擬え, aesthetic comparison) and *awase* (合わせ, matching contests) were central in poetry and courtly culture, highlighting the political and aesthetic role of similitude. Unlike *monomane*, *modoki* implies a relational, even agonistic, form of imitation.
4 See Saito (1996) for a discussion of representational features of Japanese tea gardens.
5 There were important heterodox Chinese landscape painters who rejected this approach, such as Mi Fei (米芾, 1051–1107) and Shih T'ao (石涛, 1642–1707).
6 "the men of the Renaissance said, a window. . . . But in the final analysis the window opens only upon *partes extra partes*, upon height and breadth merely seen from another angle – upon the absolute positivity of Being"; "Descartes was right in liberating space: his mistake was to erect it into a positive being" (Merleau-Ponty 1993)
7 Throughout western art history, copying was a common practice for learning and homage. Renaissance and Baroque artists like Leonardo, Michelangelo, Raphael, and Rubens studied and replicated earlier masters. In the seventeenth to eighteenth centuries, Velázquez, Greuze, and Goya did the same. The nineteenth century saw Manet's *Olympia* echoing Titian, while Van Gogh copied Millet and Delacroix. In the twentieth century, Picasso, Duchamp, and Lichtenstein reworked historical and popular imagery. Unlike these, contemporary artists Sherrie Levine and Elaine Sturtevant present copies as their own to critique originality and authorship.
8 Thank you to Enrico Fongaro for sharing this idea with me.
9 Exact duplication of books is referred to by the terms *rinmo* (臨模) and *rinsho* (臨書). See Kenzo (1991).
10 Koga Kenzo (1991) elaborates a similar distinction in teaware reproduction between "internal imitation" and "external imitation", where the former involves producing technically perfect realistic facsimiles of physical form, and the latter sought ideological or spiritual resonance.

10 Inner Roji

1. State Shintō (国家神道, *Kokka Shintō*) emerged in the early Meiji era as a political ideology affirming the Emperor's divine authority. Though presented as a non-religious moral tradition compatible with religious freedom, it was used to suppress rival beliefs, especially Buddhism, which was tied to the Tokugawa shogunate. During this period, thousands of Buddhist temples were destroyed, underscoring State Shintō's role in ideological control.
2. There is some debate as to the accuracy of Shinto being labelled an "indigenous religion". While some (Sokyo Ono) promote this notion, others (Earhart, Kuroda, Kitagawa) give a more complex picture where Buddhist and even Chinese influence prevails to such an extent that it is problematic to exclude these influencing factors in service of some purely Japanese Shinto practice. See: Earhart (1982), Toshio et al. (1981), Kitagawa (2021)
3. In his *A Popular Dictionary of Shinto* (2005) Bocking writes; "Some scholars suggest we talk about types of Shintō such as popular Shintō, folk Shintō, domestic Shintō, sectarian Shintō, imperial house Shintō, shrine Shintō, state Shintō, new Shintō religions, etc. rather than regard Shintō as a single entity. This approach can be helpful but begs the question of what is meant by 'Shintō' in each case, particularly since each category incorporates or has incorporated Buddhist, Confucian, Taoist, folk religious and other elements."
4. The treatment of Shinto as a "way" (道) complicates references to Shinto as strictly religious, and how it is understood to have been influenced by the Imperial state. See Picken (1994), Cali, Dougill (2012)
5. Over time, efforts emerged to standardize Shinto rituals and practices. One of the earliest surviving texts documenting this formalization is the *Engi-shiki* (延喜式), a 50-volume work compiled in 927 ce. This text not only systematized various Shinto rites but also provided a detailed record of over 3,000 *kami* and nearly 3,000 shrines across Japan, reflecting the expansive and organized nature of Shinto worship during that period.
6. Throughout Japanese history, the understanding of *kami* shifted with societal and political changes. Their roles ranged from securing harvests and rain to legitimizing imperial rule. As needs changed, so did perceptions and rituals, leading to evolving interpretations over time.
7. The earliest texts referring to *kami* are the eighth-century *Kojiki* (古事記) or "Records of Ancient Matters" (Ō no Yasumaro 1969), and the *Nihon Shoki* (日本書紀), "Chornicles of Japan" (Ō no Yasumaro 1972).
8. Kondo (1985), Anderson (1987), Colby (1991), Suzuki (1999).
9. Shinto shrines are central to agricultural rituals like *jichinsai*, where sake is poured to purify construction sites. Some, like Tonami's sake offering to carp to cleanse waters of spirits, have faced animal rights criticism. In another winter festival, young men

drink sake before defending a shrine from torch-bearing challengers using only pine branches.
10 Although Plato's version is the best known, Symposia also appear in the works of Xenophon and Theognis of Megara. It's also conjectured that there might have been earlier and later versions, earlier with the Etruscan people, and later Roman *convivia*.
11 Sometimes also *Tome-ishi* (止め石), or "stopping stone".
12 These are sometimes positioned to enable the tea guest to view a wooden tablet on the tea hut bearing the often poetic name of the hut.
13 Arte Povera figures such as Jannis Kounellis, Michelangelo Pistoletto, Mario Merz make use of "poor" or raw materials (earth, stone, rags, wood, industrial waste) to celebrate material vitality. In Process Art, artists such as Richard Serra, Eva Hesse, Robert Morris, Lynda Benglis work with a material form of agency where work is often shaped by gravity, time, and chemical properties, with artists giving up full control. In Abstract Expressionism Jackson Pollock, Helen Frankenthaler, Willem de Kooning paint as a medium becomes expressive in itself. Other movements include Assemblage or Junk Art, Kinetic and Bio-Art, and Land Art.
14 Kazashi (1999), Schultz (2013), Kopf, Park (2009), Loughnane (2019)
15 Many terms invoking the negative, including; "perceptual negation"?, "Mutual negation" (where he argues against Sartre's "absolute nothingness" (*nullité absolue*), which he claims is really a positivist philosophy). As early as *Phenomenology of Perception*, Merleau-Ponty writes "the world, in the full sense of the word, is not an object, for though it has an envelope of objective and determinate attributes, it has also fissures and gaps into which subjectivities slip and lodge themselves, or rather which are those subjectivities themselves." (2002. p. 389) And, later, he writes: ". . . a certain hollow opened up within the [object] in-itself, a certain constitutive emptiness—an emptiness which . . . sustains the supposed positivity of things", (1993 p. 144)and for objects to be perceived "one sole condition is laid down for their coming on the scene . . . that they could present themselves to me as *other* focuses of negativity." (1968, p. 59).
16 I use David Dilworth's translation of "表現的関係" (NKZ, 10:347.) as "Interexpression" for both this term as well as a more literal, expanded translation ("the mutual relationship between absolutely opposed things must be expressive." *zettai ni aihan suru mono no sōgo kankei wa, hyōgen-teki denakereba naranai* 絶対に相反するものの相互関係は、表現的でなければならない).

11 Wabi-Sabi, Raku and Zen

1 Unlike in the west, where ceramics are often relegated to anthropological museums, Japan places them at the center of fine arts. Major museums such as the Ōtsuka Museum of Art, Tokyo, Kyoto, Nara, and Kyushu National Museums, and the

Ishikawa Prefectural Museum of Art feature top ceramic works. Japan also has specialized institutions, including the Aichi Prefectural Ceramic Museum, Arita Porcelain Park, Fukuoka Oriental Ceramics Museum, Kyushu Ceramic Museum, Noritake Garden, Museum of Oriental Ceramics (Osaka), and Okayama Bizen Ceramics Museum.

2. The name "*Raku*" (楽) was a shortened form of "*Juraku-yaki*" (聚楽焼), which was derived from the Jurakudai Palace, built by Toyotomo Hideyoshi, which Rikyū lived within and Chōjirō close by. Hideyoshi bestowed upon Chōjirō a seal of the character for raku. Yet, during his lifetime, the famous pottery would have been known as *ima-yaki*, or "now wares", only later taking on the moniker it is famous the world over for. Raku Museum: https://www.raku-yaki.or.jp/e/history/essense.html

3. Hirota writes, "both of these changes are apparent in the poetry of Sogi" (1995, p.84).

4. *Wabi* expresses a sense of lack and melancholy, tied to solitude, poverty, encouraging reflection on impermanence. Rooted in the verb *wabu*, it evokes despondency from social or material absence. As Hirota (1995, p. 128) notes, its adjectival form *wabishi* suggests helplessness and the bleakness of life in threadbare conditions. Yet, *wabi* also carries a reflective, positive aspect, guiding awareness of impermanence as a path to reduce suffering.

5. Similarly, Murata Skukō was quoted as claiming that the "full moon is boring if there are no clouds". Akira Amagasaki claims that "both explain that the true value of something beautiful is recognized only when it is gone. At such time, the beautiful object is no longer in reality, and can only be viewed in one's imagination" Amagasaki (2017).

6. The phrase "a special transmission outside the scriptures" (*chiao-wai pieh-ch'uan*), often linked to Bodhidharma, first appears in the *Tsu-t'ang chi* (Collection of the Patriarch's Hall, 952). It's also found in a tomb inscription for Linji Yixuan (臨済義玄, ?–866), attributed to his disciple Yen-chao and later added to the *Linji lu*. Rinzai scholar Yanagida Seizan questions its authenticity, but its presence in the *Linji lu* suggests it helped shape Chan identity in the Linji lineage during the Song.

7. Nōami stated, "the Buddhist path exists within Chanoyu." In the Momoyama period, Yamanoue Sōji claimed "tea originated from Zen," citing Shukō's advice to "understand the taste of tea and the taste of Zen . . . and don't concern yourself with worldly matters" (*Yamanoue Sōji Ki*). In Rikyū's *Namporoku*, he writes, "Chanoyu of the small room is above all a matter of practicing and realizing the way in accord with the Buddha's teaching" ("Oboegaki" chapter). Shukō told Ikkyū, "the taste of tea is the same as the taste of Zen." Hisamatsu Shin-ichi called *Chanoyu* "the creative completion of Zen culture" (1987), and Sen Sōshitsu XV described it as "a popular

expression of Zen." Others highlighting the Zen–Chanoyu link include D.T. Suzuki (1973), Shōkin, Furuta Shōkin, and Haga Kōshirō, though Haga also notes other influences (Ludwig 1974, 1981).

8 See Hirota (1995) for a fascinating discussion of further subtleties in the meaning of "*suki*", including how the term implies "both knowledge and love", which Hirota discusses in relation to Nishida Kitarō's similar understanding of knowledge as love. A further fascinating aspect of Hirota's elaboration is the relation between Pure Land conceptions of "other power" (*tariki* 他力).

12 Space and Time

1 Although *ma* began as a conception of space in China, as the idea was imported and evolved in Japan, it came to refer equally to time, or together as space-time. See Pilgrim (1986).
2 For Nishida's comments on phenomenology, see: Nishida (1970 pp. 114, 122–26, 196–99; 1958 p. 97–103). For a discussion of Nishida in relation to the phenomenology of Husserl, see; Maraldo (2017), Stevens (2009), Park, Kopf (2012), Tadashi (2012), Loughnane (2019), Ishihara (2011), Elberfeld (2011). For a discussion of the early, pre-Kyoto School reception of phenomenology in Japan see Noe (2017).
3 Some of those include: Nishi Amane (1829–97), Fukuzawa Yukichi (1835–1901), Nakae Chōmin (1847–1901), Inoue Tetsujirō (1855–1944), Inoue Enryō (1858–1919), Ōnishi Hajime (1864–1900).
4 See Grandy (2006), Loughnane (2020), Rubenstein (2009).

13 The Tea Hut

1 A 1996 Statistics Bureau survey records over 2.5 million tea ceremony practitioners of which 2.2 million were women. See Kato (2002a, 2015),
2 Kato (2004, 2015), Lebra (1985), Rosenberger (2000).
3 It is possible that Blake's familiarity with Sir William Charles' (1785) translation of the Bhagavadghita explains his use of "holographic" logic in his writings.
4 Sukiya in the original Chinese meant "abode of fancy", in the sense of the imagination or creativity of the designer. When translated into Japanese, it was later rendered as the "abode of vacancy" (since it had no furniture) or the "abode of the unsymmetrical" (due to the avoidance of design or object placements approximating regularity or symmetry). Kumarasuriyar (2011)

5 Prior to Rikyū, that door was called *kuguri* (潜り) or *kugurikido* (潜り戸), and there was a separate entrance for aristocrats and nobility. Rimiko (2003).
6 Rikyū introduced a sword rack (*katanakake* 刀掛け) under the eaves adjacent the *nijiriguchi*.

14 Alcove and Hanging Scroll

1 There are various stories as to the origin of the alcove. Those include; a raised recess for sleeping; a space of honor reserved for the off-chance of a visit from the emperor; an adoption from Zen monasteries where a sacred Buddhist image or statue would have hung for worship during tea ceremony. Gunsaulus (1924).
2 In the *Namporoku*, Rikyū is reported as claiming that "No utensil ranks with the hanging scroll in significance," and that "writings done by men in secular life should not be displayed [in the tearoom], though scrolls inscribed by poets with verses expressing the Way maybe sometimes be used."
3 Nagashima Fukutaro (1983) and Haga Koshiro (1983) trace the shift in alcove display from imagery to calligraphy between Shukō and Rikyū. Their study of tea records like the *Tennojiya Kaiki* shows that while pictorial works were initially more common, preference gradually shifted toward *bokuseki*—calligraphy by Buddhist monks. The *Sotatsu Ta-kaiki* (1548–66) lists 100 pictorial works to sixty calligraphic; the *Sokyu Ta-kaiki* (1565–85) shows near parity (147 vs. 150); the *Sotan Nikki* (1586–1613) records 23 pictorial works and fifty-eight *bokuseki*; and the *Matsuya Hisashige Ta-kaiki* (1604–50) notes twenty-five pictorials to 115 *bokuseki*. Rikyū ultimately favored *bokuseki* over *zenkiga* and other pictorial scrolls.
4 Okimoto Katsumi claims that, despite being pictorial, *Zenkiga* were fundamentally no different than the single line of poetry that came to be the norm. Katsumi (1993).
5 Rikyū's use of scrolls is detailed in *Rikyu Hyaku-kaiki* (利休百回忌), which was a record of his tea gatherings.
6 The Japanese unit of measure *on* (音) accounts for both syllable number and length. A short syllable counts as one *on*, a long vowel as two, and a final "n" adds another. This makes counting in Japanese poetry more complex than in western forms, as lines may contain more *on* than syllables.
7 The term "*haiku*" (俳句) came into common currency only in the nineteenth century partly by way of the writings of Masaoka Shiki.
8 Shinkei was an early advocate of everyday aesthetics. In *Hitorigoto* (独言), he writes, "The finest *renga* are like drinking water . . . one never tires of them." Unusual things, he notes, "gradually lose their interest." In *Sasamegoto* (細言), he adds, "A style that stresses simplicity and ease . . . manifests the true way". Bullen (2016).
9 https://worldkigodatabase.blogspot.com

10 See later works of Heidegger's on poetic language: ". . . Poetically Man Dwells . . ."; "What are Poets For?" in Heidegger (2001).

15 Flowers for Tea

1 As opposed to *ikebana* flower that are "arranged" (*ikeru* 生ける), a *chabana* arrangement is said to be "placed", or "put in" (*ireru* 入れる). See Kondo (1985).
2 The original, more general meaning in Zen of "attaining the Way with One Heart/Mind", refers to complete realization of the entire complex world through single-minded focus on one, simple thing. See, Shokin (1989).
3 Another major Japanese philosopher also talks about flowers in terms of emptiness, that is Dōgen who reinterprets the Japanese term *kuge* (空華), which typically meant illusion. He writes, "When and where one supreme vision is, there are the flowers of emptiness and the flowers of vision. The flowers of vision are called the flowers of emptiness." Kim (2004).
4 *Kao irai no Kadensho*, (花王以来の花伝書, 1486. "The Flower King's Treatise on the Art of Flowers") is the oldest extant manuscript of *ikebana*, while *Sendenshō* (仙伝抄, 1992) is the oldest published manual. Other notable texts include *Senno Kuden* (千能口伝, 1542) by the founder of the Ikenobō school, the monk Senno; as well as the *Kawari Kaden Hisho* (替花伝秘書, Senno 1992), *The Kokon Rikka-shu* (古今立花集 Anonymous 1672), *The Kokon Rikka-taizen* (古今立花大全 Anonymous 1683). *The Rikka Imayō Sugata* (立華時勢粧 Anonymous 1688).
5 The eighth-century *Man'yōshū* (万葉集, "Collection of Ten Thousand Leaves") (Lurie 2023) and tenth-century *Kokin Wakashū* (古今和歌集, "Collection of Japanese Poems of Ancient and Modern Times") (McCullough 1985) were anthologies of Waka poetry from the Heian period which contained many poems with elaborate descriptions of flowers.
6 *Ikebana* was originally known as *rikka* (立花). Along with the *Nageirebana* (投げ入れ花) style, these two remain not the only but the two dominant styles. *Rikka* was known for being the more formal and decorative style whereas *Nageirebana* was less formal.
7 Often thought to be based on a conversation with Kuki Shuzo, but was in fact an adapted conversation Heidegger had in 1954 with the Japanese scholar of Germany poetry Tezuka Tomio.
8 Burik (2010), Heine (1985), Loughnane (2022a), Ma (2024), May, Parkes (1996), Parkes (1992).
9 *Le Langage des Fleurs*, (Martin, 1830) was the first dictionary of floriography. Another notable work, Joseph Hammer-Purgstall's *Dictionnaire du Language des Fleurs* (1809) was one of main texts of the floriography movement in Europe.

10 One of the central principles of *kadō* was set out by the Japanese landscape painter Sōami (相阿弥 −1525). According to him, different elements of a flower arrangement represent the seasons, the heavens above, earth below, or humans who dwell between the two.
11 See the *Dōtoku* fascicle in Nishijima, Cross (2008).
12 For a discussion of Dōgen's notion of language in relation to Japanese stone gardens, see Berthier, Parkes (2000).
13 "Being-in is thus the formal existential expression for the Being of Dasein, which has the essential constitution of Being-in-the-world. But we must observe that 'Being-in' is distinct from the categorical relation of something present-at-hand 'in' something else that is present-at-hand as well. Being-in is thus the way in which Dasein is its 'there' . . . Being-in is thus the formal existential expression for the Being of Dasein, which has the essential constitution of Being-in-the-world." (Heidegger 2008).

16 Sitting

1 Prior to Rikyū, huts were also oriented on a north–south axis, but the windows and doors were north facing, so as to be able to minimize the variability of illumination due to the movements of the sun. It is thought that Rikyū changed the entrance and windows to face south precisely to bring more light and shadow into the hut.
2 *Hassun* (八寸): The second course, usually sushi accompanied by several smaller side dishes. This course typically reflects the main seasonal theme of the entire meal. *Mukōzuke* (向付): sashimi. *Takiawase* (煮合): meat, fish or tofu dish accompanied by vegetables. *Futamono* (蓋物): usually a soup in a lidded dish. *Yakimono* (焼物): flame-grilled food, usually fish. *Su-zakana* (酢肴): vinegared appetizer of vegetable to cleanse the palate. *Suimono* (吸い物): clear broth soup. *Hiyashi-bachi* (冷し鉢): lightly cooked vegetables. *Naka-choko* (中猪口): an acidic palate-cleansing soup. *Shiizakana* (強肴): typically the largest course. *Gohan* (御飯): a rice dish. *Kō no mono* (香の物): pickled vegetables. *Tome-wan* (止椀): miso or vegetable soup with rice. *Mizumono* (水物): seasonal dessert; fruit, confection, ice cream, or cake. *Sakizuke* (先附): an appetizer. (https://kitchen-theory.com/kaisekidining/)
3 The appearance of sake in the tea ceremony closely approximates and may have been inspired by the Shinto *naorai ritual*. Anderson (1987).
4 *Cha-kai* (茶会) is the less formal ceremony lasting under an hour. It includes only one tea serving (*usucha*) and can accommodate much larger groups than *Cha-ji*.
5 Rikyū is known for having said that "in the making of thick tea (*koicha*, considered formal) there is an element of the especially informal (*sō*); in the making of thin tea (*usucha*, considered informal) there is an element of the extremely formal (*goku-shin*)." Hirota (1995).

17 As if in a Dream

1 「人生七十 力囲希 咄 — 吾這宝剣 祖仏共殺」 "Life at seventy—strength is hardly enough. — With this treasured sword, I slay both ancestors and Buddhas." Hirota (1995)
2 Japanese cinema has won more Academy Awards for Best International film than any other Asian country. Ozu's *Tokyo Story* (1953) often ranks in the top five of major international film-critics lists of best movies of all time. Kurosawa's *Seven Samurai* (1954) is likewise highly ranked internationally, including having been voted "greatest foreign-language film of all time" in the BBC's 2018 pole of critics from over 40 countries.
3 Heidegger (1982), Also see Naas (2005).

Bibliography

Abe, M. and S. Heine (1997). *Zen and Comparative Studies*, University of Hawai'i Press.

Aherne, C., Moran, A. P., and Lonsdale, C. (2011). "The effect of mindfulness training on athletes' flow experiences and competitive performance." *Journal of Applied Sport Psychology*, 23(3), 329–42.

Amagasaki, A. (2017). "What Can Be Seen and What Cannot Be Seen—the Aesthetic Sense of Japanese Medieval Arts." The Gakushuin Journal of International Studies 4.

Anderson, B. (2006). *Imagined Communities: Reflections on the Origin and Spread of Nationalism* (Rev. edn). Verso.

Anderson, J. L. (1987). "Japanese Tea Ritual: Religion in Practice." Man 22(3): 475–98.

Anderson, J. L. (1991). *An Introduction to Japanese Tea Ritual*. State University of New York Press.

Anesaki, M. and T. Barrow (1964). *Art, Life & Nature in Japan*, Tuttle Publishing.

Anonymous. (1980). *Chanoyu hyōrin* [茶湯評林; Evaluative grove of tea]. [Attributed to Endō Genkan (遠藤元閑)] In *Chadō zenshū* (Vol. 12, pp. 201–289). Shibunkaku Shuppan.

Anonymous. (13th–14th century/1971). *Kissa ōrai* [喫茶往来; Letters on drinking tea]. In S. Okada (Ed.), *Ōrai-mono shūsei* (Vol. 1, pp. 212–19). Kazama Shobō.

Anonymous. (14th c./1992). *Taiheiki* [太平記; Chronicle of the Great Peace] (N. Owada, Ed.). Iwanami Shoten.

Anonymous. (1486/1980). *Kao irai no kadensho* [花王以来の花伝書; The Flower King's Treatise on the Art of Flowers]. In *Kadenshū*. Tokyo: Kazama Shobō. (Original work written 1486)

Anonymous. (13th century/1992). *Sendenshō* [仙伝抄]. In M. Kasuga (Ed.), *Chadō koten shūsei* (Vol. 1, pp. [insert page range]). Shibundō.

Anonymous. (1661/1992). *Kawari Kaden Hishō* [替花伝秘書; Secret Notes on Alternative Flower Treatises]. In M. Kasuga (Ed.), *Kadenshū*. Shibundō.

Anonymous. (1672/1992). *Kokon Rikka-shū* [古今立花集; Collection of Standing Flower Arrangements Past and Present]. In M. Kasuga (Ed.), *Kadenshū*. Shibundō.

Anonymous. (1683/1992). *Kokon Rikka-taizen* [古今立花大全; Great compendium of standing flower arrangements past and present]. In M. Kasuga (Ed.), *Kadenshū*. Shibundō.

Anonymous. (1688/1992). *Rikka Imayō Sugata* [立華時勢粧; Contemporary Styles of Standing Flower Arrangements]. In M. Kasuga (Ed.), *Kadenshū*. Shibundō.

Aristotle (2013). *Poetics*, Oxford University Press.

Beaty, R. E. (2015). "The neuroscience of musical improvisation." *Neuroscience & Biobehavioral Reviews*, 51, 108–17. https://doi.org/10.1016/j.neubiorev.2015.01.004

Beaty, R. E., Silvia, P. J., Nusbaum, E. C., Jauk, E., & Benedek, M. (2014). "The roles of associative and executive processes in creative cognition: Insights from the default mode network and frontoparietal network." *Neuropsychologia*, 64, 92–8. https://doi.org/10.1016/j.neuropsychologia.2014.09.002

Benesch, W. (1997). *An Introduction to Comparative Philosophy*: A Travel Guide to Philosophical Space, Palgrave Macmillan UK.

Bengtsson, S. L., Csíkszentmihályi, M., & Ullén, F. (2007). "Cortical regions involved in the generation of musical structures during improvisation in pianists." *Journal of Cognitive Neuroscience*, 19(5), 830–842. https://doi.org/10.1162/jocn.2007.19.5.830

Berkowitz, A. L. (2010). *The improvising mind: Cognition and creativity in the musical moment*. Oxford University Press.

Bernier, M., Thienot, E., Fournier, J. F., & Cutton, N. (2009). "Mindfulness and Acceptance Approaches in Sport: Theoretical Considerations and First Applications." *Sport Psychologist*, 23(3), 321–32.

Berthier, F. and G. Parkes (2000). *Reading Zen in the Rocks: the Japanese Dry Landscape Garden*, University of Chicago Press.

Bocking, B. (2005). *A Popular Dictionary of Shinto*, Taylor & Francis.

Breen, J. (2010). "Conventional Wisdom" and the Politics of Shinto in Postwar Japan." *Politics and Religion Journal* 4(1).

Breen, J. and M. Teeuwen (2011). *A New History of Shinto*, Wiley.

Brinkley, F. (1901). *Japan: Its History, Arts, and Literature*, J.B. Millet Company.

Bullen, R. (2016). "Chinese Sources in the Japanese Tea Garden." *Studies in the History of Gardens & Designed Landscapes* 36(1): 5–16.

Burik, S. (2010). *End of Comparative Philosophy and the Task of Comparative Thinking, The: Heidegger, Derrida, and Daoism*, State University of New York Press.

Cali, J. and J. Dougill (2012). *Shinto Shrines: A Guide to the Sacred Sites of Japan's Ancient Religion*, University of Hawaii Press.

Carriger, M. L. (2021). "ElasticiTEA?: Preliminary Theses on Cross-Cultural (re)Presentation and the Japanese 'Way of Tea.'." *Global Performance Studies* 4(1).

Chiba, K. (2011). *Japanese Women, Class and the Tea Ceremony: The Voices of Tea Practitioners in Northern Japan*. Routledge.

Colby, B. N. (1991). *The Japanese Tea Ceremony: Coherence Theory and Metaphor in Social Adaptation. Beyond Metaphor: The Theory of Tropes in Anthropology*. J. W. Fernandez, Stanford University Press.

Copeland, R. (2018). "Transbeauty IKKO: A Diva's Guide to Glamour, Virtue, and Healing. In L. Miller & R. Copeland (Eds.), *Diva Nation: Female Icons from Japanese Cultural History* (pp. 232–49). University of California Press.

Corbett, R. (2018). *Cultivating Femininity: Women and Tea Culture in Edo and Meiji Japan*. University of Hawai'i Press.

Corbett, R. (2014). "Crafting identity as a Tea Practitioner in Early Modern Japan: Ōtagaki Rengetsu and Tagami Kikusha." *U.S.-Japan Women's Journal*, 47, 3–27.

Corbett, R. (2009). "Learning to be Graceful: Tea in Early Modern Guides for Women's Edification." *Japanese Studies*, 29(1), 81–94.

Cross, T. (2009). *The Ideologies of Japanese Tea: Subjectivity, Transience and National Identity*. Brill.

Cross, T. (2013). *Rikyū has Left the Tea Room: National Cinema Interrogates the Anecdotal legend. Japanese Tea Culture: Art, History and Practice*. M. Pitelka, Taylor & Francis.

Cseh, D. S. (2017). "Reflections of Ambiguous Realities: A Comparative Analysis of Mimesis and Monomane in the Writings of Aristotle and Zeami." *SZITU Kötet*.

Csikszent, M. (1991). *Flow: The Psychology of Optimal Experience*, HarperCollins.

Davidson, G. (1970). *Classical Ikebana*. New York, A.S. Barnes.

Decreux, E. (2014). "The Tea Ceremony Room in Traditional Japan: a Stylized Organization of Space and Time." Imago. *A Journal of the Social Imaginary*: 160–96.

Deutsch, E. (1975). *Studies in Comparative Aesthetics*. Honolulu, University Press of Hawaii.

di Berardino, F. (2018). *The Abode of Fancy, of Vacancy, and of the Unsymmetrical*, University of Iceland.

Dietrich, A. (2004). "Neurocognitive mechanisms underlying the experience of flow." *Consciousness and Cognition*, 13(4), 746–61. https://doi.org/10.1016/j.concog.2004.07.002

Dōgen. (1969). *Dōgen Zenji zenshū* [Complete Works of Zen Master Dōgen] (Vol. 1, "*Shōhō jissō*" 諸法実相). T. Nakamura (Ed.). Chikuma Shobō.

Dōgen. (1985). *Moon in a Dewdrop: Writings of Zen Master Dōgen* (K. Tanahashi, Ed.). North Point Press.

Dōgen. (2008). *Shōbōgenzō: The True Dharma-Eye Treasury* (G. W. Nishijima & C. Cross, Trans.). Numata Center for Buddhist Translation and Research. BDK English Tripiṭaka Series.

Dōgen. (2009a). "Mountains and waters as sutras" (G. Parkes, Trans.). In W. Edelglass & J. L. Garfield (Eds.), *Buddhist philosophy: Essential readings*. Oxford University Press. p. 89.

Dōgen. (2009b). "The Insentient Preach the Dharma" [*Mujō seppō*]. In G. W. Nishijima & C. Cross (Trans.), *Master Dōgen's Shōbōgenzō* (Vol. III, fascicle 54). Windbell Publications.

Earhart, H. B. (1982). *Japanese Religion, Unity and Diversity*, Wadsworth Publishing Company.

Elberfeld, R. (2011). "Handelnde Anschauung (*kōiteki chokkan*): Nishida und die Praxis der Künste. Stuttgard: Frommann-Holzboog Verlag." *Allgemeine Zeitschrift für Philosophie: Kitarō Nishida* (1870–1945), 36(3).

Fukutaro, N. (1983). "Picture versus Word: Trends in Tokonoma Display." *Chanoyu Quarterly* (35).

Gadamer, H.-G. (2004). *Truth and Method* (ed., J. Weinsheimer & D. G. Marshall, Trans.). Continuum.

Garza Villarreal, R. I., & Fujinami, T. (2017). *Characterization of Tea Whisking by Japanese Tea Ceremony Performers* (Master's thesis). Japan Advanced Institute of Science and Technology.

Gardner, F. L., & Moore, Z. E. (2007). *The Psychology of Optimal Athletic Performance: A Mindfulness-Acceptance-Commitment Approach*. Springer Publishing Company.

Ghilardi, M. (2015). *The Line of the Arch: Intercultural Issues between Aesthetics and Ethics*, Mimesis International.

Goto-Jones, C. (2013). "What is (Comparative) Philosophy?" *Philosophy* 88(1): 133–40.

Graham, Patricia (1993). "Documents and Monuments in the History of the Sencha Ceremony in Japan." 関西大学東西学術研究所紀要 (Kansai University Institute for East-West Cultural Exchange Bulletin) 26, 1–30.

Grandy, D. (2016). "Sunyata in the West." *Comparative Philosophy*, 7(1), 39–58.

Gunsaulus, H. C. (1924). "Japanese Temples and Houses." *Leaflet* (14): 1–20.

Hammer-Purgstall, J. von. (1809). *Dictionnaire du Langage des Fleurs*. Paris: Chez l'auteur.

Harris, P. (1986). "Chanoyu: A Mediator of Bihemispheric Interaction." *Chanoyu Quarterly* (48).

Hayakawa, M. (1995). "The Microcosmic Space Created by Sen Rikyu." *Chanoyu Quarterly*, 80, 7–37.

Heidegger, M. (1966). *Discourse on Thinking*, Harper & Row.

Heidegger, M. (1969). Letter to the organizers of Heidegger and Eastern Thought conference. (In L. Ma, *Heidegger on East–West Dialogue: Anticipating the Event*, pp. 138–139). Routledge, 2008.

Heidegger, M. (1982). *On the Way to Language*. San Francisco, Harper.

Heidegger, M. (2001). *Poetry, Language, Thought*, Perennial Classics.

Heidegger, M. (2001a). ". . . Poetically Man Dwells . . . ." *Poetry, Language, Thought*, Perennial Classics.

Heidegger, M. (2001b). "What are Poets For?." *Poetry, Language, Thought*, Perennial Classics.

Heidegger, M. (2008). *Being and Time*. New York, Harper Perennial.

Heine, S. (1985). *Existential and Ontological Dimensions of Time in Heidegger and Dōgen*, State University of New York Press.

Heisig, J. W. and J. C. Maraldo (1995). *Rude Awakenings: Zen, the Kyoto School, & the Question of Nationalism*, University of Hawai'i Press.

Hioki, N. F. (2013). "Tea Ceremony as a Space for Interreligious Dialogue." *Exchange* 42(2): 125–42.

Hiroishi, T. (1982). "The Essence of Chanoyu Lies Precisely in What Isn't Chanoyu." *Chanoyu Quarterly* (32).

Hirota, D. (1995). *Wind in the Pines: Classic Writings of the Way of Tea as a Buddhist Path*, Asian Humanities Press.

Hisamatsu, S. i., James, P. M., & Abe, M. (1970). "The Nature of 'Sadō' Culture." *The Eastern Buddhist*, 3(2), 9–19.

Hisamatsu, S. i. (1971). *Zen and the Fine Arts*, Kodansha International.

Hisamatsu, S. i. (1987). 茶道の哲学 (*Philosophy of Tea*). Tokyo, Kodonsha.
Hisamatsu, S. i. (1993). "The Way of Tea and Buddhism." *Chanoyu Quarterly* (74).
Hobsbawm, E., & Ranger, T. (Eds.). (1983). *The invention of tradition*. Cambridge.
Hori, V. S. (2000). *Koan and Kensho in the Rinzai Zen Curriculum. The Koan: Texts and Contexts in Zen Buddhism*. S. Heine and D. Wright, Oxford University Press.
Husserl, E. (2009). *Logical investigations* (J. N. Findlay, Trans.; D. Moran, Ed.; 2 vols.). Routledge.
Ino, D. (1970). "Introduction to the Aestheticism of Chanoyu." *Chanoyu Quarterly* 1(2).
Inoue, N. (2003). "Introduction: What is Shinto?" *Shinto: A Short History*. N. Inoue, E. Jun, M. Mizue and I. Satoshi, Taylor & Francis.
Ishihara, Y. (2011). "Later Nishida on Self-awareness: Have I Lost Myself Yet?" *Asian Philosophy* 21(2): 193–211.
Isozaki, A., Ando T., & Fujimori T (2007). *The Contemporary Tea House: Japan's Top Architects Redefine a Tradition*. Tokyo, Kodansha International.
Jakuan Sōtaku. (1995). *Zen Tea Record. Zencharoku* (禅茶録) In D. Hirota (trans.), *Wind in the Pines: Classic Writings of the Way of Tea as a Buddhist Path* (pp. 263–86). Asian Humanities Press.
Jōō, T. (1956). *Jōō Wabi no Fumi* (紹鴎詫びの文) "Letter on Wabi." Kuwata Tadachika, Shinshū Chadō Zenshū. Tokyo, Shinjusha.
Jung, H. Y. (2011). *Transversal Rationality and Intercultural Texts: Essays in Phenomenology and Comparative Philosophy*, Ohio University Press.
Kalmanson, L. (2023). "How to Change your Mind: The Contemplative Practices of Philosophy." *Royal Institute of Philosophy Supplements* 93.
Kanazawa, S., et al. (2015). "Experience Factors Influence on Motion Technique of "The Way of Tea" by Motion Analysis." In V. G. Duffy (Ed.), *Digital Human Modeling: Applications in Health, Safety, Ergonomics and Risk Management*. (Vol. 9185, pp. 155–63). Springer International Publishing.
Kanazawa, S., et al. (2016). "Research on the Motion Technique of Japanese Tea Ceremony." In V. G. Duffy (Ed.), *Digital Human Modeling: Applications in Health, Safety, Ergonomics and Risk Management*. (Vol. 9745, pp. 150–58). Springer International Publishing
Kasoku, Y. (1982). "On the Arts as Ways: Kenko and Zeami." *Chanoyu Quarterly* (31).
Kasulis, T. (2011). "The Philosophical Truth: Comparatively Speaking." University College Cork: Philosophy Conference. Cork, Ireland.
Kato, E. (2002a). "'Art' for Men, 'Manners' for Women: How Women Transformed the Tea Ceremony in Modern Japan." In S. Shifrin (Ed.), *Women as Sites of Culture: Women's Roles in Cultural Formation from the Renaissance to the Twentieth Century* (pp. 139–149). Ashgate.
Kato, E. (2002b). "The Sword Behind the Chrysanthemum: Modern Japanese Tea Ceremony Practitioners' Self-Empowerment Through Explicit and Implicit Motifs." *Semiotica* 141.

Kato, E. (2004). *The Tea Ceremony and Women's Empowerment in Modern Japan: Bodies Re-Presenting the Past*, Taylor & Francis.

Kato, E. (2015). "Can Tea Save Non-warriors and Women? The Japanese Tea Ceremony as an Empowering Public Sphere." *Internationales Asienforum* 40(1).

Katsumi, O. (1993). "Zenkiga: Expressing the Spirit of Zen." *Chanoyu Quarterly* (75).

Kazashi, N. (1999). "Bodily Logos: James, Nishida, and Merleau-Ponty." In D. Olkowski and J. Morley (Eds.), *Merleau-Ponty: Interiority and Exteriority, Psychic Life and the World.*, State University of New York Press.

Keane, M. (2002). *The Art of Setting Stones & Other Writings from the Japanese Garden.* Berkeley, CA, Stone Bridge Press.

Keane, M. (2014). *The Japanese Tea Garden*, Stone Bridge Press.

Keisen, U., et al. (2019). "A study on Interior Light Environment in Japanese Teahouse and its Relation with Tea Ceremony." In *Intelligent & Informed: Proceedings of the 24th International Conference of the Association for Computer-Aided Architectural Design Research in Asia (CAADRIA) 2019* (Vol. 1).

Kenkō, Y. (1967). *Essays in Idleness: The Tsurezuregusa of Kenkō* (D. Keene, Trans.). Columbia University Press.

Kenzo, K. (1991). "Utsushi: The Aesthetics of Imitation." *Chanoyu Quarterly* (67).

Kikawada, I. (1973). *The Tea Ceremony and the Communion of Equals.* California, University of Berkeley.

Kim, H. J. (1985). *Flowers of Emptiness: Selections from Dōgen's Shōbōgenzō*, Edwin Mellen Press.

Kim, H.-J. (2004). *Eihei Dōgen: Mystical Realist.* Boston, Wisdom Publications.

Kisiel, T. (1995). *The Genesis of Heidegger's Being and Time*, University of California Press.

Kitagawa, J. M. (2021). *On Understanding Japanese Religion*, Princeton University Press.

Kojève, A. (1969). *Introduction to the Reading of Hegel: Lectures on the Phenomenology of Spirit* (A. Bloom, Trans.; R. Queneau, Ed.). Ithaca, NY: Cornell University Press.

Kondo, D. (1985). "The Way of Tea: A Symbolic Analysis." *Man* 20(2): 287–306.

Koshiro, H. (1983). "The Appreciation of Zen Scrolls." *Chanoyu Quarterly* (36).

Kreeft, P. (1971). "Zen in Heidegger's Gelassenheit." *International Philosophical Quarterly* 11(4): 521–45.

Krummel, J. (2021). "The Symposium on Overcoming Modernity and Discourse in Wartime Japan." *Historická Sociologie* 2.

Kumakura, I. (1980). 『近代茶道史の研究』 (The Study on the History of Modern Tea Ceremony),. Tokyo, Nippon Hōsō Shuppan Kyōkai.

Kumarasuriyar, A. (2011). "Tea Ceremony and Sukiya: Negating Social Hierarchy. Sharing Cultures." 2nd International Conference on Intangible Heritage., Portugal, Green Lines Institute for Sustainable Development.

Kuroda, T., Dobbins, J., & Gay, S. (1981). "Shinto in the History of Japanese Religion." *Journal of Japanese Studies* 7(1): 1–21.

Kyōto-fu. (1916/1996). *Kyōto bōmoku-shi* [京都某目誌; Kyoto sectional survey]. In Y. Nishikawa (Ed.), *Zoku fukkoku Nihon chishi taikei* (Vol. 2). Yūzankaku.

Kobori Nanrei Sohaku, (1988) "Zen and the Art of Tea." *Chanoyu Quarterly* (55).

Larson, G. J. and E. Deutsch (2014). *Interpreting across Boundaries: New Essays in Comparative Philosophy*, Princeton University Press.
Lau, K.-Y. (2016). *Phenomenology and Intercultural Understanding: Toward a New Cultural Flesh*, Springer International Publishing.
Laozi. (2007). *Daodejing* (H.-G. Moeller, Trans.). Open Court.
Lebra, T. S. (1985). *Japanese Women: Constraint and Fulfillment*, University of Hawaii Press.
Limb, C. J., & Braun, A. R. (2008). "Neural substrates of spontaneous musical performance: An fMRI study of jazz improvisation." *PLoS ONE*, 3(2), e1679. https://doi.org/10.1371/journal.pone.0001679
Loughnane, A. (2019). *Merleau-Ponty and Nishida: Artistic Expression as Motor-Perceptual Faith*. State University of New York Press.
Loughnane, A. (2020). "The Birth of Fire, Indescribable Light, and the Limits of Philosophy's Violence: Nāgārjuna and Plato Seeing and Speaking of Nothing." *Comparative and Continental Philosophy* 12.
Loughnane, A. (2022a). "Poetic Language in the Philosophies of Ueda and Heidegger." In R. Müller, (Ed.), *Language, Experience and Zen: The Works of Ueda Shizuteru*. Springer.
Loughnane, A. (2022b). "Japanese Aesthetics as Intercultural Double Bind: Philosophical and Artistic Practice between Nishida and Sesshū." *APA Newsletter on Asian and Asian American Philosophers and Philosophies, 21* (1–2).
Loughnane, A. (2023). "Flowers of Dim-Sightedness: Dōgen's Mystical Negative Ocularcentrism." In R. Müller, (Ed.), *Dōgen's Text: Philosophy of/as/and Religion.*, Springer.
Loughnane, A. and G. Parkes (2024). *Japanese Aesthetics*. Stanford Encyclopedia of Philosophy.
Loy, D. (1990). "The Non-Duality of Life and Death: A Buddhist View of Repression." *Philosophy East and West* 40(2).
Loy, D. (2012). *Nonduality: A Study in Comparative Philosophy*, Prometheus Books.
Lucken, M. (2016). *Imitation and Creativity in Japanese Arts: From Kishida Ryusei to Miyazaki Hayao*, Columbia University Press.
Luders, E., Toga, A. W., Lepore, N., & Narr, K. L. (2009). "The Underlying Anatomical Correlates of Long-term Meditation: Larger Hippocampal and Frontal Volumes of Gray Matter." *NeuroImage*, 45(3), 672–78.
Ludwig, T. M. (1974). "The Way of Tea: A Religio-Aesthetic Mode of Life." *History of Religions* 14(1): 28–50.
Ludwig, T. M. (1981). "Before Rikyū. Religious and Aesthetic Influences in the Early History of the Tea Ceremony." *Monumenta Nipponica* 36(4): 367–90.
Lurie, D. B. (Trans.). (2023). *Man'yōshū: A New English Translation Containing the Full 20 books*. Columbia University Press.
Lutz, A., Greischar, L. L., Rawlings, N. B., Ricard, M., & Davidson, R. J. (2004). "Long-term Meditators Self-induce High-amplitude Gamma Synchrony during Mental Practice." *Proceedings of the National Academy of Sciences*, 101(46), 16369–73.

Ma, L. and J. v. Brakel (2016). *Fundamentals of Comparative and Intercultural Philosophy*. Albany, SUNY Press, State University of New York Press.

Ma, L. (2024). *Heidegger on Eastern/Asian Thought*, Cambridge University Press.

Macadam, J. P., M. Nakamura and S. Hayashiya (1974). *Japanese Arts and the Tea Ceremony*, Weatherhill.

Maraldo, J. (2017). *Nishida's Ontology of History. Japanese Philosophy in the Making: Crossing Paths with Nishida*. Nagoya, Japan, Chisokudō.

Martin, L. A. and L. Cortambert (1830). *Le Langage des Fleurs*, L. Hauman.

Masao, H. (1995). "The Microcosmic Space Created by Sen Rikyu." *Chanoyu Quarterly* (80).

May, R. and G. Parkes (1996). *Heidegger's Hidden Sources: East Asian Influences on his Work*, Routledge.

McCullough, H. C. (Trans.). (1959). *The Taiheiki: A Chronicle of Medieval Japan*. Columbia University Press.

McCullough, H. H. (Trans.). (1985). *Kokin Wakashu: The First Imperial Anthology of Japanese Poetry*. Stanford University Press.

McPherson, G. E., & Limb, C. J. (2013). "Bringing neuroscience to music research: A conversation between music psychology and neuroscience." *Music Perception*, 30(3), 239–43. https://doi.org/10.1525/mp.2013.30.3.239

Megumi Sata, "Aristotle's Poetics and Zeami's Teachings on Style and the Flower", *Asian Theatre Journal*, 1989/1, 47–56.

Merleau-Ponty, M. (1968). *The Visible and the Invisible*, Northwestern University Press.

Merleau-Ponty, M. (1973). *Prose of the World*, Northwestern University Press.

Merleau-Ponty, M. (1993). *The Merleau-Ponty Aesthetics Reader: Philosophy and Painting*. Evanston, Northwestern Univ. Press.

Merleau-Ponty, M. (1993a). "Cézanne's Doubt." *The Merleau-Ponty Aesthetics Reader: Philosophy and Painting*. Evanston, Northwestern Univ. Press.

Merleau-Ponty, M. (1993b). "Eye and Mind." *The Merleau-Ponty Aesthetics Reader: Philosophy and Painting*. Evanston, Northwestern Univ. Press.

Merleau-Ponty, M. (2002). *Phenomenology of Perception*. New York, Routledge.

Miner, R., R. E. Morrell and H. Odagiri (2020). *The Princeton Companion to Classical Japanese Literature*, Princeton University Press.

Moeller, H.-G. (2004). *Daoism Explained: From The Dream Of The Butterfly To The Fishnet Allegory*. Chicago, Ill., Open Court.

Moeller, H.-G. (2015). *Daodejing*, Open Court.

Müller, R., R. Bouso and A. Loughnane (2022). *Tetsugaku Companion to Ueda Shizuteru: Language, Experience, and Zen*, Springer International Publishing.

Naas, B. (2005). "Rashomon and the Sharing of Voices between East and West." In D. Sheppard, S. Sparks, & C. Thomas (Eds.), *On Jean-Luc Nancy: The sense of philosophy*. Taylor & Francis.

Nietzsche, F. (1974). *The Gay Science: With a Prelude in Rhymes and an Appendix of Songs*, Knopf Doubleday Publishing Group.

Nietzsche, F. (1999). *The Birth of Tragedy*, Cambridge University Press.
Nishida, K. (1941). 歴史的形成作用としての芸術的創作 *Rekishi-teki keiseisayō toshite no geijutsu-teki sōsaku*. *Nishida Kitarō Zenshū*. Vol. 10. 10: 177–264.
Nishida, K. (1958). *Intelligibility and the Philosophy of Nothingness*, Maruzen.
Nishida, K. (1970). *Fundamental Problems of Philosophy: The World of Action and the Dialectical World*. Tokyo, Sophia University Press.
Nishida, K. (1973). *Art and Morality*, University Press of Hawaii.
Nishida, K. (1998). *The Historical Body. Sourcebook for Modern Japanese Philosophy*. Westport Conn., Greenwood Press.
Nishida, K. (2003). 歴史的形成作用としての芸術的創作 "*Rekishi-Teki Keiseisayō Toshite NoGeijutsu-Teki Sōsaku*." In *Nishida Kitarō Zenshū*, Vol. 9, Tokyo: IwanamiShoten.
Nishida, K. (2012). *Place and Dialectic: Two Essays*. Oxford University Press.
Nishida, K. (2017). "The Beauty of Calligraphy." In M. Yusa (Ed.), *The Bloomsbury Research Handbook of Contemporary Japanese Philosophy*. Bloomsbury Academic.
Nishihara, K. (1968). *Japanese Houses; Patterns for Living*, Japan Publications.
Nishitani, Keiji. (1995). *The Japanese Art of Arranged Flowers* (G, Parkes. Trans.). In R. C. Solomon & K. M. Higgins (Eds.), *World Philosophy: A Text with Readings* (pp. 23–27). McGraw-Hill.
Nishitani, K. (2011). "The Meaning of Nihilism for Japan." In J. W. Heisig, T. P. Kasulis, & J. C. Maraldo (Eds.), *Japanese Philosophy: A Sourcebook*. University of Hawai'i Press.
Noe, K. (2017). "Phenomenology in Japan: Its Inception and Blossoming." In M. Yusa (Ed.), *The Bloomsbury Research Handbook of Contemporary Japanese Philosophy*. Bloomsbury Publishing.
Norgaard, M. (2011). "Descriptions of improvisational thinking by artist-level jazz musicians." *Journal of Research in Music Education*, 59(2), 109–27. https://doi.org/10.1177/0022429411405669
Odin, S. (1988). "Intersensory Awareness in Chanoyu and Japanese Aesthetics." *Chanoyu Quarterly* (53).
Ōhashi, R. (2010). *Japanese Worlds*. In H. R. Sepp & L. Embree (Eds.), *Handbook of Phenomenological Aesthetics*. Springer Netherlands.
Ogura, S. (2005). *Yoshū fūshi* [輿州風姿; Topography of Yoshū]. In T. Kawai (Ed.), *Nihon meisho fūkeiki shūsei* (Vol. 3, pp. 45–112). Bensei Shuppan.
Okakura, Kakuzo (1964). *The Book of Tea*. New York: Dover.
Okuda, Shōzō. (1990). "The Taste of Tea: Excerpts from the Chami." *Chanoyu Quarterly*, (64).
Ō no Yasumaro. (1969). *Kojiki: Records of Ancient Matters* (D. L. Philippi, Trans.). Princeton University Press.
Ō no Yasumaro (Ed.). (1972). *Nihongi: Chronicles of Japan from the Earliest Times to A.D. 697* (W. G. Aston, Trans.). Tuttle Publishing.
Kopf, G., Park, J. Y. (2009). *Merleau-Ponty and Buddhism*, Lexington Books.
Parkes, G. (1992). *Heidegger and Asian thought*, University of Hawaii Press.

Parkes, G. (1995). "Ways of Japanese Thinking." In N. Hume (Ed.), *Japanese Aesthetics and Culture: A Reader*. State University of New York Press.

Parkes, G. (1996). *Composing the Soul: Reaches of Nietzsche's Psychology*. Chicago, University of Chicago Press.

Parkes, G. (1997). "The Putative Fascism of the Kyoto School and the Political Correctness of the Modern Academy." *Philosophy East and West* 47(3): 305–36.

Parkes, G. (2009). *Mountains and Waters as Sūtras*. In W. Edelglass & J. L. Garfield (Eds.), *Buddhist Philosophy: Essential Readings*. Oxford University Press.

Parkes, G., & Loughnane, A. (2024). *Japanese Aesthetics*. In E. N. Zalta (Ed.), *The Stanford Encyclopedia of Philosophy*.

Parkin, A. (1993). "Crossing cultural bridges in search of drama: Aristotle and Zeami." In S. W. Lott, M. S. G. Hawkins, & N. McMillan (Eds.), *Global perspectives on teaching literature: Shared visions and distinctive visions* (pp. 181–92).

Picken, S. D. B. (1994). *Essentials of Shinto: An Analytical Guide to Principal Teachings*, Greenwood Press.

Pilgrim, R. (1986). "Ma: A Cultural Paradigm." *Chanoyu Quarterly* (46).

Pinho, A. L., de Manzano, Ö., Fransson, P., Eriksson, H., & Ullén, F. (2014). "Connecting to create: Expertise in musical improvisation is associated with increased functional connectivity between premotor and prefrontal areas." *Journal of Neuroscience*, 34(18), 6156–63. https://doi.org/10.1523/JNEUROSCI.4769-13.2014

Plutschow, H. (1999). "An anthropological perspective on the Japanese Tea Ceremony." *Anthropoetics*, 5(1).University Press.

Porcu, E. (2008). *Pure Land Buddhism in Modern Japanese Culture*, Brill.

Sen no Rikyū. (1995). *Nampōroku*. In D. Hirota, *Wind in the Pines: Classic Writings of the Way of Tea as a Buddhist Path*. Asian Humanities Press.

Senno. (1992). *Senno Kuden* [千能口伝]. In M. Kasuga (Ed.), *Kadenshū*. Shibundō.

Surak, K. (2013). *Making Tea, Making Japan: Cultural Nationalism in Practice*. Stanford University Press.

Rimiko, H. (2003). "Sen no Rikyū and the Japanese Way of Tea: Ethics and Aesthetics of the Everyday." *Interiors: Design, Architecture, Culture* 4(3).

Rosenberger, N. R. (2000). *Gambling With Virtue: Japanese Women and the Search for Self in a Changing Nation*, University of Hawaii Press.

Roth, T. J. (Director). (2015). *The Voice of Nothingness: Zen Buddhism and the Kyoto School Philosophy* [Documentary film]. Germany/Japan: DokHaus Berlin Filmproduktion.

Rubenstein, M.-J. (2009). *Strange Wonder: The Closure of Metaphysics and the Opening of Awe*. Columbia University Press.

Sacchet, M. D., Ehmann, C. S., & van Lutterveld, R. (2024). "Mindfulness, Cognition, and Long-term Meditators: Toward a Science of Advanced Meditation." *NeuroImage*, 284.

Sadler, A. L. (1962). *Cha-no-yu: The Japanese Tea Ceremony*. London: K. Paul, Trench, Trubner & co., ltd.

Said, E. W. (1978). *Orientalism*. Pantheon Books.

Saito, Y. (1996). "Japanese Gardens: the Art of Improving Nature." *Chanoyu Quarterly* (83).

Saito, Y. (1997). "The Japanese Aesthetics of Imperfection and Insufficiency." *The Journal of Aesthetics and Art Criticism*, 55 (4).

Sata, M. (1999). *"Modoki": The Mimetic Tradition in Japan*. In M. Marra (Ed.), *Modern Japanese aesthetics: A reader*. University of Hawai'i Press.

Schultz, L. (2013). "Creative Climate: Expressive Media in the Aesthetics of Watsuji, Nishida, and Merleau-Ponty." *Environmental Philosophy* 10(1): 63–82.

Shinkei. (1906). *Sōzu teikin* [宗祇庭訓; Rules of Conduct for Monks]. In *Zoku gunsho ruijū* (Vol. 17). Zoku Gunsho Ruijū Kanseikai.

Shinkei. (1991). *Sasamegoto* [心敬ささめごと; Idle words]. In Y. Shimizu (Ed.), *Shinkei zenshū*. Kyūko Shoin.

Shirane, H. and L. E. Marceau (2002). "Early Modern Literature." *Early Modern Japan* 10(2).

Shokin, F. (1989). "Philosophical Aspects of the Chashitsu." *Chanoyu Quarterly* (59).

Shukō, M. (1980). *Kokoro no fumi* [心の手文; Letter on Heart's Mastery]. In *Chadō Kyōiku Kenkyūkai* (Ed.), *Chadō koten zenshū* (Vol. 3, pp. 1–24). Shibunkaku Shuppan.

Slusser, D. (2013). *The Transformation of Tea Practice in Sixteenth-Century Japan*. In M. Pitelka (Ed.), *Japanese Tea Culture: Art, History and Practice*. Taylor & Francis.

Smart, N. (1998). *The World's Religions*, Cambridge University Press.

Smethurst, Mae J. (1989). *The Artistry of Aeschylus and Zeami – A Comparative Study of Greek Tragedy and Nō*, Princeton UP, Princeton,

Smethurst, Mae J. (2013). *Dramatic Action in Greek Tragedy and Noh – Reading with and beyond Aristotle*, Lexington Books, Plymouth.

Sen Sōshitsu XV. (1970). *Understanding cha-no-yu. Chanoyu Quarterly*, (1).

Sen Sōshitsu XV. (1971). "Hin and Shu." *Chanoyu Quarterly* 2(2).

Sen Sōshitsu XV. (1978). *"Cha no sugata* (Tea as it really is)." *Urasenke Newsletter* 15.

Sen Sōshitsu XV. (1979). *Tea Life, Tea Mind*. New York, Published for the Urasenke Foundation, Kyoto by Weatherhill.

Sen Sōshitsu XVI. (1992). "The Spirit of Tea is Global." *Chanoyu Quarterly* (71).

Sen Sōshitsu XV. (1997). *The Japanese Way of Tea: From Its Origins in China to Sen Rikyū*, University of Hawai'i Press.

Sōshun'ō. (1956). *Sōshun'ō chadō kikigaki* [宗舜翁茶道聞書; Sōshun'ō's recorded teachings on the Way of Tea]. In *Chadō Kyōiku Kenkyūkai* (Ed.), *Chadō koten zenshū* (Vol. 3). Tankōsha.

Stevens, B. (2009). *Self in Space: Nishida philosophy and the Phenomenology of Maurice Merleau-Ponty*. In J. Y. Park & G. Kopf (Eds.), *Merleau-Ponty and Buddhism*. Lexington Books.

Surak, K. (2012). *Making Tea, Making Japan: Cultural Nationalism in Practice*, Stanford University Press.

Suzuki, D. T. (1973). *Zen and Japanese Culture*, Princeton University Press.

Suzuki, M. (1999). 「茶事の構造」 (The Structure of Tea Ceremony). 戸田勝久（編）『茶道学大系，第3巻，茶事・茶会』. Compendium of Tea Studies. T. Katsuhisa. Tokyo, Tankosha. 3: 397–427.

Tadashi, O. (2012). "The Kyoto School of Philosophy and Phenomenology." *Analecta Husserliana*: Japanese Phenomenology: Phenomenology as the Trans-cultural Philosophical Approach VIII.

Taiichi, K. (1970). "Science of Tea, Part I." *Chanoyu Quarterly* 1(2).

Takehara, S. (Ed.). (2005). *Miyako meisho zue* [都名所図会; *Illustrated Guide to Famous Places in the Capital*]. Kadokawa Gakugei Shuppan.

Tamura, Y. (2000). *Japanese Buddhism: A Cultural History*, Kosei Publishing Company.

Tanaka, H. (2007). 『近代茶道の歴史社会学』 (The Historical Sociology of the Modern Tea Ceremony). Kyoto, Shibunkaku Shuppan.

Tanikawa, T. (1979), "The Esthetics of Chanoyu, Part I." *Chanoyu Quarterly* (23)

Tang, Y. Y., Hölzel, B. K., & Posner, M. I. (2015). The neuroscience of mindfulness meditation. *Nature Reviews Neuroscience*, 16(4), 213–225.

Tanizaki, Jun'ichirō. (1977). *In Praise of Shadows*, Leete's Island Books.

Teiji, I. (1982). "Kekkai: The Aesthetics of Partitions." *Chanoyu Quarterly* (32).

Ueda, Makoto. (1967). *Literary and Art Theories in Japan*, Press of Western Reserve University.

Ueda, S. (1965). *Die Gottesgeburt in der Seele und der Durchbruch zur Gottheit : Die Mystische Anthropologie Meister Eckharts und ihre Konfrontation mit der Mystik des Zen-Buddhismus* (Unpublished doctoral dissertation, University of Marburg). Gütersloher Verlagshaus.

Ueda, S. (1991). "Freedom and Language in Meister Eckhart and Zen Buddhism II." *The Eastern Buddhist* 24(1): 52–80.

Ueda, S. (1991). *Nishida Kitarō o yomu* 西田幾多郎を読む. Tokyo, Iwanami.

Ueda, S. (1993). "Zen and Philosophy in the Thought of Nishida Kitarō." *Japanese Religions* 18(2).

Ueda, S. (1995). *Nishida, Nationalism, and the War in Question*. In J. W. Heisig & J. C. Maraldo (Eds.), *Rude awakenings: Zen, the Kyoto School, & the question of nationalism*. University of Hawai'i Press.

Ueda, S. (2011). "Language in a Two-fold World." In J. W. Heisig, T. P. Kasulis, & J. C. Maraldo (Eds.), *Japanese Philosophy: A Sourcebook*. University of Hawai'i Press.

van Briessen, F. (2011). *Way of the Brush: Painting Techniques of China and Japan*, Tuttle Publishing.

Van Norden, B. W. (2017). *Taking Back Philosophy: A Multicultural Manifesto*. New York, Columbia University Press.

Viswanathan, M. (2017). "The Measure of Comparison: Correspondence and Collision in Japanese Aesthetics." In A. M. Nguyen (Ed.), *New essays in Japanese aesthetics*. Lexington Books.

Watsuji, T. (1996). *Rinrigaku: Ethics in Japan*, State University of New York Press.

Ward Lott, Sandra, Maureen S.G. Hawkins and Norman McMillan (Eds.) (1993). *Global Perspectives on Teaching Literature: Shared Visions and Distinctive Visions*. National Council of Teachers of English, London,

Williams, D. (2014). *The Philosophy of Japanese Wartime Resistance: A Reading, with Commentary, of the Complete Texts of the Kyoto School Discussions of the Standpoint of World History and Japan*, Taylor & Francis.

Wittgenstein, L. (2009). *Philosophical Investigations* (G. E. M. Anscombe, P. M. S. Hacker, & J. Schulte, Trans., 4th ed.). Wiley-Blackwell.

Young, J. (1970). "Chanoyu for the West." *Chanoyu Quarterly* 1(2).

Yamanoue, S. (1995). *The Record of Yamanoue Sōji*. In S. Sen Sōshitsu XV (Ed.), *The Japanese Way of Tea: From its Origins in China to Sen Rikyū* (P. Varley, Trans.). Asian Humanities Press.

Yanagi, S. (1989). *The Unknown Craftsman: A Japanese Insight into Beauty* (B. Moeran, Trans.). Kodansha International.

Yusada, K. (1995). "Approach to Haiku and Basic Principles." In N. Hume (Ed.), *Japanese Aesthetics and Culture: A Reader*. State University of New York Press.

Zhuangzi. (2009). *Zhuangzi: The Essential Writings with Selections from Traditional Commentaries* (B. Ziporyn, Trans.). Hackett Publishing Company.

Index

absence 75, 80, 106, 109, 113, 119–20, 122–27, 133, 135, 138–39, 183, 189, 202–3, 229, 231, 246–47, 254–55, 263
absolute nothingness (*zettai mu* 絶対無) 216. *See also* Nishida
abyss 308
actuality 106–8, 238, 254, 258. *See also* Ueda, Hollowness
aesthetic
　authorization (*konomi* 好み) 50
　experience 59, 138, 243
　ideal 44, 49, 208. *See also sōan*
　object 34, 145, 269, 290
　of death 63, 64
　practice 28, 31, 68, 74, 126, 129–30, 132, 166, 207–8, 236, 246, 248, 268, 297. *See also geidō*
alcove (*tokonoma* 床の間) 46, 147, 231–32
Alltäglichkeit (everydayness) 95
allusive variation (*honka-dori* 本歌取り) 170
almanac, seasonal "Year Time Chronicles" (*saijiki* 歳時記) 241
alterity 86
ambiguity 41, 84, 125, 139
An Inquiry into the Good (*Zen no Kenkyū*, 善の研究) 215. *See also* Nishida
ancestors 36, 52, 64, 113, 178, 296. *See also* killing
aniconism 184
animism 178. *See also* Kami, Shinto
anthropocentrism 263
archer metaphor
　hiki-bishaku 引き柄杓 294
　kiri-bishaku 切り柄杓 294
　oki-bishaku 置き柄杓 294
architecture 15, 24, 48–49, 52, 69, 71, 86, 123, 135, 179, 219, 226
Aristotle 61, 69, 74–75, 79, 155. *See also* law of non-contradiction

art history 60–62, 153, 156, 166, 168–70, 237, 257
artificial intelligence 113
artistic competition, games 158
　cha awase. see awase
　paragone 156
　tōcha 闘茶 28
ash 146, 201, 284–85. *See also* charcoal
Ashikaga Shogun 288
asymmetry (*fukinsei* 不均整) 82, 205
Asuka period 26
attachment 36, 38, 48, 50, 68–71, 80, 119, 207, 249, 296–98, 300, 302, 306–7
authenticity 300–301
Avatamsaka Sutra 207
awase 26, 146
　cha- 茶合わせ 26
Azuchi-Momoyama period 49

basara 婆娑羅 28, 30, 51
Bashō Matsuo 157, 189, 240, 241
basho 場所 215–220, 237, 239
basin, stone (*tsukubai* 蹲踞) 175–77, 188, 219, 289–90
beauty 16, 30, 37–38, 43, 46, 49–50, 58–62, 67–68, 71, 84–85, 108, 115, 134, 138, 147, 157, 179, 183, 185, 192, 199, 202–4, 255, 258, 260, 265, 267, 285, 287, 290
Being and Time 101, 259, 269, 273. *See also* Heidegger
being-in-the-world *in der Welt sein* 271. *See also* Heidegger, *Being and Time*
being-towards-death *sein-zum-Tod* 259. *See also* Heidegger, *Being and Time*
Bergson, Henri 257
Bhaghavad Gītā 224
binding energy (*musubi* 結び) 178
Blake, William 224. *See also* holographic metaphysics, *sōsoku*

Blue Cliff Record (*Hekiganroku* 碧巌録) 207
Bodhidharma 24
Book of Tea 85, 143, 181. *See also* Okakura Kakuzō
boundary 67, 89, 115–16, 134, 139, 197, 220, 226, 233, 287. *See also* partition
brazier portable (*furo* 風炉) 277
Buddha 66, 67. *See also* killing
    Amida 208
    Siddhartha 66
Buddhism
    Cáodòng 29
    Chan 24–25, 27, 66, 206–8, 232
    Mahāyāna 10, 67, 69, 71, 122, 207
    Mādhyamika 10, 67, 69–71, 302. *See also* Nāgārjuna
    Pure land 29, 50, 208
    Rinzai 28, 64, 70, 206, 207, 251. *See also* Eisai
    Sōtō 29, 206, 207, 221. *See also* Dōgen
    Tiāntóng 29
    Zen. *See* Zen
Butsudō fascicle 209. *See also* Dōgen
Butterfly, dream of 148, 234, 306–8. *See also* Zhuangzi

calligraphy 15, 35, 42, 86, 120, 130, 147–48, 169, 199, 213, 221, 231, 233–37, 239, 244, 248–49, 266
    ink trace (*bokuseki* 墨跡) 233
    way of (*shodō* 書道) 130, 231–32, 234
camellia sinensis 23
Camellia Well (*Tsubaki-no-ido* 椿の井戸) 20
cardinal directions 278
Cézanne, Paul 162, 164, 196
cha zen ichimi ("Tea and Zen are one taste" 茶禅一味) 208
cha-ji ceremony 茶事 289
chakai ōyose 茶会大寄せ 23
chanoyu 茶の湯 15–16, 18, 23, 34, 38–39, 43–45, 49–50, 52, 85, 89, 109, 113, 115–16, 130, 150, 170–72, 181, 208, 214, 221–22, 232–33, 240, 296–97
charcoal 47, 275, 277, 284,
    base (*shitabi* 下火) 284

ceremony, first (*shozumi* 初炭) 277
ceremony, second (*gozumi* 後炭) 284
cherry blossom 50, 55–60, 62–63, 148, 156, 204
    forecast 57
    sakura 桜 56–57
    viewing (*hanami* 花見) 56–57, 60, 78, 195, 237–38, 276, 291
"chill and withered" (*hiekareta* 冷え枯れた) 36, 43
Chinese
    art manuals 158
    literati tradition 23
    philosophy. *See* Buddhism, Daoism, Confucianism 6
    teaware (*meibutsu* 名物) 28, 31, 41.
christian 67, 181, 183, 209–10
    asceticism 210
    jesuit missionaries 210
Christ 62–63, 178–79, 184
Chōmei, Kamo no 30
chōra χώρα 216
chōrizō χωρίζω 79
cinema
    domestic Japanese (*hōga* 邦画) 303
    Japanese (*nihon eiga* 日本映画) 303–5, 307
circumscribere 115–16
clinging
    shūshu 執著 8
    upādāna 8
co-dependent origination. *See* dependent origination
colonialism 82–84, 87
comparative philosophy 80–82. *See also* intercultural philosophy
Confucian ethics 151
Confucianism 15, 17, 24–25, 47, 86, 121, 130, 149–51, 157, 177, 186
connoisseur
    of poetry (*uta suki* 歌数寄) 49
    of tea (*sukimono* 数寄者) 49
continuity 140, 189, 214, 220, 233, 236–39, 244–45, 263, 265, 302–4. *See also* cut-continuance
contradictory self-identity 217. *See also* Nishida
conventional truth (*saṁvṛti*) 10, 41, 122. *See also* Nāgārjuna, twofold truth

copy-original binary 166–67
cosmology 175, 181, 186, 278
craftsman (*shokunin* 職人) 268
crawl in entrance (*nijiriguchi* 躙り口) 52, 227–29, 253, 280, 289–90
creativity 115, 118, 165, 167–71, 192
   ex nihilo 118
   sakui 作意 169, 171–72
cultural
   appropriation 82, 86, 88, 92
   exoticism 88
   imperialism 82–83, 88, 91–92
cutting (*kire* 切) 113, 133, 135–36, 138–39, 149, 214, 233, 244–45, 302–4
   word (*kireji* 切れ字) 244
cut-continuance (*kire-tsuzuki* 切れ続き) 139, 304
Csikszentmihalyi, Mihaly. *See* flow.

Daitoku-ji 44, 205–6, 209
Dao 道 55, 103–5, 121–22, 124, 127, 130–31, 177–78, 231, 246–47, 280, 291, 298
Daodejing 100, 103, 121–22, 208, 245, 299
Daoist cosmology 175, 278
Daozi, Wu 158–59, 163–67, 307
Dasein 269, 271–72, 300. *See also Being and Time*, Heidegger
da Vinci, Leonardo 106, 168
de Beauvoir 97
death 34, 39, 53, 62–64, 151, 166, 256–61, 296
   aestheticization of 63, 64
   poem 296
degenerate age of the dharma (*mappō* 末法) 30
dependent
   co-arising 78
   origination 75, 78, 79 250, 257
   pratītyasamutpāda 78, 270
Descartes, Rene 160, 269
directional cosmology 278
disciplinary practice (*shugyō* 修行) 268
divination 278
Dōgen Zenji 29–31, 34, 206, 209, 263–265. *See also Butsudō fascicle*, *mujo seppō*, polycentric perspectivism

double bind 80, 84, 88, 92–93. *See also* intercultural philosophy
dream 61, 77, 148, 234, 285, 295, 297, 299, 301, 303, 305–8. *See also* Zhuangzi
dualism 121, 134, 186, 191
   copy-original 153, 154, 166, 167
   life-death 64, 260
   two-fold truth 41, 67, 72, 102–3, 122
   yin yang 122–129, 136, 186, 247, 248, 293
dust
   hole (*chiriana* 塵穴) 223
   of worldly concerns 119

Eckhart, Meister 102. *See also via negativa*
ecstatic body 195. *See also* Merleau-Ponty
Edo period 100, 148
Edosenke school 8
egalitarian ideal 41, 51–52, 146, 227. *See also* Shukō, Rikyū
Eihei-ji 263. *See also* Dōgen
Eisai Myōan 27–28, 34. *See also* Rinzai
Emperor Saga 26
Emperor Shōmu 26
emptiness 37–38, 51, 69–70, 72, 74, 76–80, 98, 102, 105–6, 117–18, 124, 127, 184, 211–12, 216–18, 250, 257, 261, 275, 298, 301–2, 308
   of emptiness *śūnyatāyāh śūnyatā* 70, 72, 302
   mu 無 37–38, 216, 250
   śūnyatā 70, 76, 78, 106, 122, 127, 211, 216, 270, 275, 301–2, 308
engi 縁起 78. *See also* dependent co-arising
enlightenment 17, 23, 41, 71, 80, 143, 149, 212, 236, 267, 293
entering one's seat (*seki-iri* 席入) 229
entrance, tea hut. Nobleman's (*kininguchi* 貴人口) 227
equipmentality *zeughaftigkeit* 271–75. *See also* Heidegger
eros 183
Essays in Idleness. *See* Kenko
essence 17, 32, 45, 49, 75–79, 105–7, 132, 154–55, 170, 214, 237, 246, 260, 273–74, 282, 305. *See also* Plato

eurocentrism 9, 81. *See also* Said
European
    aesthetics 192
    art history 61–62, 153, 166, 168, 170, 237, 257
    philosophy 17, 60, 81, 183
everydayness. *See Alltäglichkeit*, Heidegger
existential phenomenology *see* phenomenology
experience
    pre-reflective 93, 96–99, 164, 188, 190, 212, 216, 220, 259, 262, 270, 274
    reflective 93, 96–99, 111, 164, 188, 190, 194, 212, 216, 220, 259, 262, 270, 274
expression of spirit (*sha-i* 写意) 169–70

fan, folding (*sensu* 扇子) 147, 233, 280, 292
feminism 222
feminization of tea ceremony 222
feudal lord (*daimyō* 大名) 171, 209, 225
fine arts (*bijutsu* 美術) 16, 256, 266
finitude 300
fire 149, 176–78, 182, 201, 220, 223, 275, 277–78, 290
    festival (*himatsuri* 火祭り) 177
    ritual purification 119, 175, 177–78, 222–23, 284, 292
floriography 261. *See also* flower language
flow 98, 111, 121, 128, 131–32, 146, 151, 186, 237, 246, 256, 285, 298
flower
    arranging (*ikebana* 生け花, *kadō* 華道) 44, 67, 130–31, 220, 221, 231, 232, 253–54, 256–59, 262, 266, 280
    -language 30, 85, 89, 93, 98–99, 103–10, 195, 220, 227, 231, 235, 237, 242–49, 259, 261–65, 267, 272, 303
Flower Garland Sutra (*Kegon-kyō* 華厳経) 78, 255
flowers in the sky (*kuge* 空華) 111, 113, 146, 281, 296, 298, 302, 307=B308. *See also* Dōgen
following mood of stone (*kōwan ni shitagau* 石の乞はんに従う) 191–92, 195–96. *See also* Sakuteiki

formlessness 76, 102, 115–16, 124, 127, 149, 169, 211
    musō 無相 116
    arūpa अरूप 76
    mushiki 無色 76
four heavenly kings (*shitennō* 四天王) 293
freedom from convention (*datsuzoku* 脱俗) 205

Gadamer, Hans-Georg 100–101, 108
garden
    inner (*uchi roji* 内露地) 148, 152, 176
    outer (*soto roji* 外露地) 148, 152
gate 113–14, 118–19, 133–34, 139–40, 143, 152, 159, 176, 213, 229, 255
    -middle (*chūmon* 中門) 176
    -outer (*soto-mon* 外門) 114
geidō 芸道 127, 129–32, 156–57, 166, 169, 171, 178, 201, 207, 231–32, 246, 255, 265–66, 268, 292. *See also chadō, kyudō, sadō, shodō*.
gender 92, 146–47, 175, 221–22
    equality 38, 42, 52, 222, 226
    ryōsai kenbo. *See* good wife
globalization 168
good wife, wise mother ideal (*ryōsai kenbo* 良妻賢母) 222
grand master (*iemoto* 家元) 88–89, 221
grass roof/tea hut style. *See Sōan*.
Greek 47, 61, 67, 69, 74–75, 101, 103, 115–16, 154–55, 157, 182, 194, 258
    philosophy 101
    symposium 26, 183. *See also* Plato
guest
    main- (*shōkyaku* 正客) 143, 152, 229, 280
    Final- (*otsume* 御詰) 143, 152, 229,

Hadot, Pierre 69
haiku 俳句. *See* poetry
Han dynasty 25
harmony (*wa*, 和) 47–48, 121, 123–24, 128, 130, 146, 151–52, 177–78, 202, 205, 214, 234, 250, 256, 282, 284, 293. *See also* tea – values
head tea house (*sōke* 宗家) 34
Heart Sutra 207
hearth 34, 277
    recessed (*ro* 炉) 35, 277

Heian period, 26, 255
   court life 28, 30
Heidegger, Martin
   authenticity 300–301
   non-willing 299–300
   ontological difference 258
   stimmung 239
   "will to will", 299
Heraclitus 61
hermeneutic phenomenology. *see* phenomenology
hermit-style hut 31, 34
Hideyoshi 51–53, 226, 254
Higashiyama culture 64
Hiroshima Shukkeien garden 57
Hirota, Dennis 37, 43, 49–51, 171, 203–4, 208
Hirst, Damian 62
Hisamatsu Shin'ichi (久松真一) 16, 32. *See also* killing Buddha
holographic metaphysics 225. *See also* Blake, infinity
hospitality 92
Husserl, Edmund 80, 94–95, 97, 99–100, 212, 214
hypokeimenon 75 *See* ontology – substance
hypostasis 75. *See* ontology – substance
Hōnen 208
horizon 94–96, 100, 102, 108, 158, 275
   fusion of *Horizontverschmelzung* 100, 102, 108. *See also* Gadamer

I Ching 278–79
ichigo ichie 43–44, 117, 234
identity 15, 17, 44, 84–88, 102, 125, 168, 217, 297
Ikkyū Sōjun 35
imagination 137–39, 242, 254. *See also yūgen*
imitation 115, 154–55, 157, 170–71. *See also* mimesis, *utsushi*.
immanence 170. *See also* Transcendence
imperfection 201–2, 206
Imperial University 73, 257. *See also* Kyoto Daiguku
impermanence 37–38, 44, 50, 55, 57–63, 66–67, 106, 172, 201–3, 206, 208, 238, 256–61, 285
   mujō 無常 37, 264

In Praise of Shadows 205. *See also* Tanizaki
inauthenticity 298, 300. *See also* Heidegger
incense (*kōdō* 香道) 45, 130, 284, 285, 289
   container (*kōgo* 香合) 284
   sandlewood 284, 288
Indra's Net 78
Infinite 40, 41, 78, 79, 118, 223–225. *See also* Blake
   within finitude. *See also* holographic metaphysics, mutual containment.
inter-expression (*hyōgen-teki kankei* 表現的関係) 193, 195. *See also* Nishida
intercultural. *See also* comparative philosophy
   aesthetics 68, 72
   double bind 80, 84, 88, 92
   encounter 71, 92, 102, 109, 140, 218, 301
   philosophy 73–74, 81, 271
interpenetration 224, 247. *See also* holographic metaphysics, mutual containment
invocations (*yorishiro* 依り代) 255

Jakuan Sōtaku 296
Japanese
   aesthetics 43, 57, 62, 65–67, 85, 115, 120, 146, 157, 185, 205, 214, 237, 247, 298, 303
   architecture 69. *See also* grass hut, *sōan*
   art history 156, 169
   calligraphy 234–36
   cinema (*nihon eiga* 日本映画, *hōga* 邦画) 303
   identity 15, 17, 44, 84–87
   nationalism 87. *See also nihonjinron*
   paper. *See* Paper – *washi, kaishi*.
   philosophy *See* Kyoto School
   poetry. *See* haiku, renku
   uniqueness discourse *nihonjinron* 87
Jaspers, Karl 101, 268
Jesuit missionary 210
Jisho-ji temple 65
joint repair, golden (*kintsugi* 金継ぎ) 287–88
Jukō Murata. *See* Shukō
Jukō-in, tea hut (聚光院) 209
Jōmon period 199

Jō'ō Takeno:
    tea values 39, 47–48, 53

kadō. see flower arranging
Kamakura period 30, 49
kami 神 48, 178, 255, 282. See also animism, Shinto
kamikaze 神風 63–64
Kasulis, Thomas 81–82
Kawakami Fuhaku 8
Kenkō Yoshida 59. See also Essays in Idleness
Kierkegaard, Søren 257, 268
killing 52, 64–65, 70–72, 296–97
    ancestors 7, 14, 52, 296
    Buddhas 297
Kissayōjōki ("The Account of Drinking Tea and Prolonging Life" 喫茶養生記) 28
Kojève, Alexander 8
Korea 24, 26, 66, 177
Kuki Shūzō 259
Kurosawa, Akira 303–4, 307
Kyoto
    Daigaku 54, 72–75, 77, 79, 81, 83, 85, 87, 89, 91, 93, 95, 97, 99, 101, 103, 105, 107, 109, 111
    Imperial University 257
Kyoto School 56, 73–76, 102, 215, 257. See also Nishida, Nishitani, Ueda
kōan 207, 224
Kōbō Daishi 26, 236

lacquered dish for sweets (fuchidaka 縁高) 287
ladle (hishaku 柄杓) 176
language 30, 85, 89, 93, 98–99, 103–10, 195, 220, 227, 231, 235, 237, 242–49, 259, 261–65, 267, 272, 303. See also non-speaking
    correspondence theory 103
    non-correspondence 103
    of flowers (hanakotoba 花言葉) 261–63.
Laṅkāvatāra Sutra 207
Laozi 103, 121–22, 130, 245, 299
law of non-contradiction. See Aristotle
Leibniz, Gottfried Wilhelm 78
"Letter on Heart's Mastery" 36. See also Shukō

lifeworld Lebenswelt 94, 212
Linji Yixuan 70
logic 75–77, 85–86, 138, 173, 182, 216–17, 224, 244, 251, 255
    a=not-a 77, 86
    Aristotelian logic 217
    of absolutely contradictory self-identity 217. See also Nishida
Lotus Sutra 149, 207, 255
Lu Yu (733–804 陸羽) 25, 28

ma 間 134, 211, 213–14. See also space
martial arts (budō 武道) 130, 206
material agency 193
meditation 24–25, 32, 66, 128–29, 132,182, 196, 206–8, 267
    group (sesshin 接心) 206
    walking (kinhin 経行) 206
    zen (dhyana) 66, 207
Meiji period 16, 85
Merleau-Ponty, Maurice 97, 101, 160–64, 193–96, 214, 270
metaphysical continuum 186
Michelangelo 60–61, 155, 159, 168
middle way 67, 105–6, 257. See also Buddhism – Mahāyāna
Midorikai 88–89. See also Urasenke
mimesis 153–57, 170, 261, 263. See also imitation
Momoyama period 32, 49, 199, 233
monastery 25–26, 28–29, 31, 44, 48, 51, 66, 68, 102, 133, 135, 172, 202, 208, 232
monasticism 15, 25, 30
Monet, Claude 155, 166
Monk pizza restaurant 65, 71
mono no aware 物の哀れ 15, 55, 57–63, 67, 238, 256
Mount Fuji 189
movement and stillness 127
mujō 無常. See impermanence
mujō seppō 無情説法 264. See also Dōgen
multi-perspectivism. See also Dōgen – polycentric perspectivism
Murasaki Shikibu 58
Muromachi period 24, 28, 64
mutual containment (sōsoku 相即) 224. See also holographic metaphysics

Nāgārjuna 10, 70, 302, 306. *See also* emptiness of emptiness, two-fold truth, mādhyamika
Nampōroku 51, 149–50, 171. *See also* Rikyū
Natorp, Paul 99
negative
　ontology. *See* ontology
　space (in painting) 137–139, 213, 242, 247, 248
negativity 81, 84, 106, 108, 124, 126–27,135–40, 243–44, 246–49, 258, 302
　linguistic 246, 248. *See also* non-speaking
Newton:
　space-time 214, 218
Nietzsche 61, 257, 305
Nishi Amane 16
Nishida, Kitarō 56, 73, 102, 139, 193–96, 214–19, 236, 257
Nishitani, Keiji 102, 113, 215, 256–61
　"the Japanese Art of Arranged Flowers", 258, 260
"no guest no host" (*mu-hin-shu* 無賓主) 250–51
no-mind (*mushin* 無心) 236
noh drama 36, 60, 135
non-action (*wu wei* 無為) 74, 105, 120, 127, 129, 131–33, 171, 195, 245, 261, 298–99. *See also* Daoism
non-attachment 70, 302
non-conceptual wisdom (*prajñā*) 207
non-dualism 8, 104, 105, 121–25, 127, 129, 133, 258, 260
non-object 37, 74, 79–80, 94, 105–7, 116, 118, 192, 212, 269, 287, 298
non-self 37, 76–77, 79–80, 105–9, 115–18, 120, 127, 138, 159, 184, 192, 194, 196, 218–20, 228, 240, 257, 265, 271, 301
　anatta अनात्मन् 79
　muga 無我 79, 208
non-speaking (*bù yán*, 不言) 105, 108, 110, 127, 245–49, 261
non-willing. *See* Heidegger
Norinaga, Motoori 58
nothingness 13, 37, 51, 102, 105, 136, 217, 268. *See also* emptiness, formlessness

obey—break—transcend (*shu-ha-ri* 守破離) 170
Okakura Kakuzō 85, 143, 181
Omotesenke, tea house 表千家 34
One Page Testament of Rikyū. *See* Rikyū
one soup three dishes (*ichijū sansai* 一汁三菜) 282
Ōnin wars 38
Ontic. *See* Heidegger
ontology 15, 37, 61, 74–76, 81, 102, 105, 116, 137–38, 140, 193, 195, 213, 215–16, 233, 249–50, 263, 271, 273
　negative 11–13, 37, 51, 74, 76–78, 81, 82, 105–107, 127, 195, 219,
　ontological difference 258. *See also* Heidegger
　relational- 74–76, 81, 102, 105, 116, 213, 233, 250, 271, 273
　substance- 74–75, 105, 116, 137, 249, 271
orientalism 83, 110. *See also* Said
originality 115, 165–68, 170–72, 192
Ōtomo Sōrin 209
Otsume. See guest
Ozu Yasujirō 303–4

painting 15, 24, 57, 60, 63, 68, 86, 135, 139, 145, 153, 155–59, 161–66, 168, 187, 193, 199, 205, 213, 219, 233, 241–43, 247–48, 285, 307
　Chinese 187, 166, 167
　Japanese 57, 86, 135. *See also* Sesshū
　Landscape 135, 157, 158, 166, 242, 247
　Zenkiga 禅機画 233
paper
　kaishi 懐紙 147, 283, 291
　tassles (*shide* 紙垂) 255
　washi 和紙 234
paradox 80, 105, 172–73, 197, 226, 243
Parrhasios 155–56. *See also* Zeuxis
partition (*kekkai* 結界) 133–34, 140, 284
patriarchy 222
perception 15, 87, 94–95, 104, 154,160–61, 211, 237, 244, 289
percussive cues 229, 284, 289, 294
perigraptos 115–16, 194

perspective 77, 81, 84, 92–93, 99, 101, 126, 137, 159, 162–63, 167, 194–95, 197, 224, 238, 241, 260, 265, 304–5, 308
perspectivism 265, 304–5, 307–8
　polycentric 265, 305. *See also* Dōgen
phenomenological
　method 41, 91, 95–96, 259
　space and time 15, 41, 133, 144, 197, 211–17, 219
phenomenology
　existential 80–81, 99, 268–70
　finitude 300
　hermeneutic 98
　intercultural 102
　and aesthetics 101
　and pre-reflective experience 97–98, 164
philosophy
　comparative 80–82
　intercultural 73–74, 81, 271
　as a way of life 69. *See also* Hadot
physics 212
　Einstein 212
　Newton 212
place of absolute nothingness (*zettai mu no basho* 絶対無の場所) 216. *See also* Nishida
place of true nothing (*shin no mu no basho* 真の無の場所) 216. *See also* Nishida
Plato 26, 61, 74, 79, 151, 154–57, 163, 166, 183–84, 216. *See also chora*, *Republic*, symposium
platonism 61, 154
Pliny 156
poetry
　haiku 60, 135, 157, 204, 224, 234, 240–46, 248–50.
　renga 36, 38, 240, 244
　renku 240, 244
pottery 15, 24, 46, 51, 78, 183, 197, 199–201, 205, 254, 280. *See also Raku*
practice-realization one and same (*shushō-ichinyo*, 修証一如) 267
Prajñāpāramitā Sutras 207
pre-reflective. *See* experience – pre-reflective

presence 80, 102, 106, 113, 119–20, 122–27, 129, 135, 138–39, 178–79, 202, 204, 238, 243, 247, 249, 254–55, 263, 284
process art 193
psycho-physical continuum 191. *See also qi*
purification 119, 144, 150, 175–80, 222–23, 284, 288, 292
　cloth 147, 285, 290–94
　dust 49, 69, 71, 119, 140, 143–44, 149–50, 176, 223, 284
　fire 149, 176–78, 182, 201, 220, 223, 275, 277–78, 290
　incense 45, 130, 284–85, 289
　shinto ritual 183, 282
　water 19–23, 25, 27, 29, 31, 34, 45, 57, 119, 143, 145, 148, 175–81, 218–20, 237, 265, 273, 278, 281, 283, 285, 288–91, 293–94, 305
　harai 祓い 177

qi 気 186–87, 191, 236–37, 239

Raku 46, 197, 199–201, 203–5, 207, 209
　clan 46, 199
　Kichizaemon 199
　museum/workshop 197, 199
　Ware 46, 199, 201
Raphael 166
Rashomon 304, 307. *See also* Kurosawa
realistic representation (*shasei* 写生) 170
recitation (*nenju* 念誦) 206
refined taste, person with (*chasuki* 茶数寄) 49
reflection 96–97, 99, 118, 189, 191, 219–20, 238–40, 259, 298
relational 74–79, 81, 94, 96, 102, 105–6, 116, 118, 125, 127, 179, 211–14, 217–20, 233, 241–42, 250, 262, 271–75, 289
　field 78–79, 217–18
　ontology 74–76, 81, 102, 105, 116, 213, 233, 250, 271, 273
　self 127, 218–19. *See also* non-self
Renaissance 58, 61, 69, 156, 158–62, 164
　art 160
　perspective 162
representation 15, 124, 154, 156–57, 167–68, 170, 233, 236, 239, 249, 287

respect (*kei* 敬) 39, 47–48. *See also* tea
– values
reverence (*kin* 欽) 39, 47, 178, 187, 276.
See also tea – values
rhythmic progression (*jo-ha-kyū* 序破急)
292
Rikyū, Sen no:
    death tea 53
    One Page Testament of Rikyū (*Ichimai Kishōmon* 利休一枚起請文) 208
    - no i (Rikyū's well 利休の井) 19–20, 34, 175, 289–90
    Tea hut 46–51
    tea values 47–48
Rinzai. *See* Zen, Buddhism
ritual
    drinking 24–26, 28, 179–81, 183–84, 208, 232, 266, 268, 282, 298
    gesture 36, 127, 131, 148, 169, 176, 196, 262, 276, 283–85, 291–92, 294
    purification 119, 144, 150, 175–80, 222–23, 284, 288, 292
Rokkaku-dō Temple 256
rootlessness 260–61. *See* Nishitani
ropes, shinto (*shimenawa* 注連縄) 135, 255
Ryōkō-in 85
Rūjìng 29

sabi 寂 15, 30, 197, 199, 201–7, 209, 287.
See also wabi
Saichō 26, 34
Saigyō 30
Saito Yuriko 157, 192, 196
Sakai 19, 39, 42, 45, 50, 226, 228, 233
sake 酒 31, 115, 151, 183, 282–83
Sakura. *See* cherry blossom
Sakuteiki 作庭記 191
samurai 15, 28, 30, 32, 39, 51–53, 130, 225–27, 303
sandalwood. *See* incense
Sasaki Chōjirō 200
scenic locale (*meishō* 名勝) 157
screen divider (*tsuitate* 衝立) 284
seasonal word (*kigo* 季語) 240–41
seasonality:
    food 15, 115, 179, 183, 220, 269, 281–83
    implements 48, 51, 147, 203, 270, 276, 280, 283, 290–92
    sweets 115, 285–89

seat, upper (*kamiza* 上座) 280
selfhood 66, 68, 71, 74, 76, 85, 108, 130, 165, 167–69, 172–73, 265, 271–72
Sen Sōshitsu 26, 45, 53, 88–89, 181, 208, 214, 250–51. *See also iemoto, Urasenke*
Sengoku period 225
Sesshū Tōyō 68, 242. *See also* "Splashed Ink Landscape"
Seven Samurai (*shichinin no samurai* 七人の侍) 303. *See also* Kurosawa
Shinkei 36, 38, 43, 171
Shinto 20, 24, 47, 55, 119, 175–77, 255
Shoin 書院 31–32, 34–35, 39–40, 46–47, 51, 204, 226, 232
    style 226
    daisu 書院台子 232
Shukō, Murata 34–44, 46–47, 171, 208, 233
Shōkoku-ji 102
silence 104–7, 109–10, 213–14, 229, 245–48, 263
silk bag (*shifuku* 仕服) 290
simplicity 45, 48, 80, 151, 199, 202–3, 205–6, 225, 253, 265
    kanso 簡素 205
simulation 48, 306
Soami 64
Socrates 53, 68, 151, 184
Song dynasty 26
Sōshun-ō chadō kikigaki 172
soteriology 17, 46
space
    ma 134, 211, 213–14
    newtonian 212, 217
spatial 40–41, 118, 133–34, 137, 139, 144, 179, 218–20, 271, 275, 278
    field 220
    trigram 278, 280
spatiality 118, 144, 164–65, 204, 215, 219–20, 224–25, 227, 275
    phenomenological 215
    of the body 219
speech 104–5, 109–10, 183, 227, 229, 231, 245–48, 263
speech-silence binary 105, 246
splashed ink landscape 242. *See also* Sesshū
stoicism 17, 69, 182

stone 60, 78, 119, 143, 148, 150–52, 157, 175–76, 185–92, 202, 205, 218–20, 239, 264–65, 281–82, 285, 288
    barrier (*sekimori ishi* 関守石) 188–89
    lingering stone 190
    master (*shuseki* 主石) 192
    stepping (*tobi ishi* 飛石) 190
sublime beauty, doctrine of (*bimyōgaku* 美妙学) 16
substance 74–75, 77, 79, 81, 105, 116, 137, 186, 249, 256, 271, 274
    ontology 74–75, 105, 116, 137, 249, 271
substantial 106, 157, 207, 210–11, 215, 244, 287, 307
suffering 17–18, 38, 59, 66–69, 119, 143, 149, 172, 203, 237, 267–68
suicide (*seppuku* 切腹) 53, 63
suki 数寄 48–50, 208, 296
    ideal 49–50
    uta- 歌数寄 49
    house of (*sukiya* 数奇屋) 48–52, 225–27
    wabi- 侘数寄 49
sukiya architecture 48–51, 226
Suzuki D.T., 100, 204
sweets 115, 285–89
    wagashi 和菓子 285–86
    dry (*higashi* 干菓子) 285, 289
    moist (*omogashi* 主菓子) 285
syllabaries (*kana* 仮名) 235–36
symbolism 119, 139, 209, 263, 293
symposium 26, 183
sōan 草庵 34, 39–42, 224–26, 240
    ideal 39–41
Sōgi 43, 203
Sōtan 208
Sōtō. *See* Zen, Buddhism

Tanabe Hajime 215
Tanizaki Jun'ichirō 205
tatami 34, 40, 89, 223, 278, 280–81, 284, 290–91
Tathāgatagarbha sutras 207
tea
    -bowl (*chawan* 茶碗) 75–79, 202, 270, 273, 280, 287–88, 290–94
        Brick- (*tuánchá* 團茶) 25

    -caddy (*chaire* 茶入) 290
    -cloth (*fukusa* 袱紗) 147, 291–94
        folding ritual 293
    -contest (*tōcha* 闘茶) 28
    dawn- (*akatsuki-no-chaji* 暁の茶事) 175
    evening- (*yobanashi-no-chaji* 夜咄の茶事) 175
    -gathering (*chaji* 茶事) 23, 115, 175
    -gathering closed to outsiders (*chakai* 茶会) 23
    -gathering large groups (*ōyose* 大寄せ) 23
    -garden (*rōji* 露地) 114, 116, 143, 145, 147–49, 151–52, 175–77, 179, 181, 183, 185, 187, 189, 191, 193, 195, 197, 211
    internationalization of 88–90
    -kettle (*chagama* 茶釜) 290
    -master 18, 20, 25, 34, 36, 42, 44, 50, 53, 80, 85, 91, 117–18, 120, 123, 125–26, 131, 152, 167, 171–72, 179, 189, 202–3, 214, 221, 226–28, 231, 238–39, 242, 245, 254, 262, 265, 270, 280, 288, 290
    -meal (*kaiseki* 懐石) 281, 288
    ritual offering to shinto tea gods (*okensha* 御献茶) 23
    -party (*chayoriai* 茶寄合) 28
    powdered- (*matcha* 抹茶) 23, 26, 28, 31, 289–91, 294
    -scoop (*chashaku* 茶杓) 47, 280, 290–91, 293
    -shelf 32. *See also Daisu*
    -stand (*daisu* 台子) 31–32, 34–35, 232
    -room (*chashitsu* 茶室) 40, 226, 285
    -room in townhouse (*machiya* 町家) 39
    thick- (*koicha* 濃茶) 285, 289, 291
    thin- (*usucha* 薄茶) 285, 289
    -values 39, 47–48, 53
    vulgar (*fūryū-cha* 風流茶) 31
    -ware Chinese (*meibutsu* 名物) 28, 31
Tea Classic (*Chajing* 茶經) 25
Tetsugaku no michi 哲学の道 Philosopher's Walk 55–56, 178
Republic 155. *See also* Plato
theology 21, 109
    negative theology 109. *See also* Eckhart
    via negativa 12–13. *See also* Eckhart

three ways (tea—flower—incense) (*san-dō* 三道) 289
thrown-in flowers (*nageirebana* 投げ入れ花) 253
time
   phenomenological 41, 95–96, 110–11, 160–61, 163, 193, 211, 214–16, 218, 224, 259, 263, 269–70
   relational 74–79, 81, 94, 96, 102, 105–6, 116, 118, 125, 127, 179, 211–14, 217–20, 233, 241–42, 250, 262, 271–75, 289
Tokyo Story 303. *See also* Ozu
tool 15, 53, 77, 92, 103–5, 110, 126, 133, 193–95, 236, 266–67, 269–70, 272–74
   Merleau-Ponty 97, 101, 160–64, 193–96, 214, 270
   Nishida 56, 73, 102, 139, 193–96, 214–19, 236, 257
traditional inn (*ryokan* 旅館) 133, 281
traditional restaurant (*ryōtei* 料亭) 281
tranquility (*seijaku* 静寂) 39, 47–49, 205, 225, 234
transcendence 170, 180
transmission outside scripture 105, 207. *See also* zen
trigrams (*bagua* 八卦) 278, 280
truth 41, 44, 66–67, 72, 102–4, 117, 122, 155, 209
   correspondence theory 103
   daoist critique 104
T'ang dynasty 25

Ueda Shizuteru 76, 102, 215, 238, 242, 258, 261
   two-fold world 102–3, 105–9, 124.
   I in not being I, am I 76
Unheimlichkeit 301. *See also* Heidegger
Urasenke Institute 33–35, 37, 39, 41, 43–45, 47, 49, 51, 53–54, 88–89, 169–70, 200, 209, 221, 223, 225
utsushi 写 169–70

van Gogh, Vincent 168, 307
van Norden, Bryan 81
Vermeer, Johannes 167–68
via negativa 12–13. *See also* Eckhart

Vimalakirti 41, 278
   Nirdeśa Sūtra 41
virtue 16, 25, 31, 44, 69, 76, 82, 91–92, 94, 143, 151–52, 183, 206, 234, 261, 278
vision 44, 83, 89, 160–61, 226, 307

wabi 侘 15, 30–31, 36, 42–43, 46, 49, 51, 197, 199, 201–9, 286–87, 296
   aesthetic 43, 46, 203–4, 286
   -*sabi* 侘寂 15, 30, 197, 199–209, 287,
   -*cha* 侘茶 23–24, 28–32, 34–36, 38–39, 42–44, 46, 48–49, 51–53, 104, 146–47, 150, 183–84, 199–202, 206, 210, 213, 226–27, 232, 240, 266, 278, 289, 296–98
waiting 33, 55, 72, 96, 116, 148–49, 152, 173, 176, 197, 223, 225, 229, 277, 287, 295, 301
   arbor, outer (*koshikake machiai* 腰掛待合) 149
   bench, outer (*soto koshikake* 外腰掛) 152
   bench, inner (*uchi koshikake* 内腰掛) 223
wallet (*fukusabasami* 袱紗挟み) 147
water 19–23, 25, 27, 29, 31, 34, 45, 57, 119, 143, 145, 148, 175–81, 218–20, 237, 265, 273, 278, 281, 283, 285, 288–91, 293–94, 305
   and non-self 218
   purification 288
   bucket fresh (*mizusashi* 水指) 20
   waste water container (*kensui* 建水) 290
Watsuji Tetsurō 215
Way (*dō* 道 / *geidō* 芸道)
   of kami (*kannagara no michi* 惟神の道) 178
   of incense (*kōdō* 香道) 130
   of flowers (*kadō* 華道) 130, 232, 253
   of the bow (*kyudō* 弓道) 130
   of the brush (*shodō* 書道) 130, 231, 232, 234
   of tea (*chadō, sadō* 茶道) 15–16, 18, 23, 34, 38–39, 43–45, 49–50, 52, 85, 89, 109, 113, 115–16, 130, 150, 170–72, 181, 208, 214, 221–22, 232–33, 240, 296–97
   See also Daoism, *Daodejing*

western
  art history 60
  chauvinism 88, 92
  metaphysics 186, 236, 299
  philosophy 17, 30, 61, 74, 80, 96, 101–4, 110, 153, 239, 270, 299
wild fox zen (*yako-zen* 野狐禅) 207
women 74, 145–46, 221–22
  in *chanoyu* 221–22
pre-reflective. *See* experience
world
  two-fold. *See* Ueda
  "in-between", 101–2
worldview 92, 95, 159, 163
Wu Daozi 158, 307

Yabanouchi school 39
Yayoi period 177
yin yang 25, 122–27, 129, 136, 139, 247–48, 300
yojohan chashitsu 四畳半 34, 278
Yoshihiro Imai 71
yūgen 幽玄 15, 30, 115

zazen 座禅 206, 267
Zeami 170

Zen 禅 15, 18, 26–30, 32, 34–36, 41–42, 44–48, 51, 53, 64, 66–70, 80, 85, 98, 102, 104–5, 109–11, 126, 130, 182, 184, 196, 199, 201, 203, 205–9, 215, 220–21, 224–25, 233, 236, 246, 249, 251, 263, 265–70, 282, 289, 296–97
  meditation 25, 32, 66, 128–29, 132, 182, 196, 206–8, 267
  aesthetic 28, 46, 85. *See also Geidō*
  devil 207
  monastery 208
  philosophy 105
  practice 45, 109, 126, 208, 220, 266
  Rinzai 64, 70. *See also* Eisai
  Sōtō 29, 221. *See also* Dōgen
  silence 104–5
  temple 64, 69, 208–9
Zencharoku "Record of Zen Tea" (禅茶録) 208
Zeuxis 155–56. *See also* Parrhasios
Zhuang Zhou 148, 306–8
Zhuangzi 121, 148, 234, 305–07. *See also* dream of the butterfly
Zuihō-in Temple 209